P9-CMW-470

12-25-94

To the budding politician,

"Fischbach for President"

Billy Flaherty

ALSO BY ELIZABETH DREW

Washington Journal:
The Events of 1973–74

American Journal:
The Events of 1976

Senator

Portrait of an Election:
The 1980 Presidential Campaign

Politics and Money:
The New Road to Corruption

Campaign Journal:
The Political Events of 1983–1984

Election Journal:
The Political Events of 1987–1988

ON THE EDGE

SIMON & SCHUSTER
New York • London • Toronto • Sydney • Tokyo • Singapore

THE CLINTON PRESIDENCY

ELIZABETH DREW

SIMON & SCHUSTER
Rockefeller Center
1230 Avenue of the Americas
New York, New York 10020

Designed by Levavi & Levavi
Photo research by Natalie Goldstein

Manufactured in the United States of America

1 3 5 7 9 10 8 6 4 2

Library of Congress Cataloging-in-Publication Data.
Drew, Elizabeth.
On the edge : the Clinton presidency / Elizabeth Drew.
p. cm.
Includes index.
1. Clinton, Bill, 1946– .
2. United States—Politics and government—1993. I. Title.
E886.D74 1994
973.929′092—dc20 94-34873
CIP
ISBN 0-671-87147-1

(Left to right on title page)
Thomas F. McLarty (AP/Wide World); Donna Shalala (Reuters/Bettmann); Roger Altman (Reuters/Bettmann); Warren Christopher (Reuters/Bettmann); Anthony Lake (Reuters/Bettmann); Robert Reich (AP/Wide World); Strobe Talbott (© Robert Nickelsberg/Gamma Liaison); Leon Panetta (AP/Wide World); Hillary Rodham Clinton (Reuters/Bettmann); President Clinton (AP/Wide World); Vice President Gore (Reuters/Bettmann); Margaret Williams (AP/Wide World)

(Left to right on half-title page)
George Stephanopoulos (Reuters/Bettmann); Bruce Lindsey (Reuters/Bettmann); Lani Guinier (AP/Wide World); David Gergen (Reuters/Bettmann); Stanley Greenberg (© Richard Bloom/SABA); Laura D'Andrea Tyson (AP/Wide World)

ON THE EDGE

THE CLINTON PRESIDENCY

Acknowledgments

I am indebted to a large number of people for their help in the writing of this book. People at all levels at the White House—policymakers, aides to policymakers, press aides, secretaries—made it possible for me to do my job. It wouldn't necessarily do some of them much good for me to name them, and I wouldn't want to exclude anyone, so I'll leave it with the fact that they know who they are, and that I am very grateful. The same thing goes for various people in the Cabinet departments and on Capitol Hill.

Some extraordinary friends gave me moral support and more, and they know how grateful I am. John Bennet and Tom Oliphant were noble. I also want to thank Melissa Price, my assistant, who jumped into a big project and handled it with great intelligence and good nature. Others who deserve thanks are Leslie Sewell, Jim Jaffe, Collette Rhoney, Kathy Glover, Christine Haynes Myers, and Sarah Baker.

My agent, Sterling Lord, offered wisdom, judgment, and a sympathetic ear. My editor, Alice Mayhew, brought to this book the energy, brains, and tough-mindedness for which she is famed.

My husband, David Webster, was involved in this book at every stage. He was a total partner. I cannot imagine how I could have done it without him.

Acknowledgments

For David

Contents

Introduction

One of the most distinctive things about the Clinton Presidency in the crucial first eighteen months was the aura of danger. His Presidency was constantly on the edge—because of his past and what came to be called his "character," and because of the legislative gambles he took. A friend of his said to me while I was reporting for this book, "Bill has always been someone who has lived on the edge, politically and personally." Time after time, it appeared that his Presidency was in jeopardy, that its effectiveness and authority could come to an end. People have found it difficult to understand this complex and often perplexing man. His great strengths and his great flaws seemed constantly at war over his Presidency.

Clinton's has been a very personal Presidency—he has been his own commentator, telling the American people how he thought he was doing and sharing his feelings. The American people sensed the danger and the tension—and got caught up in the drama. His ups and downs were followed closely—and sometimes exaggerated—and they strongly affected, and were affected by, the national mood.

Even "success" and "failure" were being measured in a new way when it came to Clinton. Though his legislative achievements were considerable, they were often discounted. His and his aides' basing his success on legislative achievement carried its own danger. But, absent an ideological identification with Clinton on the part of the large segment of the public, or a strong personal following, and given the increasing questions about his character, it was all they had to work with.

Why were all these things the case?

This book attempts to answer that and other questions. It tries to draw a picture of this unusual President and his unusual Presidency.

In order to write this book I set out to watch, up close, what happened after Bill Clinton took office. In the fall of 1992 I decided that if Clinton were to win he would win on the promise of "change," and the stakes would be high. If he didn't succeed—if he were deemed to have failed—an already cynical electorate might become still more jaded, with potentially dangerous consequences.

What I didn't anticipate—no one did—was that the first phase of the Clinton Presidency would be so turbulent. This book follows the turbulence as well as the achievements—and tries to explain the phenomenon.

I wanted to discern some patterns, and draw some conclusions, and I have done so. This book is intended to help contemporary Americans, as well as future historians and others, understand this most complex man and his—to so many people—perplexing Presidency.

Elizabeth Drew
Washington, D.C.
August 1994

1

INAUGURATION

"The Era of Deadlock and Drift Is Over"

When William Jefferson Clinton, as he now called himself, retiring momentarily the informal "Bill," took the oath of office on a brilliant, cold January 20, hopes and expectations of what he could achieve were high. He had a large amount of public goodwill behind him, which could help him persuade the Congress to pass his program. The excesses of Inaugural Week—the multitude of white stretch limos (more characteristic of Republican inaugurations), the exploitation of national symbols (a concert at the Lincoln Memorial was sold to Home Box Office), the overstaged and overearnest national bell ringing (various Indian tribes and the space shuttle were beamed in by satellite), the Las Vegas–like Presidential Gala at the mammoth Capital Center, with self-indulgent Hollywood celebrities (liberals, of course) lecturing the President-elect and the country—did nothing to dampen the public's enthusiasm. The Clintons' arrival in Washington was via an elaborate route that mixed the message—stopping first in Charlottesville, they then traveled, by bus (with the Gores, in a reenactment of a popular campaign gambit), the route Thomas Jefferson had taken to reach Washington for his inauguration.

While Hillary Clinton, dressed in a royal-blue coat and a large blue saucer hat that met with much criticism, held a Bible his mother had given him, Clinton, coatless, repeated the oath of office at 11:59 A.M., a minute early. The Clintons' Hollywood friend the television producer Harry Thomason, who was in charge of the inaugural festivities, had wanted to change the oath—which is prescribed in the Constitution—so that it would sound better. He thought that the phrase "preserve, protect, and defend" would sound stronger if it started with "defend." A Thomason representative who broached this at a meeting of the Joint Congressional Inaugural Committee was met with laughter.

Clinton's coatlessness, like a number of other gestures, seemed a deliberate attempt to evoke the memory of his idol, John F. Kennedy. Earlier in the week, he had made an "unscheduled" but much photographed visit to Kennedy's grave, in Arlington National Cemetery. There were pictures of Clinton, kneeling "alone," by the gravesite, head bowed, having laid a long-stemmed white rose at the site.

The preparation of Clinton's inaugural address was to set the pattern for his Presidency. His speechwriters worked through two nights, meeting with Clinton when they could. On the eve of the inauguration, they worked with him until three-thirty in the morning. Clinton read the speech aloud, editing it as he went. The TelePrompTer operators at the Capitol were becoming highly anxious—they were accustomed to getting a major speech hours in advance, so that they could test it on their machines. They didn't get Clinton's until 11:30 A.M., thirty minutes before the ceremonies were to begin.

The address didn't meet the rhetorical standard set by Kennedy thirty-two years before, but it was more than adequate to the occasion, if not memorable. Like Kennedy, Clinton made it clear that a new generation had come to power—"a generation raised in the shadows of the Cold War." The sight of the forty-six-year-old President, of Al Gore, the forty-four-year-old Vice President, and of the young staff, made that clear. "This is our time," Clinton said. Now the nation had its first "baby boomer" President, a member of the first generation that hadn't experienced the Second World War, whose formative experience was Vietnam. The first President elected after the Cold War had ended talked of a "new world" that was "more free but less stable." And he stressed the theme of "renewal." Kennedy-like, he exhorted: "My fellow Americans, you, too, must play your part in our renewal. I challenge a new generation of young Americans to a season of service."

The brevity of Clinton's speech—only fourteen minutes—was a relief to his staff as well as to others who had begun to wonder whether he was capable of such discipline. The two most important speeches of his life—the first nominating Michael Dukakis at the 1988 convention, and his acceptance speech at the 1992 convention—had gone on much too long.

Clinton invoked many of the themes that had been prominent in his campaign; in fact, the speech was a continuation of the campaign. Clinton had figured out a formula for getting elected, and it was by this same formula that he hoped to create and maintain a governing majority. He had laid out this approach in a series of speeches at Georgetown University, his alma mater, in December 1991—the beginning of his campaign—under the heading the "New Covenant." He wouldn't be a traditional liberal; he would be "a different kind of Democrat," one who found "a third way" between the either/ors of politics. So now he reiterated his campaign theme that with opportunity came responsibility. His speech was blessedly unprogrammatic (Clinton loved to talk about programs, in detail). He spoke about "service" and his pet idea of offering college scholarships in exchange for national service, which had come from the Democratic Leadership Council, a centrist group that he had helped found in 1985 in order to search for a way to break the Democrats' Presidential losing streak and change the party's image as too liberal for the country. "The era of deadlock and drift is over," Clinton said.

Clinton and his advisers were keenly aware that he had received only 43 percent of the popular vote and that he needed a broader base in order to govern—and to be reelected. Therefore, a fair amount of the inaugural speech was aimed, as some of his campaign rhetoric had been, at winning support from voters who backed Ross Perot, the eccentric Texas billionaire who had seized the public's attention through his folksy anti-Washington rhetoric and his focus on the budget deficit and ended up with 19 percent of the vote. Clinton needed the backing of a sizable number of Perot's voters.

So, in his speech, Clinton talked of the need to reduce the deficit—he had seldom mentioned it in his campaign and as yet had no real plan for achieving it—and criticized Washington, which he portrayed as a land more foreign to him than it actually was. He said, "Powerful people maneuver for position and worry endlessly about who is in and who is out and who is up and who is down." He added, in Perotian terms, "Let us give this capital back to the people to whom it belongs," and in another nod to Perot's constituency, he called for political reform. For the first time, he spoke of the need for "sacrifice," leaving the details for later.

On Clinton's capacity for leadership rested not only his political fate but also that of the country. Another failed Presidency, for whatever reason—another dose of disillusionment, more cynicism—could poison the political well to the point where the country could turn to a demagogue or give up on trying to deal with its problems. The high hopes that were invested in Clinton were his opportunity and the nation's danger. If those hopes were dashed, anything could happen.

Clinton's taking the oath of office marked the end of what was actually his second campaign: to build support so that he could arrive in Washington with the people clearly behind him, to convince the Washington institutions, especially the Congress, to do his bidding. But in a contradiction that was to mark his Presidency, he also courted the powers that be. In two highly successful trips to Washington, he had dazzled Members of Congress, especially the numerous newly elected Democrats in the House of Representatives, with his knowledge of the issues and with his ability to call congressmen by their first name—the latter perhaps being the more important.

In those earlier visits, the energetic Clinton had jogged in the early-morning streets; the populist Clinton had jawed with customers at the McDonald's on 17th Street, just around the corner from the White House. The highly connected Clinton, who had, along with his wife, spent years developing networks, dined with many of the capital's elite at the homes of attorney Vernon Jordan, a longtime Clinton friend, who had been cochairman of the transition, and Pamela Harriman, the hostess and Democratic fund-raiser.

Because Clinton's political advisers were concerned about the picture that would be presented by Clinton's hobnobbing with the Washington wealthy, a brief walk down Georgia Avenue, in a predominantly black neighborhood, was added to his schedule.

Clinton began his Presidency after staying out until 2:00 A.M., making appearances at eleven inaugural balls, including one thrown by MTV (the hottest ticket in town), and playing the saxophone at a couple of them. At the "open house" at the White House the next day, he and Mrs. Clinton, in a Jacksonian gesture, spent six hours shaking hands, which provided boffo television pictures and kept the adulation coming.

But the truth was that as the confident new President took the oath of office, he, his wife, and his staff had no idea how unready they were to govern. Nor did the public.

2

TRANSITION

"A Cabinet That Looks Like America"

The Clinton transition had been located in Little Rock and Washington, under, respectively, Warren Christopher—the prominent California attorney who had previously served in the Johnson and Carter administrations and had won the Clintons' trust by his discreet and successful handling of the search for a running mate—and Vernon Jordan. The idea was that the Cabinet would be picked in Little Rock, while the background work—the vetting of candidates—and the work of "cluster groups" to draw up policy papers would take place in Washington. Jordan would commute to Little Rock, and the sub-Cabinet search would be headed by Richard Riley, a former Governor of South Carolina and a close friend of Clinton's.

As the work began in the governor's mansion the morning after the election, Clinton was exhausted. From then on, every day, Monday through Friday, a small group of people sat around a six-foot round table in the family room, off the dining room—and picked the Cabinet. At the table were Clinton, Gore, Christopher, Bruce Lindsey, a Little Rock attorney and close friend of Clinton's who had traveled with him through most of the campaign, Roy Neel (who was to be Gore's Chief of Staff), and, about half the time, Thomas "Mack" McLarty, the chief executive of an energy company and a lifelong friend of Clinton's. Hillary Clinton was at the table about 80 percent of the time. Clinton would sometimes sprawl in one of the room's two large overstuffed chairs. This was the room where Clinton used to have people in to watch sports events on television. He was particularly hooked on basketball.

Clinton had pledged to announce all of his Cabinet by Christmas, and that goal was soon in jeopardy. The meetings sometimes began an hour or two late, and they usually commenced with Clinton and Gore talking about what was going on in the world, or a discussion of whether Clinton should call Boris Yeltsin, the Russian President, or some such. Clinton would talk discursively about what he thought a given Cabinet department's mission was, about people he knew, about the past. Sometimes he'd break off to phone someone he knew to talk about who had served in certain positions before. Eventually, Warren Christopher would prod Clinton to discuss particular candidates, and Clinton would lead a discussion about the principle of getting the right people for certain jobs. There was a certain lack of confidence to the exercise. The Democrats had been out of power for twelve years and didn't have a deep talent pool.

There were also long discussions in Little Rock among the Clintons, their friends, and their advisers about what, actually, Mrs. Clinton's role was to be, and though it was never announced, she was basically put in charge of domestic policy for the administration. Economic policy excluded, she would oversee the agencies (Health and Human Services) and issues (children, welfare) she was interested in. Her formal role in health care would be announced later. That would give her a specific project and some protection from the idea that she was corunning the government. Mrs. Clinton had served on the board, and as chairman, of the Children's Defense Fund (CDF), a child advocacy group. Her opinion was deferred to on appointments in this field. When Clinton named Donna Shalala, an official in the Carter administration and now chancellor of the University of Wisconsin, as Secretary of Health and Human Services, he picked someone who had served with Mrs. Clinton on that board. On many issues, Shalala was to report to her. So would Carol Rasco, who was chosen as chief domestic policy adviser. Rasco had worked for Governor Clinton in the statehouse and was very close to Mrs. Clinton. They had children the same age. Other White House staff members who dealt with the issues Mrs. Clinton was interested in—immunization, Head Start, and so on—were to report to her.

But this large role was kept under wraps. A lengthy debate took place in Little Rock, and among Clinton's friends around the country, over whether Hillary Clinton should have a title. Some of her friends thought she should; others thought that the country wasn't ready for this. The title Domestic Policy Adviser was seriously considered, but it was decided that Mrs. Clinton would essentially have the role without the title—it would be less threatening. Some of her friends and advisers felt that if she didn't have a "real" job, she would be seen as a full-time meddler. She was worried that she might be seen as a Lady Macbeth figure. A close friend remarked, "Hillary had to pick and choose, and wanted to focus on an issue, and the quasi Chief of Staff role would have been attacked viciously. For those two reasons—one is enough—she decided to do health care." Taking the health care job seemed to solve a lot of problems at once: the issue would need a great deal of attention and visibility, and she would have a specific task. A friend of both Clintons said, "She decided not to be clandestine. It was a risk she was willing to take."

Fairly early in the transition it was also decided that Mrs. Clinton would have an office in the West Wing, where the President and his top staff had their offices. The decision—which would break the tradition that First Ladies' offices were in the East Wing—had been the subject of controversy in Little Rock. Vernon Jordan strongly opposed a West Wing office for Mrs. Clinton because he thought it was, in effect, an announcement of a copresidency and was too much to spring on the public. But Mrs. Clinton's advisers—Susan Thomases, a New York attorney and a close friend (who also served on the CDF board), and Margaret Williams, who was to be her Chief of Staff (Williams was a former staff member of the CDF)—were insistent, and they (and Mrs. Clinton, of course) carried the day. Williams was to serve as an assistant to the President as well as the First Lady's Chief of Staff, another innovation.

This decision had all sorts of implications, as did other early ones about real estate generally. In December, Susan Thomases went to Washington to get a floor plan of the White House offices. "That sent a chill through everyone," a transition adviser said later. Thomases, a blunt, strong-willed, and controversial figure in the campaign, drew her power from her close relationship with Mrs. Clinton and had used it often to second-guess other campaign officials. There was a rebellion against her, and campaign officials took the issue to the Clintons. Thomases was forced to draw back some, but no one doubted now that she had tremendous power in the formation of the Clinton White House.

Mrs. Clinton and Williams chose prime office space, limiting the space for the President's staff in the West Wing. They would also have offices in the Old Executive Office Building, next door to the White House. A transition adviser said, "It was a statement from which other things flowed: Hillary was the first First Lady to not only have her own office but also have an office for her Chief of Staff in the West Wing. This had important implications for Hillary's role."

A friend of both Thomases and Mrs. Clinton said later, "Susan gets into everything, protecting Hillary Clinton. She's her campaign manager for President of the United States, and I'm not kidding. Susan believes that somewhere down the road Hillary will be the first woman candidate for President of the United States. She's positioning her. Not that anybody thinks it's a bad idea—it's just a little early."

Mrs. Clinton was vested by her husband with selecting an Attorney General, and she and Thomases were to choose not only the person to fill that role but also the other major Justice Department officials. It was understood that the Attorney General would be a woman. For a while, Thomases herself entertained the idea of taking the job—only a very tight group knew about this—but then it was decided that the fact that she had no experience at the criminal bar was too big a hurdle. Thomases had also harbored the idea of becoming the President's Chief of Staff, which would certainly have led to a revolt among other Clinton advisers, but the idea was never seriously considered. Thomases had a young child. Anyway, Clinton had his own thoughts about that position.

It wasn't long before Clinton's pledge of a diverse Cabinet, one that "looks like America"—a pledge that was strongly backed by Mrs. Clinton and that soon caused problems. No formal presentation of nominees could have on display only males, and this led to scrambles to get the right combination before the cameras. And the interest groups kept up the pressure. In Washington, on December 21, Vernon Jordan was visited at the transition offices at 1120 Vermont Avenue by a delegation representing a half-dozen women's groups, which demanded that one of the "big four" Cabinet posts—State, Treasury, Defense, Justice—be a woman. Afterward, outside the transition offices, the members of the delegation complained that Clinton had set a "glass ceiling" of three women in the Cabinet. After the visit by the women's groups, the Clinton camp began to leak the names of possible women for Attorney General, giving the impression that Clinton, who in his campaign had successfully avoided being tagged as the candidate of the Democratic Party's interest groups, was, at this stage, yielding to their pressure.

Women's groups weren't the only ones who went to see Vernon Jordan to demand adequate representation in the Cabinet. So did Hispanic groups and environmentalists.

As a result, there arose early the sense that Clinton could be rolled—and that he was, or would act as if he were, beholden to the party's interest groups. Sensing that he might be able to recapture the White House for the Democrats after a long hiatus, these groups had held back their demands during the campaign. But they had supported him, and now they wanted to collect. And he appeared to be a willing hostage. The "different kind of Democrat" label he had affixed to himself in the campaign was in jeopardy, at a very early moment.

Another Clinton trait was in evidence during the transition: his inability to tell people bad news to their faces. (Toward the end of the Vice Presidential search, with Gore about to be announced, Clinton had Senator Bob Kerrey meet with him in the governor's mansion late at night and told him, "If it were up to me, it would be you.") As a consequence, he could leave some people with the impression that they had a job when they didn't. Brooksley Born, a little-known attorney at the Washington firm of Arnold & Porter, who was active in bar association activities that involved women's issues, thought after being interviewed by Clinton in Little Rock that she had the job of Attorney General, and was toasted at the firm's Christmas party. Born was criticized in Democratic circles and the press as lacking the stature to be Attorney General, but what bothered Clinton was the fact that she was being openly pushed by some women's groups, which made it look as if he was bowing to them. He was particularly annoyed when one group claimed Born's seemingly all-but-announced appointment as a victory for the women's movement. On the same day that the women's groups criticized him for not appointing enough women, Clinton threw a little fit at a press conference, calling these groups "bean counters." But the fit had been planned, with his definition as a "different kind of Democrat"—and 1996—in mind. Then he went back to counting beans. He was determined to equal George Bush, or go him one better, in naming a diverse Cabinet.

There had never been much question that if Lloyd Bentsen, the silky, seventy-one-year-old chairman of the Senate Finance Committee, wanted to be Secretary of the Treasury, he would get the job. Bentsen was an eminent figure in the party (he had been the star as Vice Presidential nominee in 1988) and a power in the Senate. Bentsen did want the job—and there would be little point in annoying him, given Clinton's ambitious domestic goals. So Bentsen was the first potential Cabinet officer interviewed in Little Rock, and the first one offered a job.

As Clinton selected Bentsen, he had an economic mix in mind. He was determined to have better coordination of economic policy than most of his predecessors had, and less infighting. Drawing on an idea that had been discussed in Democratic policy circles for years, Clinton had decided to establish a new National Economic Council, to coordinate economic policy making, including foreign economic policy. (At one point, the new body was called the Economic Security Council, but it was decided that this sounded too nationalistic.) Managing this council called for a person with standing in the economic world who dealt well with others—especially others with big egos—and Clinton thought he had found such a person in Robert Rubin, the cochairman of Goldman Sachs, a major fund-raiser for Clinton and an adviser to his campaign. Rubin, it was thought, would get along well with Bentsen (he had managed Bentsen's personal investment portfolio).

Roger Altman, another New York investment banker, an assistant Secretary of the Treasury in the Carter administration and a friend of Clinton's from their Georgetown University days, was installed as Deputy Secretary of the Treasury. Bentsen didn't know him well, but was pleased to get as his deputy someone with a direct line to the Clintons. Robert Reich, a close friend of Clinton's since they were Rhodes Scholars together at Oxford, a certified Friend of Bill (FOB), was more difficult to fit. Reich, who taught at Harvard's Kennedy School of Government, was a prolific writer and a popularizer of ideas, but he wasn't actually an economist or, as one of the better idea salesmen of his time, particularly self-effacing. There was concern about his possible chemistry with Bentsen, and therefore the NEC job was out. Eventually, he was named Secretary of Labor, a suitable testing place for some of his ideas.

Within the inner circle, it was assumed that Clinton would choose as chairman of the Council of Economic Advisers Laura D'Andrea Tyson, a professor of economics at Berkeley, whose work, especially her writings on trade policy, he admired. Tyson believed in subsidies and other devices if other countries employed them, to help major industries compete internationally and to bolster high-tech industries. This made her less than a purist in the trade debate, and controversial among the economic mandarins, but Clinton was looking for people who would cut through the old debates, find a "third way."

Clinton put a lot of stock in the chemistry when he met with potential nominees, and chemistry played a big role when Clinton chose his candidate for the important job of director of the Office of Management and Budget. He had been urged by House Majority Leader Dick Gephardt to select Leon Panetta, a popular member from California and chairman of the House Budget Committee, and in interviews with Panetta, Clinton was quite taken with him. Panetta was a bright man with a deep knowledge of the budget and a ready laugh, and—though he was quite serious about deficit reduction—he had the kind of pragmatic approach Clinton liked. Panetta could help him get hold of the budget and also be a valuable emissary to Capitol Hill. Clinton had earlier thought of Alice Rivlin, a former director of the Congressional Budget Office and a respected economist, for the post, but their interview hadn't gone so well, and now here was Panetta, an appealing man with powerful support. So Clinton picked Rivlin, who was also serious about deficit reduction and knowledgeable about the budget, to be Panetta's deputy. The members of the economic team—Bentsen, Rubin, Altman, Tyson, Panetta, and Rivlin—were announced on December 10.

There was some urgency about naming the economic team, because Clinton was to host an economic summit in Little Rock on December 14 and 15. The idea for the summit started small—a way of trying to get a consensus on economic policy—but then, being a Clinton project, it became inclusive. As the size grew to about three hundred participants, it became impossible to hold the meeting in secret, and so it lost much of its original purpose. Several advisers thought it a poor idea to interrupt the transition for this meeting, but Clinton was a smash at the two-day meeting —which was carried on CNN and C-SPAN—making a strong impression as an informed and serious figure. Clinton had got to do what he loved most: talk policy and show off his knowledge. Clinton had studied domestic policy for years and had a lot of ideas and anecdotes stuffed in his head. His knowledge may have been more wide than deep, but his interest was real, and for a busy politician, he was very well informed. In the end, the conference did take precious time out of the transition.

Warren Christopher wanted badly to be Secretary of State. As Deputy Secretary of State under Carter, Christopher had been bitterly disappointed at Carter's passing him over in favor of Edmund Muskie when Cyrus Vance resigned as Secretary in the aftermath of the failed hostage rescue mission in Iran. He hadn't started out as Clinton's preference—Clinton didn't really have one—but Christopher had worked his way into that position by getting close to Clinton, proving himself a trustworthy and discreet adviser on choosing the Vice President and the Cabinet, and benefited from Jordan's strongly advocating him for the job. When Christopher was announced as one of the codirectors of the transition, he issued a lawyerly statement that appeared to less than careful listeners to take him out of consideration for a Cabinet job: "I told Governor Clinton I assumed in undertaking this role that I would not have a major responsibility in the future." Clinton considered naming Sam Nunn, the senator from Georgia, who was chairman of the Armed Services Committee, but Nunn's conservative voting record had made him anathema to much of the liberal wing of the Democratic Party as a possible running mate, and this remained a factor as Clinton studied his options for the Cabinet. Besides, the chemistry between Nunn and Clinton wasn't great, and some Clinton advisers felt that Nunn hadn't helped enough in the election. Senator Bill Bradley, of New Jersey, whose name was floated, wasn't seriously considered. Bradley's stock had fallen after he won reelection in 1990 by only three points, and he hadn't made himself much of a presence in the 1992 Presidential campaign.

Clinton finally settled on Christopher, whose role was to be to not let foreign policy get in the President's way as he focused on domestic policy. Clinton felt he could trust Christopher on this score.

There was never much question that Anthony Lake, a former Carter administration official and professor of international relations, who as Clinton's foreign policy adviser during the campaign had successfully kept Clinton out of difficulty, would be the National Security Adviser. He had the same assignment as Christopher: keep foreign policy from distracting the President from his domestic agenda.

The job of ambassador to the United Nations was first offered to Ronald Brown, to whom the Clintons were very grateful for the way he played his role as Democratic Party Chairman in 1992, but Brown wanted to be Secretary of State. He felt that in the UN job he would be just another in a line of blacks who had filled the post, and he turned it down. After it was made clear that the State Department wasn't to be his, he accepted Secretary of Commerce. The Clinton people had thought of offering the UN job to Condoleezza Rice, who had served on the Bush National Security Council staff and was an eminent black woman, but they finally decided to stay within the party. Clinton named Madeleine Albright, a professor of foreign policy who had worked in the Carter administration and the Dukakis and Clinton campaigns.

After Clinton interviewed candidates, his wife interviewed them. Delays occurred because someone didn't do well in an interview or because Clinton didn't like the list of four or five candidates presented to him for a certain job. He would ask for more names, saying that the list didn't have enough people of stature or didn't contain the name of anyone who had helped him get elected. Sometimes he thought that the vetting report on a candidate didn't make the case for choosing that person. "His indecision was about a lack of knowledge," one adviser said. But sometimes Clinton's indecision stemmed from his own indecisiveness.

On occasion, Gore, to get closure on a nominee, would say, I think we should go for so-and-so. Gore and Clinton brainstormed about each person, saying what they knew about him or her, and sometimes Mrs. Clinton joined in. Sometimes Neel or McLarty was asked his view. McLarty's presence at the table was the first clue that he would play a role in the administration.

Not only was there a lack of a deep bench to pick from, but generally speaking, people who had served in the Carter administration weren't held in high favor, unless they had distinguished themselves in some way since. And there was a great reluctance to take people out of the House or the Senate, lest that narrow the already slim working majorities Clinton would have in each chamber. But Les Aspin, the chairman of the House Armed Services Committee, had been a big help in the campaign and was a bona fide defense intellectual. There was some discussion as to whether Aspin was too abrasive to be Secretary of Defense and whether the military, with whom he had tangled, would accept him. Serious consideration was given to naming Colin Powell, the Chairman of the Joint Chiefs of Staff, to the Defense job, but this would have required a change in the law that bars a former military official from taking the job for ten years. There was also the question of whether it was a good idea to name someone who had served two Republican Presidents. Once it was determined that letting the House Armed Services Committee fall into the hands of Ronald Dellums, a California product of the radical politics of the sixties and a leading defense critic, wasn't dangerous—Dellums had played a responsible role as a member of the House Intelligence Committee—the Defense job went to Aspin.

Henry Cisneros, the talented former mayor of San Antonio and an old friend of Clinton's, was a natural for the Department of Housing and Urban Development. Cisneros had had a publicly messy domestic situation and had to give up running for mayor again. Clinton's selection gave him a new chance at public life.

The biggest complications were over filling the jobs of Secretary of Interior, Energy, and Transportation. Both William Daley, brother of the mayor of Chicago, and James Blanchard, a former governor of Michigan, a friend of the President's, and an eager helper in the campaign, wanted Transportation. The Daleys had supported Clinton in the Illinois primary, and Mayor Daley warned the Clinton people not to let his brother dangle in the wind. But Bill Daley was dangling in the wind.

Timothy Wirth, a former Democratic senator from Colorado, wanted to be Secretary of Energy but was also interested in the Interior Department. Wirth, an environmentalist, had been pretty much of a loner in the Senate and then had enraged his colleagues when, after deciding not to run again in 1992, he wrote a piece for the *New York Times* Sunday Magazine castigating life in the Senate and the role of campaign contributions. At least two of his Senate colleagues who were well connected with the Clinton group sent negative reports. The energy community disliked his record as an environmentalist and strongly opposed his being given that department.

Senator Bennett Johnston, who represented the oil state of Louisiana and was very close to McLarty because of his energy business, pressed the case against Wirth. He told Wirth that he backed him for Interior (which would keep him out of the Energy job). Nonetheless, Wirth had been led to believe that he would get the Energy post. He and Gore (also a Senate loner) had once been strong rivals but had made peace in recent years, and Gore pressed Wirth's case in Little Rock. Wirth was allowed to dangle for seven weeks, with a lot of stories in the press about whether he was up or down, until Clinton called him on December 21, a half hour before he named Hazel O'Leary to the job. (Wirth was later given a high State Department post dealing with global issues such as the environment and population.)

Clinton had suddenly learned about O'Leary when an acquaintance in the energy business mentioned her at a reception at the Arkansas Arts Center during the transition. O'Leary, Clinton was told, was a black woman who had served in the Energy Department in the Carter administration and since then had been executive vice president of Northern States Power, in Minneapolis. "Hazel just fell out of the sky," said someone involved in the transition. "They didn't want Wirth to have it, and there was no one else outstanding. She was the closest thing to an affirmative action selection." Jordan and McLarty had known O'Leary slightly. O'Leary's name came up one day, and the next day she was in Little Rock, and on December 21 she was named, along with Richard Riley as Secretary of Education.

There still weren't the required number of Hispanics in the Cabinet. (Bush had had two.) Clinton and his advisers considered putting Bill Richardson, a congressman from New Mexico, who was Hispanic, in the Interior post—for which he had lobbied—but environmentalists rebelled, saying his record on their issues wasn't good enough. Wirth, who knew by this time that he was out for Interior as well as Energy, also argued strongly against Richardson. He proposed solving the Hispanic shortage by picking Federico Pena, the former mayor of Denver, as Secretary of Transportation. For the people in Little Rock, this would break the Daley-Blanchard impasse, which had become bitter. Neither would accept the selection of the other, but if they were told that the job had to go to a Hispanic, they might be more understanding.

A problem was that Pena had been a transition "cluster leader" on the Department of Transportation, and the understanding had been that cluster leaders wouldn't get the top jobs in the departments they were studying. But time was closing in on Clinton's vow to pick his Cabinet by Christmas.

Pena couldn't be found. He was finally tracked down at the Denver airport on the night of Wednesday, December 23. (He had left Washington wondering what sort of part-time job he could get with the administration.)

Daley, who had at some points been led to believe that he had the job, finally got the negative news from Clinton at about ten o'clock Wednesday night.

Blanchard, who had returned to Washington, where he practiced law, from Michigan (where he had gone to get his family's Christmas tree and settle in for the holidays) to be vetted, and had been assured by the vetters that no one else was being considered for the Transportation post—that Daley had been out of the running for a couple of weeks—was told to prepare to come to Little Rock on Wednesday the twenty-third, for the announcement of his appointment the next day. So he bought plane tickets for Wednesday night, for himself, his wife, and his son. But no final word came from Little Rock, so he waited. At last, Blanchard heard on CNN Wednesday night that Pena was to get the Transportation job.

Clinton, typically, tried to make it up to both men in the end. After the inauguration, Blanchard and his wife were invited to the White House several times, and he was named ambassador to Canada. Daley was invited to play golf with Clinton and then was made special coordinator for the fight over the NAFTA treaty.

Although they didn't know it, Daley and Blanchard had been on the other end of a mad scramble that was taking place in Little Rock on the night of December 23.

On that day, Bruce Babbitt, the former governor of Arizona and a popular figure from his classy, if futile, run for the Democratic nomination in 1988, went to Little Rock expecting to be named United States Trade Representative. But two things happened to that: Clinton now needed for the Interior post someone whom the environmentalists would accept; and some people, including Vernon Jordan, were arguing that the President had to give a good job to Mickey Kantor, who had been his campaign chairman. Kantor, a prominent Los Angeles attorney, was a longtime friend, particularly of Mrs. Clinton's, with whom he had served on the board of the Legal Services Corporation. Kantor and others had thought he might be Chief of Staff in the Clinton White House, but he had fallen afoul of other campaign officials, and George Stephanopoulos, a high campaign official who had become close to the Clintons, blocked Kantor from heading the transition, as he had expected and had begun to do. (At this point, Mrs. Clinton was unhappy with him too, for some things that had happened during the campaign.)

As a way of mending matters, Clinton asked Kantor to run the economic summit, which he did extremely well. (Mrs. Clinton made a point of sitting with him in the audience.) But going into the night of December 23, Kantor hadn't been offered a job.

In the end, Kantor was to be given U.S. Trade Representative—a post he had hoped for—and Babbitt, who thought that was why he was in Little Rock, was given Interior. This meant, however, that there wouldn't be enough Hispanics in the Cabinet, and that was what led to Pena.

Mike Espy, a black congressman, filled the bill as Secretary of Agriculture, in several respects. Espy had been for Clinton as early as the New Hampshire primary. He was a member of the Democratic Leadership Council (DLC) and had voted for gun control.

At this late date, the important post of Attorney General was still open. Some other women after Born were eliminated, because their interviews with Clinton didn't go well or there were other problems. It was now approaching Christmas Eve, and Clinton's advisers were beginning to panic. Zoe Baird, the general counsel of Aetna Life and Casualty, was on the list for White House counsel and had been vetted for that job. Unlike Born, Baird had little experience in bar activities, and her legal experience was narrow.

Some Clinton advisers—among them Harold Ickes, a New York attorney and a close friend of Mrs. Clinton's who had run the New York primary and the convention—were opposed on the grounds that Baird lacked the stature for Attorney General and that she wasn't close enough to Clinton. Ickes argued that the Attorney General should always be someone a President can trust completely, for whom the President's interests have the highest priority; John F. Kennedy knew what he was doing when he chose his brother for the job. But Christopher championed her for the job, as did Jordan, who had known her for some years, and Lloyd Cutler, a prominent attorney who had worked with Baird when he served as White House counsel during the Carter administration. Baird had worked in Christopher's law firm, and Christopher's firm did a lot of business with her as Aetna's general counsel. The Clintons had known Baird through their annual attendance at Renaissance Weekend, in Hilton Head, South Carolina, over the New Year's weekend. This gathering—characterized by self-conscious seminars and earnest talk as well as recreation—was just the thing for serious networkers like the Clintons. At these weekends, they made many connections that would spill over into their administration.

What seemed to be a minor matter had turned up in the course of vetting Baird. She and her husband had hired illegal immigrants as nanny and chauffeur in the summer of 1990. Baird had told the vetters and then Christopher that she and her husband had sought legal advice after hiring the couple and were straightening things out. Christopher, in turn, told Clinton that Baird had employed illegal immigrants but her lawyer was taking care of it; the transition lawyers didn't think it was a problem. Vernon Jordan confirmed later, "Nobody in the transition thought it was a problem." No one in the small group sitting around the table at the governor's mansion sensed that it would be a problem to appoint as Attorney General someone who had violated the law. (This was an even more fundamental point than the fact that she had violated a law that would be under her jurisdiction.) Besides, they were in a rush.

And so, on Christmas Eve, Clinton announced his last set of Cabinet appointments: Baird, Espy, Babbitt, Pena, and Kantor. He had just made it under the wire. He had obtained his diversity, though too publicly, and this diminished some of the people who got the jobs.

After the new year—the Clintons kept up tradition by attending the Renaissance Weekend—Clinton had still to select his White House staff. Harold Ickes had been asked to take on this job a couple of weeks after the election, and had been working with Susan Thomases and Mrs. Clinton on drawing up the list. Bruce Lindsey, who was close to Clinton and knew his wishes, had a quiet voice in the matter, as he would on most things.

It was all very casual. No "cluster group" had been established to study the White House, as there had been for the departments and agencies. The Clintons didn't want anyone to get ideas. The Clintons and Susan Thomases were focused on not having people on the White House staff who were independent powers. They said frequently that they didn't want "a Darman" —referring to the freewheeling and talkative (to the press) Richard Darman, a White House official in the Reagan administration, later Bush's budget director.

Almost all of the people working on staffing the White House were inexperienced in Washington, and Mrs. Clinton—to an extent that was not yet understood—and Thomases felt hostile toward Washington and were determined that the Clinton administration wouldn't come under its spell. The only experienced Washingtonian (other than Stephanopoulos, who had worked on Capitol Hill) chosen for the White House staff was Howard Paster, a lobbyist who was to be the legislative director. The Paster exception was in part a reaction to the Carter experience of putting in the job someone from Georgia who was too unfamiliar with Congress and didn't work out very well. Also, it was understood that numerous people from the campaign were to come into the White House. Bruce Lindsey later explained why so few people with Washington experience had been chosen. "We came here, we thought, to change things," he said. "Some people whose life has been around here don't want to challenge conventional wisdom. If Washington, D.C., had decided who would be President, Bill Clinton would not have been President." (Lindsey was correct on that point.) He said, "You do need a broader view than if you'd spent your whole life and career here." And then he added, smiling, "We overdid it."

Long before he told others, Clinton had settled on Mack McLarty as Chief of Staff. A childhood friend of Clinton's from Hope, Arkansas (they had been in Miss Mary's kindergarten together), McLarty was CEO and Chairman of the Board of Arkla, a large natural gas company. Before that, he had run the family's successful Ford dealership and had served one term in the Arkansas legislature. He was also a member of the DLC. McLarty was torn between taking the White House job and becoming Secretary of Energy, into which he could slip more easily. At least one Arkansas friend with Washington experience advised him that he wasn't ready to be Chief of Staff—he should be Deputy Chief of Staff or take the Energy job until he learned his way around Washington. Eventually, McLarty decided to take the top White House job, and his appointment was announced on December 13. The fact that he knew little about Washington, and was to be an "honest broker" rather than a strong Chief of Staff, was fine with others (such as Stephanopoulos) who wanted to have an influential role in the White House. McLarty would be no John Sununu, going off and making policy without consulting political advisers about the consequences. And Clinton didn't want a strong Chief of Staff. Stephanopoulos had wanted to be Deputy Chief of Staff, but Susan Thomases had prevented that. Stephanopoulos had conducted the briefings during the transition, and the Clintons thought he had done a good job—and they trusted him absolutely—so they made him head of the White House Communications Department and asked him to conduct the briefings for at least the first six months; but he was to also serve as a major policy adviser.

Clinton had trouble facing up to the question of who would work in the White House until Ickes forced the issue one night at the governor's mansion. It wasn't until January 14, six days before the inauguration, that Clinton announced his White House staff. Its most striking features, as the staff members stood on risers (looking as if they were going to break into singing "We Are the World") while Clinton made the announcement, were its diversity, its lack of towering figures, and its intensely political nature. Ickes—who at the last minute wasn't named Deputy Chief of Staff, as had been expected, because of questions yet to be answered about alleged ties between his law firm and a union that federal prosecutors said was run by organized crime—was still working on the staff arrangements on Inauguration Day.

Work on the sub-Cabinet was very far behind schedule, because the Clintons wanted to approve those appointments as well (they had been told that one of Carter's mistakes was his not sufficiently taking over the bureaucracy) and because choosing the Cabinet had taken so long.

Toward the end, the transition period took on a sour note, with Clinton and the press carping at each other. The press irritated Clinton by asking about campaign pledges he had already gone back on: that he would propose a tax cut for the middle class and that he would reverse the Bush administration's policy of returning Haitians who were fleeing to America on boats. A few days before the inauguration, Stephanopoulos said at a briefing that there had been some "bumps in the road" and he was "relieved to have the transition end."

Clinton was to pay a very heavy price for waiting so long to choose his staff and for preferring inexperience.

3

EARLY TROUBLES

"They Hit the Ground Barely Standing"

Other administrations had had shakedown cruises, but this one was unusually rough—and it went on for quite some time.

The administration came to Washington with a "team" of people who hadn't worked together as a team and whose job descriptions weren't clear. A few weeks after the inauguration, Bruce Lindsey said he had concluded that the White House staff should have been chosen before the Cabinet. Clinton himself came to the same conclusion later. One experienced Washington observer said, as the new administration started to flounder almost immediately, "These problems stem from the fact that too much of the transition was spent picking too few officials, and everyone else was in abeyance. They hit the ground barely standing."

Astonishingly, there was no real plan for what the new administration would do after it got to Washington. George Stephanopoulos said that a memo covering the first two weeks had been drawn up before the Clinton people left Little Rock. And that was it. (The plan was to be updated every two weeks.) But the first two weeks didn't go according to what little plan there was. Lindsey said, "We had working groups during the transition—welfare, economic—but we hadn't put it all together. They each came up with plans and legislation in their area, but that's as far as it went. We had no time line before we came. No one sat down and said, 'If you do A, B, C, is your plate too full?' A couple of weeks into it, we realized that we had to think about it more strategically."

Lindsey also said, referring to Clinton's decision to put his campaign headquarters in Little Rock, "I'm absolutely convinced we shouldn't have had the campaign in D.C., but maybe the transition should have been here. It would have put us more in the frame of mind of how this city works."

Another senior White House official said that part of the problem was the headiness, if not arrogance, that came out of the election victory. "There was a legend developing from the fact that we won. It was only in part because we were smart. The truth was that eighty percent of the American people felt the country was headed in the wrong direction. 'Giddiness' is the right word for how the White House team was at the beginning. Some of the campaign people were glorified in *Time* and *Newsweek,* and it carried over into the administration. It suggested that we were more masters of our fate than reality allows, or we were in a position to be coming off the transition. We just weren't ready—emotionally, intellectually, organizationally, or substantively."

Then there was sheer fatigue. As Stephanopoulos said later, "A lot of the mistakes we made in the first weeks were because we were so tired." For many, there had been no respite from a long year of campaigning to straight into the transition, straight into the week-long inauguration festivities, straight into the White House. Weariness clouded their judgment and robbed them of the energy to cope with something that was a lot bigger and more difficult than they expected. Even the equipment—computers, faxes, telephones—they encountered was antiquated or didn't work. Clinton was stunned to discover that in order to make an outgoing call, he had to go through the switchboard. He quickly got this changed.

Most fatigued of all was the new President. Early on, a Cabinet officer said, "He said to me he's dog tired, that he's sixteen months tired. During the transition there were things he didn't want to take on. He needs to go to Camp David with Hillary and Chelsea and just hang out. Someone else asked him, When was the last time you and Hillary were together for a day? He couldn't remember."

The President had hoped to have his entire Cabinet confirmed by Congress and ready to be sworn in shortly after the inauguration. But one of his nominees was in trouble. On the day after Christmas, a Washington attorney who had vetted Zoe Baird for the White House counsel job told Howard Paster, who was to head the White House congressional liaison, that there was a problem with her record. Paster pressed for details and, upon learning the facts about the hiring of illegal immigrants, decided that it was a major problem, and he told this to McLarty. In a conference call a couple of days later with McLarty, Baird, and her husband, Paster expressed his concerns, hoping that Baird would withdraw—but she showed no interest in doing that. After the Renaissance Weekend, Baird told Paster that Clinton had told her that she would be OK.

In early January, Paster dispatched Baird to Capitol Hill, to tell Joseph Biden, the chairman of the Senate Judiciary Committee, and other committee members about the nanny problem. Biden sensed big trouble. When someone in Baird's entourage said that this violation of the law was the equivalent of a parking ticket, Biden replied, "No, this is like a wreck on a Los Angeles freeway."

On January 14, the *New York Times* ran a front-page story saying that Baird and her husband had hired illegal immigrants and hadn't paid Social Security taxes on them until earlier that month.

As soon as the *Times* story appeared, some Clinton advisers argued that Baird should be dumped. Clinton's and some of his advisers' failure to focus on trouble in this case was in part an unwillingness to face cutting someone loose and in part an angry reaction to press calls for someone to be dropped. It was, an adviser said, "A 'f—— you' attitude toward the press. 'Who the f—— is the press to tell us this?' " It was to be replicated in several other instances. Clinton's seeming unwillingness to face such decisions was based in large part on loyalty—but it had the effect of leaving people dangling all the longer.

Biden tried to warn the President's staff that Baird's nomination was in trouble, but he felt that he wasn't getting through. He then tried to convey this information to Christopher and to Cutler, Baird's sponsors, but neither seemed concerned. Biden was reading the Baird situation with the Clarence Thomas hearings still in mind, and he wasn't keen on presiding over another controversial television spectacular.

Reluctantly, Biden began the hearings on Baird's nomination on January 19. The next day, Inauguration Day, as Clinton lunched in the Capitol with members of Congress after his swearing in, Biden took him aside and said, "Tomorrow I will call you with one of two requests: either weigh in on her behalf and help the center hold, or take her down." Clinton seemed surprised that it had come to that, and indicated to Biden that he wasn't particularly eager to weigh in on Baird's behalf.

As Biden, who came from a blue-collar background, had foreseen, the Baird "nanny" issue set off a class conflict. Baird, who earned over five hundred thousand dollars a year, was seen by less affluent people to have bought her way out of a difficulty many working mothers faced. It was an issue easily digestible and usable by radio talk show hosts, who could stir up a strong enough public reaction on certain issues to give politicians pause, and sometimes to change their vote. This plebiscitary decision making wasn't necessarily a good thing, since it short-circuited an intended deliberative process and further undermined an already eroding willingness of politicians to take an unpopular stand. But it was a real phenomenon, and the specter of such a call-in campaign was enough to make politicians hide under their desks.

One of Baird's problems was that she didn't have a constituency—except for the older, establishment male lawyers who had championed her. A Clinton adviser said later, "When the old-boy network meets diversity, you get Zoe Baird." One reason she had been chosen over Brooksley Born was that she *wasn't* backed by women's groups. Moreover, when she got in trouble, it was hard to make the case that Baird had the stature or breadth of experience to be Attorney General.

On the second day of Baird's hearing, the day after the inauguration, she made a poor impression on the Judiciary Committee members. Several found her too cool and self-assured, her ambition too much on display. Asked whether she thought she had the credentials to be Attorney General, Baird replied, "I think that my overall record gives me the potential to be a great Attorney General."

And there was something else, which didn't become public, that caused problems for her confirmation. Word reached the Judiciary Committee and the White House that the immigration lawyer to whom Baird and her husband turned had a different story about how soon they had sought legal help.

As Baird's hearing on the President's first full day in office went on, her position deteriorated rapidly. The phone calls to the Hill were running over three hundred to one against her. At his daily briefing, Stephanopoulos, looking gray, gave her less than full support. One could hear the saw in the background. Alan Simpson, Republican of Wyoming and a member of the Judiciary Committee, said that he couldn't support Baird because she had broken the immigration law, which he had written. Moderate to conservative Democrats—Bennett Johnston and John Breaux, of Louisiana; David Boren, of Oklahoma—came out against her confirmation. There was now a real question as to whether there would be sufficient votes to confirm her. Nancy Kassebaum, a moderate Republican from Kansas, came out against her.

At the White House, there was a rolling meeting all day about what to do. Around noon, the President summoned Paster and Bernard Nussbaum, the White House counsel, to the Oval Office. Nussbaum had just begun lunch in the Mess with his deputy, Vincent Foster. (Foster was one of three of Mrs. Clinton's former partners at the Rose Law Firm who were placed in strategic positions in the administration. The others were William Kennedy, who was also given a job in the counsel's office, and Webster Hubbell, who was made Associate Attorney General, the number three job in the department and, under the circumstances, a very powerful position. On Inauguration Day, an administration official said, "Webb went over to Justice and planted the flag.")

Mrs. Clinton may not have followed the dictum that a President should pick an Attorney General who's close to him, but she did other things to see to it that her husband's—and her own—interests would be looked after. Not only did she put her Rose partners in strategic places, but she had known Nussbaum, a corporate-takeover lawyer in New York, since she worked for him in 1973–74 on the legal staff of the House Judiciary Committee's impeachment proceedings. They had stayed in touch over the years, and Nussbaum had contributed to Clinton's campaigns. One day, Ickes suggested Nussbaum as White House counsel, and Mrs. Clinton and Thomases concurred. Nussbaum, reached in New York, got to Little Rock that same day.

The President, sitting in the Oval Office, looked glum. The First Lady, McLarty, Paster, and Stephanopoulos were also there. Clinton addressed Nussbaum: "It looks like Zoe Baird isn't going too well. What do you think I should do?" Nussbaum replied, "I think you should fight." Paster said that he thought they had a serious problem. Nussbaum and Paster were dispatched to Capitol Hill to meet with Baird and her husband and make sure they understood how serious the problem was.

Baird said she wanted to fight. Paster canvassed several senators on and off the committee and, returning to the White House, reported to the President, "We're losing ground." The committee Democrats weren't happy, he reported; the White House would have to depend on Republicans just to get her cleared by the committee for a vote in the full Senate. McLarty called David Pryor, a Democratic senator from Arkansas, who was trying hard to help his friend the new President. Pryor said, "Cut your losses."

Meanwhile, Biden had decided, "This thing is over." In the early evening, the President called George Mitchell, the Senate majority leader, to get his assessment, and Mitchell called Biden. Biden had kept the hearing going that night until matters got settled at the White House, as senators asked Baird softball questions, which Baird misinterpreted as a sign that she was doing well. Biden thought that if the hearings went over to the next day, matters would only get worse. From Mitchell's office the two men called Clinton. They couldn't get through to him. Biden told Mitchell to tell the White House that if they didn't get a call back from the President within fifteen minutes, he would go public with an announcement that Baird's nomination was finished. Biden and Mitchell then called Paster to tell him they couldn't get through to the President; they asked him to tell Clinton that the situation was hopeless.

Clinton called and said, "Joe, what's the situation?" Biden told him, and Clinton replied, "Oh, God." The President and his aides were still trying to figure a way out of this morass, to do something that would have Baird's participation and perhaps preserve her dignity. They couldn't stop the hearings, because that would alert the press to a crisis.

The hearing adjourned at about 9:30 P.M. Warren Christopher and Vernon Jordan went to Lloyd Cutler's law firm to meet Baird and tell her that her nomination was going to fail. Baird wouldn't accept the fact that her chances were nil. The senators had been kind to her this evening, she said, and large numbers of people had stopped her on the street to wish her well.

After midnight, Paster reached Biden, back home in Delaware (where he commuted every night), and asked him to call Baird and explain to her that it was over. Baird's pride and confusion were understandable. She wasn't blameless, but she paid a big price that stemmed from other people's actions. She had come face-to-face with some of Washington's hypocrisy; her case had been mishandled by the Clinton people.

That night—the night Clinton had promised himself that he would start to catch up on his sleep—he was up until well past midnight, as an exchange of letters between himself and Baird was arranged. Paster, Stephanopoulos, and others were camped out in Stephanopoulos's office, where the President, dressed in a jogging suit, joined them. The negotiations ended, and the White House put out its statement at 1:30 A.M. By this time, cleaning women were clearing up the West Wing offices, and the new President went around introducing himself to them.

On Friday, Clinton admitted error, saying that he shouldn't have been rushed by the Christmas Eve deadline for naming the Cabinet. In response to a reporter's question, Clinton said, "In retrospect what I should have done is to basically delay the whole thing for a few days and look into it in greater depth."

The Baird episode on day one demonstrated that the congressional Democrats weren't going to roll over for the new Democratic President, and it brought Clinton's judgment into question before his term really got started. White House aides were reeling.

Without a substantive program to put forward, the only early actions Clinton could take were by executive order. He had signed an executive order on new ethics guidelines for government appointees immediately after the luncheon in the Capitol that followed his swearing in. Now, on Friday, his second full day in office, in a televised Oval Office ceremony, he was to sign a group of executive orders that were aimed at undoing some of those by Ronald Reagan and George Bush. (Clinton's new executive orders had been cobbled together quickly by a group headed by an outside attorney, Walter Dellinger, a constitutional law professor at Duke, who was first contacted only a week earlier.) In the ceremony, Clinton signed orders lifting restrictions on abortion counseling (the "gag rule") and on federally sponsored research on medical use of fetal tissue; ending restrictions on the use of U.S. funds for UN population programs that included abortion counseling, and restoring the right of U.S. military hospitals overseas to perform abortions paid for with private funds; and ordering a review of the government ban on private importing of the French abortion pill, RU-486.

What most of the Clinton people—including Clinton—didn't realize until later was that by making his first order of business the undoing of these orders, all of them on social issues, the President, who had run for office as a centrist, was placing himself on the left side of the spectrum, appearing to be responding to interest groups on that side. Stan Greenberg, Clinton's campaign pollster and still a major adviser, had argued against issuing the abortion orders right away. At the same time, Clinton and his aides were struggling to figure out how to act on his campaign promise to issue an executive order lifting the ban on gays serving in the military.

In October 1991, through the good offices of his friend David Mixner, a major gay leader and fund-raiser in California, Clinton had met in Los Angeles with ANGLE, a group of twenty major gay and lesbian campaign donors nationwide. Gays were a major force within the Democratic Party, as organizers and fund-raisers, and, covertly or openly, Democratic candidates had regularly courted them, especially in California. At the time Clinton met with this group, he was running third among gays, after Paul Tsongas and Jerry Brown. In the meeting, Clinton was warm, as usual, and empathetic. Asked if he would issue an executive order to end the ban on gays serving in the military, he said that he would do it as one of the first acts of his administration. There was no room for compromise on this, Clinton told the group. This wasn't the issue of paramount importance to gay groups; a gay and lesbian civil rights bill, including a ban on discrimination in public accommodations, was of greater moment to them. But this seemed the issue Clinton was most comfortable with. (In a typical straddle, in the course of the campaign, Clinton, as opposed to all of his Democratic rivals, declined to support the gay and lesbian civil rights bill.)

Nevertheless, Mixner said, "Clinton became the Abraham Lincoln of our movement," which, he said, raised $3.5 million for him over the primary and general elections, and the gay and lesbian vote went strongly for Clinton in the general election. After the election, it was estimated that one in seven of those who voted for Clinton were homosexual. (Gays are generally estimated to make up 10 percent of the population.)

During the campaign, Clinton said that the military ban should be removed, and his campaign's official position paper said: "Bill Clinton has called for an immediate repeal of the ban on gays and lesbians serving in the United States armed forces." But not much attention was paid to the fact that Clinton had taken this position. In the course of the campaign, Sam Nunn did meet with Clinton and warn him that the issue was complicated and highly controversial within the military. He told Clinton that whatever he did, he shouldn't have an immediate de facto policy of permitting gays in the military. "The military isn't ready for it," Nunn said. The issue wasn't actually whether gays could serve in the military; despite the military's policy banning their serving they had done so for a long time. The issue concerned the existing ban on gays serving, as well as the services' practices of asking applicants if they were gay and rooting out gays—the Navy was the most vigorous about this—or dismissing an avowed gay. As the argument unfolded, Clinton took the position that homosexual status shouldn't count but certain sorts of conduct would. Nunn took the position that status *was* conduct.

Shortly after the election, following a Veterans Day event at the Arkansas statehouse, Andrea Mitchell, of NBC, asked Clinton whether he intended to fulfill his campaign pledge on gays in the military. Clinton replied, "Yes, I want to." He also said that he would consult with the chiefs of the armed services on the best way to go about this, and on the appropriate timing. Clinton's comments set off an uproar, especially among veterans groups. (A week before the election, Mixner had flown to Little Rock to urge that the postelection priority be the civil rights bill, rather than gays in the military, which he warned was the more difficult issue.)

Two days after Clinton's Veterans Day remarks, Colin Powell, who had openly expressed his opposition to lifting the ban, said that the Joint Chiefs of Staff and the senior commanders "continue to believe strongly that the presence of homosexuals within the armed forces would be prejudicial to good order and discipline."

During the transition, Powell met with Clinton at the Hay-Adams Hotel, in Washington, and, according to a Powell associate, told Clinton that he couldn't leave the meeting without telling him that the gays issue was a very hot one within the military. Without being committal, Clinton said he would take that into account.

Paul Begala, a major campaign adviser and now a consultant to Clinton, said later, "It wasn't a big thing in the campaign. We clearly had no appreciation of the offense that would be taken at a Presidential directive ending the ban."

The thought had been that the work on the order, involving various consultations, would be done by Inauguration Day, so that Clinton could keep his pledge to issue the order as one of the first acts of his administration. But, like a lot of other things, this didn't get done in time.

As Inauguration Day approached, some of Clinton's political advisers—especially Begala and Greenberg—wanted him to just get rid of the issue, put it off. But other campaign advisers argued that the commitment had been made. Clinton was caught in a vise: he could please the gays and anger the military, or appease the military and make the gay community bitter. And he was already being criticized for abandoning some campaign pledges.

On the Sunday night that the Clintons arrived in Washington for the inauguration, after the performance at the Lincoln Memorial, Clinton met at Blair House with Aspin, Powell, and some of the Pentagon officials. Powell and the others were there to brief the President on SIOP (Single Integrated Operational Plan), the codes and options for waging nuclear war. After the briefing, Aspin stayed behind to meet with Clinton and National Security Adviser Anthony Lake, and Samuel Berger, Lake's deputy, and Stephanopoulos. Aspin had already cleared with Stephanopoulos a proposal to get Clinton out of his immediate bind: rather than issue the executive order right away, Clinton should refer the matter to Aspin and direct him to report by July 15 on an executive order and how it should be implemented. This would buy Clinton some time. Meanwhile, Aspin suggested, Clinton could decline to answer questions on the subject, referring them to the Pentagon. It took Clinton a long time to learn this. And it cost him.

By the time of the inauguration, several other people had come to the conclusion that a postponement was a good idea. George Mitchell had told the Clinton people that if Nunn or Republicans moved to write the existing policy into law, he didn't have the votes to defeat that. The Democrats were planning to bring up a bill (twice vetoed by Bush) called the family leave bill, to give workers up to twelve weeks per year of unpaid leave for the birth or adoption of a child or the illness of a family member, and the Republicans (or Nunn) could try to attach an amendment codifying existing policy on gays in the military. Mitchell needed something to point to that would defer the collision and would enable his flock to avoid casting a difficult vote at the outset of the new session.

On the day after the inauguration, Aspin presented the plan to the Joint Chiefs, in the "tank"—the soundproof (but not leakproof) room where sensitive meetings were held. He told the Chiefs, "Nobody's going to change anybody's mind. We need to talk about how we would do this thing if it is done." The meeting was a stormy one, which lasted for an hour and a half and ended with a request by the Chiefs to see the President.

Colin Powell and Bill Clinton had an uneasy relationship from the beginning. Powell wasn't happy about Clinton's pledge on gays, and he was worried that Clinton intended to make deep cuts in the military budget. And Powell was in an uncomfortable position. Many of the officers with whom he worked, and whom he represented, saw Clinton as a draft-dodging naïf on military policy and his young staff as arrogant. (The story, which was true, of a young woman on the White House staff, upon being greeted by a senior military official, saying, "I don't talk to the military," shot like a shell through the Pentagon.)

Clinton, in turn, was uneasy about Powell, an independent force who had played more of a policy role than most Chairmen of the Joint Chiefs and was known to have at times let the press know of his policy differences with his bosses. Clinton knew that he had to establish a working relationship with the military and try to win its respect—and that to fail to do so would be harmful politically and in terms of trying to govern. Yet he was starting out with a very bad issue for that relationship.

Powell also wasn't overly fond of Les Aspin, with whom he had had collisions when Aspin was Chairman of the House Armed Services Committee and whom (like some others) he regarded as a publicity hound. Aspin clearly intended to play a more active role as Secretary of Defense, through setting up new policy shops under his direction, and to be a more assertive boss than Dick Cheney, his Republican predecessor. Moreover, Powell was tired and wanted to get out. His retirement date wasn't until September 30, but he had told Cheney that he would like to leave early, have a nice vacation, and get on with his life. He had never owned a home, and he wanted to make some money. Later he told friends that he wanted to be out early in 1993, but they advised him that it would look bad if he left when a new President was coming in. Then, in late January, when rumors started to circulate—fanned by Powell's "friends"—that he wanted to leave, the White House let it be known that the President hoped he would stay. At that point, Powell had no choice but to stay until the end of his term.

Powell had said in a speech on January 12, to the midshipmen at Annapolis, that if they found the new plan on gays in the military "completely unacceptable and it strikes the heart of your moral beliefs, then I think you have to resign." This was hardly an endorsement of the direction the President-elect had pledged to take. Powell added, "Homosexuality is not a benign behavioral characteristic such as skin color. It goes to the core of the most fundamental aspect of human behavior." Powell, according to associates, bridled at suggestions that integrating gays into the military was a latter-day parallel to integrating the races in the armed forces. Race wasn't a matter of choice, he said. As the nation's first black Chairman of the Joint Chiefs, and as a national hero, Powell's voice counted for much in this debate. A military friend of Powell's said, "For some reason, Colin is emotional about this."

A high military official said, "The Chiefs didn't have to gear Powell up to talk to the President about it. Everybody in the Joint Chiefs is hard over against doing this, including Colin." Some of the military leaders took their stand on the issue as a matter of "unit cohesiveness"—the military doctrine that members of a unit fight for each other in battle. Some put it on grounds of "privacy," since servicemen share bunks and other communal facilities, and some raised the inflammatory issue that straights shouldn't have to share showers with gays.

And there was something else, which the Chiefs, and Nunn, didn't talk about publicly. Senator David Boren, a close friend of Nunn's, said, only a few days after Clinton took office, "It's not about allowing gays in the military—not to Sam and Powell and some others. It's about assuming gays will next push for nonregulation of behavior and fearing that Clinton won't resist. A lot of people think that if they get in they'll want to act out the gay culture—kissing, holding hands, dancing on the dance floor. So their worry is that Clinton will allow the gay *culture* in addition to the status, and they think gays are going to push for that. They're worried whether Clinton will be strong enough to let the Chiefs write rules that the gays don't like." Clinton had been in office less than a week.

On Monday, January 25, the new President sat down in the Roosevelt Room for a two-hour meeting with Powell and his deputy, Admiral David Jeremiah, and the Chiefs of Staff of the four military services. Also present were Gore, Lake, Berger, Aspin, Stephanopoulos, and Leon Fuerth (Gore's representative on the staff of the National Security Council). It was a rough meeting. Starting at one end of the table, each Chief had his say. All of them were opposed to the President's proposed order. Each of the Chiefs came at it from a slightly different point of view. General Carl Mundy, the Marine Commandant, who was the most opposed, spoke of it as a moral issue. (Mundy later circulated a videotape showing gays as black-leather-clad sex fiends.) The Army Chief of Staff, General Gordon Sullivan, said it was an issue of the morale of the forces. General Merrill McPeak, the Air Force

Chief, the most pragmatic, said a compromise could be found. Chief of Naval Operations Admiral Frank Kelso took a middling position.

Clinton told the Chiefs that he had made a campaign commitment and had taken the oath of office to defend the Constitution. "If I felt I couldn't do this and defend the Constitution, I wouldn't do it," Clinton said. Clinton was very temperate. He didn't tell the Chiefs that he was the Commander in Chief and this was what he was going to do—as even some military people thought he should have.

At the end, Mundy said, "Mr. President, I hope we don't come over here and have many more meetings like this." Clinton replied, "This country has gone wrong sometimes because there haven't been meetings like this."

An adviser to Clinton said that the meeting was "an example of Powell's political savvy. He was able to be intimidating and helpful all at once." But the meeting left a lot of people uneasy. The Chiefs were testing Clinton.

At the same time, Nunn was bringing pressure on the President. He wouldn't accept suspension of the policy of ejecting gays from the services during the six-month period before a new policy went into effect, while the Pentagon studied the matter—as Stephanopoulos, who was in touch with gay leaders, was arguing should be the interim policy. Nunn made it clear that if the President didn't satisfy him on this point, he would encode existing policy through a rider on the family leave bill.

Nunn was testing Clinton too, giving him a lesson on power in Washington. After extensive negotiating with Nunn, who rejected one tentative agreement, the President arrived at the new approach. (Stephanopoulos said later, "We were trying to figure out a way to close it down.") The Secretary of Defense would present him with a draft executive order on July 15; in the meantime, the services would no longer ask applicants about their sexual orientation, and avowed or discovered gays would be put on standby reserve, losing all pay and benefits, and would have to petition for readmission if the ban was permanently lifted. This met Nunn's demands. Clinton announced the policy on Friday, January 29, at a news conference in the White House briefing room. Standing in front of the blue curtain, Clinton said, "This compromise is not everything I would have hoped for or everything I have stood for." Clinton looked pale and uncertain—he conveyed no sense of command. The scene was alarming to many people. It was his second capitulation in his first nine days in office.

Democrats on Capitol Hill weren't impressed, and some were appalled. An important senator said privately, "A lot of people can't understand why he's breaking his promise to the middle class and fulfilling one to gays." Even though Clinton had postponed issuing the executive order, his having the issue arise so early in his Presidency—as he had promised, even if he didn't do all that he had promised—was seen as bowing to interest groups, as were his continuing to seek a female Attorney General and his issuing the first executive orders on reproductive rights. He didn't look like "a different kind of Democrat."

A senior military official said that the Chiefs had come very close to insubordination on the gays issue and that Clinton should have established his authority over them at the outset. The fact that he didn't worried a number of people. It gave the impression that Clinton saw the military as another constituency to be wooed, one he was afraid to be tough with because of his own vulnerabilities. This was a potentially dangerous situation.

The controversy over the gays issue raised serious questions about Clinton's judgment and his strength. According to Stan Greenberg's polls, the issue caused a sharp decline in Clinton's favorability ratings—nearly 20 percent in his first two weeks in office. And the effect was to last.

In the face of criticism for making gays in the military such an early priority of his Presidency, Clinton blamed the Republicans for forcing the issue to come up when it did by threatening to add a rider to the pending family leave bill preserving and writing into law the existing Pentagon ban on gays in the military. This of course was untrue. Though Republicans were making the threat, Clinton had introduced the subject. A Clinton adviser, one who had helped propagate the claim that the Republicans had started it all, later privately called it "a lie"—and this was perhaps the first example in his Presidency of his tendency to lay blame off on others.

On the second weekend that Clinton was in office, at six-thirty Saturday morning—it was still dark, and very cold—the Cabinet members, their deputies, and top White House staff members pulled themselves into buses to take them to a retreat at Camp David, the rustic Presidential weekend place in the Catoctin mountains, in Maryland. The Camp David retreat, with the Clintons and the Gores attending—complete with two "facilitators"—was just the sort of thing the aging baby boomers now in charge of the White House liked. It had a sense of Renaissance Weekend. Many aides thought that the idea, as one put it, "was nuts." There were two purposes. The first was to make sure that the team understood the working hypotheses and the goals of the Clinton administration. The second, of course, was "bonding."

The lead-off session that Saturday in Laurel Lodge, in a large, nondescript dining-hall-like room, was conducted, appropriately enough, given the prominent, and unprecedented, role they were to play in the Clinton administration, by three veterans of the campaign who were to be President Clinton's floating consultants: Greenberg, Begala, and Mandy Grunwald, who had run the campaign's media strategy. (The fourth consultant, James Carville, who had ended up in charge of Clinton's campaign, was traveling.) The consultants told the Cabinet officers why Clinton had won and what the continuing political strategy should be.

Begala, laying out "the people's idea of Bill Clinton," explained that Clinton was seen as a very human person, a tribune of economic change, very rooted in the middle class and its values, and a big break from both George Bush and traditional Democrats. He said that people had come to see that Clinton believed what he was talking about. They saw Clinton, Begala said, as a President of hope and optimism, at a time when they were in economic pain.

A key phrase all weekend was that this was "a rare moment in American history." As Mandy Grunwald put it, people were more frightened of the status quo than of change; seared by the loss of the idea of America, they now felt that if you played by the rules you couldn't win, because the system was rigged. People were fed up with Congress and with Washington, she said, because very little of what touched people's lives seemed to penetrate the discourse of Washington. The cynicism about Washington shouldn't be underestimated, Grunwald said. People were very focused on the economy, health care, and the need to reform the political system. Words wouldn't be enough; the politicians had to produce results. Candor really matters, Grunwald said. There was a reason Ross Perot had done as well as he had in the election: he had cut through the bull and talked directly to people.

Greenberg's topic was "What must be communicated." The President's pollster told the Cabinet officers that the people were hopeful but skeptical and that leaders who got in trouble were those who pursued policies with arrogance. Greenberg said that while the public discourse was ostensibly about the economy, it was really about living standards, because the middle class had suffered during the Reagan-Bush era. People want to know that there is a sense of direction, he said. They had taken a chance on the person with a plan. The welfare issue, Greenberg said, was one of stressing responsibility. This had been one of the major themes of Clinton's three addresses at Georgetown University in 1991, to define Clinton as turning from the standard Democratic "handout" programs. Clinton's campaign pledge was to "end welfare as we know it," by insisting that recipients be moved off the rolls after two years. They were to be given job training and, if they couldn't find jobs, be given public sector jobs. The Clinton administration was to find out over the next year and a half how difficult it was to draft such a program and find the money to pay for it. More than once in Clinton's Presidency, Greenberg would urge that Clinton give a speech on the subject, as a way of reasserting his supposed centrism.

Greenberg stressed that Clinton had run as a national Democrat, not as a vehicle of disaggregated groups. The campaign discourse, he reminded them, was activist, and its most critical aspect was that it showed Clinton with people, connecting with them. This, he said, was why Clinton insisted on wading into crowds, why he rode a bus, why he had spoken out against big government and bureaucracy and about taxing the wealthy.

People want big change, Greenberg said. They believed that they had been lied to going back to the Vietnam War and Lyndon Johnson. They want things to move now; they want to see an end to gridlock. The risk the assembled group faced, he said, was further political decay, and a volatile reaction to that. Therefore, the Clinton administration should do things to capture these feelings: find visible things to do to reorganize and streamline the bureaucracy.

The campaign aides who were to be outside political consultants—an arrangement that would be made formal later—weren't much in evidence during Clinton's first couple of weeks in office, except for Begala, who was helping on the economic program. Carville was in and out of the White House. In the course of the Camp David retreat, Clinton told Begala, Greenberg, and Grunwald that he wanted them to be more involved. He was upset that as a result of leaks by his own advisers, the stories about his economic plan, still in formulation, talked almost solely about deficit reduction. He wanted his various goals to be better understood. "The President wanted a more strategically driven administration," Greenberg commented later. Within two weeks, the consultants were attending regular White House meetings, where they discussed with top aides the President's schedule and speeches, and White House announcements.

Greenberg was concerned that Clinton hadn't come to office with a governing coalition. The day after the inauguration, he told the Democratic National Committee that though according to the public polls Clinton had been more popular than anyone who entered office since polling began, the 1992 election wasn't a realigning one. Unlike Richard Nixon, who in 1968 also won by 43 percent, and had cultivated the George Wallace constituency so that it became part of a Republican coalition, Greenberg warned, "we have not yet formed a new Democratic majority." The obvious partner, he pointed out, was Perot's following, whose chief characteristic was that it was angry at government. "I view this as our primary task," Greenberg said. Forming that coalition was going to be a lot more difficult than the Clinton people thought. The attempt would lead at times to a bifurcated Clinton: a Clinton who was trying to get things done in Washington and a Clinton who attacked Washington; a Clinton who had to work with the barons and other congressional powers to get his program through Congress and a Clinton who called for political reform.

The next panel at the Camp David retreat, shortly before noon the first day, was billed in the program as "A free-flowing discussion of how the Government, the Nation and the World will be different as a result of the Clinton-Gore administration."

Clinton told the group, "If we have a vision, it enables us to make it through tough times." He went on, "For twenty years, our ability to generate opportunity and to live together has been eroding." This led, he said, to the importance of inspiring hope, then of providing opportunity and of pulling people together. He added that opportunity is not enough, that they had to change things, help people take responsibility for their own lives.

"The key vision," Clinton said, "is that at the dawn of a new century we can make the twenty-first century an American century." He added, "We must be driven by something that is bigger than ourselves. We must find ways to make people triumphant in the face of change, make our major institutions friendly to change and change friendly to them." Someone had told him, he said, that it's scary to be "little people."

Gore said that the process of governing is different from the campaign, where there is a defined "enemy"—"a way of thinking" that doesn't care about people. But, Gore added, there is a way for an administration to provide focus on an enemy. We must achieve a new way of thinking about the future, and make the government work. We are at a crossroads, Gore said.

Then Mrs. Clinton addressed the group. Hillary Clinton spoke to this group in a way no previous President's wife, however influential through her husband—or even, like Eleanor Roosevelt, in part on her own—would have found imaginable. It made very clear the strong and central role she would be playing. She pointed out that in Clinton's first term as governor of Arkansas, he had tried to do too much in too short a span of time, but that after he lost after one term and recouped by changing his approach (and his wife changed her last name from Rodham to Clinton), they had focused on education reform. (Mrs. Clinton had taken on the project.) She said that they had made "the enemy" the educational establishment. (Establishing opponents of Mrs. Clinton's goals as "enemies" was to be a feature of the Clinton Presidency.)

In her charge to the group, Mrs. Clinton said that the story of what we want to accomplish has to be written before the plan; then we must fill in the details, and be sure to make that story human. We need an administration that is responsive, she said, that makes people feel included, involved in the process. Perquisites should be limited, she said; there should be few differences between people in and out of government.

At a later point in the program, Mrs. Clinton instructed the group, "Don't believe what the press says or writes that someone on the team says about you."

In another session, Clinton laid out his five priorities for the first year. It was an ambitious list: a stimulus program to reinvigorate the job base; an economic program that reduced the deficit and shifted priorities from consumption to investment; a political reform bill, including reform of campaign financing and new restrictions on lobbying; a national service bill; welfare reform; comprehensive reform of health care. Beyond this list, Clinton said, there were other things the government could do: work on policies that protect the environment and sustain jobs; teach everyone who works to read; stress training and apprenticeship programs; adopt a trade policy that recognizes the competitive dimensions of world realities; reduce the homeless population.

That evening, after a long day, there was a fireside chat in a living room setting in Laurel Lodge. The two facilitators—Gore had proposed one of them, a management consultant who had worked with his Senate office on "team building" and other organizational problems—led a discussion in which these assembled leaders of the world were to tell something about themselves that people didn't know; tell some ways they would like to change; and say how their subordinates, the people closest to them, would reflect their management style.

As the forty-odd top officials of the new administration, all of them casually dressed, sat around an open fire, Bill and Hillary Clinton on one side of the fireplace, Al and Tipper Gore on the other, with Cabinet members and White House staff seated on couches or on the floor, they made their confessions. The President revealed that he had been taunted in school when he was five and six because he was a fat kid. Donna Shalala said people didn't know she was a twin. Henry Cisneros revealed that even though he lived in Texas, he had been a Washington Redskins fan for twenty years. Richard Riley, bent from a spinal disease, said he had been cocaptain of his high school football team and had never lost that competitiveness. Warren Christopher, the seemingly buttoned-up Secretary of State, said that he liked jazz and enjoyed going to piano bars.

The bonding went on over Sunday, with sessions on Connecting with the

White House Staff: Key Interfaces, White House/Cabinet; Policy Development; Congress/Communications Strategies; Conflict Management. An afternoon session was devoted to "If We Are Serious About Team Work . . . ," which was described in the program as "Everything about the history of the federal bureaucracy, the agency structures dictated by statute, the ethos of this town, and the interfaces with Congress, lobbyists, and the media will work against cross-agency cooperation. Real teamwork is definitely counterculture; we will have to dedicate ourselves to build a new culture at our level and throughout the federal bureaucracy."

A Cabinet officer said later, "It would be easy to make fun of a weekend like this, but it was a very productive exercise." Others, less enthusiastic, generally didn't comment.

On Friday, February 5, members of the White House staff were exhausted but in a good mood. That morning, the President signed the family leave bill into law in a ceremony in the Rose Garden. It was the first truly positive thing that had happened, providing the first truly positive story since they had taken over the White House. Maybe, some speculated, the curse was behind them.

And Clinton was about to name a new candidate for Attorney General. Stephanopoulos, feeling upbeat at last, hoped that this could be done by Sunday or Monday, "to close out this period." He was looking forward to a good ending to Clinton's first two and a half weeks in office. It was very odd that this new Presidency was already being measured—internally and by the press—in terms of a week at a time: Could Clinton get through a week without a pratfall? The internal weekly assessment was whether the public relations of the week had been positive or negative. While it was important that a President get off to a good start, make a good impression—which Clinton did not—praise for a given week would be ephemeral, have little to do with his ultimate record.

As their next nominee for Attorney General, Mrs. Clinton and Susan Thomases had settled on Kimba Wood (who had been suggested by Harold Ickes), a forty-nine-year-old federal district court judge in New York. The President agreed. Mrs. Clinton and the President had interviewed her, as did Nussbaum, but, oddly, all this took place before Wood had been thoroughly vetted. On Thursday night, February 4, the White House confirmed to two major newspapers that Wood was to be named. At just about that same time, the vetters found that Wood and her husband, the political writer Michael Kramer, had employed an illegal alien as a baby-sitter—though before the law was passed that made such employment illegal. Also, the Social Security taxes had been paid. Still, there was great perturbation among the President's aides. Stephanopoulos and Lindsey felt that this would be too difficult to explain, that again the talk show hosts—especially Rush Limbaugh, the conservative nemesis of the Clinton administration—would have a field day. Moreover, they felt that they hadn't been leveled with. Late that night, the newspapers were called back and asked to hold the story.

So the next day, behind the facade of happiness over the President's first bill signing, there was high anxiety in the White House. Clinton decided that he couldn't go forward, that the nomination should be put on hold, a nondecision. Nussbaum met Wood and her husband at the law office of one of the vetters and told them that they should act on the assumption there would be no nomination. Wood and Kramer said they wanted to put out a statement saying that she was withdrawing from consideration; they insisted, over Nussbaum's objections, that since there had been a leak that she would be named, there would probably be a leak about this (a reasonable assumption). They wanted to get the story out in time for the network news broadcasts that night. Nussbaum begged them to wait. The White House definitely didn't want this to be the day's story. Stephanopoulos pleaded for forty-five minutes. He hoped, unrealistically, that if Wood didn't make a statement, the story would just fade away. But the statement was issued, and it of course overtook the pleasant story about the signing of the family leave bill. Another week was ruined.

A few days later, Clinton went to Michigan to conduct his first town meeting as President. He got wrong some answers to questions put to him by the audience, took jabs at Washington, and said the gays-in-the-military issue had come up so early because the Republicans had forced it.

A troubling aspect of the Clinton Presidency was beginning to surface and was noticed at this early point by some experienced observers in Washington, including leading Democrats. Clinton was running the risk of being too informal and too accessible. From his and his advisers' point of view, his showing up for a town meeting in the third week of his Presidency and making many appearances on television were attempts to get through to "the people." Furthermore, by getting out of Washington he could work around it. This was a perfectly plausible goal, but he was overdoing it—and in the process risking the dignity and majesty of the office that he had so ardently sought. These aspects of the Presidency are needed—at times they are crucial—if a President is to lead. Similarly, his frequent trips to Capitol Hill, in an effort to be accessible—there had been two during the first week in February—caused some members of Congress to feel that he was trying too hard to be their buddy. He should be a little more distant, they thought.

On Thursday, February 11, Clinton had been in office for three weeks and a day.

George Stephanopoulos, presiding in the crowded briefing room, said, "The President will have an announcement today regarding the Attorney General." There were teasing cheers and applause from the press, and Stephanopoulos broke into a relieved grin. Clinton was, as usual, running late that morning, and therefore so was Stephanopoulos. It was by now understood within the White House that Clinton usually ran late and one never knew when a scheduled event would actually take place.

The President was meeting with a group of congressmen, Stephanopoulos said, and would do so every day, straight through to the following Wednesday, when he was to present his economic plan in a televised speech to the Congress.

In his office after the briefing, Stephanopoulos, who had turned thirty-two the previous day, looked older than he had a few months before. His face was more angular, the baby-faced innocence gone. He was very weary.

The large office he had inherited from previous press secretaries—looking out over the North Lawn, the sun streaming in through the floor-to-ceiling windows—was strewn with birthday items: a "Curious George" monkey wearing a cap that said "Attorney General"; helium-filled silver balloons (from the press) labeled "Stimulus," "Bosnia," "Spending Cuts," "Nominees." There were three vases of roses and some leftover chocolate cake.

Stephanopoulos was popular within the White House. He was extremely intelligent, and he had a sense of humor and proportion. He had been a Rhodes Scholar, but not the sort who had to tell people about it. Though his diminutiveness (five feet seven inches) made people feel protective toward him, he could be a killer. But Stephanopoulos was overworked and very nearly overwhelmed. He was in charge of the Office of Communications, with its staff of some fifty-two people, which dealt with all the ways Clinton communicated—in speeches, through surrogates, by satellite (getting around the Washington press corps), coordinating "the message" with members of Congress—and he sat in on all meetings the President had with Cabinet officers and all important meetings on domestic policy. He also worked on legislative strategy, often with people he knew from his days as House Majority Leader Dick Gephardt's chief assistant for legislation.

As Stephanopoulos sat at a circular table, eating a dry turkey sandwich from the White House Mess, Bernie Nussbaum came in, smiling, his sleeves rolled up. "Everything's OK," he said. Stephanopoulos broke into a smile. Their long nightmare over an Attorney General was ending. Janet Reno, the Dade County state attorney, was to be named that afternoon, to much applause.

After Nussbaum left, Stephanopoulos said, "I keep thinking this will get better. It's so much. We've had a lot of bad luck. You lose an Attorney General on your first day, and it's very tough to recover." This wasn't the "spin" that the outside world was getting about how wonderful it was that the President was focusing on his economic program. He continued, talking about the second Attorney General fiasco, "Last Friday, we had a great week until 5:20 P.M. Family leave was looking very good."

Asked what he had learned in the first three weeks, Stephanopoulos replied, "We've learned about the power of the President's voice. When he says something, it pretty much drives everything else away." While stepping around the subject, Stephanopoulos alluded to the fact that Clinton hadn't learned to discipline himself about what he said. As a Cabinet officer put it, Clinton tended to toss off ideas that he hadn't yet fully considered. It was his long-standing method of trying out thoughts. But it could be confusing to the public and lead Clinton to put out half-baked ideas.

Stephanopoulos said that they had learned that "you have to make decisions faster. The longer it takes, the more likely that the process gets spoiled."

Continuing on that point, Stephanopoulos said, revealing a great deal about the decision-making process in the early Clinton White House, "We have to work on our internal decision-making structure. We have to come up with a system that lets Clinton be Clinton—even more, *help* Clinton be Clinton. He needs the time to talk, to bring people together. What we have to do to help him is shorten the frame between his discussions—let's say on an Attorney General—and his decision. If he wants to talk to a lot of people, make sure the work has been done, and then he does the deciding. All the backup work has to be done more quickly, more precisely, so that he can get on with the decisions. Things that come out of his seeing more people and talking to people—more questions—we should get that work done fast. When you talk to so many people, there's a danger of it leaking."

Though Stephanopoulos recognized early some of the problems with the way the Clinton White House functioned, it was to be a very long time before the needed changes were even addressed.

4

FACING THE FACTS

"The Dynamic Is Inside Himself"

Bob Rubin hadn't enjoyed the inaugural festivities. Rubin, the chairman of the new National Economic Council, was to coordinate the drawing up of the President's economic program. While others attending the inauguration partied, Rubin, a slim fifty-four-year-old man with soulful brown eyes and a soft voice and slightly graying hair, was becoming increasingly worried about the fact that he had to have an economic program ready within thirty days—in order to meet the goal of beating Ronald Reagan's timing for presenting his economic program.

During the transition, Clinton had promised that his economic program would be ready on Inauguration Day. But on the day of the swearing in, the program was far from ready. So that afternoon, while the inaugural parade was going down Pennsylvania Avenue, Clinton's economic team met in Lloyd Bentsen's Senate office. The issue at hand was whether there was something that the new administration could put out about its economic plans before Congress took its annual February recess honoring George Washington's and Abraham Lincoln's Birthdays, so that the subject could dominate the news.

Earlier in January, Gore had pushed the idea that the President should ask the Congress not to take a recess, so that it could work on the Clinton program, but House Speaker Thomas Foley and Senate Majority Leader George Mitchell nixed that idea, arguing among other things that there was no Clinton program. Clinton had earlier entertained the idea of simply preparing an outline of an economic program and negotiating it with the Congress, to have a final program ready on Inauguration Day. When Clinton called Foley in Barbados over the Christmas holiday, to try this out on him, Foley quickly scotched the idea and said that Clinton should propose his own program.

On Inauguration Day, Stephanopoulos was worried that a long gap before an economic program was produced would cause problems with the press—which was hungry for details of Clinton's proposals—and that unwanted stories would fill the gap. Stephanopoulos couldn't make it to the meeting in Bentsen's office. Gene Sperling, the thirty-four-year-old economic issues adviser for the campaign, who was now to be a deputy to Rubin, made the case on his behalf. Roger Altman; W. Bowman Cutter, a deputy budget director in the Carter administration, who was to be the other deputy to Rubin; Leon Panetta, the new director of the Office of Management and Budget; Laura Tyson, the new chairman of the Council of Economic Advisers; and some aides listened as Bentsen argued that the economic program shouldn't be rushed out, that it would be the President's program for a long time and care should be taken with it. His argument prevailed.

Rubin had taken over the economic plan from Robert Reich when Reich was named Secretary of Labor, but the two had pushed ahead together and, with some staff working through two nights, got briefing books (five large notebooks plus a smaller summary notebook) done in time to deliver them to the governor's mansion—one set for the President-elect and one for Hillary Clinton—by the designated deadline of December 21. Clinton was to spend some time on the briefing books during his "holiday" at Renaissance Weekend.

Reich and Rubin assumed that Clinton would make some of the basic decisions on his economic program over that weekend, but he didn't. "That wasn't procrastination," Reich said later. "It was more a matter of crystallization. The overall framework hadn't quite come together for him." But it was also another sign that Clinton wasn't inclined to make decisions until he absolutely had to.

Clinton faced some daunting problems in drawing up his economic program. He was caught—not for the only time—in contradictions he had set up in his campaign and hadn't been forced to resolve. The figures in his election manifesto, "Putting People First," a 232-page document issued in September, didn't add up. They relied on very optimistic assumptions and evaded some of the hard questions. Only one program—a subsidy for beekeepers, which had eluded budget cutters for years—was to be totally eliminated. The only money-saving proposal in the large entitlement programs—Social Security, Medicare, veterans' benefits, agriculture supports—was a proposal to raise the Medicare premium for better-off recipients.

The campaign document also proposed a sweeping reform of the health care system. In the campaign, Clinton had said—unrealistically, as it turned out—that reforms in the health care system would provide the revenue for extending coverage to the estimated thirty-seven million people without insurance and for reducing the deficit.

Clinton was faced with his campaign promise to cut the federal deficit in half in four years. At that time, in June, the estimated deficit four years out was $193 billion, but by late July 1992, the deficit was projected to be about $60 billion higher in four years. Though the Clinton people were perfectly aware of this new number, they had not revised their campaign pledge, or even acknowledged the change. (Neither did George Bush or Ross Perot.) One Clinton economic adviser said later, "The campaign knew about it but didn't want to talk about it." Similarly, in early January 1993, the Clinton camp professed "unsettling shock at the revelation" by OMB (still in the hands of Richard Darman) of yet another deterioration of the deficit picture, though Clinton's economic policy advisers had in fact received an early tip about the new estimates. Thus, by the time Clinton was to take office, the deficit had become $125 billion larger over the four years than when he had pledged to cut it in half.

This new deficit estimate put Clinton in a very deep hole if he wanted to carry out his campaign pledges of both cutting the deficit in half and spending more federal money on "investments"—on programs such as education and job training and "high tech" (a particular passion of the Vice President's), on children's programs and rebuilding infrastructure—all in the name of spurring economic growth and competitiveness. Even after the first deficit increase, in the course of the campaign, the Clinton people figured that they could still offer at least a partial tax cut for the middle class. Clinton pledged such a tax cut sporadically during the campaign (it was mainly used as a club against Paul Tsongas in the primaries). After the election, following the second bad turn in the deficit, the Clinton camp became enmeshed in a debate over whether they should raise taxes on the middle class.

During the campaign, Clinton hadn't dwelled on reducing the deficit. If he had, he would have been under pressure to specify how he would accomplish that, and if he complied (if he could), he would have alienated interest groups and large numbers of voters. If he had been honest about it, he would have had to say that he would raise taxes, but ever since 1984, when Walter Mondale said that taxes would have to be raised and then lost forty-nine states—for a number of reasons—this was considered the equivalent of political death. During the campaign, the closest Clinton came to leveling on the matter of raising taxes on any but the wealthy was in a debate in Lansing, Michigan, on October 19, when he said, slyly, "I will not raise taxes on the middle class to pay for these programs." (This left open the possibility of raising taxes on the middle class to do something else; and since much of the federal money was fungible, his distinction made no difference.)

Clinton's self-definition as "a new kind of Democrat" was designed, among other things, to camouflage his big government tendencies, which were real enough.

Following the election, Clinton came to realize that there was little he could do about raising spending for his investments if he didn't tackle the deficit. (Each year's deficit adds to the debt, which at this point amounted to four trillion dollars, three trillion more than when Reagan took office.) During the transition, a number of forces were pushing Clinton toward serious deficit reduction. (In August, during the Republican convention, in a four-hour meeting with a group of economists he had convened in Little Rock, he asked, "Why do I hear about deficit reduction all the time?") He gradually came to see that the debt posed a threat to what he wanted to do to spur competitiveness and economic growth, as well as to revive the economy, and was using up capital that could otherwise go to public and private investment. And the public mood was changing. Ross Perot, of course, had made deficit reduction one of his main themes, and now Clinton and his people were in quest of Perot's following.

Traditionally, politicians had seen little profit in casting difficult votes to achieve a goal—such as a lower deficit—that was amorphous in the public's mind. But in the 1992 elections, a number of politicians got wind of the new public mood. Democrats elected to the House for the first time had stressed the issue in their campaigns. When Democratic congressional leaders—Mitchell, Foley, and Gephardt—met with Bill and Hillary Clinton and Al Gore over dinner in the governor's mansion shortly after the election, on November 15, they pressed the case for deficit reduction. After drinks in the living room, the group settled into the big dining room, which had a large display case of silver items—punch bowls, trays, pitchers—from the decommissioned battleship *Arkansas.* Over a dinner of beef, cheese-potatoes, vegetables, and a salad, the discussion got down to the agenda for the Clinton Presidency. The congressional leaders had a message for the President-elect. Gephardt emphasized the importance of deficit reduction as the first order of business, saying, "I've believed since '81 [when Reagan's tax cuts were enacted] the day would come when we'd have to face this problem." He went on, "We all know what 1981 did to this country, and this is the first chance we've had as a party to fix this problem." He told Clinton that "We all believe in the micro things that you've talked about—training, education, infrastructure, health care reform, and more government backing of high-tech research." And he added, "But we'll never get to those things unless we solve the larger economic problems." He argued, "As difficult as it is, as nasty as it is, we have to do it." The Clintons nodded their heads in agreement. Gephardt added that the House Democratic leaders had met with the freshmen, "and they felt we had to do it."

At the dinner, Foley, too, emphasized that the freshmen were particularly keen on making deficit reduction a priority. Many of these freshmen had been elected with the support of Perot voters as well as Democrats—and thus they had higher margins of victory than Clinton, and they wanted to retain those margins. (In all, sixty of the sixty-four Democratic freshmen had run better than Clinton in their districts.)

Introducing a factor that was going to be a source of tension after Clinton got to Washington, Foley advised him not to listen to the urging of those who told him that he should "take on the Congress." Foley said that traditionally, the incumbent President's party loses seats in midterm elections, and the losses are blamed on the President. Therefore, Clinton shouldn't go out and weaken the Congress by attacking it. So Clinton was to be torn between two poles: the large swath of the electorate, including the Perotites, that was fed up with the Congress; and the Congress, upon which he was dependent on getting his program through. At this dinner, Foley also persuaded Clinton to drop his pursuit of the line-item veto, which would enhance the power of the President by allowing him to zero out any item in an appropriations bill rather than force him to veto the entire measure. Clinton complied, and this backtrack on his part was noted by other politicians.

On the occasion of this dinner, Hillary Clinton's deep involvement in her husband's activities got its first postelection public airing. The subject was of all the more interest because of the public role Mrs. Clinton had played during the campaign. After coming under criticism for her unusual aggressiveness (as candidates' wives had gone) and her famous line, "I suppose I could have stayed home, baked cookies, and had teas," she had switched to the role of the demure spouse, nodding her head in agreement during her husband's speeches and sometimes holding an umbrella over him. (Actually, the line was longer and in a context that was lost. She also said, "The work that I've done as a professional, as a public advocate, has been aimed in part to assure that women can make the choices that they should make —whether it's full-time career, full-time motherhood, some combination, depending on what stage of life they are at—and I think that is still difficult for people to understand right now, that it is a generational change.") Clinton, asked at a press conference after the dinner whether his wife had been there, replied, "She was. She stayed the whole time. She talked a lot. She knew more than we did about some things. I think they would agree with that." In fact, Mrs. Clinton had weighed in on a number of subjects, and her political acumen was clear on several issues, including the question of what to do about remaining S&L problems—a subject that, as it happened, she knew a lot about.

There were also strong pressures on Clinton from within his new economic circle to emphasize deficit reduction. Panetta and Rivlin had long been advocates of reducing the deficit, and both were pushing an energy tax. (During the campaign, Panetta, as House Budget Committee chairman, had openly criticized candidate Clinton's budget as not adding up.) Both Bentsen and Rubin argued that only if Clinton was seen as serious about deficit reduction would the financial markets have confidence in his program—and lower interest rates—and would the Federal Reserve keep rates down. They warned that if nothing was done, there would be a real risk of a financial crisis.

The economic situation that Clinton had inherited was daunting. Unemployment was 7.7 percent, growth was erratic. The recovery was shaky, and it wasn't producing jobs. Corporations had "downsized," suggesting a fundamental change in the employment structure. Worldwide growth was stagnant. The questions facing Clinton and his advisers were how to spur investment without igniting inflation and how to eliminate a significant portion of the deficit without contracting the economy too much. To ward off the latter, he and his advisers were considering a program to stimulate the economy in the short term, largely by spending to create jobs; the idea was received wisdom among many Democratic economists and had been given a large boost at the economic conference.

On January 7, Clinton held his first meeting with his economic team, at the governor's mansion in Little Rock. (Reich, undergoing his confirmation hearing in Washington, was hooked up by speakerphone.)

Rubin, anxious about having such a short time to prepare a new budget, was facing the NEC's first meeting with the President. He had rehearsed his troops carefully at preparatory meetings in Washington. Having obtained a commitment for five or six hours of Clinton's time for the meeting, he said to his charges, several times, "We have five or six hours to discuss three months' work. If you go off-subject, or if you go overtime, I'll cut you off."

Just before the meeting, Rubin, who was beginning to know his new boss's ways, told the President-elect how important it was to stay on schedule and urged him to resist getting into substantive debates on such questions as taxes and health care. Clinton put his arm on Rubin's shoulder and said, "Don't worry, Bob. I'll be good." So at that meeting in Little Rock, in the dining room of the governor's mansion, with Hillary Clinton in attendance, the various performers explained the budget process, and the discussions began over what deficit-reduction number should be the goal: $270 billion? $240 billion? $220 billion? $180 billion?

According to two witnesses, it was Lloyd Bentsen who, in a feat of economic acrobatics, supplied Clinton with a way out of his jam—the problem of how to live up to his pledge to cut the deficit in half in four years, when he was now facing a far higher deficit ($350 billion in fiscal year 1997) than when he had made the pledge. At another meeting between the economic team and Clinton in Little Rock, on January 13, Bentsen said to Clinton, "When you said you'd cut the deficit in half, the deficit for that year was to be $290 billion, so what you promised people was $145 billion in cuts. I think that's what your goal should be." Bentsen argued, "Forget what the number will be in four years; the number could be anything in four years. These numbers keep changing. So pick an objective number that represents a real cut in the deficit and use that." In effect, Bentsen elided the question of what the deficit would be in four years and took a recent figure—before the numbers had turned worse. He had come to the rescue.

Bentsen had an uncommon influence on Clinton virtually from the start. Clinton looked up to the gray, elegant, street-smart aristocrat from south Texas as he did to none of his other advisers, except perhaps Warren Christopher. Bentsen, seventy-one, and Christopher, sixty-seven—both of them wealthy and accomplished, and both of them men who spoke slowly and as from depths of experience—were unique in the life of the fatherless Clinton. Bentsen, a settled, confident person, gave others confidence in him. These men were to become strong rivals within the Clinton administration, the relations between them tense. Each wanted to be the second among equals, the President's prime confidant in the Cabinet—and both of them couldn't be. A Clinton adviser said later that Bentsen became highly influential with Clinton because he "had four things going for him, whereas the rest of us had two or at most three." Bentsen, he said, "could give Clinton economic, political, and congressional advice—and fourth, he could look him in the eye as a political peer and say, 'I know what this means politically.' "

Clinton gratefully accepted Bentsen's advice on the deficit reduction figure and laid out his position in a preinaugural interview on January 14 with Judy Woodruff on PBS. Greenberg said later, "He knew what he was doing. He picked a figure that was half of the deficit when the deficit was lower."

George Stephanopoulos said later that when Clinton committed himself to the $145 billion cut, "He knew exactly what he was doing. He put himself on the path of significant deficit reduction. He felt that this was his time, and unless he had a big, bold package he'd be a failed President." So Clinton committed himself to a large deficit reduction program at the same time that he sought increased spending for his "investments." Though this made sense as a shift in priorities, it turned out to be a troublesome combination.

Stephanopoulos said, "The dynamic is inside himself. There is always a tension between wanting to get this big program and knowing you have to reduce the deficit and get future growth and also make investments. It's a conflict among several sides of him: the part of him that's committed to children's programs and investing in jobs and highways; the part of him that knew the middle class had gotten screwed in the 1980s, that the middle-class tax cut was an important symbol; the part of him that's cut spending time and time again in Arkansas but also the part of him that knows the intense pain caused by each cut; the part of him that understands the role of Wall Street and the part of him that knows that ordinary people have been screwed by those sources."

At a meeting at the transition office in Little Rock on the night of January 14, the political advisers were surprised when they heard that Clinton had set his deficit reduction goal at $145 billion. As Gene Sperling laid out the options for meeting that new goal—which included taxing a higher proportion of Social Security benefits and a possible energy tax—they were incredulous. Greenberg said his research indicated that the public had no expectation of the deficit being cut in half, regardless of what Clinton had said in the campaign.

He added that in the focus group interviews he'd conducted, people didn't think that Clinton had made a firm commitment to a middle-class tax cut. Greenberg said, "In every focus group I've done, people don't think he made a 'read-my-lips' pledge on the middle-class tax cut." The division among Clinton's advisers ran along the fault lines of temperament and experience; in the view of some of the younger Clinton advisers, it was "change" versus the "status quo." It pitted James Carville and Paul Begala, who wanted Clinton to stick to the economic populism he had preached (or they had imposed on him), as well as Stephanopoulos and Sperling, against more traditionalist advisers such as Panetta, Bentsen, and Rubin. The division arose on several issues, but it has been overstated. As the arguments unfolded, political consultants were themselves divided on several issues—even on the economic program.

On January 29, nine days after the inauguration, there commenced an extraordinary series of meetings of the President and his advisers to draw up an economic program. Over the next two and a half weeks, the group met almost every day and often into the night—spending ten hours on Sunday, February 7—for a total of nearly fifty hours, with Clinton and Gore in attendance during most of them. Not long after the sessions began, Bentsen was to remark privately, "This is the meetingest crowd I've ever seen." Never before had a President got so involved, in such detail, in the huge federal budget. How Clinton conducted these meetings told—and foretold—a lot about his governing style.

Arrayed around the long mahogany table in the Roosevelt Room, on the first floor of the West Wing of the White House, just steps from the Oval Office, were a large group of people making a multitude of decisions. At the center of one side of the table sat the President, with the Vice President across from him. On the President's right was Bentsen, on Gore's left was Panetta. The seating of the other key figures—Rubin, Tyson, Ron Brown, Reich—was rotated (McLarty was there occasionally). Deputies Rivlin and Altman were at one end, and at the other were Cutter, Alan Blinder, a member of the Council of Economic Advisers, Stephanopoulos, and Sperling. Paul Begala attended some of the meetings—to protect the President's political interests, as he saw them. (Soon Begala began working full time on the economic program—mainly the marketing of it.) Aides to Bentsen, Panetta, and Gore sat along the wall. Sometimes Howard Paster attended.

Bentsen, to whom Clinton turned frequently, was good at reading the room and, utterly secure, was amused by "the kids"—Stephanopoulos and Sperling, who spoke up strongly, especially to protect "investments."

In an interview while the meetings were still going on, one of the economic advisers said, "The political people keep saying, 'You said this during the campaign,' and that some of the tough choices were politically dangerous. Bentsen and Panetta would reply that the package as a whole would be progressive, that they were trying to help the middle class—that the program would create more jobs and that higher-income people were being asked to make the biggest share of the contribution in the effort to get the deficit down."

In addition to the division between most of the campaign veterans and Clinton's new economic advisers over the President's economic program, there was a division between some of the Cabinet members and economic officials at the table. Reich, a true liberal, a believer in using the federal government to increase workers' skills, provide jobs, and other seemingly desirable things, fought hard for as many programs as possible to be offered as part of the President's "investments" and in the stimulus proposal that was to accompany the budget. Ron Brown, the Commerce Secretary, questioned the sanctity of the deficit reduction figure. He asked, "What's the magic of the number? Suppose we went to $130 billion? What's magic about $145?" (Without much press or public notice, this number soon got "rounded off" to $140 billion.) But the liberals at the table were outnumbered and outgunned by the "deficit hawks," who included people—such as Bentsen, Panetta, and Rivlin—who had a great deal of experience in the budget process. One person who attended the meetings said, "Bentsen could talk about his experience as former chairman of the Finance Committee, Panetta could talk about his experience as former chairman of the House Budget Committee, Alice Rivlin could talk about her experience as former head of the Congressional Budget Office. Rubin, Altman, and Cutter all had business or government experience. If you have Bob Rubin and Lloyd Bentsen saying, 'the financial markets will not believe this is real deficit reduction unless . . . ,' it's real hard to argue with them." Another participant said, "The reason Bentsen was so effective with the President was that he could look at him and say, 'I know this is going to cause pain. I understand that this is going to be tough on a lot of people. It's the right thing to do, and we have to do it.' "

There were other pressures. Howard Paster cautioned against cuts that might cost the President's program needed congressional votes. He especially warned against cutting agriculture subsidies—Stephanopoulos joined him—and the cuts under consideration were reduced. (On the other hand, to attract votes some "investment incentives" were added for rural America.) Paster joined Stephanopoulos in arguing against charging Medicare beneficiaries more. Stephanopoulos was of the pragmatic-liberal school. To him, it was more important to get a result than to strike a pose. Someone who attended the meetings said, "The question was, What can you do without gutting the entire package. Howard Paster would say, 'Mr. President, if you make that cut, you're going to lose these two senators and put your whole package at risk, and it's not worth it.' "

One senior official who attended the Roosevelt Room sessions said, "The meetings were like the economic conference in Little Rock. Clinton was the master of ceremonies and the star. He both conducted the discussion and dominated the discussion." (When, during a special television program with children, on ABC on Saturday, February 20, Clinton was asked what subject he had trouble with in grade school, he replied, "I made my lowest grade in conduct, because I talked too much in school and the teachers were always telling me to stop talking.") In part, as it had been in the Little Rock conference and often in the campaign, it was Clinton showing how much he knew. Clinton seemed to have a compulsion about this—though, as he must have known, no one who dealt with him doubted that he was a very smart man. Clinton seemed to have an outsize need for reassurance. In many cases, Clinton drew on his experience as governor, talking about which programs worked and which ones didn't. His predilection was to believe in the programs. Another attendee said, "We're still in the stage of the administration where labels matter. If something is called the Community Development and Goodness Fund, it is seen as just that."

Clinton's participation slowed things down. (For one thing, he was often late.) On a number of occasions, when the President was going on and on, Rubin and Reich would glance at each other. The two men had private discussions about the absurdity of spending forty-five minutes of the President's time on a five- or ten-million-dollar program—in an annual budget of $1.6 trillion. From time to time, one or the other would intervene and say, "Mr. President, we really need to move ahead." Usually, he disregarded their admonitions. Gore, also no slouch at talking, on occasion conducted little seminars, for instance about the environment. But sometimes Gore would gently try to steer the President toward closure on some issue, saying, "We have to make a decision now."

One participant said, "Clinton is not sequential. When you put a list in front of some people—setting forth what is most important and what is least important—they go down the list. Clinton goes around the problem. He circles it and circles it."

One of the reasons for the indecisiveness Clinton demonstrated in these meetings, an adviser said, was that "Clinton never stops thinking." Another said, "There were a lot of last-minute decisions and changes. That's Clinton's way." Another participant in these meetings said, "His decision-making style is not to make a decision the way others do—toting up the costs and benefits. He makes a decision when he absolutely has to. Sometimes when he must make a decision that he's not ready to make, the decision doesn't get made." One Roosevelt Room attendee said, "You couldn't really tell when he was making a decision and when he wasn't." He continued, "One of the problems of the switch from being king of the hill in Arkansas to here is that a lot of the decisions are fifty-one to forty-nine, and they pile up on you. You have to be pretty orderly pretty early."

As some of the meetings stretched to 8:00 or 9:00 P.M., someone would say, "Mr. President, do you have time to go on?"—hoping, along with others who were also exhausted, that he would call it quits. And Clinton would respond, "Sure. Let's continue." One participant said, "There'd be almost audible groans in the room, and he'd go on for another couple of hours." Sometimes an aide would come into the Roosevelt Room and say, "Mr. President, you have a meeting." And Clinton would respond, "I prefer this" —but would eventually duck out for the other meeting, then return to the budget deliberations. One time, returning after a half hour's absence, he said, simply, "Bosnia." As a meeting went on and on, he would often remark, "This is fun." (When his aides ordered in pizza, Clinton, a junk-food lover, could only look at it longingly, because the Secret Service forbade his eating carry-in food. Later he admitted to an MTV interviewer—perhaps with his audience in mind—that he had actually nibbled some pizza. No matter how long the meetings lasted, rarely was a meal offered. The group otherwise subsisted on fruit and Pepperidge Farm cookies.)

Finally, as February 17, the date for the President's first speech to Congress, approached, a number of advisers were alarmed. Each new decision forced the Office of Management and Budget to reestimate all the numbers. All-night sessions in the large, ornate Old Executive Office Building, where the OMB officials dwelled, were becoming common. Neither the President nor his advisers who were new to drawing up a budget understood the extreme pressure they were putting on the OMB staff. Decisions were made and remade. As the week of the speech neared, some of Clinton's advisers secretly colluded to bring the deliberations to an end. Panetta was becoming particularly anxious; he had a budget document to write. One participant remarked, "People around the President—Sperling, Stephanopoulos, Gore, Rubin—said you have to keep pushing him to make a decision." Finally, Panetta and Rubin implored Gore to bring things to a close. So as the last week began, Gore said, as a participant recalled it, " 'Mr. President, here's the procedure I recommend. Monday we do this, Tuesday we do this, Wednesday we do this, etc., and here's where we should be by Friday.' " The schedule was largely followed, and the others were relieved and grateful. This person remarked later, "Until then we were having an intense seminar on government minutiae, led by Bill Clinton."

Chief of Staff Mack McLarty concluded later that the President had spent too much time in these meetings as opposed to getting his administration —and in particular his White House staff—going. McLarty and others also felt that the meetings distracted Clinton, and his top advisers, from dealing effectively with some of the controversial issues that arose in the early weeks of the administration. McLarty also felt, he said later, that these meetings "took a lot out of him and took away time for reflection and rest."

In order to make the (new) goal of reducing the deficit by $140 billion by fiscal 1997, the deficit had to be cut by about $500 billion during that period. After that, the deficit was set to rise again, because of the rising costs of health care—which were to be dealt with separately.

Clinton had of course made more pledges than it would be possible to carry out. He and his campaign veterans were now up against the distinction between campaigning and governing. An economic adviser said privately at the time, "The campaign people act as if 1996 is tomorrow."

Clinton encouraged Reich and Sperling to play the role of defender of the investments. He told them privately that he wanted to be sure there was balance around the table. He had put together a very strong deficit reduction team and wanted to be sure that the investments got a fair chance. So he would call on Reich and Sperling to give their views. Thus, in deliberate Rooseveltian style (he had been reading up), Clinton created some of the conflict.

Clinton's political advisers were divided. Carville and Greenberg were open to a broad-based tax, as evidence that Clinton was doing something "big." On the basis of his survey data, Greenberg urged the President to be "bold." The people were ready for deficit reduction, Greenberg said. In other words, deficit reduction was good politics. Stephanopoulos and Begala were opposed. Begala said later, "My concern was that the focus of the entire process was becoming deficit cutting. That wasn't what Clinton was elected on—he was elected on helping people. When we run for reelection, people won't focus on our budget number. The question will be: Did you create jobs? Did we deliver on the change people wanted?"

Greenberg's research with "focus groups" showed, he said later, "surprising openness to the tax piece if it seemed fair. We concluded there was more support for an across-the-board tax than for a partial one and that the elites would be more open to it if we hit the middle class." Carville ended up with the attitude, "If that's what you have to do, sign me up." In one meeting, Carville told the President, "I don't care what you do, but just make damn sure it's big and different." Gore argued several times, and eloquently, that if you do something bold you can change the terms of the debate. This was an early example of many eloquent arguments—not all of them appreciated by Clinton's staff and other advisers—that Gore would make in meetings in the course of the Clinton Presidency.

A deliberate leak that the group was considering a freeze on cost-of-living allowances for Social Security recipients set off the predictable controversy on Capitol Hill and protest from the interest groups. But the COLA leak served the intended purpose of making more acceptable what was ultimately proposed—an increase in Social Security taxes on recipients making over $25,000 for individuals and $32,000 for couples. Panetta, Rivlin, and Cutter were major proponents of a COLA freeze. Gore also made a strong argument for it, saying that it would enable the administration to do other things. One economic adviser said privately at the time: "We made a calculation that if we get it up there, and people throw themselves over it, we pull it back, and there is something else we can do—raise the taxes on Social Security recipients. Without the float of the COLA freeze, the tax would be harder." One problem with the let's-float-it gambit was that it gave the impression of Clinton backing down, and—even at this early stage of his Presidency—he didn't need that. Merely considering the possibility of freezing COLAs aroused the political advisers, because Clinton had accused Bush of intending to cut Social Security and Medicare. A political adviser said later, "The COLA leak suggested that once Clinton got in office, he'd disregard past promises." In the end, Bentsen persuaded the President that the Congress wouldn't accept a freeze on Social Security cost-of-living increases—that it might be good policy but was politically deadly.

Stephanopoulos argued that on the basis of recent history, such a proposal would set off an uproar among the elderly, and therefore in the Congress, and would likely be blocked.

Clinton continued to agonize over the budget cuts. He was reluctant to take anything away from people, and in addition there were many new things he wanted to do. He also worried about the possible negative reaction to the cuts. One participant at the meetings said privately at the time, "What's really hard for him is that what he likes in policy and what he's learned and honed in a national campaign make it very hard for him to come to grips emotionally and intellectually" with the need to cut the deficit. Exhibiting the dichotomy in his own mind, Clinton would say in the meetings, "What you all have to understand is that no one enjoys deficit reduction. While we may have to do it, it's not a good thing."

The populism that was part of his campaign was also apparent at several points in the Roosevelt Room meetings. Clinton was a complex mixture of the Southern boy who grew up poor white, the young man who matriculated at Georgetown University, Oxford, and Yale Law School, and the adult who traveled in sophisticated intellectual and moneyed and international circles—but had not lost his good-old-boy, down-home, southern core. One or another of these aspects of his nature might come to the fore from time to time, but all of them remained within him. Sometimes it appeared that Carville and Begala, who specialized in populist campaigns, had appliquéed Clinton's populism onto him in his Presidential campaign, but Clinton had given them something to work with. Populism was also in the tradition of Arkansas Democratic politics. That Clinton wasn't consistently populist suggested not so much that this part of his persona was phony but that there were several Bill Clintons: the populist and the wonk, the poor southern kid and the well-read, well-connected networker, struggling for his mind and his voice.

Clinton was particularly uncomfortable about the prospect of taxing the middle class—through an energy tax that would fall on the middle class as well as on the wealthy. He had, after all, based much of his campaign on the middle class, saying, "I want a country where people who work hard and play by the rules are rewarded," and talking about "the forgotten middle class"—pointing out that the middle class had suffered an erosion in real income in the past decade. The Clinton campaign was determined to demonstrate to middle-class voters that here, at last, would be a Democratic President who understood their disappointments and their struggles.

An adviser who attended the meetings said, "His emotional instincts are very populist. His instincts are always distributional. If you say to him, 'This is a tax where somebody earning forty thousand dollars will pay the same amount as someone earning two hundred thousand because they drive the same number of miles and use the same amount of heat,' he'll get very perturbed. But he has the added merit of being smart. Bentsen, Panetta, Rivlin, and Cutter would say, 'Wait. Look at the package as a whole,' and he'd see the point." Their argument was that because of the proposed increase in income taxes on the rich, that group would carry the burden of the deficit reduction.

This same person commented, "He'll say, 'This is a rich man's issue.' But if you say, 'On the contrary, standing between us and being poised to be a more competitive nation in the world is the deficit,' he can carry both points of view on his shoulders at the same time." But an effect of Clinton's being conflicted was that in pushing his program later, he sounded an uncertain trumpet.

Toward the end of the deliberations, the President decided to go with a tax on energy sources, based on the heat content of fuels as measured in British thermal units, or Btu's, as advocated by Gore, because it was broad-based—and because taxing pollutants, such as coal, more than any other energy source would be beneficial to the environment. (Bentsen had been pushing a value-added tax on energy sources, as simpler to administer than a Btu tax and as an opening to a broader-based value-added tax later.) The idea of a Btu tax had been around for a while. It was even considered briefly by members of the Bush administration during the great deficit reduction struggle of 1990.

Right up to the end, the policymakers in the Roosevelt Room, spurred on by the campaign veterans, attempted to find a way to provide some relief to the middle class. One thought was to charge enough in energy taxes that there could be a giveback. Eventually, after three weeks, the search for a way to do that was given up. It was felt that the message of a tax and a giveback would be too complicated and confusing, and there was concern that if the energy tax was set high enough to allow a giveback, it would be too high to be acceptable to numerous members of Congress. The policymakers also looked for a way to give something back to the middle class through a still higher Earned Income Tax Credit than was planned. But that, too, failed because it would be too expensive.

The President was very troubled about not being able to do some of the things he had talked about during the campaign. There would be less room for his "investments" than the campaign had anticipated. But Clinton was insistent that Head Start be fully funded—that is, that every eligible child would have a slot—and that there be a new program guaranteeing immunization of every child against polio, diphtheria, and tetanus. These two programs were at the top of the agenda of the Children's Defense Fund, whose founder and president, Marian Wright Edelman, was very close to Mrs. Clinton. Edelman had shrewdly urged them at the economic conference as things that could get done quickly. These programs were also consistent with Bill Clinton's beliefs.

But as a consequence of pressures by some at the table—especially Gore and Reich—the "investments" program ended up being indiscriminate, and not all of the "investments" met the test of the term. This reflected logrolling ("change" hadn't completely taken over the Roosevelt Room) as well as a deliberate strategy of trying to win the support of as many Democrats as possible. In all, increased spending was proposed for sixty-one government programs, from a "forestry research" initiative to boosting research on "information highways" (another Gore pet) to an "urban partnership" against crime to Head Start and a youth apprenticeship program to more research for NASA. Clinton's national service program, the program he felt most strongly about—to provide loans for college tuition for everyone in exchange for two years of national service or repayment as a percentage of income—would have to be begun on a more modest basis than he had hoped; but his original proposal, to make it available to all students, had been extravagant.

Though there wasn't real debate in these meetings on whether the President should also propose a stimulus package to give the economy a near-term boost, the amount agreed upon—roughly $30 billion, about half for new spending and half for tax breaks—was much smaller than was proposed by some at the economic conference.

Toward the end of the deliberations, there was much pressure, and temptation, to slip even the $140 billion noose. The taxes and spending cuts agreed upon thus far didn't add up to that amount. But Rubin, Bentsen, Panetta, and Rivlin argued that while in macroeconomic terms it didn't much matter whether deficit was cut by $130 billion or $140 billion in the final year (and the numbers were sheer guesswork), it was very important to stay with the amount that had already been made public: this would be an important signal to the financial markets. So only a few days before the President was to address the Congress, more cuts were made.

The result was an economic program that was bold by conventional standards and did seek to reverse Reaganomics and redirect the country's economic resources from consumption to long-term investment, and at the same time to take a major bite out of the federal deficit. Clinton proposed deficit cuts of $493 billion over five years; increased spending, most of it for "long-term investments" such as job training, rebuilding the nation's infrastructure, education, and promoting high tech; tax increases of $246 billion over five years; and net cuts in federal spending of $247 billion. The spending cuts were phased in more slowly than the tax increases. (This gave the Republicans room to charge that Clinton was proposing to raise taxes more than he was to cut spending.)

The final economic plan proposed $60 billion in "tax incentives"—a tax break on investment by the high-tech industry, which the administration hoped would back its program, and tax breaks for small business, whose opposition it hoped to forestall. And it included $100 billion in additional spending over five years. It proposed to cut defense spending by about 9 percent. (A larger cut, Clinton felt, would put him too far to the left.)

Despite the Btu tax, the tax increases were to fall mainly on the wealthy, to a far greater degree—by as much as one-third over existing law—than Clinton had proposed in his campaign. The top rate was moved from 31 to 36 percent (on couples earning $140,000 and above), and the "millionaires' surtax"—a 10 percent surtax on people earning a million dollars a year—that Clinton talked about in the campaign became a surtax on couples earning over $250,000. To the campaign veterans at the table, those people were millionaires. Further tax revenues would be brought about by removing the limit on the income against which Medicare taxes would be applied. The actual top tax rate, as a result of these various changes, was over 42 percent. Corporate taxes were to be raised by 2 percent.

The gamble was that these increases wouldn't change the behavior of those being hit. It was a gamble, backed by a populist animus toward the rich, based on the assumption that politicians wouldn't protest tax increases on "the rich." The truly wealthy men in the Roosevelt Room—Rubin (estimated worth of over $100 million) and Altman (estimated worth of from

$40 million to $60 million) and Bentsen (comfortably into double digit millions)—did not protest. And there were to be tax breaks for business investments. The administration even proposed relaxing the rules on passive losses. This was a bald attempt to get the support of the realtors and home builders for the economic program, and an acceptance of the reality that such a proposal had over three hundred cosponsors in the House of Representatives. Though few in the press noticed, Clinton had committed himself in New Hampshire to restoring passive losses, because of complaints about the sad situation in real estate there, where the recession had hit late but ferociously.

In several respects, therefore, the Clinton administration was proposing to undo the Tax Reform Act of 1986, which created low and few rates in exchange for elimination of many tax breaks (including passive losses). Clinton's program would be much criticized, and not just by Republicans, for having set its deficit reduction too low, but the budget cuts represented the President's and his assembled advisers' best judgment of what sort of and how large a deficit reduction program could be got through the Congress. Clinton and his advisers wanted to limit the number of fights they picked, so that their program wouldn't be so shredded that it would cease to exist. Though the President and his advisers were more serious about deficit reduction than any of their predecessors (including Ronald Reagan), some of his advisers thought at the time that there was a miscalculation—that the group was viewing unconventional times, when deficit reduction had gained a vast number of new adherents, through a conventional construct.

Clinton's program wasn't as bold as it might have been, and as it turned out, he and his people had underestimated the public's desire for deficit reduction. Though administration officials boasted that they were proposing cuts in one hundred fifty programs, only seven minor programs—including the subsidy for beekeepers—were to be completely eliminated. (Five of the seven, including the beekeeper program, were later spared by Congress.) No major assault was made on entitlement programs—Social Security, Medicare, veterans' benefits, and the like—which made up about half of the federal budget. A certain amount of courage was displayed in the new administration's taking on of powerful western interests by proposing increases on the fees for mining and grazing and timber cutting on federal lands—but that wasn't the end of the story. A large spending cut in Medicare was to be charged against "providers," that is, against doctors and hospitals, rather than the more politically powerful beneficiaries. This was described by the administration as a "down payment" on health care reform, a term that, one official conceded privately, made no sense, because this cut would actually make it harder to find funds for expanding health care. (In any event, the costs to providers of Medicare and Medicaid were routinely shifted to the cost of taking care of other patients.)

The President and his advisers had gone as far as they thought possible within the political parameters—that is, what they thought they could get through the Congress. What they didn't fully realize was that the political parameters had changed.

5

STARTING AGAIN

"I've Just Been Here Four Weeks"

Two days before Clinton's first major address to Congress, on Wednesday, February 17, he gave a televised talk from the Oval Office. Ronald Reagan had done a similar thing and had won the large part of his program from the Congress in fairly short order. The Clinton people were trying to model the new President's presentation of his program after Reagan's, even if the aim of his program was to reverse Reaganism. During the transition, some Clinton aides had sought the advice of Michael Deaver, Reagan's impresario, and David Gergen, Reagan's first communications director. From them they got the idea of running the effort to win the economic program as if it were a political campaign, as well as for an Oval Office speech before the one to Congress—to "make it big," as George Stephanopoulos put it later.

The Oval Office speech was also intended to get out of the way the news, which by this time was really no surprise, that not only would there be no tax cut for the middle class, but there would be an energy tax (the Btu tax) that would hit the middle class as well as the wealthy. Clinton's aides didn't want this to be the headline after his big speech to Congress. To this end, Clinton said in his Oval Office speech, "I've worked harder than I've ever worked in my life" to be able to increase investment in (spending on) various domestic programs "without asking more of you," but "I can't, because the deficit has increased so much beyond my earlier estimates." In saying this, the new President came close to groveling.

Later Stephanopoulos explained, "You know that there's going to be one day in this whole process when the front page of the newspaper says, 'Clinton breaks promise to middle class.' We got the middle class point out of the way on Monday, and the Thursday papers said, 'Clinton presents bold plan.' "

Clinton, seated at what was once John F. Kennedy's desk (behind him were gold damask drapes and a table laden with a bust of Abraham Lincoln and the requisite family photographs), was obviously ill at ease. Despite all the supposed communications wizards surrounding him, he was seated in a chair that was much too large, even for a man of his bulk. (It was shortly got rid of.) Moreover, the brief, ten-minute speech was crammed with so many thoughts and facts that it became confusing. He was still running against Reagan and Bush. James Carville had argued strenuously against the President's presenting a distribution table to show that by far most of the new taxes would fall on the wealthy; he didn't want the discussion to be centered on taxes. But Carville's concern was moot: the table wasn't ready anyway.

The President had asked McLarty to invite both Arkansas senators, Dale Bumpers and David Pryor, to come to the White House to watch the speech on television. Clinton was closer to Pryor than to Bumpers (whom he once nearly challenged for his Senate seat), but both senators were trying to be helpful to the new President. Both men were able, earthy politicians (and populists). They watched the speech in Gore's office, and then joined the President, Mrs. Clinton, McLarty, and Gore in the living quarters for dessert and decompression. The critique of the speech was that it was a good beginning but it had been too partisan, and too much like a campaign speech. In fact, the Oval Office speech was a semi-disaster. It was unconvincing and didn't give people confidence in Clinton. The next day, the stock market dropped eighty-three points, the biggest drop in fifteen months.

There was bedlam in the White House as the President and his advisers prepared for the big speech to Congress on Wednesday. Though this was a special speech for a special occasion, the way it was put together reflected some of the characteristics of the new administration. Several Clinton aides worked through the night—this was becoming a badge of honor in the Clinton White House. Some worked through two nights. Staff members were still fiddling with the budget until 2:00 A.M. the night before the speech. About a dozen people worked on the speech, some from the outside. As can happen, the rewrites didn't always constitute an improvement, and the many hands didn't provide a clear voice. On the day Clinton was to give the speech, the draft at hand was flat.

One of the speechwriters recalled later, "When it became clear there was too much work to do, Hillary took charge. She read the draft out loud, and people would make suggestions. Groups would go off to rewrite the opening, the close, and flabby parts." Mrs. Clinton did some rewriting herself. Clinton himself spent a lot of time rewriting certain sections. In midafternoon, Anthony Lake, the National Security Adviser, offered what became a key line (and a Kennedyesque one): "The test of our program cannot simply be what is in it for me; the question must be what is in it for us." At a 6:30 P.M. practice session, Clinton made several ad-libs, which were incorporated into the text. There was a 7:30 P.M. version of the speech, and then an 8:30 P.M. version. Clinton didn't leave the family theater until twenty minutes before the ceremonies were to begin, at 9:00 P.M. He continued to work on the speech as his limousine made its way to Capitol Hill, and as he waited in the Speaker's office, just off the House floor, for the moment he was to enter the House Chamber.

As Clinton entered the chamber of the House of Representatives, he was given a warm reception. Familiar as these ceremonies had become, there was still an excitement to them—especially when a new President made his first such appearance. The presence, according to tradition, of the Cabinet, the Supreme Court, the diplomatic corps, the top military officials, all added to the sense of occasion. As Clinton, at the podium, acknowledged the ovation, the frenzied TelePrompTer operator was still making changes. Mrs. Clinton, in a bright red wool dress with a high neck, her hair swept up, looked triumphant. She had worked for this as hard, and as long, as her husband had. On one side of her was John Sculley, the chairman of Apple Computer, who symbolized the affinity between the Clinton campaign and the high-tech industry. On the other side was Alan Greenspan, the chairman of the Federal Reserve Board. (There was some criticism of Greenspan afterward for appearing to lend himself to the Clintons' cause.) Also in the First Lady's group were Vernon Jordan and his wife, Ann.

And then the fresh-faced young President took over the hall. At first his delivery was flat and he stepped on applause lines. He said, in what was intended as the defining phrase but was little remembered, "Our nation needs a new direction." Then Clinton seemed to grow more confident and to speak more energetically. And he ad-libbed extensively. His obvious command of the material and his almost physical relationship with his audience, his clear and urgent call for change, lifted his speech from its prosaic text. He laid out the "four components" of his program: "It shifts our emphasis in public and private spending from consumption to investment"; It would honor "work and family" (by which he meant a substantial increase in the Earned Income Tax Credit, or EITC, which gave a tax credit to the working poor); "It substantially reduces the federal deficit honestly and credibly," by using conservative estimates of revenue; and "It earns the trust of the American people" by paying for his plans with cuts in government waste, with real cuts in government spending, and with "fairness for a change in the way the burdens are borne"—by which he meant, but didn't say, taxes.

The Clinton people had set great store by using honest numbers and having a credible proposal, and the result was relatively gimmick-free, especially as these things had gone in the past. When, at one point in the speech, the Republicans mocked him for saying that he would use nonpartisan numbers of the Congressional Budget Office as the basis of his deficit reduction, Clinton shot back—with a slight slip—"Well, you can laugh, my fellow Republicans," and argued that the CBO had been closer to accurate than Reagan and Bush had been. It seemed that the new President was taking charge of the debate, and that he was up to the rough-and-tumble.

Pausing and biting his lip—a device seen often in his campaign—and, to make sure, saying, "I feel so strongly about this," he launched into a lengthy ad-lib about health care. He interpolated statistics, as he often did (sometimes his aides would give him one statistic in a speech, and he would add three more). Clinton carried a lot of information in his head, something that didn't always work to his advantage. Reagan, being underinformed, could be utterly clear about simple goals; Clinton, being exceedingly informed, sometimes got lost in his facts.

He laid out an ambitious legislative program: a thirty-billion-dollar stimulus program, featuring increased spending on job training and infrastructure, and tax breaks; a permanent investment tax credit for companies with revenues of under five million dollars; special assistance for defense industries hurt by cuts in defense spending; more spending for immunization of children, Head Start, and the Women, Infants and Children Act, which was targeted at children under the age of five; more spending on, and reform of, education; "a partnership between businesses and education and the government" for apprenticeship programs in every state; community development banks; a streamlined worker-training program to deal with the fact that "the average eighteen-year-old today will change jobs seven times in a lifetime"; national service; expansion of the EITC program to the extent that no one who worked a forty-hour week and had a child in the house would be in poverty; welfare reform; an anticrime bill; a campaign finance reform bill and a lobbying reform bill; and to "reinvent government to make it work again" (an idea that Clinton had mentioned from time to time in the campaign and that was the rage among the "new ideas" people in the Democratic Leadership Council and elsewhere). The "policy wonk" had been turned loose in the greatest playpen on earth.

He spelled out clearly the necessity for deficit reduction and offered a challenge that some of his staff believed was the way to stay on the offensive: "all those who say we should cut more [should] be as specific as I have been." He made a careful case for the fairness of his tax program, stating that only the 1.2 percent at the top level of income would see an increase in their income tax rates (leaving out the energy tax). Clinton also made clear his grasp of the connections between investment and education and training and trade and competitiveness. He had probably thought through the nation's essential problems more than any of his recent predecessors. This, plus his obvious energy and enthusiasm, was what made his Presidency seem so promising.

Raising hopes that things might truly change in Washington, and trying to throw up a protective wall around his plan, Clinton said that he knew that interest groups would be lobbying against various pieces of it. He said, "Our people will be watching and wondering, not to see whether you disagree with me on a particular issue, but just to see if it's going to be business as usual again, or a real new day." He urged against picking his plan apart. He was trying to make people see that the whole of his program —the shift from consumption to investment—was what mattered. But his talk of "sacrifice" was gone. His political consultants thought the term too downbeat.

The speech won much enthusiastic (if largely partisan) applause in the hall and high praise from commentators. It was a triumph, in part because by this time expectations were low.

Clinton's Presidency had already gone through one great mood swing on the part of the press. This was to be a pattern. The highs were usually too high, and the lows usually too low. Clinton was the object of the mood swings because so much had been expected of him and because, dropping so many of the protective walls around the Presidency, he insisted on establishing such a personal relationship with the public. Through his acts, he was out there all on his own, without institutional protections, calling attention to and often commenting on his every up and down. The success of his first speech to Congress was hailed in some quarters as a "restarting" of his Presidency. It was odd that a Presidency needed to be "restarted" so soon.

One reason Clinton's speech was so successful, especially compared to the unfortunate Oval Office address two nights before, was that Clinton was far better at playing to a room. The room happened to be on television.

(Clinton's aides had already learned that he needed an audience. After his first Saturday-morning six-minute radio address, with virtually nobody in the room, hadn't gone very well, they made sure that aides, campaign workers, and friends were present in the Oval Office for future talks.)

The two big questions when Clinton left the House chamber were whether he could win the battle for the definition of his program, and whether he could surmount the special interests by getting the great swath of the American people (many of whom might be part of a particular interest group) behind his program. It all came down to the question—one in many people's minds by then—of whether Clinton could lead.

On the day after Clinton's speech, the bond market went up. This was variously interpreted as confidence in the President's program and lack of confidence in the President's program.

Two days after the speech, the President's program received an important boost when Greenspan, in testimony before Congress, called it "a very positive force in the American economy." He said that it was "serious" and "credible." This complimentary testimony followed direct and indirect discussions that began during the transition, when Greenspan went to Little Rock. (It was akin to his assurances to negotiators in the 1990 nonpartisan deficit reduction agreement, during the Bush administration, that if they reached a certain reduction level, he could back them up in his monetary policy.)

The public debate over the plan quite soon settled on whether more spending cuts could be made and whether the tax increases were too great. (Panetta, in his confirmation hearings, before the inauguration, had said that he thought that the proportions of deficit reduction should be two dollars of spending cuts for one dollar in tax increases, but in Clinton's program it was about one to one.) The White House asked Democrats who were unhappy with the economic program to hold their fire, giving Clinton time to go out and try to sell it. Republicans started attacking the President's program right away. In fact, the Republican attacks began before the speech was delivered. Trent Lott of Mississippi said, "This is the biggest tax increase ever proposed by a President." (It may have been the largest proposed, but the Tax Equity and Fiscal Responsibility Act tax increase program, signed into law by Reagan in 1982, was larger.) Senator Pete Domenici, Republican of New Mexico and formerly chairman of the Senate Budget Committee, said, "People don't want tax and spend." Domenici had not been particularly partisan in the past, but the new dynamic within the Senate Republican Caucus changed his style. Senate Minority Leader Robert Dole and Domenici had decided that if Domenici continued in his past role, that would reveal a deep split among the Senate Republicans. Phil Gramm, Republican of Texas and head of the National Republican Senatorial Committee, a man with national ambitions despite his dismal performance as keynote speaker at the 1992 Republican convention, called Clinton's program "cradle-to-grave government paid for by cradle-to-grave taxes."

Other opponents were homing in on the tax increases and making it appear that everyone was going to be hit hard by them. Reagan and Bush had poisoned the well on the subject of taxes (though both had raised them), and now it was nearly impossible to have a rational political discussion on the subject. Local taxpayers' revolts, and the poor delivery of some government services, had also fed the national mood over the past decade or more. Political consultants advised their clients not to talk about raising taxes and perhaps even to talk about cutting them—in the face of clear evidence that taxes would have to be raised. This had led to the increasing cynicism about government and politics.

On the very day he presented his program to Congress, Clinton, in a photo opportunity, said, "I've made more specific cuts that affect me personally than I can think that any of my predecessors have made and I intend to find more as I go along." And then he said, "I've just been here four weeks." This was a surprising and odd statement from a man who had portrayed himself as ready to go, sleeves rolled up; it was apologetic and defensive.

The administration settled on the strategy of demanding that critics who said spending hadn't been cut enough come up with their own proposals. In a hearing before the House Budget Committee on the day after the President's speech, when Republican after Republican said the administration should cut spending more, the usually affable Panetta slammed the witness table and fairly shouted, "The time has come to put up or shut up." Less than a week after his speech to Congress, Clinton appeared before the U.S. Chamber of Commerce and said that he was looking for more budget cuts. "There are more cuts coming," he said.

Members of Congress had found during the Washington's and Lincoln's Birthday recess that their constituents were demanding deep spending cuts. Of course, many people are for cutting the deficit as long as they themselves are not disturbed.

At first, Clinton's aides thought that if Congress wanted to make more budget cuts, fine. One senior aide said, "It's a gift, as long as it comes from the Congress." He added, "But you can't take this reaction to mean that we could have come up with more. We already have western troubles—on grazing and mining—and we have agriculture troubles." What they didn't see for some time was that the public discussion about the President's entire economic program had turned into a discussion of how to cut the deficit more. Nor did they see how costly this was to the President's overall program, or that such a frame of reference would keep Clinton on the defensive. Almost imperceptibly, he was losing the battle over the definition of his program: it gradually became identified as a tax-and-spend program rather than one that was shifting government economic policy from consumption to investment and redistributing the tax burden. Though the new taxes on the middle class, through the Btu tax, would be small (according to the administration, $17 a month per household), people came to believe that Clinton was imposing a major tax increase on all but the poor. If the Republicans, who kept up a drumbeat of opposition and had clear points to make, won the definition battle, Clinton helped them do it. His arguments were complicated; he did have a more complicated case to make, but he could have made it more effectively. As President, he had the largest megaphone, but he didn't use it adeptly.

Clinton complained frequently to his staff and the consultants that they had given him "only two weeks of strategy." The consultants publicly shouldered the blame, but they were only partially at fault. Clinton himself dropped the ball; his instincts weren't strong, and he didn't bring a sharp focus to the issue. He was soon on to new subjects, and he only sporadically argued his budget case. Within a little over three weeks after his speech before Congress, he was beginning to hold meetings on the health care proposal. Leon Panetta said later, "After February 17 the message became confused. The President began to push health care and enterprise zones, community development banks, immunization. And foreign affairs—especially Bosnia—took more time than he expected."

Later in the month, the economic report issued by the government said that in the last quarter of 1992 the economy had grown by 4.8 percent, a quite high number. This might seem to raise a question about the necessity for some of Clinton's measures. But, the report said, a lot of this growth was due to greater efficiency—that is, "downsizing"—and there had been little growth in employment. So Clinton was at pains many times to say that though a recovery might be taking place, it wasn't producing jobs, and his program, including the stimulus, was as necessary as ever.

Though Clinton didn't talk much in this way, there was a coherent idea —he called it "lifelong learning"—behind his array of programs, which he mentioned in his speech to the Congress and which was spelled out in the budget blueprint issued on February 17, "A Vision of Change for America." This concept—that the opportunity to learn and develop skills would be available throughout a person's working life—encompassed expansion of Head Start (to move toward being a full-day, year-round program and be newly available to children from birth to age three, all of which would help working mothers); an education program (Goals 2000) stressing specific proficiency goals for students; reauthorization and reform of the existing Elementary and Secondary Education Act; a school-to-work program to provide apprenticeship training that connected formal education and workplace experience for high school students not going on to college; direct government loans to college students, to be paid as a percentage of income; national service, which would provide stipends for higher education and advanced technical training; and a revision of the various government training programs for workers who had lost their jobs, to provide one-stop shopping.

Had Clinton consistently explained this coherent idea, he might have been less on the defensive about "spending."

Later James Carville observed, "After February 17, we got into a poker game on the deficit. We were presenting a fiscal plan and not an economic plan. No one was telling people how we want to make their lives better. The deficit strategy was the wrong strategy. I would have talked about an economic plan, of which deficit reduction is a part. An economic plan that has a fiscal component to it is not a fiscal plan."

Though it was Clinton who allowed himself to be driven into a deficit reduction battle, some of his political advisers later blamed the economic advisers for setting him on this course. Paul Begala said, "They came to the President and said, 'We're talking to the business community, and they say you're being punitive and judgmental and participating in class warfare. Every American wants to be rich, and you're suggesting there's something wrong and dirty about that, and you're going to hurt yourself in the business community.' So our rhetoric became focused on deficit reduction." In the simplistic view of some of the consultants, the issue was deficit reduction or class warfare, overlooking the basic premise of Clinton's program—that a lower deficit would help the middle class.

The real problem was that there was an apparent contradiction at the heart of Clinton's program: he was for deficit reduction *and* increased spending. He had reasons for this, and they had been thought through, but he couldn't get that across. Another Clinton adviser said, "An essential element of Clintonism is that there is a desirable category of public investment that is distinguishable from consumption and the private economy. One, is that the case? Two, do the American people believe that that's the case—that it's not just 'spending'? I think we haven't made the case. Clinton has made pieces of the case over and over again. Whether the American people have heard it and accept it I doubt. I fear that people in the administration and his political advisers think November 1992 was a binding endorsement of that proposition. But '92 was as much a negative reaction to George Bush as an endorsement of Bill Clinton."

The President pushed the case for his program in town meetings, in satellite interviews to local stations, to local anchors who were brought to the White House, and on MTV. Cabinet officers were pressed into service (they were sent to their home states to make speeches). People were invited to send messages to the White House via E-mail. The communications department's young, hip "techies" were immensely proud of the volume of their product, but this had little to do with its substance.

On the day after his speech, Clinton himself traveled to St. Louis (site of an especially successful rally during the campaign) and then to Chillicothe, Ohio (a political adviser said that if Clinton could sell his program in this predominantly white, middle-class area, he could sell it anywhere).

In St. Louis, he said to a large and enthusiastic rally that since he was in Missouri, he would demand that people who said he should cut the deficit more should "Show me. Show me where, and be specific." He added, "I've been there four weeks and I'm still looking." The next day he traveled to Hyde Park and unsubtly drew a parallel between himself and Franklin Delano Roosevelt.

In Chillicothe, he did an "Ask Bill" event, walking around with a microphone in a town meeting setting. In this event, Clinton yielded to his old impulse of airing an idea before he'd thought it through, and mentioned a value-added tax, in effect a sales tax, as "something I think we may well have to look at in the future." Afterward, Dee Dee Myers, the press secretary, said that "there is no other discussion of a broad-based tax at this point." His advisers thought that this was a poor time to be mentioning another tax and persuaded Clinton to stifle his thoughts on this subject.

This was one of the areas where Clinton was having trouble making the adjustment from governor and even campaigner to President; it was taking him some time to recognize the impact of whatever he said. He had to learn to discipline himself in many ways once he gained the Presidency. Clinton was a learner, usually a fast one, but in certain particulars of the Presidency, learning took him some time.

Not long afterward, there was a change in strategy: Clinton's aides decided that it wasn't such a good idea for him to be telling audiences that he was looking for more cuts. Though Panetta actually had drawn up a list of some other potential cuts, it was decided that proposing them would undermine the administration's arguments that it had cut everything it could. Moreover, it would just up the ante, and the Republicans would demand more. Howard Paster was stressing that the administration had narrow majorities in the Senate and the House; that proposing more cuts might sink the economic package. But by the time the strategy was changed, it had already backfired.

Then something else happened to the President's program, which received little notice but had a profound effect on his investment strategy. On March 3, the Congressional Budget Office, whose numbers the Clinton administration had vowed to adhere to, issued figures indicating that the Clinton administration's estimate of how much its program would cut the deficit was off by sixty billion dollars.

On Friday afternoon, March 5, in a meeting in the Roosevelt Room, the President was very unhappy. The weather outside wasn't conducive to cheering anyone up: it was a gloomy, gray day, the second day of rain. Clinton's economic advisers had just given him the bad news that the deficit-cutting fever on Capitol Hill, and the sixty-million-dollar gap, could lead to a 25 percent cut in his proposed investments. Some Clinton aides had already been saying among themselves that they had created a "Frankenstein's monster" in setting the target of $140 billion for deficit cuts.

Gore was nearly as glum as Clinton. The investments, some of them for Gore's pet projects, were to have been their innovations, their break with the past and their change in emphasis. Reich was depressed; some of the programs to be cut represented his ideas for new kinds of worker training. The group feared that if the investments were cut very much, the appearance would be, as one adviser put it, "status quo versus change."

The question was whether to at least fight to preserve the investments. Clinton said to the assembled group, "If we don't do that, we are rewarding Reagan and [David] Stockman [Reagan's budget director]. What's the use of getting elected?" One adviser said later, "The President was mystified by the CBO estimate. He couldn't understand why that happened." Gore said that they should fight for the investments as if in a political campaign. Like Clinton, Gore argued that the investments were what the election was about. Paster, trying to reassure Clinton, said, "I know, Mr. President, this isn't perfect. But everyone in this room has to know that this is your budget, and your budget is getting through virtually intact, and if it does it's a major victory." He added, "While twenty-five percent of the investments might be cut, it will still be a major victory."

Clinton was particularly upset that his investments were in jeopardy despite the fact that interest rates had dropped since he had announced his program and the lower interest rates would bring down the deficit number. He was also upset that he wasn't getting credit for that. He wasn't pleased when Panetta told him that the Office of Management and Budget's new estimates, taking the lower interest rates into account, wouldn't be issued until July, per normal schedule.

But despite the strong statements in the room that the investments shouldn't be allowed to be cut too much, because that was what the election had been about, it was Clinton who, revealing the dichotomy in his mind, in the end suggested a note of balance. He said, "We shouldn't push investments so hard that we lose our deficit-cutting message."

At lunch the following Friday, George Stephanopoulos, a born worrier, was, for him, optimistic and in a good mood. The President was away, visiting the aircraft carrier USS *Theodore Roosevelt,* as part of his effort to establish warmer relations with the military. (The visit didn't turn out too well. To Clinton's fury, press reports focused on complaints and wisecracks the sailors made about Clinton's gays-in-the-military proposal. Also, the pictures of Clinton weren't wonderful. An adviser who traveled with him said afterward, "The jacket they gave him on the Roosevelt was two sizes too small. He looked like a sausage. We were paranoid. We thought it was deliberate.")

The White House staff was always in a lighter mood, less pressed and edgy, when Clinton was away. That morning, Janet Reno had been sworn in as Attorney General—to the President's great relief.

Stephanopoulos was sitting at a round table next to one of the long windows in his office, this time eating a dry chicken sandwich from the White House Mess. As always, he was nattily dressed. (His preference was for sharp Boss suits and slim, arty ties.)

He launched into one of his current frustrations: "The press has lost, in the wake of 'read my lips,' any sense of proportion on campaign promises. It's one thing to say 'a middle-class tax cut' and another to say 'read my lips.' "

Stephanopoulos continued, "If you took on all the responsibilities of governing when you campaign, almost by definition you can't win. Why should we accept the OMB number"—he affirmed that the Clinton camp had known about the higher deficit figures before it professed shock at learning them—"if the opponent doesn't? All the 'breaking promises' assumes an opponentless campaign." He added, "If you ran governing-responsible, you'd be assuming the legacy of what your opponent created.

"Here's our central problem with the economic plan: our whole enterprise is premised on the idea that there's a difference between wasteful government spending and productive government spending. The complication, the dilemma, is that the political system—the Congress and the public—finds it hard to absorb that. Polls show people want you to do more about education and job training, and they want you to cut spending more. The system chews it up and tends to turn everything into 'spending.' "

Stephanopoulos said, "Our job is to lift the veil and show the difference." Earlier in the week, in an attempt to do this, Clinton had given a speech before the National League of Cities, in which he made a strong and closely reasoned case for his investments, arguing that there were differences among types of government spending programs. Stephanopoulos commented, "The National League of Cities speech was one of the most important he's given, and one of the best, but it got little attention because so much else was going on."

Thus Stephanopoulos put his finger on another of Clinton's big problems.

6

ADJUSTING

"Let's Have Them All In and Talk About It"

Despite the disappointments and frustrations of the early weeks, Bill Clinton loved the Presidency. He loved the trappings and the unmatchable opportunity to put his ideas into national policy. He loved showing off the White House to visitors—he gave guided tours to dinner guests—and quickly became an expert on its history. He spent most of his working time in the Oval Office, rather than in the small study next to it. Sometimes he worked in his study in the East Wing, the family quarters—especially if his wife was away, so that he could be near Chelsea.

Clinton had put his own touches on the rooms that made up the West Wing Presidential quarters. He reinstated John F. Kennedy's large desk, from HMS *Resolute,* a British ship rescued by Americans (Queen Victoria gave America the desk); he moved some pictures around on the walls, and installed family photographs. On the wall facing the main door to the Oval Office, Clinton hung a striking, colorful painting by Childe Hassam called *The Avenue in the Rain.* On one shelf was a small replica of Rodin's *The Thinker,* lent to the Clintons by a friend.

In the small hallway just off the Oval Office—leading to the study and a private dining room—there was a photograph of John F. Kennedy shortly before he was shot, and one of Robert Kennedy. There was always a small pile of serious books on the table behind the desk, unlikely as it was that he had much time for reading books in the Oval Office. (Clinton read serious books, and mysteries for relaxation, with a self-imposed rule of reading two serious books for every mystery. Later he confessed to a group of journalists that he was so busy and tired that his ratio had become one to one.)

Clinton worked and talked until all hours of the night. After a party for his staff on the night of his first speech to Congress, he stayed up until 2:00 A.M., talking to Rubin and others. It wasn't uncommon in those early weeks for him and his wife and an aide or two to stay up talking until that hour. Cabinet officers and friends became accustomed to getting a Presidential phone call at any time—late at night, on a weekend, during mealtime, while at a restaurant. Sometimes there was a sudden summons to the White House. Not a man to do one thing at a time, Clinton often watched an old movie on television while talking on the telephone. He could get quite absorbed in watching basketball games on television. (At a moment of distress, a friend found him, in jeans, standing in the upstairs kitchen, eating ice cream and watching a basketball game.) Clinton worked on his "days off." Usually, especially in the first few months, there were weekend meetings.

For this and other reasons, the Clintons very rarely made use of the Presidential retreat at Camp David. Reagan and Bush had regularly used the rustic retreat, with its many amenities—swimming pool, bowling alley, bicycle paths, movie theater. When Clinton called on Reagan in California after the election, at Thanksgiving time, Reagan stressed the importance of getting away to Camp David. The story line out of the White House was that the Clintons didn't go there because of the President's allergies and because their teenage daughter wanted to be able to see her friends on weekends. But those reasons, however important, were only part of the story. The Clintons hadn't liked Camp David when they were there on the Cabinet retreat in January. They felt a lack of privacy—there was always staff around—and the isolated location didn't suit their gregarious natures or their desire to conduct business on weekends. Also, Clinton liked to play golf on weekends; among his favorite partners were Vernon Jordan and Webster Hubbell. Clinton played golf with more enthusiasm than skill, and he presumed the right to take a second shot, a "mulligan," if the first one didn't go well. (There was no golf course near enough to Camp David, the President complained.)

The Clintons actually had great difficulty adjusting to living in the White House. For all the President's pleasure in showing it off, he and his wife were unhappy with the lack of privacy there, as well, and with its formality. When they had arrived at the White House, they were dismayed to find Secret Service agents stationed inside the second-floor family living quarters and, in time, got them moved outside the door; the size of the second-floor detail was reduced and some agents were transferred downstairs. Clinton couldn't understand why a Secret Service man had to ride in the elevator that carried him from the living quarters to the ground floor. He also had difficulty adjusting to the Secret Service culture at the White House: agents assigned to the President (as opposed to those protecting a Presidential candidate) are trained not to speak to anyone, to stay completely focused on the President's safety. For a long time, it bothered Clinton, the talker, that when he would get into his limousine with the two agents there to protect him, neither would talk to him. He was also taken aback by the large number of agents who guarded his office: one stood on the walkway outside the Oval Office, two in the hallway outside his door, and a third in the hall outside the Roosevelt Room. Whenever Gore traveled the few steps from his own office to the President's, he was accompanied by two agents—making four agents outside the Oval Office door. When both Clinton and Gore attended a meeting in the Roosevelt Room, there was quite a jam-up of agents in the hallway outside.

In Arkansas, the Clintons had made the governor's mansion, where they lived for twelve years, into a warm and personal place, but there was limited opportunity to do that to the White House. Early on, Mrs. Clinton brought in a Little Rock decorator (Kaki Hockersmith) to redo a number of the rooms—a subject of some controversy later on. To recapture a bit of their earlier way of life, Mrs. Clinton installed a wooden table and chairs in the family kitchen, for people to gather around as they had in Little Rock, and the Clintons took many meals there. Chelsea's friends often came to dinner at the White House, with the Clintons joining them. In the early months in particular, Clinton might work in the Oval Office until about 8:00 P.M. and on the spur of the moment invite a staff member to dinner (which might consist of leftovers served buffet style). But despite their efforts, the White House wasn't homey, and the Clintons chafed at the constrictions on living there—though they were careful not to complain publicly lest they seem ungrateful for what to many was a palace.

The White House is a place of splendor (not opulence), but it can be a velvet trap for those who live there. It is like living in a grand apartment over the store, with some employees always hanging around. There are some private spots on the South Lawn, where the occupants can lunch, or walk—and the Clintons did these things—but they couldn't pop down the street to see a neighbor (as they had in Arkansas) or just take a walk outside the iron fence that surrounds it. In fact, it's nearly impossible for a President and his wife to do anything spontaneously outside the White House grounds—and the Clintons liked spontaneity.

Perhaps Clinton's first real sense of the imprisoning nature of the White

House came when, at the end of a mid-February visit by Michael Dukakis, Clinton offered to walk him back to his hotel and got as far as the White House gate, where a Secret Service agent told him he couldn't go any farther. So Clinton and Dukakis stood inside the fence and talked for about ten more minutes, the President captive within his own grounds. When the President wanted to go anywhere, it took thirty minutes to "move" him: station agents along the way, check his destination, load up the long motorcade.

One evening in March, Clinton, having been back and forth on the matter all day, decided he wanted to go to a book party for his friend Strobe Talbott (then ambassador at large for Russia and the other former Soviet republics) and Talbott's coauthor, Michael Beschloss. The party celebrated the publication of *At the Highest Levels,* an account of the relationship between George Bush and Mikhail Gorbachev. But though the event was being held only three blocks from the White House, by the time Clinton decided he wanted to go his transportation couldn't be arranged to get him there before the party was over. Later, after he complained, the time needed to "move" him was reduced.

Mrs. Clinton occasionally managed to go out in enough disguise to remain undiscovered. (Once, she and Chelsea did this at Disney World, where Mrs. Clinton was to make a speech, but after a couple of blissful hours a German tourist recognized Chelsea.) In the early months, the Clintons' entertaining was quite casual. They would invite friends, many of them from Arkansas, in for small, informal suppers—usually with Chelsea and perhaps one of her friends present. Often, the meal was followed by watching a basketball game, or a movie in the family theater—a small viewing room in the East Wing. Sometimes they had people in for a movie and popcorn, peanuts, and diet Coke. The Clintons often checked to see who was in town—whether old friends or someone they didn't know but would like to meet—to invite to dinner. And they liked going out for dinner to Washington restaurants, usually with friends, and, when they could, did so about once a week.

From early on, the Clintons were attracted to Hollywood figures. Harry Thomason and Linda Bloodworth-Thomason, who stayed at the White House frequently (and had passes entitling them to go anywhere in the building), were of course old friends. They had even bought a beachfront house near Santa Barbara for the Clintons to vacation in—the unwisdom of which the Clintons didn't grasp at first. (They spent the Thanksgiving weekend there in 1992.) The Clintons gave a birthday party for the actress Mary Steenburgen, an old friend from Arkansas. Singer Judy Collins was an overnight guest, and so was Barbra Streisand, who made herself something of a fixture on the Washington scene, discussing issues with officials. A stay at the White House was such a status symbol that one prominent Hollywood couple wrote a friend a condolence note on White House stationery. (The friend was enraged when she discovered that the note was not from the President.) Bill Clinton in particular evinced a notable interest in meeting celebrities—another perquisite of being President. The poor boy from Hope could now meet anybody in the world. Though Clinton occasionally had scholars in for dinner, to discuss a particular subject (say, Russia), usually before a trip, these were set pieces; generally speaking, the Clinton White House wasn't a place of intellectual ferment or much high culture.

In part the difference between the way the Clintons and their predecessors entertained was generational. It was to be a long time before they had a state dinner (the large formal dinner given for Kim Young Sam, the President of South Korea, at the end of November 1993, and even this was technically not a state dinner). In part it had to do with their concept of Clinton's job. In early March, a friend of theirs said, "He understands why he got elected. The country wanted action. He's going to give it to them. Coming down the stairs to a state dinner isn't about action." It wasn't until June, after some urging by friends and staff, that they began to have larger dinners of about forty people, including journalists. The idea was, among other things, to get to know people and enlarge their network and build a constituency in Washington.

The Clintons'—in particular Mrs. Clinton's—hostile view of the press was a hangover from the campaign. She remained angry over the hard time her husband had been given in New Hampshire about Clinton's alleged affair with Gennifer Flowers, the onetime lounge singer and then Arkansas state employee, and about whether Clinton had tried to avoid the draft during the Vietnam War. The odd thing about the Clintons' view was that much of the press was highly (and sometimes overtly) partial to Clinton's candidacy; some reporters even brought pressure on their colleagues—successfully—to put an end to the questions and stories about these subjects. An adviser said, "They both carry that in them about New Hampshire, her more than him." An aide said that Mrs. Clinton also felt "seared" by the criticism of her during the campaign.

Some advisers tried to convince the Clintons that this attitude was self-defeating, but to little avail. In fact, it had led to one of the big controversies of the early months—the closing of the corridor between the press briefing room and Stephanopoulos's office. The Clintons didn't want the press to have access to Stephanopoulos's reception area, because he was to be involved in policy, and high officials, including perhaps the President, might drop by. But the decision was also prompted by the continuing animus of the Clintons, who had seriously considered moving the press's workspace out of the White House entirely and over to the Old Executive Office Building.

The Clintons rarely went to other people's dinner parties, because they wanted strict control over who would be there (they didn't want to encounter members of the press) and because they felt that once they started, there would be no end to it. Numerous Washington hostesses were, of course, crushed. In private, among friends, they liked to laugh—Mrs. Clinton had an almost raucous laugh—and to have fun. Both of them serious people, they also needed to let loose, to have people around them with whom they could let down their hair.

Clinton was a man of large appetites. He ate a lot. He worked hard and talked a lot. By his own fuzzy admission during the campaign, he had indulged in extramarital sex. And now that he was President, he wanted to get a lot done. And fast. His keen intellect and ability to absorb a lot of material caused him to immerse himself in a great many issues—which wasn't altogether to his benefit.

Despite many warnings by members of the former Carter administration and other seasoned observers that one reason for Jimmy Carter's troubles was that he had overloaded the agenda, Clinton soon compiled a very large one of his own. By March, only five days after his speech to Congress, he had proposed his policy to promote high tech (announced in California, where he and Gore appeared together at Silicon Graphics); and a defense conversion plan (offered at a Boeing plant in Seattle), actually more a white paper than a program, was rushed out before the first round of base closings to be announced later that month. A study of how to "reinvent government," promised in the campaign, to be headed by Gore, was announced on March 3, with a six-month deadline.

On March 1, the thirty-second anniversary of John F. Kennedy's announcement of the Peace Corps, an irresistible date, Clinton gave a speech at Rutgers University about his national service program—though there were still many issues to be thrashed out. In early March, a friend and sometime adviser of Clinton's described the President's activities thus far as "frenetic, crazy." He said, "They're overexposing him, wearing him out. They need to pace things, be more thoughtful, slow down."

There were several reasons why Clinton was in a hurry to get a lot done. His political calculation, which was correct, was that he would have the most leverage early in his Presidency. Further, he believed that the issues he was proposing were interrelated, and beyond that, he felt that he would have no standing to challenge other countries to do things to strengthen their economies if he had not undertaken such an effort himself.

There may have been deeper reasons too. In 1991, Clinton said, according to the *Boston Globe,* "I had been living with the idea of my father's death and therefore my own mortality since I was a kid, and that's maybe why I competed so hard and wanted so much."

A Clinton aide said, "He knows that one way or another all of this is fleeting. One of the things he learned in his devotion to the Kennedy Presidency, and having been turned out of office, is that he has no idea how long he's going to govern. He could lose an election, or time could pass faster than his ability to make things happen, and that explains his impatience, and his desire to always be doing more. That's why we don't stop, why we're always on to the next initiative."

Clinton liked to travel, to leave Washington and "get in touch" with the people. Canned and planned as his, or any President's, trips were, Clinton was recharged by contact with the public. He had an almost mystical sense of his relationship with "the people," felt that he derived his strength from them. A friend said, "He'll be tired until he gets to a meeting, where the people are, and then he gets pumped up again. He'll complain that he just doesn't want to go to an event, and then he sees the people's faces and everything is OK."

Travel was also one of Clinton's ways of reaching around the Washington press corps. His people thought that he was at his most effective—and he seemed to share this view—in "town meetings" and other formats that brought him into direct contact with individuals. In these settings, which Clinton was to use a lot, people told him their problems and he would bite his lip; occasionally a tear would appear. He would express his sympathy with their plight—and then spell out some program he had proposed that would deal with it. Clinton's empathy, actual or feigned, became one of his trademarks.

But it raised the question: Was it leadership? Did it display the commandingness people want in a President? Did the American people want a Phil Donahue in the Presidency? Clinton slipped into the culture, became a part of it. He made himself available to MTV. But there was a price for that.

In early February, Clinton looked so exhausted—his face ashen, his eyes puffy—that an alarmed Howard Paster called Robert Reich, knowing he was a close friend of Clinton's, and said, "You have to talk to him. He's trying to do too much too soon." (Reich did speak to Clinton, but it didn't seem to do much good.) Moreover, Clinton, who was pushing himself to the limit and beyond, and tried always to appear to the public relaxed and happy, as a President must, wasn't so easygoing in private. An aide said, "Clinton worries a lot. He'll say, 'I was up in the middle of the night last night thinking about X or Y.' "

And then there was his temper. Other Presidents had tempers. Eisenhower's was famously bad. Clinton's temper was much less intimidating than Lyndon Johnson's. The real significance of Clinton's temper was what it said about his deeper nature. There was a self-indulgence in Clinton's tantrums, an immaturity, a part of him that never grew up and a part—shared by other politicians who took advantage of their powers over others—that felt free to chew out aides, who couldn't argue back and weren't likely to quit.

Clinton would blow up easily, venting a frustration that some event hadn't gone right, or a plan to do something wasn't ready, or a speech wasn't in good shape. He was especially angered by leaks out of the White House, so much so that he didn't seem to understand that this sort of thing would happen and that some of the leaks reflected deliberate efforts by his aides to further his objectives. (He had a better case when they were to further themselves.)

The temper was strong, and big. Clinton, a large man, would swing his left arm forcefully as if to make a sidearm pitch and bring it forward, with his index finger pointed; sometimes his right arm slapped the air as if hitting something out of the way, and he would yell. The terms used by aides were "yell and scream"—especially "scream." One top aide, having just experienced the temper, returned to his office shaken and said to two visitors, "You don't want to be in the room when Clinton gets angry." The aides most subject to it were the ones who were around him most, and were among the younger aides—but not exclusively. Sometimes, on the road, he inadvertently lost his temper—chewing out an aide over logistical details—before the television cameras. In the White House, Stephanopoulos, who saw a great deal of Clinton, was a frequent target; but Stephanopoulos's colleagues credited him with handling this situation well. One said, "George doesn't get fazed. He'll sit there and say, 'Mr. President, I know you're upset. Now, there are two things we have to deal with.' He appeals to Clinton's intellectual side, stays focused on the discussion at hand. He doesn't get silent."

There grew up a myth that no one in the Clinton White House was willing to take the President bad news (this was often said about Presidents), but it wasn't the case. When Clinton got bad news, he'd sometimes say,

"Whaaa?" Stephanopoulos and McLarty were among the aides who were willing to take Clinton bad news (another would be Ickes, who joined the White House staff in early 1994). A colleague of Stephanopoulos's said, "George is willing to tell the President he's got something wrong, and then he gets yelled at. Sometimes he has to try three times, but he makes his point."

And there was in the temper a kind of petulance—a word used by an Arkansan who knew him well. There was in fact a kind of unmaturity about Clinton. There seemed to be something unfinished about him. Compared to many men his age, or even younger, he didn't seem quite grown up. To what extent this was because he was his proud mother's perfect son, or because for all the rough-and-tumble of politics he hadn't lived in the real world very much and had so many of his needs, psychic or material, catered to, or it was simply some innate personality trait, was impossible to know. There was much that was appealing about him—his brain, his zest, his resilience, his charm—but he didn't come across as a settled person, and the public seemed to sense that. A lot of people in politics aren't settled and come across as spoiled or particularly needy. But Clinton demonstrated these traits in large measure, perhaps in part because the spotlight was so often on him. This could have been one reason why, even in those periods when he was doing well, when his poll ratings were high, the public seemed to be holding something back.

By all accounts, Clinton's temper was tolerable, if momentarily unpleasant, because the storms subsided almost as quickly as they arose. He didn't stay angry, and he didn't carry grudges or resentments. His other side was sunny and warm and often good-humored. An aide who had been a target of his wrath said, "When he's in a good mood, he's easy."

Mrs. Clinton was more difficult to deal with. She could be extremely thoughtful toward someone, but if angered, she could make cold and cutting remarks—and she remembered. An associate who knew her well said, "She's a complex person. She can be extraordinarily warm, personable, very kind and loyal—and she can be combative and tough. If you take her on, you had damned well better know what you're talking about. She has a very incisive mind and is a rigorous questioner. She's very hard-hitting and formidable in debate." Mrs. Clinton didn't hesitate to pick up a phone and tell one of her husband's aides of her displeasure about something. A Presidential aide said, "She's the only person around here people are afraid of."

Clinton's pace and his appetite for work, his proclivity toward talking long and working late and holding meetings at all hours and on weekends, had a nearly ruinous effect on some aides' lives. As early as February, one remarked privately, "I'm not sure how long I can take this." True, many of the aides were young: of the roughly four hundred fifty members of the extended White House staff, about one in seven was under twenty-four. Many others were under thirty. The legend of "the kids" quickly took hold. Their informal dress (this wasn't true of all of them), their bars, their taste in music, and their wizardry with computers were solemnly chronicled. It was noted that the Clinton White House was the first one where women wore pants to work. But most of these young people were stashed over at the Old Executive Office Building, handling communications and advance work for Presidential trips. If they wanted to work all hours, that was largely their business. The ones directly affected by Clinton's work habits were nearer by, and at higher levels, and a few of them were older and had children.

Clinton's inclusiveness was initially a joy to his staff. The unhierarchical structure and the collegial style of the Clinton White House seemed, at first, wonderful. Clinton himself contributed to the informality, often wandering the halls and dropping in on aides or on the Vice President. Aides felt fairly free to drop in on him. In early March, Bruce Lindsey said, "More people tend to walk in on him than probably any of his predecessors." A peephole in the door leading from the back corridor to his office enabled an aide to see if he was on the phone, or talking with people, before going in.

A large number of people were in on meetings with him. Clinton encouraged it. An adviser said, "You can go to him and say, 'So-and-so thinks this' and 'So-and-so thinks that,' and go down the list, and he'll say, 'Let's have them all in and talk about it.' " Harried Presidential aides were typically scheduled to attend wall-to-wall meetings—with the President or otherwise—with little time to think. And then spontaneous meetings would be added. When the President was in the White House, his top aides knew that their schedules were meaningless.

Even an official who wasn't a great fan of Clinton's governing style said that Clinton made a real contribution to meetings, by asking good questions, penetrating questions that took things further down the road—questions about an aspect or implication of a proposal, or its connection to something else, that others hadn't thought of. This official said, "You know where he's going. He verbalizes as opposed to just sitting there quietly." He added, "So you know what he's carrying away. But you don't necessarily know the decision of the meeting."

A Cabinet officer suggested that Clinton's idiosyncratic governing style had a purpose. This person said, "What Clinton does instinctively is carry around in his head a lot of feedback from people, whether or not it's consistent. He sends out the sonar, tests out ideas, gives a speech and watches and listens for responses. He'll talk to people, asking, 'What do you think?' This is a process of constant sonar, and he'll carry in his head different views from different people until they evolve into policy, or he'll try to set forth a problem and leave it to other people to come up with proposals and solutions. What this means is he's sitting in the middle of a cacophony of voices and ideas. It also means that those who have the most time with him have the most influence, so there's a great deal of stampeding around him to have the most time with him."

Therefore, this person continued, "What happens in the White House is a reflection of the way he thinks. He doesn't want hierarchy. He doesn't want a strong Chief of Staff. He doesn't want a single economic adviser. He wants all kinds of advisers swirling around him constantly."

One symptom of Clinton's indecisiveness—and also his insistence upon micromanagement—was the personnel problem. The Clinton White House was very slow to fill the jobs at the agencies below the rank of Secretary. It was so slow, in fact, that Cabinet officers complained privately that they were understaffed and overloaded. As part of the last-minute staff shuffle in January, Lindsey was put in charge of personnel. A soft-spoken former Little Rock lawyer, with a gentle sense of humor, Lindsey, who was to be a general counselor to the President, was a longtime Clinton loyalist. When Clinton was turned out of office in 1980, Lindsey's law firm took him in. And while Lindsey was clearly overloaded—the piles of papers on his desk and on the surrounding floor were testimony to this—others were also responsible for the lag in filling jobs. Foremost was the President, who, in the midst of everything else he had to do, insisted on signing off on the appointment of every assistant secretary, and sometimes deputy assistant secretaries.

Though Lindsey, defensive about the subject, gave out figures indicating that Clinton was further along in making appointments than Bush or Reagan at a given stage, other figures showed that Clinton was behind Carter (and Reagan and Bush weren't as interested in governing). Hillary Clinton (and her friend Susan Thomases) remained involved often in certain kinds of appointments—particularly at the Justice Department—or in seeing to it that certain people were rewarded with jobs. The appointments process was complicated by the Clintons' insistence on diversity.

The Clinton people had been urged by former members of the Carter administration to insert their own people into the agencies, so as to ensure where the loyalty lay; but the Clinton people carried this caution quite far. The shrewder Cabinet officers picked enough Clinton loyalists and put enough diversity into their list of candidates to get White House approval relatively early. But this was rare. Sometimes a whole slate would be returned to a Cabinet officer because it wasn't diverse enough. Sometimes Clinton would question a single potential appointee's credentials, and the whole group of nominations would be returned so that it could come back in correct balance.

Defense Secretary Les Aspin and the White House were at a long standoff because his slates were judged insufficiently diverse. The continuing insistence on diversity led to a certain amount of tokenism, of putting people in jobs they weren't ready for, and was to lead to some highly controversial appointments. The Clintons were looking not only for racially diverse appointees, as well as a high percentage of women, but also for people who had helped in the campaign or came from the heartland—including such electorally valuable states as Ohio, Michigan, and Illinois. One whole personnel desk was devoted to making sure that California, the biggest electoral vote prize of all, was amply taken care of. Around the White House, the criteria for jobs became referred to as EGG—ethnicity, gender, geography. Numerous Democrats who lived in Washington and who had waited twelve years to enter, or reenter, the government were to be sorely disappointed. People who contributed to Clinton late—after it was certain he had the nomination—weren't especially appreciated, and weren't offered jobs.

The increasingly complicated process for clearing nominees also slowed things down. With each government scandal, the requirements for government service became more stringent and the forms more burdensome. After the President signed off on a nominee, that person had to fill out three forms: an FBI form, a financial disclosure form for the Office of Government Ethics, and a new form developed by the Clinton White House. Some of the delay was caused by the FBI. A "full-field" FBI investigation could take from one to two months. Occasionally, the White House leaned on the agency to speed things up, but the Clinton people had been warned by their predecessors that this wouldn't work often.

The nomination of the President's close friend Strobe Talbott to the important post of handling policy with Russia and the other former Soviet republics was announced January 19, the day before the inauguration. For his previous job as a *Time* correspondent and columnist, and for some of the books he had written, Talbott had taken dozens of trips to the Soviet Union. Whether that made the FBI suspicious, or for whatever reason, his name languished for a long time, until the White House asked the FBI to get on with it, since the President wanted him at the table at the forthcoming summit meeting in Vancouver in early April. His name was finally sent to

Capitol Hill on March 16. (Clinton swore him in in a Portland, Oregon, hotel room, en route to the summit. Since no Bible could be found, Talbott solemnly rested his right hand on briefing books. A proper ceremony took place in Washington later.)

The strict conflict-of-interest rules and the lengthy forms kept some people away from government jobs, and the long wait for a decision on whether the job was available caused some people to give up. The fact that Clinton valued Bruce Lindsey's company, and wanted him along whenever he traveled, contributed to the pileup on and around Lindsey's desk. A friend of the President's urged him to leave Lindsey at home when he traveled, and the President replied, "I *need* Bruce." When they traveled, Lindsey and Clinton played hearts—at which Clinton was fiercely competitive. Lindsey was the President's political radar on the road—and in the White House as well. A friend of both men said that Clinton also looked to Lindsey to tell him how he had done at a certain event or in a certain situation.

Senator David Pryor, a friend of both men, said, "Bruce Lindsey is Bill Clinton's conscience. Bruce can get in his head. He knows how he thinks, knows how he's going to react, what he's going to do." Pryor said it was Lindsey who rescued Clinton at what was one of the lowest points in his political life—when Clinton had just given the disastrously long and strangely ill-suited speech nominating Michael Dukakis. Pryor said, "He literally picked him up, got him out of bed, and made him face people. It was Bruce who got him to go on the Johnny Carson show [where he played the saxophone to show what a regular guy he was]. It was Bruce who made it clear he had to handle it with humor." Lindsey watched out for Clinton's political network and commitments, and kept his secrets. Pryor said, "Bruce and Clinton can communicate with body language or facial expression. Bruce can wiggle his eyebrows in a certain way, and the President will know whether he's on board or not."

Another friend said, "Bruce Lindsey is more and more able to challenge the first conclusion about something. He's also a security blanket. That's why the President wants him on trips."

Mrs. Clinton's abandonment of the pretense of her role in the latter part of the campaign—as the adulatory and largely silent wife—was complete once she reached Washington, and, to many people, jarring. Her reinstitution of her maiden name, so that she was now Hillary Rodham Clinton, was a strong statement—too strong for some—and her staff was busy trying to get across that this didn't represent a change, even though, of course, it did. There were some transparent efforts to try to keep things in balance. The first press interview she gave was with the food correspondent of the *New York Times,* whose front page displayed an evening-gowned Hillary checking the place settings for the Clintons' first large, formal dinner (for the governors). The story was about how much Mrs. Clinton liked going over menus for dinners and wanted more emphasis on American dishes and less on the French cuisine that had been in vogue during the Republican reign. (Later, she fired the chef.) One morning in early February, Mrs. Clinton's social secretary, Ann Stock, was on all three networks' morning shows, talking about how much Mrs. Clinton loved her role as hostess.

But Hillary Clinton remained involved in most major decisions made by her husband—and some minor ones as well. Whatever the state of their marriage at any point, they had long been a political team; Bill Clinton valued and even needed her advice. And some of the staff wished that she were even more available, because of her effect on him. A former campaign aide said, "He was never focused on health care in the campaign, but he began to see this as a monster, and he saw Hillary as his smartest, toughest adviser. She *is* his closest adviser. She's terribly well organized and always pushes him to more decisive action. Part of his deliberative process is to keep everything open as long as he can. Everyone realizes they have to keep Hillary informed and posted, and they do that. If they don't, he'll always ask her for her opinion anyway. It's not that she forces her way into the process. He invites her into the process. They talk about every issue—they enjoy it. They sit around at dinner talking policy."

It was understood within the White House that Mrs. Clinton ferociously protected her husband and that aides would have to answer to her for any perceived misservice to him. She reviewed his schedule, and told staff members off for setting up events he wasn't prepared for. Later in the year, an aide said, "She has sometimes felt that the President's schedule was abusive to him and harum-scarum. She concerns herself with the overall management of the White House and what she feels is a failure to integrate the President's politics into the workings of the White House. She expresses frustrations about the loose management of the White House and the inability to hold some people accountable." The aide pointed out that on occasion Mrs. Clinton was part of the problem, since she herself encouraged criticism from the outside, including from Susan Thomases and the consultants. Another Clinton adviser said, "McLarty is not prepared to force any issues with her. A first-rate Chief of Staff would do something about this. She has a vested interest, and a deep conviction that this guy [her husband] should get the very best, but it sends a confusing signal."

A Presidential aide, describing Mrs. Clinton's style of criticism, said, "In any number of meetings she has metaphorically pounded the table—she doesn't have to literally because of the force that she has. She'll argue that there is no plan, there's no strategy." The aide continued, "I want to put this carefully. She has in many cases served functionally in the way a Chief of Staff would in terms of accountability and discipline and sometimes unruly organization. She has made the point openly in his presence. What she does privately I can only imagine."

Another adviser said, "More than anyone else in the building, she wants to see him reelected."

No one doubted that Mrs. Clinton was in on anything she wanted to be in on, and some made their arguments to the President through her. One Presidential adviser said that he could usually tell when the President was passing along a thought Mrs. Clinton had given him: the President wouldn't mention his source—as opposed to saying, I was talking to Senator X last night and he said . . .

All of the President's aides knew that Susan Thomases had the First Lady's ear. Having been closely involved in the selection of the White House staff, she kibitzed and second-guessed various White House activities—especially the communications and scheduling offices. It would become known not only within the White House but around Washington when Thomases was "down" on some member of the White House staff. Thomases publicly denied that she had such clout, but many people knew that she did. It was enough to unnerve some White House aides. At a June "roast" of James Carville, with whom she had done battle during much of the campaign, Thomases elaborately thanked Carville for being kind to Hillary Clinton during the campaign. She also thanked him for getting tears in his eyes during the Clintons' taping of their famous appearance on *60 Minutes,* where Clinton admitted that he had caused "pain in my marriage." "I appreciate that, James," Thomases said.

The real state of the Clintons' marriage was something known to very few people, most of whom didn't talk about it. It was known to have been turbulent in their pre–White House days, and therefore, inevitably, there were rumors during Clinton's first year and a half as President. The rumors were a cottage industry, but nothing was proved. There were aspects of the marriage that close observers could talk about with some validity and that gave clues about the way they governed. One longtime friend of theirs said, "They really are each other's best friend—the smartest person each of them knows. They love to discuss books, but for them discussions are very passionate, very confrontational. They probably have one of the most multidimensional marriages I know, because they turn to each other for virtually everything. They get into tough arguments about a book they've read, or what Chelsea should wear to school. They act the same way with political strategy. They don't do anything with each other without tremendous emotion behind it. They scream and yell at each other, but it's not in anger. Well, yes, there's some anger too. Chelsea participates in these passionate discussions. Hillary protects Bill's time with Chelsea. Bill gets real out of sorts if he doesn't have his Chelsea fix every day."

In early March, an item in *Newsweek* recounted that one day at school, when Chelsea needed an aspirin, a school official said she would call her mother, and Chelsea replied, "Call my dad; my mom's too busy." A White House aide remarked that the story, which made the rounds, was true. Clinton later tried to explain it away (on MTV) by saying that this happened because Mrs. Clinton moved around and traveled a lot because of her work on health care, but they always knew where to find him.

The longtime friend said that the Clintons did love each other, and added, "But it's a very taxing relationship. Hillary is better at seeing ramifications and implications; Bill is better at vision and in dealing with people." This person elaborated, "It's a more taxing relationship than most because they're so enmeshed. Neither can go off with others for the things they deal with. It's a very taxing relationship because it's so enmeshed and emotional."

In the early months, the Clintons were feeling shakier about their new roles than they let on. Their close friends knew it. One said, "As smart as they are, and as much as they knew about governance, it's impossible to anticipate the enormous pressures of that job." The fact that the Clintons considered themselves so smart made the bumpy transition from Arkansas to Washington, and the enormity of the difference, all the more disorienting. They had traveled in national policy circles and governed a small state, and they'd groomed themselves for the White House for a long time. None of this prepared them for what they faced. Some say that no one is prepared for the Presidency (though Vice Presidents have a good foundation), but for the Clintons, who wanted to do so much and had so ill equipped themselves to do it by picking such an inexperienced staff, the beginning was particularly difficult.

It was to be a long time before any repair work was done (not until mid-1994, when Clinton's Presidency seemed to many people, including some of the Clintons' intimates, dead in the water). Within the White House and outside it, there were questions from the beginning as to whether Mack McLarty was up to the job of Chief of Staff, and—especially on the outside

—whether the White House staff itself was up to the job. McLarty, a man of medium build, neatly combed, thinning brown hair, and pleasant looks punctuated by large blue eyes, was a tidy man in a generally disheveled White House. His desk was tidy; the stacks of phone messages on his desk were always tidy. He wore conservative, striped ties, navy suits, and crisp shirts with French cuffs and his initials. He was an elaborately courteous man with a pleasant demeanor, but his background as a tough businessman also showed.

Though McLarty was genial, it often seemed a studied geniality; when he was displeased, or when it was time to move on to the next thing, his face would quickly harden, and the message was clear. There was a corporate crispness to his manner. He was often brisk but rarely brusque. A senior White House aide said, "Geniality is his operating philosophy." Privately as well as publicly, he talked in a formal manner and somewhat circuitously. And he often seemed wary in conversation, as if he knew he wasn't quite at home in his new milieu and felt he was being watched. But his laugh was loud, and he could kid around—his voice often gaining substantial volume and getting higher, as if going up the scale—revealing a good-old-boy streak.

McLarty grew up in a prosperous home set in a hundred acres in Hope, Arkansas—in the same town but a long economic distance from Clinton. McLarty was devoted to the President but was hampered by both his lack of Washington experience and his own management style. More than one White House staff member said privately that "an enforcer" was needed, someone to make sure things got done and inspire discipline among the staff. Whether these people really wanted such a person was another question.

The arrangement seemed to suit the President. A Cabinet officer said, "There's an explanation for choosing McLarty, Bruce, Rubin. What's the single common denominator they share? They're not going to try to impose their views or take charge. I go over there and what do I find? The nicest people. These are the sweetest people, they're gentle, not one of them raises their voice or bangs their fist on the table. Generally, relative to other administrations, they don't hide information. The common denominator is that none of them insists that his position is necessarily the best. None of them is overly conscious of turf—or, certainly, relative to previous White Houses."

Robert Reich said, "Clinton has a preference for people who are going to collaborate, express their ideas, help him with his continuous process of thinking about policy, and help him reach conclusions about what's to be done."

By late March, the general impression outside the White House was that Clinton was recovering from his earlier problems and that things were going well. Some people inside the White House told themselves—and reporters—that, but privately they remained apprehensive. With good reason.

7

EARLY TRIUMPH

"He Doesn't Seem to Be the President"

The Congress takes its measure of every new President—the members watching and sniffing the air and feeling the pulse of their constituents. It is constantly judging how strong a President is and how popular he is, as they make their calculations of how important it is to support him and the consequences of not doing so. These judgments can change over time, but first impressions are very important. In Clinton's case, the first impressions weren't very good.

The Clinton camp was riven from the outset over what kind of relationship it should pursue with the Congress. This dispute was continued at least through the first year of Clinton's Presidency. In his campaign, as part of his promise to bring about "change"—and especially as he reached for the Perot vote—Clinton vowed to change things in Washington, to take on the "insiders" and the "special interests" and to reform the campaign-finance and lobbying laws. At the outset of his Presidency, Clinton listed campaign-finance reform as one of his top five priorities. But in order to get his ambitious domestic program approved, Clinton needed the votes of the members of Congress he was supposed to take on. So he said very little about the reform issues after the start of his Presidency, and his drive for them was halfhearted at best.

Though the Democrats controlled the Congress, the President didn't have reliable margins in either chamber. The House started out with a lineup of 258 Democrats and 176 Republicans and 1 Independent, but any Presidential initiative was vulnerable if more than 30 conservative Democrats voted with the Republicans. The Senate lineup of 57 to 43 wasn't enough to guarantee the Democratic leadership enough votes to break a filibuster (60 were needed).

The consultants—Carville, Begala, Grunwald, and Greenberg—felt that Clinton should reach around the Congress and appeal directly to the American people, who would make the Congress fall in line. They had great faith in Clinton's ability to reach the public, even when the evidence suggested otherwise. In his early months in office, through missteps, Clinton dissipated much of the strong support with which he had started out. The consultants regarded Howard Paster, the President's assistant for congressional liaison, as too concerned with the Congress's view of things, as seeing the Congress as his client. In a sense, he did see it that way, feeling that if the President wanted Congress's cooperation on issues of importance to him, it could be pushed only so far on matters of importance to it.

The President's handling of the transition had given members of Congress (as well as interest groups) their first strong clue that he was malleable. It was known that in Arkansas he had tried to please all factions, but his demonstration of this on the national stage gave it a greater dimension. And of course, his open capitulation to Sam Nunn and the Joint Chiefs of Staff on gays in the military was telling. Then came the President's direct dealings with members of Congress.

Upon taking office, Clinton put a great deal of time and energy into meeting with the congressional leadership and other members. In mid-March, Howard Paster said that Clinton had been to the Capitol five times. The idea was to get members feeling invested in his economic plan.

Many of the politicians admired Clinton's energy and thought he had a real political touch. Senator Christopher Dodd, Democrat of Connecticut, said in mid-March, "I don't know when the guy sleeps—he's on the go all the time. It seems every other day there's a meeting at the White House. He's probably wise to do that—to establish ties. He had a couple of meetings with one of my colleagues who was grumbling about the budget, and he came back and said, 'He's a regular guy.' "

But members were noticing something else as well. They noticed a passivity on Clinton's part, and that some among them played on this passivity, with apparent impunity. Very early, some saw that Clinton wasn't held in awe and inspired no fear, and they found this alarming. In early February, Senator David Boren of Oklahoma described a meeting he had just attended with the President and some senators and House members. "I found it a very disturbing meeting," Boren said. "They were patronizing to the President. They didn't show enough deference to the President. This gets to a larger point: I think the President has to become much firmer and grab these reins. He seems so passive. This is popping up in other areas—in the case of the Joint Chiefs, the image that they thumbed their nose at him."

Boren continued, "He doesn't seem to be the President. I've had this concern watching him on TV. He can be articulate in conversation and in a campaign, and not be when he's with decision makers. People were in essence saying, 'We'll bring this up when we want to, Mr. President.' And he was passive. He didn't say much. He kind of slumped and listened."

A House Democrat described an hour-long meeting in February of the President and the Vice President with forty House Democrats on Clinton's budget proposals. Mainly, the congressman said, the members made suggestions—from trivial to major, political and philosophical—and the President took notes. The congressman added, "Two things struck me about the tone of the meeting. One, it was so incredibly laid back, in terms of the President's participation. With Bush, it was scripted and stilted. Two, it was hardly a rally or strong advocacy type of meeting. It's not that Clinton wasn't engaged, or proprietary about his package. But there was no strong pitch, no 'Guys, I really need your help, we will sink or swim together.' No call to arms. It was the mood or atmosphere you would expect if you were having a Friday-afternoon book meeting—a kind of 'Let's talk about this.' "

Early on, the White House people attempted to show that the administration could play rough. It retaliated against Senator Richard Shelby, a conservative Democrat from Alabama, who, when Vice President Gore called on him on the day after the President's speech to Congress to urge his support of the economic program, had television cameras present and said that the program was "high on taxes and low on cuts." This offense to the Vice President's dignity and the open challenge of the President's program by a member of his own party could not, White House officials concluded, go unpunished. The President agreed, telling his aides, "We've got to do it." The retaliation took the form of moving a NASA project—worth $380 million a year and involving ninety jobs—from Huntsville, Alabama, to Houston, Texas. (The Office of Management and Budget had wanted to do this for years.) For their next step, White House aides leaked the story to various news outlets, to send a message to other Democrats who were considering whether they should back the President's program. The aides were quite pleased with their ploy. A top White House aide said, "Members got it, and it shot through the Hill. It broke in the papers on Monday. It gave a jolt inside the Hill that we needed. People were thinking: Should I be for him or not be for him? When they opened up the *Wall Street Journal, U.S. News,* and *Newsweek,* they saw that story."

But the White House's sense of satisfaction didn't last long. In the aftermath of the ploy, Shelby almost without exception opposed the administration's proposals, and he became a hero in Alabama. The administration drew the conclusion that this wasn't an exercise they could indulge in often.

Following an episode of a different nature, Greenberg said, "We don't have very many senators to waste." Greenberg was defending the administration's move, which came to light at the end of March, to mollify western Democratic senators by removing from its budget the proposed increases in grazing fees on public lands, royalties for mining the lands (there had been no charge for this), and elimination of below-cost timber sales. The increased charges for using public lands had been trumpeted by the administration in February as a symbol of its determination to take on the "special interests." So the retreat sent a very powerful message.

On March 16, a group of ten Western Democratic senators, led by Max Baucus, of Montana, met for a little over an hour in the Roosevelt Room with Clinton, Gore, McLarty, and Panetta. The senators raised some qualms they had about Interior Secretary Bruce Babbitt and some of his appointees, as well as their unhappiness with the proposed fee increases. The meeting and the concession occurred without any notification to Babbitt, who favored a new ethic in the use of Western lands. Babbitt, too, was seeking a "third way" on land policy, a breakthrough in the longstanding battle between environmentalists and Western economic interests. The senators pointed out that several Western states—including Colorado, Montana, and New Mexico—had gone Democratic in 1992, for the first time in a long time. The President listened intently, took notes on three-by-five cards, and for nearly the full hour made no comments and asked no questions. Then he said, "We should do something about this."

In deciding what to do, the administration went further than the senators expected or, indeed, asked. No one at that meeting asked the President to drop the fee increases from the budget. Baucus recalled thinking when the result was announced, "Uh-oh. This is a problem. They're going too far."

The administration, falling back in the face of vociferous criticism that it had caved in to the Westerners too easily, said that these changes in policy would be dealt with in separate legislation (so as to give the senators a better shot at them). But this was a weak reed. Later, in May, Clinton told a town meeting that the mining and grazing fees were new proposals and therefore would have been subject to a filibuster—an explanation that was without foundation. (After a long struggle, Babbitt tried to impose higher fees by executive action, setting off a protracted and inconclusive battle with some Western senators. As of mid-1994, the issue still wasn't resolved.)

Nevertheless, on the surface, there was a sense of momentum as Clinton's budget started to move through the Congress. The young, vigorous President was working hard for passage of his program, and he seemed a good politician. But there was also an underlying tension. Members, from liberal Democrats to conservatives, were hearing from their constituents that they wanted the deficit cut further. On March 10 and 11, the House and Senate Budget Committees, led by chairmen friendly toward the administration, cut Clinton's program by another $63 billion. This was in part to deal with the fact that the President's proposal exceeded the "caps" on discretionary spending that had been set in the 1990 budget agreement between Bush and the Democratic Congress, and in part to respond to the public pressure to make more budget cuts. In fact, in a move that was to have a major impact on Clinton's program, the House Budget Committee went beyond the 1990 budget agreement and froze discretionary spending, not even allowing increases for inflation. (This was known as a "hard freeze.") The problem of caps, and the hard freeze, bedeviled Clinton for a long time. If the caps were to be met, Clinton's "investments" had to compete with domestic programs more favored by important members of Congress. Clinton's economic advisers had known that the President's program exceeded the caps but thought that they could negotiate this with the Congress—a task that proved far more difficult than they anticipated.

The result of the Budget Committees' action was to increase the overall deficit reduction over the next five years to roughly $500 billion. This would get the deficit to below $200 billion in fiscal year 1997—which happened to correspond with the calendar year in which Clinton would be running for reelection—but then it would start to increase again (mainly because of the growth in the cost of health care programs). The restrictions on new spending and the consequent threat to the President's investments notwithstanding, both measures reflected the basic philosophy of the President's economic program: a shift of emphasis from consumption to investment, if not as large a one as the President had hoped.

Despite this progress, by just before mid-March the President had already begun to lose the argument over the definition of his economic program. Clinton continued to fret about his investments, which he saw as the touchstone of his campaign. He talked with some passion to his aides about the importance to his Presidency of doing more for children's programs, education, worker training, and the Earned Income Tax Credit, sometimes arguing that they were why he had run. He emphasized the need for more investment in infrastructure, saying, "We're way behind Germany and Japan in modernizing infrastructure." In his frequent meetings with members of Congress, Clinton often said that British Prime Minister John Major had told him in a recent visit that if you cut spending too much too fast, you could choke off economic recovery. In a speech before Treasury Department employees on March 18, Clinton said that people who were saying, "This program's all right, but we ought to do a little less of that," were known at the White House as "the 'status quo lite' crowd." He said, "Frankly, I think if we do a little less of everything, we have a little less spending cut, a little less tax cut, a little less investment—we'll get a lot less in results." His comments went largely unnoticed.

The White House and the House Democratic leaders worked together hard to guarantee House passage of the resolution incorporating the President's budget (as amended). The House leadership gave Clinton some names of House Democrats to call. Cabinet officers were dispatched to key media markets to make the case for the program.

Perhaps most important to many House Democrats was their need to demonstrate that the Democratic Congress could act. House Speaker Tom Foley said later that an important factor in Democratic members' decision on whether to support the resolution was "the desire to have a win. Democrats themselves aren't happy with the idea that the place might be faltering." They had to show that the "gridlock" between the Democratic Congress and the Republican Presidents in recent years could be broken. If it couldn't, Ross Perot and other generic critics of "Washington" would be proved right, and there would be still more cynicism about the political system. And more incumbents would lose.

And so on Thursday night, March 18, the House of Representatives approved the President's budget by a wide margin of 243–183. Republicans voted against it unanimously, but only eleven conservative Democrats defected. And then at 12:21 A.M., the House passed the President's stimulus program by a vote of 235–190, despite Republican charges that it contained a substantial amount of "pork" and the unease of some Democrats that that might be true.

At the White House the next morning, the mood was one of elation. Clinton, though pleased, reminded his staff over and over, "It's just a beginning." About a hundred forty House Democrats showed up at the White House that morning for celebratory doughnuts and coffee.

A week after the House voted, the Senate passed its own budget resolution incorporating the President's program. The vote of 54–45 was basically along party lines, with all Republican senators, plus Shelby of Alabama, voting against it. Through six days of debate and forty-five roll call votes, the White House and the Democratic leadership fended off amendments designed to put Democrats in an uncomfortable position. The party-line voting should have set off an alarm, but it didn't. Neither did Senate Minority

Leader Bob Dole's warning, "We start shooting with real bullets from here on." Nor did Louisiana Democrat Bennett Johnston's saying, "This kind of loyalty is not always going to be there." (Johnston, from an oil-producing state, had already come out against the Btu tax.)

Bill Galston, a White House aide for domestic policy and a former DLC official, said, "A strategic decision was made on our side to go for a budget that would maximally unify the Democratic Party. We clearly produced a budget in which different kinds of investments are made that leading figures in the Democratic Party have been urging. The effect was to maximize the unity of the Republicans."

While the budget resolution was moving through Congress, Clinton was adding subject after subject to his legislative proposals. In late March, Mark Gearan, the Deputy Chief of Staff, said, "Every day we are throwing a ball in the air to get through the day. There's been a growing sense here in the last couple of weeks that we can't do this every day. We thought all we had to do was throw that particular ball in the air. Now, as we approach April and May, they're all in the air. We have to juggle. That's what terrifies me."

But the ease of the White House's victories in the House and Senate led most people—on Capitol Hill, in the White House, in the press—to conclude that Clinton was sweeping all before him.

8

STIMULUS

"We Didn't Expect a Filibuster"

Clinton's attempt, early in his Presidency, to win a $16 billion spending bill—the so-called stimulus bill—to give a quick boost to the economy while his larger economic program was moving through the Congress, was more important, and had far more ramifications, than the size of the bill would suggest. By Washington standards, $16 billion was small beer. (The President also proposed tax changes that would have made the entire stimulus program cost $30 billion .) But the White House and its Republican opponents in Congress understood that the fight over the stimulus bill was about more than the stimulus bill. It was about the new President's power.

Clinton and his staff mishandled the stimulus bill at virtually every step. It was misconceived, as well as badly named. The name didn't mean anything to most people; later on, the administration took to calling it a "jobs" bill. The concept of stimulating the economy in the short term while trying to cut the deficit in the long term made economic sense in theory but was hard for people to understand.

That there should be a stimulus program to give a quick boost to the economy had been an article of faith among the Clintonites for some time. During the campaign, James Carville, the campaign's top strategist, liked the idea as a way of showing that, unlike the inattentive Bush, Clinton would do something to create jobs right away.

At the economic conference held in December in Little Rock, liberal economist James Tobin had suggested a stimulus program of $60 billion.

The conference planners, knowing that Clinton wouldn't propose a stimulus of that size—it was presumed to be too large for the Congress to swallow, and it would aggravate the deficit problem—had put Tobin on the program to take this position so that Clinton's forthcoming proposal, whatever it was, would look more middle-of-the-road.

To draw up a stimulus package, the Office of Management and Budget asked the Cabinet departments to suggest programs that could get the money into the economy relatively quickly. Indiscriminately, funding for a plethora of programs was included. Quality control, or even coherence, wasn't a consideration. The package became a playground for the Cabinet, the economic advisers—and Clinton. Offered an opportunity to propose things for the bill, the only criterion being that the money be paid out early, these people loaded it up with their favorite programs, and also used the opportunity to give an early start to programs, such as spending to rebuild the nation's infrastructure, that were in the longer-term economic package. Reich was so adept at getting his pet ideas into the stimulus package that at one point during the meetings in the Roosevelt Room, Gore looked at him and said, jokingly, "Don't you ever stop?" Two items of great importance to Mrs. Clinton and her allies—additional funding for Head Start and free immunization for all children—were included in the stimulus bill. By asking Cabinet officers to come up with "ready-to-go" projects, the administration asked for trouble.

The biggest source of controversy, and embarrassment, was money for Community Development Block Grants, which gave money to cities for local projects. In the Reagan years, federal control over such projects was loosened in the name of reducing the federal government's power. Thus, in the stimulus debate, Republicans were able to embarrass the Clinton administration by citing some of the more foolish-sounding CDBG projects in the "ready-to-go" list, which had been essentially drawn up by mayors. It included a beach parking lot in Fort Lauderdale and a cemetery in Puerto Rico, money for fish atlases and for student drawings of "significant structures" for deposit in the Library of Congress. The CDBG program—definitely not a "New Democrat" program—was in the stimulus package because it offered a quick payout of federal funds and because, a Clinton aide said later, "We had Los Angeles on the brain."

There wasn't a great deal of money for the cities in the larger economic program, and members of the new administration, like a lot of other people, feared further riots in connection with the case of the police beating of Rodney King, as there had been the year before when an all-white jury held the police innocent. The CDBG program was also attractive to the Clinton people because it was a way of building support among the nation's mayors.

Howard Paster said later, "The bill was flawed to begin with. It didn't have a theme." He continued, "Unfortunately, there was never an adequate predicate for the stimulus package. We ended up with about fifty items, some of them as small as twenty to thirty million dollars. The purpose was to stimulate the economy. It wasn't a jobs bill." The thinking was it could get through Congress as an "emergency" program. And some of the components such as one to provide fifty thousand summer jobs for poor youths—a favorite of the President's and Reich's—did have to be geared up quickly.

The first sign of trouble came when members of Congress, especially House Democratic freshmen, gave notice to the Democratic leadership that they would refuse to vote for a "spending" bill before they had voted to cut the deficit. So in consultation with the White House, the House leaders switched the order in which the economic bills were to be taken up: the big budget bill would be voted on before the stimulus package. This change was, as a House leader later admitted privately, "a charade," because the budget resolution was only a set of recommendations, and didn't actually make any cuts. Still, despite the Republican criticism of "pork," the House had seemed to pass the stimulus bill easily.

But there was a price. The administration had mortgaged itself to House liberals, in particular the Black Caucus, by pledging that if they went along with cuts called for in the budget resolution, the stimulus bill would be kept intact. In fact, the stimulus bill was essentially aimed at northern cities, the Democratic Party's urban constituency, and this was almost asking for trouble in the Senate, where western and rural interests have far more influence.

And then the administration committed a tremendous blunder. It neglected to seek support for the stimulus package from Senate Republicans. Since under the Senate's rules the budget resolution hadn't been open to a filibuster, the stimulus program offered Republicans their first shot at Clinton's economic program and their first chance to embarrass the new President. Clinton had ignored the Republicans. Now they found a way to get the White House's attention.

White House aides, riding high after their dual victory in the House, on the budget resolution and the stimulus program, simply assumed that some Republican moderates in the Senate—especially those from northeastern states with large urban constituencies—would support the stimulus package. A top White House aide said afterward, "We didn't expect a filibuster. There was no indication the Republicans would fight this." Therefore, when a filibuster did begin, the White House had no strategy for dealing with it, a failure that made the President extremely angry. Clinton complained that nobody had told him that a filibuster was possible. But this wasn't quite the case. Clinton often was to claim victimization by his staff, though in some cases his charge was exaggerated and in some he was also at fault.

Paster said later that he did expect the Republicans to hold up the stimulus bill. They had been using the filibuster increasingly in recent years and in 1993 had already filibustered the "motor-voter" bill (to allow people to register to vote when they apply for a driver's license) and forced unwelcome changes on the administration—and their strategy seemed to be to press hard and then cut as good a deal as possible. Therefore, Paster also expected the Republicans to deal.

Then the White House people committed another blunder. Rather than focus on the Republicans, they became intent on showing their strength by heading off amendments by Democrats, especially one proposed by two moderate Democrats—John Breaux, of Louisiana, and David Boren, of Oklahoma—that probably would have saved the stimulus bill in the Senate. The Breaux-Boren amendment would have deferred spending half the money in the stimulus program until actual deficit reductions had been voted by Congress. The amendment was mainly cosmetic, but it might have protected some legislators from the "spending" sobriquet, or given them an explanation to offer, but it also might have held up quick spending on stimulus programs.

The Clinton White House was convinced of its invincibility—and it had made a deal. In order to get rid of the amendment, the administration came up with an innocuous solution in which the President wrote the sponsors a letter pledging to press Congress for spending cuts.

Stephanopoulos said later, "The mistake we made is pretty clear. We had an opportunity to accept Breaux-Boren. But we were getting crosscurrents. For House liberals, not getting jammed on the stimulus package was their price for accepting cuts in the budget."

John Chafee, Republican of Rhode Island, said later, "I don't know why they didn't expect a filibuster. It's the only tool we have."

On the night of Thursday, April 1, the Republicans, expressing outrage over a parliamentary maneuver by Senator Robert Byrd, of West Virginia, that made it impossible for them to amend the bill, began their filibuster.

Subsequent mythology notwithstanding, the Republicans would have filibustered even if Byrd hadn't executed his parliamentary maneuver. Thad Cochran, Republican of Mississippi, said afterward, "The filibuster certainly would have happened anyway. Byrd was a factor, but not the reason."

The second myth was that Dole, in defeating the stimulus package, proved that he was a formidable power. Dole's victory on the bill was inadvertent. It grew out of his weakness within the Republican Conference, not his strength. The opposition of even moderate Republicans to the bill came as a surprise to Dole, among others. Chafee said, "I think Bob himself was a little surprised at the vehemence and the unity that was in his flock. It was an internal development rather than one responding to the leader's call."

For days, Paster continued to assume that Dole would offer a deal. So did Senate Majority Leader George Mitchell, to whom Dole said on the Friday, April 2, that the filibuster began, and on subsequent days, "I'll have something for you" by some appointed hour. But Dole was stymied by two things. One was the surprising (to him) intransigence of Republican moderates. The other was the unsurprising fact that the Republican senators were divided into numerous factions, and Dole couldn't control them. Dole later told a friend, "I couldn't get three people together." After the stimulus bill failed, Dole was lionized in Washington as a master strategist, a tremendous force to be reckoned with. Dole knew better.

The filibuster began on the eve of a scheduled two-week Senate recess and of Clinton's trip to the Northwest, for a summit in Portland, Oregon, on the future of the spotted owl (Clinton had pledged in the campaign to resolve the long-running issue between loggers and environmentalists), and then a summit meeting with Russian President Boris Yeltsin in Vancouver. The White House staff was distracted and spread even thinner than usual. Clinton had pledged that both he and Gore would attend the spotted owl/timber summit, so Gore would be out of town, too. As a result, no serious strategy meeting took place as the filibuster began. By Friday, so few people were on hand in the White House that Mark Gearan referred to himself as Macaulay Gearan, after Macaulay Culkin, the child star of the movie *Home Alone*.

After the President returned from his summit meetings, on April 5, the White House fell into what was to become a typical pattern of indecision and reversals of decisions. The President's advisers were divided over whether he should get highly exposed on the stimulus issue by traveling and attacking Republicans who might be converts, or whether his exposure on the issue should be limited, so that if a deal didn't come to pass soon he could cut his losses.

In the end, Clinton followed both strategies. Greenberg and Stephanopoulos thought it had been decided that the President wouldn't go to Pittsburgh the following Saturday, April 17, to bring pressure on Senator Arlen Specter, but he ended up going. (Predictably, Specter didn't change his position. Any senator who did so after such a tactic would be seen as weak.) Paster and Gore made highly publicized calls to moderate Republicans. Neither Greenberg nor Stephanopoulos believed that Republicans could be brought around. "It was too much of an organizing issue for Republicans," Greenberg said. "We thought we should redefine it as a 'jobs bill,' and move off." Besides, he said, "The program wasn't big enough for a big fight."

Despite a few efforts by the President to gin up a public outcry for the stimulus program—he pointed to kids rolling Easter eggs on the White House lawn and denounced the Republicans for wanting to deprive them of vaccinations—none developed.

Democrats who went home for the Easter recess found that they couldn't sell the program. The Republicans had won the definition of the issue: the President was pushing a spending bill that would essentially purchase pork. On April 22, Dole, after saying many times that the issue was over a "basic philosophical difference," added, "A lot of our members think paying for it is secondary. The bottom line is not to have it at all."

Just before the weekend of April 17–18, Clinton offered a compromise, partially in the hope it would break the logjam but also to try to affix blame for the "gridlock" on the Republicans. Dole rejected Clinton's compromise outright, and took to saying—as did some others—that the filibuster was over a matter of "principle": the money shouldn't be spent without offsetting cuts in the budget. The Clinton people argued that the cuts were included in the long-term deficit plan. And anyway, administration officials argued, if the spending was offset right away, there wouldn't be a stimulus.

White House officials couldn't go too far in compromising, for fear of offending House liberals, or the mayors. Also, they decided that they wanted a clean issue—that the Republicans had "killed" the stimulus package. And so, late Wednesday afternoon, April 21, as the President was preparing to greet Holocaust survivors and heads of state at a White House reception on the eve of the opening of the Holocaust Museum, the negotiations ended. The only part of the stimulus package that survived was an extension of unemployment benefits, which were about to run out. (The administration finally, in July, won a mini-stimulus bill that authorized $220 million for summer jobs.)

Shortly before the bill's ultimate demise, Greenberg said, "We are hurt by the general perception of 'gridlock.' The sense of it eats away at the hopefulness about this Presidency." Though the Democrats were blaming the Republicans for the impasse, Greenberg said, "We pay the higher price for it, and I think they [the Republicans] understand that."

Clinton, according to his aides, was highly frustrated over the loss and upset that so much time and energy and Presidential capital had gone into a fight over a spending bill. He asked them, angrily, how they could have sat there for a week and not had a filibuster strategy. At a press conference later that week, Clinton said, in what was to become a stream of open, and demeaning, confessions, "I just misgauged it. And I hope I can learn something." He added, "I've just been here ninety days."

It was also Clinton's misfortune that the impasse continued over the long Easter recess, making the stimulus bill—and Clinton's efforts to save it—a long-running story. Clinton knew that this had contributed to his image as a "spender" and detracted from the one he sought, as "a different kind of Democrat." Democrats in both chambers were dismayed by the administration's handling of the issue: by the fact that it wasn't more cognizant of the nature of the Senate, that Clinton had been so out of focus on the issue, that —as House liberals and moderates saw it—they had voted for things that the administration had then offered to give away in the Senate.

Was this, Democrats wondered, the way the administration would handle the big ones?

On Friday night, April 2, Bill Clinton went from the Portland spotted owl summit to Vancouver, British Columbia, for his first summit meeting with Boris Yeltsin. Because of Yeltsin's rocky political situation, the meeting had almost been moved to Moscow, a possibility that only further frazzled the frantically busy Clinton White House.

Clinton had gone through his first Russian crisis on Saturday, March 20, when Yeltsin, who had been locked in a struggle with his parliament over its attempts to block his economic reform program, announced in a televised address that he was dissolving the parliament, assuming emergency powers, and calling a referendum on how Russia was to be ruled. U.S. officials had been aware that such action was likely, though when Foreign Minister Andrei Kozyrev earlier that day briefed Western diplomats, he left out the bit about dissolving the parliament. Clinton watched the speech on a small television set in his study next to the Oval Office. (There was no television set in the Oval Office.)

Clinton then met with Gore, Christopher, Lake, Talbott, and Stephanopoulos to discuss how to respond. It wasn't clear whether Yeltsin's actions were constitutional. Talbott and Lake urged that the President issue a quick response supportive of Yeltsin, avoid the specifics of Yeltsin's speech, and take the position that questions of constitutionality were for the Russians to determine. In the end, it was decided to risk appearing to go too far in backing Yeltsin because, as one official put it later, "With all his faults, there's no one else." After a long delay, Stephanopoulos read a statement in which the President said that a plebiscite was a way of "letting the Russian people decide their future." He added, "We support the process of reform." Under questioning, he stuck to the formulation "We support democracy and reform in Russia" and "President Yeltsin is the leader of the reform movement." This was a way of trying to avoid seeming to give blanket support to Yeltsin, but a lot of people didn't get the distinction. (Richard Nixon sent a handwritten note to Stephanopoulos, saying: "You could not have handled a delicate situation better.")

After some lobbying on Nixon's part, Clinton had begun to call on Nixon for advice about Russia. The former President had written a congratulatory letter to Clinton on his election and (not unlike a lot of other people) received no response. He made some other efforts to get in touch with Clinton and then let it be known that if he wasn't shown proper respect, he might write an op-ed article critical of Clinton's conduct of foreign policy. Nixon was invited to the White House for a nighttime talk with the President —no press would be around—on March 8. In the days leading up to the Vancouver summit, Clinton had a two-hour NSC meeting; hosted a dinner of bipartisan members of Congress and another dinner for Russian experts; and made a lot of phone calls—including to Nixon, Jimmy Carter, Colin Powell, and Brent Scowcroft (Bush's National Security Adviser). He met with his advisers on what sort of aid program to offer Russia. Clinton was carefully cultivating bipartisan support for an increase in U.S. aid to Russia. He gave a speech at Annapolis before he left for the Vancouver summit (this, too, would become a pattern at the outset of foreign trips), in which he argued that more aid to Russia was a good investment in making certain that defense spending in the United States could be reduced.

In Vancouver on April 3 and 4, Clinton got his first chance to be the international statesman, and he carried out his part well enough. Mort Engelberg, a Hollywood producer who had arranged some of the Clinton campaign's most scenic events (including the bus trips), set up picturesque scenes, including one of Clinton and Yeltsin walking together through tall, damp evergreens. So that there could be a picture of just the two of them, interpreters were shooed away—and since neither could speak the other's language, not a word passed between them.

At the summit, Clinton promised Yeltsin loan guarantees for housing for demobilized Russian soldiers (as an inducement to get them to withdraw completely from the Baltics and Eastern Europe), funds to help state-owned industries increase their sales, and technical assistance. He also promised to encourage the Group of Seven industrial nations to increase its aid to Moscow. The commitments included but went beyond moneys that had already been approved by Congress. Clinton announced $1.6 billion, which included low-interest food credits, help in dismantling Russia's nuclear arsenal, and technical assistance for privatization of businesses—all to come out of existing funds. When Clinton submitted his budget request to Congress on April 8, he sought an additional $703.8 million in funds for Russia and the other republics. The administration also proposed using an additional $400 million of the Pentagon's fiscal year 1994 budget—on top of the $800 million that was already set aside—to help dismantle Russia's nuclear arsenal. (In the end, he won virtually all the funds from Congress.) Clinton further suggested that the two countries establish a permanent commission, under their number-two officials, to discuss various areas of possible cooperation.

By the end of the two days, the leaders were addressing each other as "Boris" and "Beel." Clinton did caution Yeltsin on Russian adventures beyond its borders, as in Georgia, where it was helping a separatist movement.

In the course of the summit, Clinton also found time to have a late-night party with movie stars Sharon Stone, Richard Gere, Richard Dreyfuss, and others who were making films in the area. He didn't seem to understand that this undermined the serious aspect he was trying to show the world.

At a press conference on Sunday, Clinton pointed out that Yeltsin came from simple roots and hadn't forgotten that—which was, of course, the way Clinton saw himself. In a painstakingly crafted sentence, Clinton said, "We actively support reform and reformers and you and Russia." But after Clinton had carefully stated the priorities of U.S. policy toward Russia, he shook Yeltsin's hand enthusiastically, bidding him farewell, and said, "Win! Win!"

Yeltsin, closing in, said, "We are partners and future allies."

And then Clinton had to return to Washington to face less worldly matters. He often complained that he didn't get enough credit for his Russia policy.

9

PROFILE

"We Were Out of Focus"

By mid-April, unbeknownst to the public, the Clinton White House was in crisis. The President was upset about his "profile." Stan Greenberg's polling indicated that he was seen as a traditional liberal Democrat rather than as the "different kind of Democrat" he had struggled to establish as his identity. Clinton was obsessed by the subject. It led to numerous crisis meetings. Moreover, the White House staff wasn't functioning at all well. Decisions were being made and then "revisited" again and again. The President's agenda was getting beyond manageable proportions. His schedule was the object of constant battles, and frequently changed. He wasn't getting across what he was about.

Everyone, from the President on down, knew that the problems were deep and went far beyond the defeat of the stimulus program, damaging as that had been. Clinton and his advisers considered the "profile" problem to be a serious one not only in terms of his reelection (a subject always on their minds) but also of his ability to govern. Governing and reelection were one seamless subject in the Clinton White House.

For Clinton, the problem evoked bad memories of being turned out of the Arkansas governor's office because he had tried to do too much, and was seen as aloof from the people of his state. In mid-April, Greenberg said, "This is somebody who lost the governorship in 1980 and spent a decade sensitive to this problem. He spent a decade making sure it didn't happen again. Now he's pushing his advisers to work on it." And so the consultants became still more engaged in the President's decision making. But a poll-driven, consultant-ridden Presidency carried risks. Leadership could be preempted by the consensus of the moment. There might not be any leadership at all.

The role of the consultants in the Clinton administration was without precedent. Previous Presidents had pollsters and other outside political advisers, but never before had a group of political consultants played such an integral part in a Presidency. Clinton's consultants were omnipresent, involved in everything from personnel to policymaking to the President's schedule. The consultants—and some members of the President's immediate staff—made a point of saying that they weren't involved in foreign policy matters, but at various times, and in various ways, they were. The consultants earned substantial amounts from the Democratic National Committee—Carville and Begala's firm, $300,000 a year; Greenberg, $25,000 a month (plus fees for polls); Grunwald, $15,000 a month (plus fees for media buys)—and there were of course substantial fringe benefits, in the form of other clients and speaking engagements, that stemmed from their much publicized connection with the President. All four consultants forswore taking on corporate or interest-group clients, so as to avoid conflicts of interest, but that didn't rule out making lucrative speeches to interest groups, which sought them out because of their inside knowledge. They weren't bound by the conflict-of-interest or disclosure rules that full-time government employees had to adhere to. (Only after this became an issue in mid-1994 did they have to disclose their sources of income.)

Their role raised problems of governance. For one thing, they contributed to the clogging of Clinton's information systems, the size of his meetings, and the policy paralysis that sometimes occurred. The omnipresence of the consultants sometimes muffled the President's instincts. Further, the consultants were accountable to no one except the President. They could sashay into the White House, offer some advice, and sashay out again, leaving the hard part to others. They didn't have to carry out their own proposals or live with the consequences.

In the eyes of several White House aides, the consultants didn't understand or accept the realities of governing; the consultants, in turn, felt that the White House aides were playing too much of an "inside" game, that they had been co-opted by Washington. There was increasing tension in particular between the consultants and Paster: They felt that Paster was too eager to please various Members of Congress, and Paster felt that the consultants weren't dealing in the realities of doing business with the Congress. But Paster was far from the only member of the White House staff who thought it was too easy for the consultants to come to meetings and say what should be done and then leave. Even the normally gentle Mark Gearan said, "Governing isn't the same as campaigning. Outsiders can bring perspective, but the difficulties of the journey aren't apparent to those outside."

The amount of weight given in Presidential decision making to polling results—close calibrations of what the public thinks at the moment—as opposed to unpopular acts that a President, as a leader, should perhaps take, can have a defining effect on a Presidency. Shortly before Truman fired Douglas MacArthur, he was at 26 percent in the polls. Woodrow Wilson and Franklin Roosevelt led their countries into what had been unpopular wars. Winston Churchill rallied his divided nation to resist Adolf Hitler. Even George Bush mustered support for a war by a previously uninterested populace. Reliance on polling can displace the role of President as educator. It can even lead him astray, or sow the seeds for future trouble. The consultants' soundings about the relative unimportance of foreign policy in the public mind reinforced Clinton's own disinclination to focus on it—with sometimes ruinous results—and eventually (and inevitably) Clinton's lack of interest turned into a negative for him in the polls.

The consultants themselves weren't the unified group usually portrayed in public. There were tensions among them. Each worried about how much time the others had with the President. Carville's having gone show biz—he was usually out on the road speaking and had become a celebrity—didn't sit well with all his colleagues; Grunwald was suspected of using her close relationship with the First Lady to her own advantage.

As of early April, there was to be nearly a meeting a week in the White House—including the President, the Vice President, and the First Lady, the consultants, and key White House aides—on the President's political situation. In addition, Greenberg met alone with the President once a week, to tell him what he was picking up in his polling, and the consultants met often with the White House staff. (On occasion, when Greenberg couldn't get on Clinton's schedule, Stephanopoulos conveyed the news. The consultants also attended the daily five o'clock staff meeting.) In April, Clinton brought up the subject of his "profile" with his staff each morning. He said, "We've got to get this back. We're not telling people a story." Stephanopoulos said, "We talk about it every day. He's concerned about being seen as too liberal; he's concerned about all the attacks on him as a 'taxer and spender.' " Clinton would tell his staff, "Nobody knows that we're responsible for interest rates coming down." (Long-term interest rates had dropped half a percentage point.) He was upset when Greenberg found that the three things people most remembered about the first months of his administration were the summit with Yeltsin, health care, and gays in the military. The subject of gays in the military particularly stuck in the President's craw.

Greenberg said, "I think gays in the military is eating away at us, and the President does too." (Clinton couldn't restrain himself from answering questions about it, despite Aspin's strategy of having the President hand the issue off to the Pentagon until July 15.)

The other issue that was defining Clinton's "profile" was taxes. The problem, a senior aide said candidly, "is that with all these proposals we're making, he's in danger of being seen as another big-taxing, big-spending, big-government Democrat—which he is." Gearan summed up: "The profile is not where he wants to be. We're all agreed on the problem."

White House aides used the shorthand "profile" to put across a whole argument. One day in April, Rahm Emanuel, the political director, glided into Stephanopoulos's office—Emanuel, a ballet dancer as well as a fund-raiser for Clinton's campaign, was always gliding into and out of people's offices—said a few words about an upcoming event, and then said, "profile," and made his exit. The "discussion" was about how the President should propose his program for "empowerment zones," an attempt through tax cuts and waiving of certain regulations to lure business investment into the inner cities (a variation of the Bush administration's proposal for "enterprise zones"). Stephanopoulos, worried that a big event would look too inner-city, was thinking "profile" too. In the end, the President introduced the program by a telephone conference call with mayors and community leaders.

On Wednesday, April 21, at Clinton's request, a political meeting was convened at 12:30 P.M. to discuss the "profile" problem. In attendance were the President, Mrs. Clinton, the Vice President, McLarty, Stephanopoulos, Emanuel, Begala, Maggie Williams (Mrs. Clinton's Chief of Staff), Greenberg, and Grunwald. Greenberg and Grunwald presented memos that caused Clinton to erupt. The memos suggested that the President focus on themes such as responsibility and accountability. Clinton replied angrily, "I know my job." He raged, "I don't need to be told what the themes are. That isn't the point. It's how do we execute them?" He continued, agitatedly, "What is the plan, and what are we doing?" One of the participants said, "He bristled and bridled, and said the problem was staff and structure. We said structure was part of it but not the most important thing." Begala said at that meeting, "It's not that we have one structure or another but that the people who speak for the administration are clear on what our core principles are."

At another "profile" meeting in April, Carville said, "The reason people didn't think our economic program was any good was we weren't telling people it was good. They'd turn on the TV, and there we were saying we can do better." He added, "There's an old saying that if you give a person a fish, you give him a fish for a day. If you give people fishing lessons, they have fish for a lifetime. The old Democratic Party ran a fish store. We should be running a fishing school."

Mark Gearan said later, "We were reeling, we were just reeling. We were out of focus. The question was what does the President stand for. Is he a New Democrat? It was gays and Zoe and Kimba."

A Presidency that was facing these questions was in trouble. A President who needed all these advisers to work out what he stood for and how to get that across was lost. This was why, particularly at this point, Clinton's voice was muffled. This was a long way from the clarity of thought and act of a Harry Truman—or a Ronald Reagan.

The problem wasn't just that Clinton was trying to do too many things. It was also, aides said later, that he had lost confidence—in himself and his advisers.

Nor was it, as some observers charged, that Clinton lacked core beliefs. Clinton saw government as the engine for improving people's lives. There was no problem in drawing distinctions between what Clinton believed and what his Republican predecessors believed. His budget priorities were quite different from those of his Republican predecessors.

Clinton's problem was that he was a big-government, or, at least, an activist-government man trying to come across as a Democrat who didn't believe in big government. Actually, he was both. He was a modern Democrat, and far from the only one, who was seeking new ways for government to help people, because of the lack of funds, because of real or perceived failures of federal programs (more were successful than was generally believed), and because big federal solutions to problems were out of style. (Even such a traditional liberal as Edward M. Kennedy had been moving in this direction.)

As Clinton sought the "third way" of governing in some areas—the environment, welfare, trade, health care—he confused a lot of people. Clinton talked privately and dismissively about "old Democrats" trying to do things in the old way. This division came up particularly in a fight over his education proposals, where much of the education establishment, as represented on the House Education and Labor Committee, was more interested in the distribution of federal funds to the status quo than in the outcome-based approach Clinton sought in Goals 2000.

The Goals 2000 program was an example of the difference between Clinton and his predecessors, and also of limits imposed by political and fiscal realities. It set voluntary national academic standards and voluntary testing by the states. (Mandatory federal standards weren't feasible.) A relatively small amount of money would finance model projects. It was a way of trying to lift educational standards and get a consensus behind those standards, with the idea that this might lead to more willingness to spend on schools. In seeking to raise standards in public schools, the program was the reverse of the Bush approach of providing vouchers for attending private schools.

Clinton was a transitional figure, the first real post–New Deal Democratic President (there were foreshadowings of this new phase during the Carter Presidency). And the transition, plus some failings on the part of Clinton and his staff, had produced a full-blown Presidential identity crisis.

Clinton was finding that it was riskier in the Presidency than in a campaign to be inconsistent. In a campaign, one can make statements and keep moving. In the Presidency, the statements have consequences and are translated into real policies. And the spotlight is much stronger. Inconsistencies are harder to hide.

Of course, much would be made of Clinton's noted flexibility on issues. As President, he may have yielded more often than was necessary—this is an impossible thing to measure—and he may indeed have tried to please too many people, but there was no real reason to question the basic things he was for. His difficulty in articulating these things stemmed in part from the ambiguity of his own beliefs, in part from his difficulty in getting past the complexities in his own mind, and in part from the fact that there were too many cooks involved in almost every significant speech he made and every important action he took. Clinton didn't have the confidence to dismiss the cooks often enough and just say what he wanted to say. Sometimes he didn't know what he wanted to say. His efforts to keep conflicting constituencies in his corner sometimes confused his purposes and muffled the sounds coming out of him.

To collect themselves after Clinton's blow-up about the "profile" memorandum, Grunwald, Greenberg, Stephanopoulos, Gearan, and others convened in Stephanopoulos's office and decided that a more detailed memo should be prepared. Two days later, on Friday afternoon, the President and his advisers had an "ideas" meeting to go over all the things Clinton had proposed, to take stock. Al From, the president of the Democratic Leadership Council, attended. In mid-April, From had sent Clinton a memo telling him that "among many moderate and conservative Democrats there is a growing feeling that you're just not dancing with the ones who brought you to the dance." He told Clinton that a lot of people, including many of his allies, "are having a hard time figuring out who you are and what you really stand for." He said that Clinton hadn't spelled out a New Democratic philosophy.

From argued that Clinton should focus more on the issues of welfare reform, preventing teenage pregnancy (to soften his pro-choice position on abortion), national service, and reinventing government. (Privately, From also told Clinton that his prominent association with Hollywood figures had reinforced the impression he had gone left.) From maintained that Clinton wouldn't have been elected if he hadn't "inoculated" himself on "values" issues: welfare, the death penalty (Clinton was for it and during the primary contest had returned to Arkansas for the execution of a brain-damaged death row prisoner; even some of his most ardent supporters thought this wouldn't have happened but for the campaign), national service, and being against "quotas" and (if ambiguously) for the Gulf War.

At the Friday "ideas" meeting, the President and his advisers discussed the issues Clinton thought had elected him: more community policing, empowerment zones, welfare reform, cracking down on deadbeat dads, more student loans, education goals, anticrime initiatives, and political reform. The meeting was resumed the following Monday, when there was still more discussion of what issues and themes to emphasize. It was decided that the President's economic program should receive renewed focus. But it was to be some time before that happened.

Whether the President should be constantly talking about something new, in order to get television coverage—of the sort that was desired—or stay with a subject or theme for days to try to drive it home was a subject of ongoing debate among his advisers. (The Reagan people had developed staying with a subject into an art form and were much envied by the Clinton group.) That question, too, went unanswered. Gearan bravely tried to get some order by convening a meeting in the Ward Room, the private room in the Mess complex, in the basement of the White House, every ten days. As was often the case in other instances, a large cast—White House aides and the political consultants—attended these meetings, which went over such questions as the President's schedule, communications strategy, political strategy. But such decisions as were made rarely stuck.

Aide after aide complained privately about the Clinton White House's inability to make a decision and stick with it. Greenberg said, of the on-again, off-again Presidential trip during the stimulus fight, "I never knew why he went to Pittsburgh." Like as not, a plan would be drawn up to introduce a program at a certain event, and when the time came the program wouldn't be ready. (To preempt some embarrassment, Clinton's aides had hoped to introduce his program for reforming the campaign finance system before a Democratic fund-raising dinner, typically replete with lobbyists, but when the time came around in May, there was no program to introduce.) A leading congressional Democrat observed, "They keep setting deadlines for themselves which, if not met, is a 'failure' according to the press." The priorities changed from day to day. Every morning at 7:45, there was a senior staff meeting, but after a while that meeting devolved into "show-and-tell."

The schedule became the focal point of the arguments over the President's profile. Greenberg said, "The fight is over the clutter, the lack of focus, the inability to communicate one main theme." Everyone wanted a piece of the President's time, and everyone had something to say about the President's schedule. The Vice President would get things added to the President's schedule. Paster got things added in order to do the President's congressional business. And the President himself contributed to the problem.

The White House staff was in over its head. During the April turbulence, Gearan and Stephanopoulos had a long talk and agreed, Gearan said later, that "We didn't know what we were getting into." Some of the White House staff concluded—as did Clinton—that Clinton had made a serious mistake in selecting the White House staff so late. And with the exception of Anthony Lake, who was on the foreign policy side, not a single Clinton White House aide had ever worked in the White House before. The lack of maturity on the part of a high percentage of the Clinton White House staff was costly.

Mack McLarty's deficiencies as Chief of Staff were becoming clear enough, but in fairness, it had to be recognized that he was the kind of Chief of Staff Clinton had wanted, and the person Clinton wanted. Friend after friend of Clinton said that Clinton didn't want "a Jim Baker" (Reagan's strong, and cunning, Chief of Staff). He wanted someone with whom he was utterly comfortable, whom he could completely trust, who had no agenda of his own, and who wouldn't get in his way. To his own great detriment, Clinton wanted to be his own Chief of Staff.

McLarty's previous business had put him in contact with moderate and conservative Democratic senators from the oil-and-gas states of the South and Southwest, and as time went on he became the White House's ambassador to members of this group, whose votes were often needed on important legislation. He came to represent reassurance to these and like-minded people that the President hadn't gone over to the liberal side.

But McLarty's lack of Washington experience, of feel for the place, led to some mistakes (such as the cave-in on mining and grazing fees) and deprived the President of someone who could see around corners in Washington. McLarty couldn't be expected to see around corners if he didn't know where the corners were.

McLarty wasn't a disciplinarian, and he didn't run the White House. No one did. Over time, this was to drive Cabinet officers, outsiders who tried to deal with the White House, and also some White House aides, to distraction. The White House was "run" by what one top aide called "ad hocracy."

April was an unhappy month for Clinton in several respects. On April 7, Mrs. Clinton's father, Hugh Rodham, died of a stroke, in Little Rock. His final illness had caused her to be absent from the White House for a lengthy period of time, starting in late March. Her long vigil by her father's bedside distracted the President and deflected his attention from some important matters. And her absence reduced the amount of advice the President got from her. (It also, as Mrs. Clinton's staff knew, shifted the image of her, softened it by showing her vulnerability and the priority she put on her family.) During his father-in-law's illness, Clinton himself went to Little Rock one weekend, and he told aides later that he had found it "restful" to be away from the White House and among friends. The Clintons' joint distraction impeded work on a number of issues and bollixed the schedule. Gearan said, "It got us off stride."

A lot of things went wrong for Clinton in April. On Monday the nineteenth, FBI agents conducted a raid on the compound in Waco, Texas, of the Branch Davidians—a religious cult led by David Koresh, who said he was the Messiah—that ended in a conflagration. Eighty-six men, women, and children were killed in the fire. There was reason to question the judgment of Janet Reno—who became a national hero by appearing on numerous television news programs on Monday evening, taking responsibility for the event—as well as that of the President and his advisers. Reno was a shrewd politician (she had been elected five times as state attorney of Dade County, Florida), and as she must have figured, the public was very impressed with anyone in Washington who would stand up and take responsibility for some untoward event.

The White House tried to give the appearance that the President hadn't known anything about the proposed raid until Reno briefed him on the plan on Sunday. Actually, the plan for the raid on the compound—driving the cult members out by ramming their building and creating a hole through which to inject nonlethal gas—reached the White House the previous Wednesday, leaving plenty of time for it to be considered. Bernie Nussbaum had known for some time that the Justice Department was working on a plan to raid the compound. During the week before the raid, Lindsey, Nussbaum, Vince Foster, and Webster Hubbell met in Nussbaum's office to discuss the matter. They had been informed that the FBI had recommended such a plan to Reno and that she was considering it but hadn't made a decision. Lindsey and Nussbaum told the President about the plan. Nussbaum claimed later that he advised the President not to get involved in the details. The President had been aware since the botched raid on the compound by the Bureau of Alcohol, Tobacco, and Firearms in February that another attempt would be made. Stephanopoulos was also made aware of the plan midweek. But no one in the White House tried to stop it.

Over the weekend, Reno decided to go ahead with the plan. The President spoke to her on the phone and, according to White House aides, asked her three questions: Have you carefully considered it? Have you looked at everything? Do you feel this is the best way to go?

On Monday afternoon, the President and his aides watched with horror as the fire consumed the compound. Lindsey and Stephanopoulos disagreed—in front of the President—over whether Clinton should make a public statement. Lindsey was for it; Stephanopoulos was against, arguing that they didn't have enough facts. Later, when the evening news programs were coming on the air—with appearances by Reno, taking responsibility —Lindsey went to Stephanopoulos and said, "I think we ought to go out there, George." Stephanopoulos replied, "We have a few confirmed deaths, and we don't know what's happening." Lindsey responded, "Everybody in America has seen it on TV, and nobody would criticize us for going out there if some of them come walking out later."

Clinton, hearing the divided advice, and lacking sure instincts, remained silent before the public. That evening, after the newscasts, the White House issued a brief statement by the President, saying that he was "deeply saddened by the loss of life in Waco today," and handing off responsibility for the raid to Reno. The statement said, "I told the Attorney General to do what she thought was right, and I stand by that decision." Later Clinton went so far as to tell a reporter that he had gone out and made a statement that night, after the early-evening news broadcasts, because having been governor he thought that there were two major newscasts a night.

Reno let it be known that night that she had been unable to reach the President—thus compounding the picture of a President hiding. The episode set off tension between Reno and the White House, tension that was to grow in the months ahead. Clinton's aides later explained that the President and his Attorney General had been "playing tag" on the telephone, and it was just one of those things that they hadn't made contact. (The President had attended a party at a Georgetown restaurant and then gone to the Holocaust Museum.) But it was safe to assume that if, say, his Secretary of State had been trying to reach him, contact would have been made. And the fact that at least two aides used the term "playing tag" left the strong impression that this was a precooked explanation, another "spin." The President did talk to Hubbell that night. Clinton's problem was that his action—or inaction—evoked "Slick Willie," something his advisers had desperately been trying to avoid.

Clinton was enraged by the stories in the next day's papers suggesting that he had been lying low. "That's shit," he said to his aides—an expression he employed often. The stories questioning his motives were the kind of press talk that drove him crazy, he said. As he saw it, he told aides, the press was once again twisting something and making it into a big issue. "A sickness," he called it. "This town is caught up in who did what to whom." But it was obvious that he would have to take questions on the matter at some point, so in a Rose Garden ceremony that day to present the Teacher of the Year award, Clinton expressed his sorrow over the loss of life, announced that he had instructed the Departments of Justice and Treasury to undertake an investigation of the siege, and reiterated his support for the Attorney General. Clinton also said that he was "bewildered" by the observations that he was trying to distance himself from the disaster.

At the time of the Waco raid, questions were raised about Reno's judgment, as well they might have been. The reason she gave for charging the compound, rather than just waiting Koresh out, was that the FBI had reported that "babies were being beaten." But the next day, William Sessions, the FBI director, said that there was "no contemporaneous information" of abuse to warrant the assault.

When Clinton was asked at an April 23 press conference about Sessions's dissent, he answered dramatically: "We know that David Koresh had sex with children. Does anybody dispute that?" And he paused, looking around the East Room. Nobody in the press corps was about to, or knew enough to, stand up and dispute it. He repeated, for effect, "Does anybody dispute that? Where I come from, that's child abuse."

The press conference came at the end of the week of April 19, in which Waco occurred, the stimulus bill went down to defeat, a White House reception before the opening of the Holocaust Museum turned into a semi-disaster, and Clinton was coming under increasing pressure to do something about Bosnia. He was stretched almost beyond endurance.

Also during that week, a major Presidential speech, and an announcement of an important new initiative, were totally lost in the confusion.

The White House reception was held on the evening of April 21 for twelve heads of state who had come for the dedication of the Holocaust Museum the following day—more dignitaries than had been gathered in Washington since John F. Kennedy's funeral—and for Holocaust survivors and Jewish leaders. Clinton had been supposed to meet with each of the foreign leaders for fifteen minutes earlier that day, but the meetings stretched far longer than that. By afternoon, he was running an hour behind schedule.

The fifteen-minute meetings turned into discussions of Bosnia, where the situation was deteriorating. (Most of the leaders urged the United States to get more involved.) The other guests were kept waiting in a white tent in a chilly rainstorm for over an hour while the President conferred by phone with Capitol Hill about the stimulus bill, as well as with the foreign leaders. The British ambassador, a major presence in Washington, and Britain's defense minister were turned away because their names weren't on the right list. At the reception honoring the victims of the Holocaust, ham was served.

The President had given a speech at the U.S. Botanical Gardens shortly before noon to commemorate Earth Day, to be observed the following day. But in the midst of everything else, his environmental speech, in which he pledged to sign the biodiversity treaty adopted at a conference in Brazil in 1992, which Bush had refused to sign, was lost on the world. So was a news conference at which Richard Riley and Robert Reich introduced the Goals 2000 education program. (Clinton was supposed to announce it, but there wasn't time.) Later Gearan described the day—on which one of the "profile" meetings with the President also took place—as "a disaster."

The next morning, Thursday, April 22, when the President was to dedicate the Holocaust Museum, Bruce Lindsey looked especially weary. He began an interview, "It's been a tough week," then spoke of Clinton's unhappiness with the administration's handling of the stimulus fight. "He was angry at himself, at the entire group of us. He doesn't know how we could have sat there last month and not have a filibuster strategy." Now, Lindsey said, "He wants to schedule his day so that he can get into and get involved in these questions, rather than being asked, 'Are you willing to go to twelve?' [The question was whether he would compromise at asking for $12 billion for the stimulus program rather than the $16 billion he had proposed.] 'Are you willing to cut Community Development Block Grants?' " Lindsey added, "We've had a running debate here about Waco. Should he, and we, have been more involved in the tactics? Are there things we might have realized? Your successes work, so you don't look at them, but you look at your failures. If a month ago we had sat down and devised a legislative strategy, could we have headed off the filibuster on the stimulus bill?"

Lindsey said there had been a series of meetings, and there would be more, on how to restructure the White House. He said, "There are only twenty-four hours in the day, and you should sleep a few of them. You can't be meeting with Boris Yeltsin, reforming health care, and working on campaign reform, lobbying restrictions, education reform, and welfare reform. If you try that, you can't be effective on anything." When asked if the problem was the size of the agenda or the way the President's time was allocated, Lindsey replied, "What he's starting to do is to figure out how to best use his time. He would say it's the way he's been scheduled, because he never thinks he has taken on too much."

The weight of recent events on Clinton showed as he sat through the dedication of the Holocaust Museum. The troubled expression on his face was only partially attributable to the solemnity of the occasion.

The weather was appropriate for the occasion—a gray sky, a mean, cold wind, unforgiving weather. Flags of the troops that liberated the camps flapped in the wind. Behind them stood the new museum building, made of brick and limestone—stark and cold and threatening. The Marine Band played sad Jewish hymns. Clinton and his wife were dressed in dark raincoats, and Cabinet officers stood shivering under their umbrellas. Behind them, the foreign leaders were announced and filed in: the President of Bulgaria, the President of Hungary, the President of Slovenia, the Prime Minister of Albania. Franjo Tudjman, the President of Croatia, who had written that the crimes committed in the Holocaust had been exaggerated, and called Israelis Judeo-Nazis for their treatment of Palestinians, was booed. (Germany sent only a foreign minister, because Germans were upset that the museum portrayed only the Nazi era, not present-day Germany.) Other heads of state—especially Vaclav Havel, of the Czech Republic, and Lech Walesa, of Poland—received cheers and applause, but everything was subdued.

Bosnia imposed itself on the ceremony. The previous week, the Muslim town of Srebrenica had been under siege by the Bosnian Serbs, and the carnage had provided ghastly television pictures. At the end of the week, the town had all but fallen to the Serbs, the final catastrophe being prevented by a UN designation of Srebrenica as a "safe area" and a demand that Serb forces withdraw. When Elie Wiesel spoke at the dedication, he turned to the President and—inappropriately, some thought—charged him with doing something about Bosnia. "Mr. President . . . I have been in the former Yugoslavia. . . . I cannot sleep since what I have seen. As a Jew I am saying that. We must do something to stop the bloodshed in that country."

Clinton's speech was a good one, strong and moving. He had spent over two hours on Monday night visiting the museum's grim displays. Clinton said, in his speech, "We are reminded again and again how fragile are the safeguards of civilization." Of Bosnia, he said, "We know, of course, that the new Europe is not yet free of old cruelties and that contemporary horrors like the slaughter of innocents in Bosnia have not disappeared."

On April 30, Clinton was to mark his first hundred days in office. On the twenty-third, he and his staff, attempting to preempt expected hundred-days analyses, staged a press conference. Clinton looked tired and was somewhat defensive. As in a lot of his public appearances, Clinton's demeanor was smiling, soft—not the commanding style most people want in a President. He just didn't pull himself up in a way that made people pay attention; they paid attention because he was the President. In television scenes of him at various events, or being shown some object, or listening to an explanation, his mouth often hung open, which didn't look Presidential. The sight of his chunky body in his jogging shorts wasn't wonderful to behold; he resisted his staff's efforts to get him to wear a track suit, just as he resisted their efforts to get him to stop making policy pronouncements as he finished his jog, sweaty, sometimes out of breath, and with a baseball cap shading his face. In his daily life, he had taken to wearing suits with big jackets and reverse-pleat trousers (he wore Donna Karan suits almost exclusively) that were fashionable in certain circles but on him looked baggy and emphasized his bulk.

In the East Room, on April 23, with red carpet stretched in the hallway behind him and ferns placed around the platform where he stood, Clinton began the press conference by claiming, "In this first hundred days we have already fundamentally changed the direction of an American government," and he enumerated features of his economic program. Clinton had some grounds for claiming to have changed the economic direction of the country, if at the time this seemed premature. If his economic program stayed on course, he would have even greater claim. But at that point, the loss of the stimulus package seemed of greater moment than the budget resolution that had been passed by the Congress—a fact that he recognized by saying, "I regret that the stimulus did not pass." He added, "I have begun to ask, and will continue to ask, not only people in the administration but the people in the Congress whether there is something I could have done differently."

"I've only been here ninety days," he said, once again making excuses for a shaky beginning and, as he was wont to do, offering commentary on his own Presidency. A couple of weeks later, when he announced that Roy Neel, Gore's Chief of Staff, would become a deputy to McLarty, he commented—to the dismay of much of his staff—"I think what we need to do, frankly, is to get the focus back on things that I have been working on from the beginning, passing the major economic program." He also said, "We've been discussing it for, oh, about five weeks now: what we can do to be more effective. After all, I just got here, and there are some things that are very different about the way Washington works, some good and some not so good."

But Clinton had run for President saying that he would get right in there and change things. He certainly didn't say, "It'll take me some time to learn my way around, so don't expect too much in the first few months." This excuse making was embarrassing and didn't evoke confidence. He was still paying for having frittered away much of the transition, and was still negotiating the huge leap from Little Rock to Washington.

In late April, Stan Greenberg said that the biggest problem for Clinton was that he was losing his sense of promise.

The celebration of the first hundred days, on April 30, wasn't a very joyous occasion, and the newspaper reviews of the period weren't exactly adulatory. White House aides accused the press of making too much of the hundred-days concept, though it was Clinton who had talked in his campaign of what he would accomplish in the first hundred days—he had promised "an explosive hundred-day action period."

On that Friday, April 30, Clinton flew to New Orleans to make a speech introducing his national service program. Each White House staff member received a single pink long-stem rose with a card saying, "I want to thank you for all the work you've done since the inauguration. We have an historic opportunity to make great things happen in our nation. Thanks for being part of the first 100 days." Each was signed, "Bill" and "Hillary."

10

BOSNIA

"Our Conscience Revolts"

During the campaign, though Clinton was challenging Bush on domestic issues, he knew he needed a threshold of credibility on foreign policy in order to play in the Presidential league. That was Bush's strength, and Clinton understood that he mustn't seem insufficiently muscular, or "weak," as some past Democratic candidates had. Anthony Lake had accomplished this for Clinton. Lake's new role, as National Security Adviser, was a derivative of his earlier one: keep foreign policy from becoming a problem —keep it off the screen and spare Clinton from getting embroiled as he went about his domestic business. Clinton had promised to "focus like a laser beam" on the economy. (Later in the year, a senior official said, "We had hoped to keep foreign policy submerged.")

The campaign strategy of maneuvering Clinton slightly to the "right" of Bush, of having him appear more the activist in some areas (such as aid to Russia, which Clinton managed to call for about an hour before Bush did), led him to say some things that he would later regret. Candidate Clinton called for a more aggressive role in Bosnia: "President Bush's policy toward former Yugoslavia mirrors his indifference to the massacre at Tiananmen Square and his coddling of Saddam Hussein. . . . Once again, the administration is turning its back on violations of basic human rights and our own democratic values."

The warfare between Muslims and Serbs (with the backing of Serbia itself) in the former Yugoslav republic of Bosnia-Herzegovina had been going on since March 1992 and it followed Serbian aggression in Slovenia and Croatia, which broke away from Yugoslavia in 1991. The war in Bosnia was marked by the driving of Muslims from their homes and towns—"ethnic cleansing"—and by the mass rape of Muslim women by Serb troops. The Bush administration had decided, amid much internal debate, that except for backing economic sanctions on Serbia and establishing a "no-fly" zone over Bosnia, the Balkan warfare essentially needed a good leaving alone. (Former Secretary of State James Baker said, "We don't have a dog in that fight.") Shortly before the inauguration, the President-elect said that "the legitimacy of ethnic cleansing cannot stand."

During the campaign, Clinton had also called for intervention to feed the starving people of Somalia, and during the transition the Bush administration obliged by sending troops—in part because it had also been attacked for its inaction in Bosnia. (Bosnia and Somalia were to continue to have reciprocal effects on each other.) Clinton also demanded a reversal of the Bush administration's policy of turning back boats carrying refugees from Haiti to the United States. Clinton reversed his own boat-people policy even before he took office. Clinton advisers said they had received intelligence reports that Haitians in large numbers were tearing up roofs to build boats, and there was too much danger some would drown at sea. The real fear was that the Haitians would make it to the United States, causing economic and social—and political—problems in Florida, as well as some other states. (Clinton had experienced that in 1980, with the Mariel boat people from Cuba, which he thought had a role in his defeat.)

After the new President retreated from his more bellicose campaign rhetoric on Bosnia and Haiti, Warren Christopher, his Secretary of State, said on *Meet the Press* in late February, "I don't suppose you'd want anybody to keep a campaign promise if it was a very unsound policy."

Clinton wanted to avoid the open warfare of the Carter administration between Secretary of State Cyrus Vance and National Security Adviser Zbigniew Brzezinski. In Tony Lake, Warren Christopher, and Les Aspin, he thought he had put together a smoothly working team. But it didn't turn out that way.

Christopher, at sixty-eight the most senior of the three, was a member in good standing of the establishment. Starting with his heading the search for the Vice-Presidential candidate, Christopher had cultivated an almost father-son relationship with Clinton. He showed traits that had attracted others to him: discretion and the aura of a certain wisdom. He spoke carefully. And he was a lot of things Clinton wasn't: controlled, accepted in all the establishment's reaches, seasoned, and even natty. Christopher wore expensive suits, crisp shirts with French cuffs and long collars, and quietly expensive ties. He was a picture of studied elegance. His jackets were lined with paisley silk. His clothes bespoke the man: careful, with a desire to be noticed. He had a dry wit, and one close friend said that behind Christopher's control, in fact the reason for the control, was a powerful temper.

Christopher was more competitive than he let on: he had gone from humble circumstances in North Dakota to the highest levels of power, and he had no intention of letting go. He was smart if not particularly imaginative or innovative. He had a lawyer's approach to issues, preferring problems that he could put in boxes and move around. Thus he was more comfortable dealing with, say, the Middle East than with the Balkans. Hard as it was, the Middle East could be approached by talking to country A, then country B, and so forth. One could draw boxes on a page. The Balkans defied a rational or linear approach.

Though Christopher had wanted to be Secretary of State for a long time, he seemed to have no strong beliefs or guiding philosophy. A number of State Department officials complained that Christopher didn't provide leadership to the department. Secretaries of State had varied on how important they thought that was. George Shultz did provide leadership, and was accessible; James Baker and his top aides treated what they called "the building" almost with contempt. One State Department official said, "Christopher's not an innovator, a thinker, a doer." By Christopher's own admission, he wasn't very interested in the new global issues of the environment, population, and the like. And he was constantly concerned about his place in the administration's firmament—more concerned than a man of his experience, who had the trust and respect of the President, should have been.

Lake, fifty-three, with his sandy hair and spectacles, his slight frame and quiet voice and mild manner, looked the part of the owlish professor many took him to be. His exceptional and genuine courtesy was also misleading. Lake was in fact a tough, highly competitive man, emotional and quite at home with four-letter words. His quiet demeanor, too, was protective coloring, his camouflage as he fought the battles of interagency rivalry and bureaucratic resistance. His fey sense of humor made him popular (mostly) within the White House and masked a serious and tough core.

At the outset, Christopher and Lake agreed to avoid the Vance-Brzezinski rivalry, with its consequent embarrassment to the President. As part of that agreement, it was stipulated that Lake would essentially stay off television, allowing Christopher to be the sole spokesman for foreign policy, and that Lake would also eschew diplomacy, leaving that to Christopher as well.

Thus Christopher was guaranteed his place in the sun. (Though, technically, the job of National Security Adviser is to bring the options to the President, most of the recent ones, from Henry Kissinger to Brent Scowcroft, weighed in with their own views as well.) But Lake wasn't acting solely out of self-sacrifice. He believed that his staying out of the limelight gave him a certain power. A close friend of Lake's said, "Tony is the most competitive person I know. He's even competitive at being obscure."

Lake's approach to his job was much affected by his own history and moral framework. Most recently a professor of international relations at Mount Holyoke College, Lake had been a Foreign Service officer in Vietnam and then served on the staff of the National Security Council under Nixon and Henry Kissinger, until he quit in 1970 in protest against the U.S. expansion of the Vietnam War into Cambodia. Later, under Carter, he was in charge of policy planning at the State Department. A colleague said of Lake, "More than anyone I've ever known, Tony is a moralist. He believes passionately in the moral aspects of foreign policy—he's a true Wilsonian." In Bosnia, he faced a situation filled with moral complexity.

Les Aspin had been of considerable help to the Clinton campaign—as an adviser on defense policy and a booster in Wisconsin, his home state. As chairman of the House Armed Services Committee and a defense intellectual (he had been one of former Defense Secretary Robert McNamara's "whiz kids"), he had what many thought were excellent credentials for Secretary of Defense. Moreover, Aspin was somewhat right of center in the Democratic defense spectrum, offering the kind of protection Clinton needed. Aspin was a large, ebullient man with a big laugh; he was like a big, friendly dog. He had a brilliant mind, but he had wandered around in his views on some defense matters and wasn't completely trusted by his Democratic House colleagues. (He was in one place and then another on the Gulf War, and ended up supporting it.) Aspin also had a flair for publicity, a little tamed in recent years. He liked to take a somewhat academic approach to defense questions, but the seminar approach didn't always suit his Pentagon job and irritated his counterparts in the administration. His loose, shambly style was part of his personal appeal, but it was one of the things about Aspin that didn't go down well with the military. He didn't have the look many thought a Secretary of Defense should have.

The three men met for lunch every Wednesday in Lake's large corner office in the West Wing of the White House. Lake and Christopher also spoke on the phone three or four times a day, Lake and Aspin fewer times. The three kept up an appearance of working together smoothly, but there were tensions among them almost from the outset. The tensions derived from conflicting ambitions, divergences in outlook, and differences in style. The State Department resented Aspin's setting up new shops in the Office of the Secretary of Defense to deal with such issues as democracy building, policy toward Russia, and economic competition. To Aspin, these were some of the new, post–Cold War issues that the Pentagon should deal with. To the State Department, Defense was poaching. Other officials said Aspin was badly organized and, as one put it, "circumlocuitous" in meetings. Christopher didn't talk much in meetings, as if unwilling to reveal his hand. But Lake liked Aspin—most people did—and the real tensions were between Lake and Christopher.

The three men differed on Bosnia from the outset. Contrary to many published reports at the time, Aspin (who was said to favor bombing) was for doing as little as possible in Bosnia. He thought it was "a loser from the start," that there was no way to deal with the problem effectively without enormous military force, and that neither the United States nor Europe was willing to pay that price. He argued that the best they could end up with was a divided Bosnia—Serb, Croat, and Muslim—with the Serbs maintaining control over most of the land they had already won in the war. When the question of bombing Bosnian Serb artillery sites arose in the spring of 1993, Aspin favored a cease-fire in place. Lake consistently pushed for the United States's taking strong action. Christopher was on different sides of the issue at different times, and not above retouching the record when he was caught on the wrong side of the opinion of the foreign policy establishment and influential members of the press.

An official who dealt with all three men said, "Christopher and Les are as polar opposite as any two men in public life. Christopher prepares every word he says on TV and in meetings and interviews. Les is spontaneous, with sometimes disastrous consequences." Christopher relied heavily on Tom Donilon, his highly influential adviser on press relations and overall policy. Donilon, forty-one, had been one of the Democratic Party's prodigies. In 1976, at the age of twenty-four, he was in charge of rounding up delegates for Walter Mondale. Since then, he had earned a law degree and had made partner in Christopher's law firm, O'Melveny and Myers. He headed the debate preparation in the Clinton campaign, and during the transition was involved in vetting possible appointees. Donilon was disappointed at not winning a White House job (Susan Thomases thought he was "too Washington," and others thought him too aggressive). In proposing his own role at the White House, he overreached—but ended up happily as Christopher's close adviser and sidekick.

Christopher didn't make many moves without consulting Donilon. Engaging, smart, baby-faced, and slightly pudgy, Donilon was a street fighter, constantly on the prowl for ways to show his boss to advantage—sometimes by implication derogating his boss's competitors, and even the President. On one occasion, another State Department official felt constrained to remind Donilon that his real boss, and his first loyalty, was the President. With Donilon's encouragement, Christopher concerned himself a great deal with his press coverage. At Donilon's suggestion, Christopher made a statement before television cameras virtually every day. It didn't seem to have occurred to either of these very smart men that having the Secretary of State pronounce on some policy every day—and not always interestingly—devalued the currency. State Department officials said that in meetings with Christopher and Donilon there was an uncommon amount of "How will this play?"

Tony Lake had been deeply affected by his Vietnam experience. He admitted to being "emotional" about Bosnia and believed that emotion had a proper role in the formulation of foreign policy.

One afternoon, in his office, in early 1993, Lake talked about "how I think about working on foreign policy, and what I've learned from Vietnam." His ground-floor office had a conference table and a sofa and several chairs; gauzy curtains let in a fair amount of light. Lake, who maintained a hundred-forty-acre cattle farm in Massachusetts, had hung a large painting of a cow over his office bookshelves.

" 'Emotional' is the right word to use," Lake said. "When George Kenney [a junior State Department official] resigned last year [over Bush administration policy in the former Yugoslavia], he was accused by some of his former associates as being 'emotional,' and when I resigned over Vietnam—the invasion of Cambodia—some said that I had been 'emotional.' I think those comments flow from a potential disease of people in my racket, because people are dying and we're deciding on whether to conduct air strikes. There's tremendous comfort in not being emotional and numbing yourself—blinding yourself—to the human consequences of your decisions. The alternative disease is to become so emotional that you lose confidence in your ability to decide. The reason Abraham Lincoln is my hero is that he knew what was happening, that while he was making decisions people were being killed, and if he *didn't* decide, people were still being killed, so he was ready to decide. Compare that to George C. Scott playing Patton, in his line 'God, I love it.' I think you should be emotional, but I don't think you should let your emotions cloud your judgment. But you can sure hate it when you turn on the television and see the carnage."

Therefore, to Lake, the response (by the Bush administration and others) that the warring factions in the former Yugoslavia had been killing each other for hundreds of years wasn't an answer to the agony of Bosnia. "In a policy sense, you want to be aware of that," Lake said. "But you look at a mother who's lost a child, and it's cold comfort to her that this has been going on for centuries. This isn't dominoes; this is the spread of hatreds."

Bosnia triggered a number of concerns in Lake. One was the balance of power. "What could be more classic than concerns about a new Balkan war with spillover that could draw in the Greeks and the Turks; and what could be more uncivilized than—I hate the euphemism 'ethnic cleansing.' And with all this you have tensions between the Islamic world and the Christian world that are filled with ancient dangers."

Finally, Bosnia was related to another concern of the Clinton administration's foreign policy: the containment of both Iraq and Iran, or "dual containment." Iran, at the time acquiring sophisticated weaponry and seeking a nuclear capability, was seen as the greater long-term danger. Lake said, "Containment of Iran requires our working to contain Muslim extremism, and we have to find a way of being firm in our opposition to Muslim extremism while making it clear we're not opposed to Islam. If we are seen as anti-Muslim, it's harder for us to contain Muslim extremism. And if we stand by while Muslims are killed and raped in Bosnia, it makes it harder to continue our policy of dual containment."

The Clinton administration had inherited difficult foreign policy questions, faced a host of new ones, and came under criticism for not sending aloft a whole new definition of foreign policy. This wasn't entirely fair. The Bush administration, coming to office as Mikhail Gorbachev was undertaking economic and political reform in the Soviet Union and offering a more peaceful face to the West, went to the drawing boards to design a new policy, and after four months came up with an uninspired slogan and a watery policy, "Beyond Containment." That the Clinton people in their first year in office didn't come up with a catchy term was understandable, given the complexity, newness, and variety of what they were facing. Most of the foreign policy issues the Clinton administration inherited involved struggles going on within nations rather than between them, and in some cases raised the question of the definition of "nation." The real problem was that Clinton had trouble defining policy, even in a given case, and seemed not very interested in foreign policy. He seemed uncomfortable talking about it. Unlike every President since Truman, Clinton had no regularly scheduled meetings with his foreign policy team. (He did see Lake almost daily.)

The Clinton administration began with high hopes that many of the new crises could be dealt with through the peacekeeping machinery of the United Nations—as a way of sharing resources and responsibilities. In the campaign, Clinton had discussed the establishment of an international rapid deployment force under the UN, which could go beyond traditional peacekeeping to preventing mass internal violence and aggression and providing humanitarian relief. Madeleine Albright, the U.S. ambassador to the United Nations, was particularly keen on enhancing the role of international peacekeeping and coined the term "assertive multilateralism." Lake had initiated a large number of inter-agency policy reviews—some saw this as an exercise in control by tying up others—with peacekeeping one of the subjects. This was to end up the object of a year-long battle.

There were two constraints on Bosnia policy. First, it was assumed that the public wouldn't accept the sending of ground troops, even if top officials wanted to send them, which, because of the opposition of the military, and the "quagmire" potential, they didn't. Second, it was felt that the administration should do nothing to embarrass Boris Yeltsin. The Russians had a long-standing friendship with the Serbs, their fellow Slavs, and Russian nationalistic sentiment was on the rise. Moreover, Russia had a veto in the UN Security Council.

Policymaking on Bosnia, as on any other important foreign policy issue, was largely done in the Principals Committee, which consisted of Lake, Christopher, Aspin, Colin Powell, CIA Director James Woolsey, and Albright. Samuel "Sandy" Berger, Lake's deputy and alter ego, and Leon Fuerth, as Gore's representative on the NSC staff (an innovation in the Presidential–Vice-Presidential relationship), also attended the meetings. Principals meetings were held in the Situation Room, a secure, three-room complex in the White House basement, where staff members monitored developments and sent out alerts when something caught their attention. Most of the Principals in the Clinton administration had worked together in the Carter administration and had attended a zillion conferences together during their twelve years in the cold. One participant said, "We're at an advantage and disadvantage because we all know each other so well. There's not much of a terror, even awe, of each other in our institutional positions. It makes it all very pleasant, but people interrupt each other and there's not enough discipline. We're there not as people brought together as representatives of institutions but as people who've been around tables with each other for a long time."

When the President attended a Principals meeting, McLarty and Gore were also present. Gore, Albright, and Fuerth represented the "hawkish" position on Bosnia—and on other issues as well. The meetings (like domestic policy meetings) sometimes meandered as the President was bombarded with conflicting advice and took his time to make up his mind. The divisions within the foreign policy group contributed to a division in the mind of a President who had few strong instincts on foreign policy questions.

The first big decision on Bosnia was made rather casually and, given its importance, received little public notice.

After three long Principals meetings had been held, at the end of the last one, on the afternoon of Friday, February 5, Lake invited Clinton and Gore to join the group in the Situation Room. In the meeting, Clinton said that the United States had to lead on Bosnia, for humanitarian reasons if no other. Several European countries had contributed ground troops to the UN "peacekeeping" force in Bosnia. "If the United States doesn't act in situations like this," the President said, "nothing will happen." He also said, "A failure to do so would be to give up American leadership."

So the President took a number of decisions: to become directly involved in humanitarian action (this led to U.S. airdrops of food into Muslim-held areas of Bosnia); to ask the United Nations for authorization of enforcement of the no-fly zone; to seek a tightening of the economic sanctions; to appoint an envoy to the talks being conducted by Cyrus Vance, representing the United Nations, and Lord Owen, representing the European Community, in an attempt to find a settlement more acceptable to the Muslims; to reiterate the Bush administration's warning to Serbia not to cause trouble in Kosovo (a part of Serbia with a large Albanian population); and, most important, to help enforce an agreement among the parties to stop fighting—provided all parties willingly signed the agreement. Lake said later, of Clinton's new Bosnia policy, "The key to it was our willingness to take part in the implementation of a peace agreement. Otherwise we wouldn't have been taken seriously."

Getting internal agreement on the airdrops, the Clinton administration's first real initiative in Bosnia, was a problem. Powell was skeptical at first that there was a way to get the food safely to the people. But not long afterward he said that the military had studied the question further, and that if small parachutes were used, the food could be dropped at night, close to where the people were. Later the plan was changed so that individual "meals ready to eat," or MREs (left over from the Gulf War), were dropped, since it was safer to be hit on the head with one of those (in a small foil package) than with food attached to wooden skids.

At the same time the administration announced the airdrops, in late February, it also sent signals to assure the public that the President was not preoccupied with foreign policy and the administration wasn't getting deeply involved in Bosnia. Before the airdrops had gone on for long, there was open confusion about the policy. On March 2, Aspin said, in impromptu remarks on Capitol Hill, that the airdrops had been suspended, because they had proved "a great success" in getting the Serbs to free up convoys carrying food to Muslim towns. But press reports from Bosnia indicated that the Serbs had stepped up their attacks on Muslim towns at which the airdrops were aimed and were holding up the convoys. (Military officials had opposed a project of indefinite length.) Aspin was publicly corrected by both Clinton and Gore, who said the airdrops would continue.

The Clinton people had deep reservations about the plan that had been drawn up by Vance and Owen to carve Bosnia into ten cantons and return less than 30 percent of it to the Bosnian Muslims. The numerous borders seemed unenforceable, and the Muslims felt shortchanged. In effect, a settlement would be forced on the Muslims, and the administration didn't want to be part of that politically or militarily. So the President decided that the United States would participate in the Vance-Owen negotiations, to try to get adjustments made in the proposal and assure the Bosnian Muslims that any agreement that was reached would hold. Though Aspin raised a lot of questions, publicly and privately, about problems with enforcement—and publicly laid out his own guidelines placing limits on the terms of the U.S. participation—the commitment was made. Powell had agreed to it at a Principals meeting, and the President later phoned him for confirmation. To Powell, one participant in the process said, this was a limited military commitment.

These decisions were made public on February 10 in a statement by Christopher, which eloquently described the situation in Bosnia—"over the past two years the states of the former Yugoslavia have descended into a dark period of terror and bloodshed"—and criticized the Bush administration for not taking action. "Our conscience revolts at the idea of passively accepting such brutality," Christopher said. A State Department official later ascribed this rhetoric to "campaign overhang."

It seemed that Christopher was leading up to something big. He said, "Beyond these humanitarian interests, we have strategic concerns as well." The destruction of Bosnia, a member state of the United Nations, "challenges the principle that internationally recognized borders should not be altered by force." He added that the United States had an interest in avoiding the spread of the hostilities, averting a "river" of refugees into Europe, and in the test Bosnia posed to the world of "how it will address the concerns of ethnic and religious minorities in the post–Cold War world."

Officials believed that if Serbia, which hadn't been stopped in Croatia, exacerbated the situation in Kosovo, with its majority population of Albanians, or moved on Macedonia, which borders Serbia, Albania, Bulgaria, and Greece, the Albanians, the Greeks, and the Turks wouldn't sit by. This wasn't a "domino theory" but an envisioning of a wider conflict. Further, they felt that with the breakup of the Soviet Union producing new tensions over borders and ethnic rivalries, as one official put it, "It was important for us to say that eliminating an ethnic minority is not acceptable." But there later developed strong disagreements over the implications for U.S. foreign policy.

The actions Christopher announced didn't match the rhetoric. "This is an important moment for our nation's post–Cold War role in Europe and the world," he said. "In the face of great suffering and the imperative of our own interest, we cannot afford to miss any further opportunities to help pursue a resolution of this conflict."

But miss them they did, for over a year.

With little progress on reaching peace in Bosnia, and in order to put new pressure on the Bosnian Serbs to stop their recently initiated assault on certain Bosnian towns, especially the town of Srebrenica, Lake called the Principals together on March 25 and told them that the situation was about to enter a new phase, and it was time for new ideas. Administration officials also thought that, as a result of the increased violence—and the television pictures of it—European attitudes might be changing. The European countries that had provided ground troops to the UN peacekeeping force opposed measures to try to even the balance in arms between Muslims and Serbs by lifting the arms embargo on the Muslims; they argued that lifting the embargo would endanger their troops and their efforts to get food through. "The old policy was running out," Lake said later. He was also looking for ways to put pressure on the Bosnian Serbs to sign a new version of Vance-Owen, which the Bosnian Muslims had agreed to sign. The next day, Clinton said in a White House press conference with German Chancellor Helmut Kohl that the two men had discussed Bosnia. He added that the Bosnian President, Alija Izetbegovic, had also been at the White House that morning, and "We're going to do everything we can to put on a full-court press diplomatically to secure the agreement of the Serbs."

The arms embargo had been imposed by the United Nations in 1991 on all of the former Yugoslavia, "for the purposes of establishing peace and stability." This left most of the weapons in Serb hands. Clinton felt there was a moral problem in not enabling people under attack to defend themselves, a view he had carried into his Presidency. Lifting the arms embargo was a cost-free way for the United States to have an effect on the war. The administration had put off asking for it because it wanted to keep the world's focus on getting the Serbs to sign Vance-Owen, and because the allies with ground troops in Bosnia were opposed. Now the idea was under serious consideration, with the hope that the allies would change their views.

One option included some limited form of American military pressure against the Bosnian Serbs. Aspin continued to favor a cease-fire in place. Powell was flatly against the use of ground forces, but in other cases his arguments were in the form of a question: Tell me what the objective is, and I'll tell you what it will take and what the consequences are. He could of course weight the argument—not out of dishonesty but out of his own deep misgivings about military involvement in Bosnia. In the meetings with the Principals and the President, Powell kept asking, "What is the end point?" He'd say, "If we bomb Serb military targets in Bosnia and that doesn't bring them to the conference table, then what?" Even the advocates of bombing—who included Gore and Albright—accepted as valid the question of what the purpose was and what they would do if the bombing didn't succeed in bringing the Serbs to the conference table.

The intelligence assessment wasn't optimistic about the use of airpower in Bosnia. The policymakers were told that while there were a number of "lucrative" targets in Serbia itself—fuel dumps, military facilities, bridges, command and control centers—bombing them might damage the position of Serbian leader Slobodan Milosevic but still not get the Bosnian Serbs to the conference table. (Saddam Hussein had survived extensive bombing of Baghdad.) The assessment was that the Bosnian Serbs weren't highly dependent upon Serbia for military supplies, and the Serb artillery would be very hard to hit since it could be easily hidden in the mountainous, wooded Bosnian countryside, and, except in the summer, much of the country was under heavy cloud cover. Moreover, the warning went, the Bosnian Serbs were capable of putting howitzers and mortars next to schoolhouses or churches and daring their opponents to bomb them.

The intelligence assessment said that the effectiveness of the ordnance for attacking Serb sites could be improved and that bombing might have a deterrent effect, but the only thing that would be truly effective would be to send in two to three divisions of ground troops and two to three air wings. That had drawbacks, the policymakers were told: you might not be able to get out, and you might not know what to do once it's over. A final problem —one that haunted some policymakers—was that any result achievable without a great commitment of force would in effect recognize ethnic cleansing.

In April, there was a series of Principals meetings with the President. Options were discussed and refined, but Clinton kept postponing a decision. He was expected to make one over the last weekend in April, but didn't. Clinton would press each advocate: What are our objectives with that option? What is the limiting principle? How do we extricate ourselves if we do X? What is controllable and uncontrollable with that option? At times, the President would express his frustration with both the limits on U.S. actions and the dangers of turning the effort to end the conflict in Bosnia into an American problem. The latter was a real consideration: if the United States acted unilaterally, it would be all the harder to get both domestic support for its actions and cooperation from other countries—which, in turn, would further undermine domestic support. Clinton determined that the United States would not act unilaterally.

He was reinforced in this view by Stan Greenberg. Greenberg's general view was that polling on foreign policy questions wasn't very useful because it could give no guide to public reaction after a President called for action. Though the administration insisted that the consultants had no role in foreign policy, Greenberg sometimes put a foreign policy question in his polls for a bipartisan group called America Talks Issues, and sometimes, using public polls, gave the President advice on foreign policy. Stephanopoulos also acted as a conduit from the political advisers to the President and to Lake. "Not everything requires a formal meeting," Greenberg said.

Greenberg told Clinton that there was increasing support for action by the United States in Bosnia in conjunction with the UN, but there was no support for unilateral action. He also told Clinton that on the basis of his findings, Bosnia was a subject on which public opinion could be shaped.

Many times, Clinton said in meetings that if he were a Bosnian, he would want the right to have weapons to defend himself, and asked, What if others told Americans they couldn't have weapons. He would say, "Jesus, at least if we're not going to help those people we should lift the arms embargo and let them help themselves." On one occasion, he said, "If there were other countries keeping us from defending ourselves, I'd be pissed as hell or goddamn resentful." On a couple of occasions, both Clinton and Gore expressed their frustrations in such strong terms that it got in the way of making decisions. As a senator, Gore had been a hawk on Bosnia, and in the campaign he had urged Clinton to take strong positions on it. Sometimes, in White House meetings, when Gore would deliver of himself on the subject of Serbian aggression, Clinton would also get worked up, his face reddening.

The long hours spent in the Situation Room, the protracted agonizing, said one high-level official, was "a bad sign." He added, "It wasn't policymaking. It was group therapy—an existential debate over what is the role of America, etc." A month after Lake had begun the new round of meetings to find a new policy, no decisions had been made.

The outside pressures on the President to "do something" had increased substantially by mid-April. The world was seeing pictures of Srebrenica under siege. On April 16, the news indicated that the town was about to fall. The evening before, television networks had showed wrenching pictures of a little boy from Srebrenica, who had had part of his face blown off, now in a hospital, where a doctor unwrapped the bandages and told the boy's mother that he would never see again. Stephanopoulos said at his April 16 briefing, "We are outraged."

That afternoon, the President held a press conference in the East Room with Prime Minister Kiichi Miyazawa of Japan. Clinton, wearing one of his baggy suits, was red-faced and clearly tired, and his bulk loomed over Miyazawa. In an answer to the first question, Clinton said, "At this point, I would not rule out any option except the option I have never ruled in, which was the question of American ground troops." He criticized the situation as one he had inherited and praised the actions he had taken thus far—including a reshaping of the Vance-Owen proposal in an attempt to get the Bosnian Muslims to agree to it—and said, "I'm going to be spending a lot of time on this today. I'm outraged that the Serbians, when given the opportunity, did not sign on to the Vance-Owen agreement." Neither the President nor Stephanopoulos used the word "outraged" casually. Asked if it was time for American leadership to try to persuade the Europeans to lift the arms embargo and approve air strikes, Clinton replied, "I think the time has come for the United States and Europe to look very honestly at where we are and what the consequences of various courses of action will be. And I think we have to consider things which at least previously have been unacceptable." Echoing Christopher's statement in February, the President said, "We have an interest in standing up against the principle of ethnic cleansing. If you look at the turmoil all through the Balkans, if you look at the other places where this could play itself out in other parts of the world, this is not just about Bosnia." It is up to the United States, Clinton said, "to force the consideration of all possible options."

Later that afternoon, Stephanopoulos slumped in his office chair with his feet on a coffee table and, looking very tired, said, "We're in an untenable position. It's been building."

As the Principals met at length over the weekend of April 17–18 and worked through the options, they arrived at two major ones. One was a combination of lifting the arms embargo, and some bombing strikes to keep the Serbs from launching serious aggression before the Muslims got their arms; the other was a cease-fire and the protection of Muslim enclaves. Lake asked the advocates of each option to prepare a paper for the President on the pros and cons of their position, to be given to Clinton Sunday night.

Lake and Christopher decided that in an attempt to depersonalize such an emotional issue, the name of the writers wouldn't be on the memos. Albright's paper, which advocated bombing strikes, was leaked to the press.

Lake, who had been for a strong policy all along, favored the option of lifting the arms embargo, with interim bombing. This was where Christopher ended up as well, and the two men went over, line by line, the paper for the President, written at the State Department, setting forth that option. In the meetings, Christopher had asked a number of probing questions about the objective of various options. He had begun favoring simply the lifting of the arms embargo. But he had since been persuaded—by Gore and by Russian Foreign Minister Andrei Kozyrev—that there might be a surge of Serbian aggression before the arms reached the Muslims. Lake and Christopher saw the lifting of the arms embargo as something that could "level the playing field" and induce the Bosnian Serbs to negotiate.

The majority within the group believed that the agreement of Serbia was a necessary condition for reaching a settlement, and so bombing it might keep it from cooperating. But they also didn't want to explicitly rule out bombing Serbia. On Saturday, Clinton, on his way to Pittsburgh to make a last-gasp plea for his stimulus program, called Lake from the plane and said he wanted an update that evening. The papers were given to the President Monday morning and a Principals meeting was set for the next day.

At this point, discontent with the Bosnian policy among the more junior ranks of the State Department, the experts on Bosnia, bubbled up once more—this time in the form of a letter to Christopher, which was made public, describing Western policy as a failure and recommending strong military action to end the Serbian "genocide" in Bosnia. Over the year, there were four resignations from the department over the policy. (And in March 1994, Warren Zimmerman, a former ambassador to Yugoslavia, resigned over this and personnel matters.)

White House and State Department officials said that Lake was the moving force behind drawing up the new policy. One White House official said, "The President will come out where Tony is." Lake also kept Stephanopoulos informed. Stephanopoulos was far more involved in foreign policy matters than was publicly known. He and Lake had become close friends in the campaign, and in the White House they had an alliance. The two men talked every morning before the senior staff meeting.

Lake saw the President nearly every day for the morning intelligence briefing by someone from the CIA (Gore, Berger, and Fuerth also attended), which took about fifteen minutes—Clinton often asked questions—and was usually followed by a foreign policy discussion based on items Lake wanted to bring up with Clinton; and Lake was often in and out of his office several times a day, as foreign policy developments that needed the President's attention arose. But when domestic issues consumed the President, the intelligence briefings could get "blown off" his schedule. (The President could still read the briefing, which was usually about ten pages of items about things going on.) Other White House aides appreciated Lake's being gracious about this, but they also thought that Henry Kissinger wouldn't have been "blown off." At times, CIA Director James Woolsey (who only occasionally briefed the President) had such trouble getting on Clinton's schedule that he called upon retired Admiral William Crowe, who had endorsed Clinton in the campaign and had great influence with him, to bring something up with the President.

By late April, senators of both parties were calling for bombing strikes in Bosnia.

On April 20, Clinton, in a photo op, said, "The U.S. should always seek an opportunity to stand up against—at least speak out against—inhumanity." There was quite a disparity within that one sentence.

Clinton was said by his aides to have been deeply affected, and influenced in his position on Bosnia, by the ceremonies surrounding the opening of the Holocaust Museum. A close adviser said, "Clinton was very anguished about it. The decisive things were the dedication of the Holocaust Museum, with Elie Wiesel's lecture, and the bad pictures on television of Srebrenica. The pictures of Srebrenica brought ethnic cleansing home." It was discomfiting that the President, after all the deliberations, was basing his Bosnia policy heavily on his emotional reactions to events. This wasn't to be the last time that television pictures out of Bosnia drove him to a new policy.

In his press conference on April 23, Clinton was asked several questions about Bosnia. He replied, "We'll have a policy. . . . The United States should lead . . . but I don't think we should act alone," and he said he had been reviewing the options and would have a new policy to announce soon. His aides thought that he would make a decision on the policy over the weekend of April 24–25—but he didn't.

By saying so often that something must be done to stop the ethnic cleansing, Clinton had got himself in a corner. Whatever his misgivings, doing nothing wasn't an option. On April 27, Clinton met in the State Dining Room for two hours with bipartisan congressional leaders and other members with a particularly strong interest in Bosnia, to go over the options he was considering. (The meeting was interrupted when Clinton had to go out to greet two athletic teams. There were a lot of events of that sort on his schedule.) Clinton opened the meeting by saying, "Listen, this has gone on too long. We have to act, and I am going to act." He also said that Gore pressed him on the matter every day.

The meeting with the congressional leaders was marked by strong emotions and sharp debate—and mixed advice to the President. Gephardt, who was strongly against any further intervention by the United States, because he thought it posed great danger to the President's domestic agenda, raised a number of questions about what he saw as "downside risks." Foley, who was worried, asked practical questions about the proposal to lift the arms embargo and about what would happen if the first steps didn't work. Others expressed their worries about how they would be seen by history if they didn't act. One leader worried that if the United States got militarily involved, the inevitable "collateral damage" caused by bombing would cause Republicans to charge that this was the result of Clinton's lack of military experience. At the same time, the military was still balking at some of the proposals. At a breakfast with reporters, Admiral David Jeremiah, the Vice Chairman of the Joint Chiefs of Staff, said that bombing in Bosnia might cause civilian casualties and wouldn't cripple the Serbian threat. From Vietnam, Powell and others had concluded that the United States shouldn't fight unless it was willing to apply overwhelming force, the objective was clear, there was an end point, and the venture had political support. These criteria were met in the war with Iraq. But Bosnia didn't fit the past.

On Thursday, April 29, Clinton met with the Joint Chiefs for two hours in the Oval Office, with Christopher, Lake, Aspin, Stephanopoulos, Berger, and Fuerth. The group went through the options—using airpower, lifting the arms embargo—and discussed the risks of each approach, and what was and wasn't achievable. Clinton asked, "Even if we introduce bombing for a limited purpose, what if the Serbs make advances anyway?" His concern was about getting drawn in deeper and deeper. He asked, "Couldn't the use of force embolden the Serbs?" He asked the Chiefs to tell him, "What can we do from the air that will have the least risk to civilians?" General Merrill McPeak, the Air Force Chief of Staff, gave a very optimistic estimate of what could be done with minimal risk to American servicemen. At that meeting, Powell acted as the "honest broker" among the Chiefs.

As the objective became more limited, Powell became more comfortable. A key foreign policy official said, "Colin Powell has made the point about the need for a set of objectives, but he's not against the grain. He recognizes that there are consequences of doing nothing."

After their meeting with the President, the military men exited by the door leading to the front driveway, thus making themselves available to the press and cameras stationed there. This was most unusual, but both

Stephanopoulos and Powell had a purpose: to show that the military would be behind whatever the President decided. Powell had planned the sound bites he wanted picked up: the U.S. had "a wide range of military options," and "the armed forces of the United States will be fully able to carry out the instructions that will have been given, and at that point, there is never any reluctance." Powell also put a damper on what he considered excessive predictions (by McPeak) of what airpower could accomplish.

For the May 1 meeting, at which the President was committed to making a decision, Lake put together a list of a dozen objectives and interests, and fostered a discussion of how the various options fit those interests and objectives. The meeting went on for five hours. At one point, Gore said, "I mean, is this a difficult problem or what?" Powell set forth the risks of using airpower on Serb artillery, saying that early success could be anticipated, but then the Serb weapons would be moved to churches and mosques. By the time the meeting was over, every option but sending ground troops (except to enforce a peace agreement) had been examined. In the end, the President arrived at a proposal to lift the arms embargo and conduct air strikes if the Serbs took advantage of the interval before the arms reached the Muslims: "lift and strike." A top policymaker said, "The basic strategy was, This thing is a no-winner, it's going to be a quagmire. Let's not make it our quagmire. That's what lift the arms embargo, and the limited air strikes, was about."

Within hours after the May 1 meeting, Christopher left for Europe and Moscow to discuss the President's proposals. Though planning for the trip had begun days before, it was, curiously, insufficiently thought through. The later vilification of Christopher for having failed to persuade the allies to support the "lift and strike" option was unrealistic. Critics who said that Christopher could have succeeded if he had been tougher with the Europeans were off base. There was no real reason for the President and Christopher to believe that the trip would succeed. They had set themselves up for an embarrassing failure. A senior official said later that Christopher knew the trip was risky but felt that it had to be taken.

The British and the French had quite specifically warned the administration not to come to them with a fait accompli. One British diplomat said later, "We told them that until we were blue in the face. We said we can't do 'lift and strike,' especially lift. Our troops are on the ground. We felt that it would inflame the situation and could cut off relief. There was nothing Christopher could have done to get a different outcome." Lake's counterpart in the British government had sent him a message that the Prime Minister could see no way in which he could obtain the agreement of the Cabinet or the Parliament to "lift and strike." In Washington, officials at the

British Embassy gave their contacts the same warning. A French diplomat said later that Christopher "knew perfectly well before he embarked on his trip that our position was negative."

Christopher's instructions were to consult with the allies, try to get them to go along with the policy, but not threaten the end of the alliance if they didn't. An official said, "Chris's mission was to seek support for this approach, but there was never a view that he should say, 'This, or else.' If we'd bet the ranch, said to the French and English, 'This threatens a fundamental breach in our relationships,' we could perhaps have got the Europeans—kicking and screaming—involved. But this would have made it an American problem. We would have taken over. We have viewed it as a European problem where we'd help out."

In the May 1 meeting, the President told Christopher, "You've been a great lawyer and advocate all these years—now you've really got your work cut out for you." One person who attended the meetings said, "Everyone knew it was a tough sell." Clinton's view was that maybe Christopher could turn the Europeans around. This represented both Clinton's unbounded faith in salesmanship, and a naïveté about nations' interests.

In his meetings with the foreign leaders, Christopher laid out the options the President had considered, explained why Clinton had come to the conclusion he had, and said that the United States wanted their cooperation and was prepared to discuss their misgivings.

People who traveled with Christopher, not all of them his sycophants, said that he did try to sell the policy. One remarked, "It was made very, very clear that this was the direction the President wanted to take." This official said, reasonably, that it was in the interest of the British and the French to tell the press—on a background basis—that Christopher hadn't really tried to sell them. The British in effect said no, but added that they might consider air strikes. British officials stated that the overwhelming majority of the Parliament opposed lifting the arms embargo, and if the British government pursued that option, it might well fall. The French opposed lifting the arms embargo but said that they would go along with air strikes if the United States sent in ground troops—which they knew was most unlikely. The Italian Prime Minister told Christopher, "This would be like throwing a log on a burning fire." The German government was the least opposed, but Germany felt it couldn't have troops in Bosnia because of restrictions it had adopted on using troops anywhere outside the NATO area. The Dutch government seemed sympathetic. The knottiest talks were with the Russians: officials didn't like the policy but didn't want to be seen as repudiating the United States.

But by the time the Christopher entourage reached Moscow, something had happened that helped give the allies, and Yeltsin, a way out of endorsing Christopher's proposal. On May 2, the day after Christopher left for his trip, the Bosnian Serb leader, Radovan Karadzic, meeting in Athens with Vance and Owen, as well as Bosnian Muslim representatives, said he would agree to the Vance-Owen proposal, subject to its approval by the Bosnian Serb parliament.

Yeltsin, meeting with Christopher and some of his entourage, said that he didn't even want to talk about the American plan; the subject now was how to enforce the peace agreement. On Wednesday, May 5, the Bosnian Serb parliament turned down the agreement and called for a referendum on the matter. In the referendum, on May 15 and 16, Bosnian Serbs turned the plan down.

During Christopher's trip, some things happened in Washington that also contributed to the doom of the "lift and strike" policy. Aspin, Powell, and Peter Tarnoff, Under Secretary of State for Political Affairs, made a visit to Capitol Hill to assess the mood there and found limited support for the policy. The Christopher entourage was given a gloomy assessment of congressional support.

One day while Christopher was in Europe, Aspin and Powell went to the White House for a photo op of the President, in the Rose Garden, presenting a Commander in Chief trophy to the Air Force Academy's football team. It was a beautiful spring day. After the ceremony, Clinton asked Powell and Aspin to return to the Oval Office with him. Once there, Clinton said he had been reading the book *Balkan Ghosts,* by Robert Kaplan, a haunting description of the Balkan people's historic propensity for war with each other. (Powell had read part of the book, and Mrs. Clinton had read it.) The book pointed out that these people had been killing each other in tribal and religious wars for centuries; the Serbs' National Day was a commemoration of the battle of Kosovo, in 1389 (which they lost to the Turks). As he heard the President talk about it, Aspin thought, "Holy shit! He's going south on 'lift and strike.' "

When Aspin got back to his office at the Pentagon, he called Lake and Tarnoff and said, "Guys, he's going south on this policy. His heart isn't in it." Aspin also told his colleagues, "We have a serious problem here. We're out there pushing a policy that the President's not comfortable with. He's not on board." Tarnoff asked if he should call Christopher and tell him. "That's why I'm calling," Aspin replied. Aspin also called Walter Slocombe, Deputy Under Secretary of Defense for Policy, who was traveling with Christopher. Aspin told Slocombe, "Walt, we're going to pull the plug on it. The

President is going south." So at the same time that Christopher was getting a negative reception in Europe, he got word that the President was wavering on the policy he was trying to sell.

During that same week, an op-ed article by Arthur Schlesinger in the *Wall Street Journal* warned of the serious effects Clinton's inclination to take a more active role in Bosnia might have on his domestic and foreign policies. This had a strong impact on Clinton, who was often swayed by op-ed pieces. Gore, who liked to work on the Macintosh computer on his desk, prepared a point-by-point rebuttal to this to give to the President, as he did with other op-ed pieces, often to little avail.

On Wednesday, May 5, while Christopher was in Europe, the President welcomed back a contingent of soldiers from Somalia. A little parade was arranged, in which the President marched with the servicemen, dressed in their camouflage uniforms, across the South Lawn. It wasn't clear where they were going, but this scene was one of many attempts, not all of them successful, to show Clinton mixing comfortably with the military. Clinton had a dreadful salute. Instead of the snappy ones that Reagan and Bush got off, Clinton's salute was limp, his raised hand curved. In greeting the troops, Clinton said that their return demonstrated that multilateral efforts, such as the one in Somalia, "need not be open ended or ill defined."

At the end of the week, Clinton and his aides were determined to put the negative reports about Christopher's trip in a positive light. They didn't want weekend stories saying that Clinton had suffered a diplomatic failure, one that would worsen relationships with the allies. So in a South Lawn news conference on Friday, May 7, Clinton said "There is a lot more agreement than you think" between the Europeans and the United States. Lake and Stephanopoulos "spun" positive stories about the talks.

When the President and his foreign policy advisers met on Saturday, May 8, to hear Christopher's report of his trip, they were given a negative account of the prospects for allied cooperation. Christopher said that the only way to get the Europeans to go along was to pressure them very hard, which carried risks, and that he didn't recommend it. One attendee said later, "Nobody recommended simply steamrollering the Europeans." This person added, "Chris made it clear that if we wanted to get this done, we'd have to push them very hard, and at the end of the day they might go along, but this would create strains." Another said, "We didn't want to stake the alliance on this, or totally Americanize the issue." Another said, "I don't think any of us were prepared for how definite Chris was and how badly his trip had gone."

The meeting went off in a number of directions, and no decisions were made. Gore proposed air strikes to take out the Serbian artillery. Christopher began to talk about shifting to a policy of containment, perhaps by giving assurances or by sending a token force to Macedonia and taking new steps to make sure that the conflict didn't spread to Macedonia and Kosovo. An official said, "Chris clearly was thinking more and more in terms of, OK, let's do containment. Let's concentrate on Macedonia and Kosovo, that we've just got to take Bosnia off the front pages. I don't think he thought it was a soluble problem." Following Christopher's return from Europe, Tom Donilon said, "Containment issues became front and center."

Lake agreed with examining the containment possibilities but said the administration should remain firm about wanting to lift the arms embargo, combined with air strikes.

One official said later, "The President took it under advisement. This was not a meeting where there was a crisp conclusion."

The trip had a strong impact on Christopher's thinking. A senior official close to him said, "I don't think it was until he made the trip that Chris focused on what a loser this policy was."

In the days following Christopher's trip, there was a fair amount of transatlantic sniping between the United States and its allies—what came to be called "rift and drift"—until American officials called their European counterparts and suggested that they knock it off. On May 10, some administration officials let it be known that the U.S. policy was being put on hold pending the Bosnian Serb referendum. There was disagreement within the administration over whether the plan was dead (Lake was holding out)—but it was dead.

And the President of the United States looked feckless. He had talked and talked about the moral imperative of doing something about Bosnia, and done nothing. He had said publicly that he would be coming up with a strong policy, one that could well involve military action, and had failed to do so. He had reacted to what he saw on television, and his mind seemed easily changed. He had also claimed, disingenuously, to be closer to an agreement with the Europeans than he was. Whatever the policy should have been, Clinton's way of making it didn't engender confidence.

Christopher and Vernon Jordan became increasingly concerned about the President's propensity for making public statements indicating strong action on Bosnia before he had a policy, and they talked to him about this. Clinton the neophyte in foreign policy hadn't understood the effects of a President talking about a policy that hadn't been decided on yet, much less never happened. One high official said later, "No question that it was a mistake for Clinton to huff and puff. It was a result of not enough understanding of the effects. There wasn't an acute enough sense at that point of the consequences of those kinds of statements." The President was also cautioned not to talk in advance about meetings where decisions were supposed to be made, as he had in the case of Bosnia, thus raising expectations. He was advised to simply announce a policy when it had been decided upon. Clinton made a partial adjustment.

A senior official who would know said, "I think Chris came back from his mission convinced the policy wasn't going anywhere and the question was how to extricate the U.S. from a highly exposed position." Christopher and Donilon became convinced that any serious U.S. involvement in Bosnia was politically unsustainable and could wreck Clinton's domestic efforts.

Christopher took a proprietary interest in Clinton's Presidency. He believed that his responsibility for helping Clinton succeed went beyond his role as Secretary of State.

In the weeks following his trip, Christopher moved methodically to shut down the Bosnia policy. He wanted to get the subject off the front pages. One way of doing this was to mask the retreat with a "containment" policy. Another was to have quiet talks with certain key people. Christopher invited Stephanopoulos to have dinner with him on May 13 at Citronelle, a trendy new Georgetown restaurant that Christopher, who liked to dine out, favored because it was California based. A few nights later, also at Christopher's invitation, Stan Greenberg had dinner with him at Galileo, Washington's top Italian restaurant. Greenberg said later, "Christopher was dead set against America getting embroiled in Bosnia. He thought it was a no-win situation." Greenberg continued, "He was clearly trying to alert the political advisers to the dangers. The main thing he was doing was making sure that others who were talking to the President were aware of the dangers." To Greenberg, Christopher related his view that the warring parties in Bosnia weren't looking for a peaceful solution and that putting the United States in the middle of it was dangerous to Clinton's Presidency.

Within the same period, Christopher had two unannounced one-on-one talks with the President. Christopher had been irritated by Gore's impassioned and often wordy advocacy in meetings on Bosnia; he felt that it was making it difficult for the President to move decisively to a policy of leaving Bosnia alone. He had complained to colleagues that he found Gore too "warlike." After one meeting, Christopher remarked of Gore, "He's going to get us into a war." One day, when Gore was going out of town, Christopher on very short notice arranged a meeting with the President to take place shortly after Gore had departed. Normally, Gore sat in on every foreign policy meeting the President had. Roy Neel, as Deputy Chief of Staff, found out about the meeting and got hold of Gore to ask if he could come back for it, and Gore, not at all happy, said that he couldn't. (Lake found out about the meeting afterward.)

An administration decision in late May to send three hundred American troops to Macedonia, where United Nations Protection Forces (UNPROFOR) from other countries were already serving, was a way of putting the emphasis on containment and of looking like the United States was doing something about the war in the Balkans. The politics of the moment superseded serious thought as to the implications of this move. (The administration had already told the European allies that it was willing to send about twenty thousand troops to police a peace agreement in Bosnia, but that possibility hadn't yet had a political airing in the United States.) On May 11, Clinton, in Chicago in an effort to get public attention refocused on his economic program, confirmed a *Wall Street Journal* report that the administration was considering sending the troops to Macedonia. Clinton, talking too much once again, said, "We have two objectives. The first is how to confine the conflict, the second is whether we can do anything to end it and to stop ethnic cleansing." In a Chicago diner, he said in answer to a patron's question about possible U.S. military action in Bosnia, "I think we can stop a lot of the terrible things without doing that." Aides scrambled to tidy this up, saying that the President meant that he wouldn't consider unilateral military action.

Then Christopher found a new way to try to shunt Bosnia to the sidelines. The Europeans were interested in the concept of "safe areas" for the Muslims inside Bosnia. On May 6, the UN adopted a resolution declaring six Muslim towns to be "safe areas" and calling for the "immediate cessation of armed attacks" and the withdrawal of Serb forces to a safe distance from these towns. This was to be one of several meaningless UN gestures about Bosnia. The French felt that they had been caught flat-footed by Christopher's mission and wanted a counterpolicy of their own, and so the "safe areas" were established. Lake didn't think much of it, because the UN wasn't proposing to do anything about the "safe areas."

Russian Foreign Minister Kozyrev, having been roused (by Christopher's trip) to get Russia involved in policy making about Bosnia, became seized with an idea, and, during the week of May 17, he called for a special meeting of the foreign ministers of the Security Council. He was pushing for the provision of actual international protection for the six Muslim "safe areas." The French backed this idea as well, and also said that the United States should commit ground troops to the venture. Clinton, asked about this during a photo op, said that he wouldn't send U.S. troops into a "shooting gallery."

On May 18, Christopher, in congressional hearings, described the Bosnia issue as "a problem from hell," a "morass" of ancient hatreds among the Muslims, Serbs, and Croats, with "atrocities on all sides." He said, "At heart, this is a European problem."

The President's and Christopher's comments were deliberately skeptical of any ambitious proposal to protect the "safe areas."

The last thing Christopher wanted was an unplanned UN meeting, and so he hijacked Kozyrev's meeting by inviting the foreign ministers of France, Great Britain, and Spain, as well as Kozyrev, to a meeting in Washington. And on Monday, May 17, as he dined with Donilon at Citronelle, Christopher listed on a yellow pad what points these countries seemed to agree on that the American public would approve. The aim was to find a way to sideline Bosnia and allow Clinton to do what he should—focus on the domestic agenda. The Europeans as well were looking for something that they and the Americans could agree on. Long, private negotiations with the French preceded the meeting—the President's and Christopher's skeptical comments were in part aimed at these negotiations—and after a long meeting at the State Department on Saturday, May 22, a bizarre ceremony took place. Flags behind them, the five foreign ministers solemnly signed a document committing their countries to a policy of protecting the six Muslim "safe areas" within Bosnia, by force if necessary (the United States committed only to contribute air support to UNPROFOR troops providing this protection). This "Joint Action Plan" was a minimalist approach—another form of containment—designed to smooth things over among the Western allies and to co-opt Kozyrev. The press interpretation of the Joint Action Plan—encouraged by the elaborate tableau at the State Department—was that this was now *the* Bosnian policy, and many of the reports were appropriately skeptical. (The plan was essentially adopted by NATO in June.)

The plan, in effect, sanctioned Serb aggression in Bosnia and offered the unpleasant possibility of six permanent Muslim camps. Lake thought that the plan had the potential of garrisoning these towns for the Serbs. He understood the need to get agreement on *something,* and though he thought the plan was nonsense, or worse, he went along because he couldn't see any realistic alternatives at that point. He didn't believe that containment would work unless the United States established credibility for what it was trying to do in Bosnia. It still had none.

Christopher saw the Joint Action Plan and the decision to send troops to Macedonia as substitutes for "lift and strike" and as initiatives that could make the Bosnia issue go away—or at least appear to. And for a while Christopher succeeded in doing that—and came under considerable criticism, in the United States and elsewhere, for the failure of the administration to do more. Christopher thought he had done what was in the President's interests.

Lake disagreed that Bosnia should, or could, be made to go away. It will be back, he warned.

11

HOUSE CALLS

"I'll Be Out There with You"

In order to get a break from the bad news of April, Clinton and his advisers had decided that he should go on the road one or two days a week. They wanted to get the press out of the White House for a while and focused on something other than Clinton's troubles.

Clinton's speeches on the road had a defensive air and no coherent theme. In Cleveland, in early May, setting up a straw man, he said, "I've been criticized for doing more than one thing at once," and then went through the list of proposals he had made, thus giving evidence that he had taken on a very large load. In California, he talked about his "investments" and why spending on them was important, but the substance wasn't conveyed in the news accounts. At a San Diego town meeting, he had a moving exchange with a gang member, who told him in halting English that a lot of gang members wanted jobs and a chance to pursue a different life. Clinton understood what the youth was saying and replied that he wanted to provide not just jobs but also education and training, because people would have to change jobs several times—a major theme of his.

In California, key to his electoral future, Clinton tried hard to reassure defense workers that he was trying to make things better for them. "I work for you," he said. He talked about his program for pushing development of high tech, but that would take time to pay off and would be of little help to the workers he was addressing. (At various stops, Clinton talked about his defense conversion proposal, which was to develop commercial applications of defense technologies, encourage retraining programs, and assist communities that had been dependent on defense contracts in developing diversification plans.) In the San Diego town meeting, he showed off his specific knowledge (having been briefed) of such things as a bridge-building program there and sewage problems in Tijuana. He came off as the Answer Man. He toured the streets of South-Central Los Angeles, visiting a sporting goods store that had been rebuilt since the riots of 1992, and shot baskets with some local kids. For many months, Clinton would complain privately that the main thing that was featured in the media, of his tour of South-Central Los Angeles, was his shooting baskets—but his aides must have known that this was what would be shown on television.

By mid-May, the White House staff had geared itself up for the fight over the reconciliation bill, the key piece of budget legislation, which dictated the changes in taxes and spending so as to reconcile them with the deficit-cutting goals set in the budget resolution. The administration got its reconciliation bill out of the House Ways and Means Committee after making numerous concessions on the Btu tax—to the oil industry, the aluminum industry, the chemical industry, on ethanol, and on energy used in agriculture—by a straight party-line vote. The Btu tax proposal was now a maze of complications. As of the capitulation on grazing and mining, the word was out on Capitol Hill that it wasn't hard to get concessions from the President. The White House was aware of the problem. A Presidential adviser said, "We can't cave anymore." A senior official said, as the Ways and Means Committee approved the bill and the White House was celebrating, "We were not astute enough about positioning the President over and above the details, instead of having him get all beat up about all the compromising and the 'caving.' " This aide argued that, somehow, Clinton should have been more like Reagan.

Many changes were made in Reagan's economic program, but people didn't think of him as "caving." Reagan knew how to look like what people thought a President should look like, conduct himself as people thought a President should (he deliberately threw back his shoulders before going onstage). Reagan's definiteness, even if it was wrongheaded, gave him a stature that Clinton's indefiniteness denied him.

The deficit reduction in the bill approved by the Ways and Means Committee on May 13 was significant—especially considering the political buffeting it had taken—and the administration's victory was a real one. The Btu tax was to raise $72 billion. The administration had agreed to drop its investment tax credit, which, it turned out, business, in particular high tech, didn't want as badly as the Clinton people had thought. (Support of the administration by the high-tech world was evanescing.) The bill also reduced the proposed increase in corporate taxes. Yet despite the compromises already made, the Btu tax was in trouble. Dan Rostenkowski, the Ways and Means Committee chairman, said, "I think that the administration, never having written a tax bill, doesn't realize that you have to get supporters out there."

Meanwhile, the President was upset that the Congress was cutting back his "investments." He complained that his staff hadn't adequately explained to him the extent to which the "caps" on domestic appropriations limited new spending. Members of the Appropriations Committees customarily sought to protect existing programs. But aides said he had been told—clearly—on at least two occasions. Leon Panetta, the OMB director, had plainly told him. The political advisers, always looking for ways to lay blame on the economic advisers, said that the problem hadn't been emphasized enough to the President. Clinton complained in one meeting, "Maybe there's nothing we can do, but I sure would feel better about this if we really had understood how difficult the caps were, that we would have had a strategy to get deficit reduction and investment and meet the caps."

While the President was fighting for his economic program, he was also trying to get his national service program and his empowerment zone program and a number of other things through Congress. Bentsen was so troubled by the overload that in mid-May he told Clinton in a private meeting in the Oval Office, "You have too many issues out there, and the public is losing focus on what you're trying to do." Clinton replied, "But I've made these promises." Bentsen said, "Yes, but you have four years." But nothing much changed.

On May 18, four days after the Ways and Means Committee approved the reconciliation bill, John Breaux of Louisiana, often an ally of the President (Breaux was a charter member of the DLC), said, "In its present form the [reconciliation] bill does not have the votes to pass the Senate." Between forty and fifty conservative House Democrats were pushing for caps on entitlement programs—which would have resulted in cuts in all entitlements, including Medicaid, Social Security, and agricultural subsidies—to replace the Btu tax. Clinton went to Capitol Hill a few hours after his return from California on May 19 to try to salvage his original proposal. In a meeting with worried-looking Democratic leaders, Clinton said that if the Congress voted the entitlement cuts, it would mean "across-the-board cuts on very vulnerable people." He argued that savings in such programs as Medicare and Medicaid should be left for his forthcoming health care program.

But the President's economic program was now under fire from all sides.

Ross Perot was also on Capitol Hill, saying that the Clinton plan was the old "tax and spend, and that's not what the American people want." Liberals were suspicious that Clinton might deal too much with the right, and resentful that the new stimulus program was so small (a $900 million program for jobs). But Clinton's real problems with the reconciliation bill were related to both the Btu tax itself and, more important, the way he had governed. Numerous Democratic House members didn't trust him to stay with the controversial tax after the House had voted for it. House members had, after all, voted for the stimulus package only to see it die in the Senate.

At that point, no one was sure that there would be enough Senate votes to pass the reconciliation bill. And there was little incentive for members to declare their support early, before they had seen what prize they could exact from the President. If a President is seen as an easy target—if there is no fear of him—his job in getting legislation passed will be all the more difficult, and expensive. There was no fear of Clinton on Capitol Hill. In a meeting with the House Democratic Caucus, Clinton assured the members that he wouldn't abandon them if they voted for a Btu tax. Clinton told Charlie Wilson, a ten-term Democrat from Texas, "If you're out there on a limb, I'll be out there with you." The House Democrats left the meeting feeling that they had been assured by the President that if they voted for the Btu tax he wouldn't make a deal with the Senate that undermined them. "I'm not going to leave you out there alone," Clinton said.

On the issue of lowering the deficit, Clinton was on Republican territory —even if Republicans hadn't done much about it. (Stan Greenberg said in late May, "He lost control of the message.") They kept up a drumbeat of opposition to the President's program, charging it was "tax-and-spend," and they got across the point that it raised taxes on the middle class. From time to time, Clinton made the affirmative case for increased government action in certain areas, but in the cacophony, the nation didn't hear it. Clinton saw himself as a descendant of FDR, but he not only lacked a perceived emergency but was up against deep skepticism, even cynicism, about government. That may have been his most effective foe. He was the first activist President in the age of cynicism.

On May 20, Senator David Boren, of Oklahoma, and three other senators —Bennett Johnston, of Louisiana, and Republicans John Danforth, of Missouri, and William Cohen, of Maine—announced an alternative proposal, which, among other things, dropped the Btu tax. To make up the money, Social Security and other pensions were cut, as was the Earned Income Tax Credit for the working poor. It was a regressive proposal that was easy for the President to argue against, but it was a huge blow to his program.

Without Boren's support on the Senate Finance Committee, where the Democrats had only a two-vote margin, the President's program wouldn't be reported out for action on the Senate floor.

Boren's proposal made it more difficult for House members from oil-producing states to vote for the Btu tax, and now House members had all the more reason to suspect that the Senate wouldn't approve it. Johnston's saying at the press conference where the proposal was announced that the Btu tax was "dead" was also very damaging.

So, suddenly, just before the House vote on May 27, the White House changed its strategy. Convinced it wouldn't otherwise get enough votes, the administration started telling oil state representatives that they could vote for the Btu tax in the House because it *would* be changed in the Senate. Thus they stood on its head the members' argument that they wouldn't vote for it because it might be substantially changed in the Senate.

At three o'clock on the day of the House vote, McLarty went into the Oval Office and was told by Stephanopoulos, "Mack, I just don't think we have the votes." So McLarty called Breaux, a friend from his Arkla days, and they agreed that they would tell House members the Btu tax would be changed in the Senate.

In an interview later, McLarty said, "I talked with Breaux. I said we're not going to be able to be specific about what we can do in the Senate, just that it'll be changed. Anybody could see there were going to be changes in the Senate." In fact, by then Breaux had been publicly championing a transportation tax—a seven-cents-a-gallon gasoline tax on all vehicles—as a substitute for the Btu tax.

On the night of the debate, Charles Stenholm, a conservative from Texas who headed the Conservative Democratic Forum, said that his vote for the bill "is predicated on the belief that improvements in the Btu tax will be forthcoming as the bill proceeds through the Senate."

The President and his advisers had bet on the support of a coalition that didn't exist. They had assumed that a substantial portion of Perot supporters could be brought around to the view that deficit reduction combined with "investments" and slowing the rate of growth of government were all a good thing. But one study said that the 19 percent of those who had voted for Perot wanted above all else deficit reduction and smaller government. In the days leading up to the vote, Clinton held a number of meetings at the White House, with House committee chairmen, with the House whips, and others. A congressman said afterward that the President seemed "distracted" and added, "He had been outmessaged by the Republicans. The country didn't understand how significant this deficit reduction was. Toward the end of the meeting there was finally some color in his cheeks and gestures, but until the very end we could have been talking about the price of Hondas rather than the survival of his Presidency."

On the day of the vote, Clinton held a town meeting at the White House, televised on *CBS This Morning.* A key House Democrat said later, "I don't believe the town meeting was a useful device. When you have those town meetings, a hundred subjects come up and there is no message." In the course of the town meeting, Clinton answered a question on gays in the military, an account of which was on the front page of many papers the next day. Congressional Democrats were appalled.

Clinton also provided further running commentary on his Presidency, saying on CBS that he understood that some of his problems were caused by an inability "to keep the public focus on the issues that we are working on."

At 1:30 A.M. on the night before the vote, exhausted House leaders, with Majority Leader Gephardt playing the key role, reached an important compromise with Stenholm on a cap on spending for entitlements. Without that, the President might well have lost the vote. The compromise gave the conservative Democrats a second cover for voting for the bill with the Btu tax in it (the first was being able to say that the tax would be substantially changed in the Senate). Some members of Congress can't get enough covers. But reaching the compromise wasn't easy: while the leadership was dealing with the conservative Stenholm group, liberals were demanding that the compromise not go too far. The Black Caucus, with forty-eight members, which had unanimously supported the bill, now threatened to vote against it if caps were put on entitlements (even though the bill contained a new program specifically intended by Clinton to win votes in the Black Caucus).

Everyone understood that the stakes were extremely high. If Clinton lost, he would be seen as powerless, treated as powerless, and therefore would be powerless. Losing the stimulus bill, a minor matter compared to this, had done him great harm. The President and the congressional Democrats had to show that they could govern. Their fates were intertwined: it was widely assumed that both would suffer at the polls if they couldn't function effectively. Therefore, the President, the Democratic leadership, and the committee chairmen threw their all into the fight. The President, the Vice President, Cabinet officers, and even some deputy Cabinet officers made call after call. It was not unusual for an "undecided" member to hear from four or five administration officials.

Clinton was a neophyte at making the phone calls to get votes. His conversations with House members tended to be discursive. He would discuss policy in great detail. Only after urging on the part of some of his aides did he understand how to ask for votes. An aide said after the vote, "Bill Clinton enjoys debating the merits of the policy. He could go into great detail about how the bill would affect cotton farmers. When you have leisure, this is a very useful thing, and members of Congress love it. As the week went on, he got to, 'Hello, this is Bill Clinton. I need your vote. This is important to me personally. Can I count on you?' "

A leading House Democrat said, "Freshmen members would say, 'I had the nicest talk with the President. We talked for a half hour. He said he understood my problem.' Question: 'Did you tell him you'd give him your vote?' Answer: 'No.' There were a lot of stories like that." Finally, this Democrat called the White House and said, "Tell him he has to *ask* for their vote." He continued, "Members have many ways to weasel. 'Mr. President, I'd like to be with you.' 'Mr. President, I really hope I can be with you.' We told the White House, *'Get their commitment.'* Then when someone from the White House called us to say they had someone's vote, we'd call to get confirmation. We try to get it four or five times."

Members who wanted protection for voting for the Btu tax were told by White House officials to fax a letter for the White House to type up and the President to sign. According to a White House aide, the letters said, in effect, "Dear [blank]. You have been a great fighter for [state]. I understand that you are concerned about the effect of the energy tax on [industry]. If you don't like the final version, I understand you reserve the right to vote against it."

But the administration had still more to offer waverers: members with personnel matters hung up in the White House were promised action; appearances by high-level officials at fund-raisers were committed; one member was promised improvements on the military base in his district. Ted Strickland, a Democrat who represented Chillicothe, Ohio, managed to prevent the moving of a spent waste facility even though the uranium plant in the area was being closed down. (After the vote, twenty wheat state representatives extracted from the administration a pledge of more government help in exporting wheat.) Cabinet members made their own promises.

On the day after the vote, Paster said, "We were careful not to have the President making offers. He didn't consummate transactions. We would tell them, 'The President is going to call you and ask for your support, and if you say yes to him we'll take care of what you want.' Some members just asked for the President to call." (By later in the year, the President was doing his own trading.) Gore made a great many calls, sometimes reminding members that he had campaigned for them. Gore and Clinton took a list and worked from opposite ends. Then Clinton called people Gore had called and vice versa. Paster said, "Gore had eight years in the House, eight years in the Senate, and ran for the Presidency or Vice Presidency in 1988 and 1992. He knows the moves."

On Thursday evening, May 27, at 8:44 P.M., the House gave Clinton a narrow victory, voting 219–213 to pass the reconciliation bill. No Republicans voted for it, and thirty-eight Democrats voted against it. The administration had in reserve another nine Democrats, who said that they would vote "yes" if their votes were needed. What saved the President in the end was the fact that enough Democrats didn't want him to lose the vote—for their sake as well as his—and that there was no acceptable alternative.

The President, the Vice President, and McLarty watched the vote in the President's private dining room. Shortly after the vote, Clinton appeared in the Rose Garden, with Bentsen and Gore standing behind him (Gore was always in these pictures, which was unusual for a Vice President) and McLarty close enough to be included in the picture (even more unusual for a Chief of Staff). Clinton called the vote "a victory for growth over gridlock." Despite the difficulties, Clinton had a right to be pleased. But the difficulties were far from over.

On Friday afternoon, Paster, in his second-floor office in the West Wing, received an unwelcome call. Roger Altman, the Deputy Secretary of the Treasury, phoned to tell him that Boren had said a Btu tax in any form was unacceptable. House leaders had told key senators that the House wouldn't accept simply a gasoline tax, that it would insist on a broad-based energy tax. Paster replied to Altman's news, "But we have to call it Btu for the House, so we should try to get a blend."

Then a call came from Eric Fingerhut, a freshman Democrat from Ohio, who had exacted from Paster a pledge that if he voted for the bill, a senior economic official would go to his district, just outside Cleveland, and explain how important and well founded the President's program was. Fingerhut wanted Treasury Secretary Bentsen to make the trip, and right away. Paster explained that Bentsen would be out of the country the next week, and that he had succeeded in getting Laura Tyson, the chairman of the Council of Economic Advisers, to go to Ohio. But Tyson, a distinguished economist and an important member of the administration, wasn't enough for Fingerhut. He still wanted Bentsen. So Paster arranged that both Tyson and Bentsen would go to Fingerhut's district.

At this point in his Presidency, Clinton's standing was so low that although, according to the *Wall Street Journal,* he got more of his economic program from the House than Reagan had in his "fabled" budget victory in 1981, much of the press coverage begrudged him his victory and focused on the slimness of his margin.

On the Friday afternoon after his victory, Clinton addressed a rally in Philadelphia. His delivery was strong and upbeat. "There were a lot of people who said we could never change the way things happen in Washington. . . . This national capital of yours is beginning to change." He went on, largely talking themes. It was as if he'd found his voice and his themes again.

A little more than a week later, in the late afternoon of Monday, June 7, after the Memorial Day recess, George Mitchell, and Daniel Patrick Moynihan, of New York and the chairman of the Senate Finance Committee, brought the White House some blunt news. In an Oval Office meeting, they told Clinton that without Boren's support, the reconciliation bill wouldn't be passed by the Senate—that there was no way the Senate would approve a bill with the Btu tax in it. The next day, McLarty was in intense discussions with Breaux and Boren.

Also, the next day, Dee Dee Myers, Clinton's press secretary, said that the President sought a "broad-based energy tax." This was the official signal that the President was preparing to abandon the Btu tax. Clinton, when asked, during a photo op, if the Btu tax was dead, said he didn't want to "get into the name game." That evening, when Bentsen was asked on *The MacNeil/Lehrer Newshour* if the Btu tax was dead, he replied, "As a Btu tax, I don't think you're going to see that."

This comment set off an explosion on Capitol Hill, especially in the House, the following day. Some energy state members who had voted for the reconciliation bill howled that they had been betrayed. Many of them had just come back from their districts, and had been given a hard time by their constituents for voting for the Btu tax. Some of the protests may have been for home consumption. But those who signed on to the Btu tax before the concessions and the switch in policy were furious.

Some liberals were angry again because they had gone along with the Btu tax as a way of paying for social programs. Charles Rangel, of New York, said, "One of the things that we got assurances from the President on is that he would not leave us out on a limb with a Btu tax if those of us who had major problems with it supported it." Other liberals were upset because the President had portrayed the tax as benefiting the environment. Oil state representatives who voted for the bill with the understanding that there would be changes in the Senate hadn't anticipated that the President would drop the tax altogether. Mike Andrews, a four-term representative from Houston, said, "Had we known that they literally were going to throw out the Btu tax, we would have acted accordingly and fought the Btu." David Skaggs, a four-term congressman from Colorado, said privately, "There's a lot of anger up here. There were comments about various anatomical parts."

At lunch in the House dining room, a youngish Democratic congressman said, "I don't know if the President can get anyone to go out on a limb again."

Even some White House aides were upset. One asked privately, "Why didn't we let *them* [senators] make the change?" Well-placed White House aides said that Bentsen's statement on *MacNeil/Lehrer* had been a mistake. The "mistake" was that Bentsen had made it appear that the administration was dropping the Btu, while the White House had wanted the death to be seen as having come at the hands of the Senate. Later that week, Paster said, "What Bentsen was saying was that we don't have the votes for the Btu tax. He could have put it better." To try to calm things down, Clinton made some calls, Panetta went to the Hill to see a group of House Democrats, and Mitchell and Moynihan met with some House Democratic freshmen. Paster said, "We had to convince them that we weren't backing away, we were simply accepting the reality of where the votes aren't. A lot of the House members' anger was tied to the issue of whether we did it or the Senate did it. I think we persuaded them that the Senate did it, that the votes aren't there."

Clinton was caught in a fight between the moderate-conservative and the liberal wings of his party—a fight within his coalition that was to go on for much of the rest of the year. Some House members, of course, were making a fuss in order to gain leverage. Some of the House Democrats' anger was caused by the institutional hatred of many House members for the Senate. House members had long felt, not without reason, that senators looked down on them. The House was traditionally more rowdy and usually more liberal than the Senate. On top of that, the Senate's killing the stimulus bill, which House members had passed with misgivings, still rankled. In giving in to the Senate on an issue—the Btu—that so many House members had voted for reluctantly, Clinton touched a raw nerve.

So, through ineptitude, the administration brought on itself a crisis it surely didn't need, and gathered more mistrust.

12

MAY TROUBLES

"Everybody Has to Get His Hair Cut"

Late in the afternoon on Tuesday, May 18, as the huge blue-and-white Boeing 747 that had been converted into Air Force One sat on the tarmac at Los Angeles International Airport, Bill Clinton, at the end of his trip to California, got a haircut. The cut, by Christophe of Beverly Hills, whose usual charge was two hundred dollars, took about forty-five minutes. The press on the President's plane, and on the backup press plane, waited. Despite the White House's subsequent strenuous denials that the President's trim had delayed other planes, the evidence, based on Federal Aviation Administration information, was that other planes were delayed as two of LAX's four runways were shut down for over an hour. (The normal security delay for a Presidential arrival or departure is about twenty minutes.)

The next day, White House Press Secretary Dee Dee Myers announced that seven longtime workers in the White House travel office, which made arrangements for the press to accompany the President on trips, had been fired because of "financial mismanagement" and "shoddy accounting procedures." She further announced that the office would now be headed by Catherine Cornelius, a twenty-five-year-old cousin of Clinton's from Little Rock, who had coordinated travel in the Clinton campaign. Further, Myers announced, for the time being travel arrangements would be handled by World Wide Travel Inc., a Little Rock agency that had handled such arrangements for the Clinton campaign. World Wide Travel had been a client of David Watkins, formerly a public relations man in Little Rock and now assistant to the President for management and administration. Watkins had also been a business partner of Hillary Clinton's, making some joint investments—for instance, in cellular phone systems.

Under questioning, Myers said that though Cornelius was related to Clinton, the move didn't constitute nepotism because she was "a distant cousin." In answer to an inquiry after her briefing, Myers also disclosed that the FBI was investigating the travel office. (A White House report later said this disclosure was "unwise" and a result of internal miscommunication.) The head of the travel office, Billy Dale, and one of his associates had worked there for thirty years. All seven workers had been summarily fired without a hearing. Among the practices the group was charged with were using lax accounting procedures; writing eighteen thousand dollars' worth of checks to cash, without any record; and not asking for competitive bidding for charters to carry the press.

Thus two ill-considered actions set off an uproar that engulfed the White House for days. In retrospect, the uproar was out of proportion to the incidents, but it was touched off by several factors. The stories about the haircut and the travel office hit at a time when Clinton's political standing was very shaky and his and his staff's competence widely questioned. The two incidents were seen as signs of a group that didn't know what it was doing. And worst of all, because the White House didn't get out all the information at once, both stories, especially the travel office story, kept growing. And the increasing antipathy between the Clintons and the press, especially a large segment of the White House press corps, fueled the reaction. The White House press corps led a more difficult life than the glamour suggested. The working quarters were cramped and airless; network correspondents sat cheek by jowl in tiny booths. The briefing room, much smaller than it seemed on television, smelled of stale air, and was stuffed with menacing equipment. This situation, when coupled with diffidence, even outright dislike, on the part of the First Couple, made for a collective bad mood in the pressroom.

And Stephanopoulos's dealings with the press contributed to that mood. Many in the press corps liked Stephanopoulos. But as a close adviser to the President, one who attended all the important meetings, he didn't have time to hold special background sessions with or return the phone calls of a great many members of the press corps. And worse, he didn't seem to care. He appeared to reflect the Clintons' attitude. His formal briefings had begun early on to stir a noticeable tension. Some members of the press corps never forgave him for shutting off the hallway to his office. They didn't know that it wasn't his idea but the Clintons'. But Stephanopoulos seemed to have no problem with it. To much of the press, it reflected arrogance in this man whom many saw as too young, too hip, and, now, a national heartthrob to boot. To his friends—and to Stephanopoulos himself—this latter development was a surprise. He was a nice-looking man, but no movie star. Yet he had been touched by the glamour that the White House can bestow, and he took to his new prominence. A lot of the press corps had been looking to put him in his place. They had felt, with reason, that he knew a great deal more than he was telling them, and to many of them he seemed flip, a bit of a smart-ass. At the same time, some of the Clintons' friends were telling them that Stephanopoulos, with his unruly mop of brown hair, his youngish face, and his bantering with the press, was hurting the administration. Stephanopoulos had become the embodiment of "the kids," and suddenly the kids weren't so cute anymore. Maybe they were what was wrong with the Clinton White House.

On Thursday, a small item about the President's haircut appeared in the "Style" section of the *Washington Post.* From there, once it was learned that the runways had been shut down, the story fanned out to the tabloids and the television networks. (The May 21 *New York Post* blared "Bill's New $200 Do.") At his Thursday briefing, Stephanopoulos was besieged. His explanations of the haircut did no good. "If he had stayed back at the hotel it wouldn't have made any difference," Stephanopoulos lamely offered. What about a two-hundred-dollar haircut? "The President has to get his hair cut. Everybody has to get his hair cut." By Christophe of Beverly Hills? Laughter. Stephanopoulos's answer didn't help at all: "The President and the First Family have a personal service contract with Christophe." More laughter. Mrs. Clinton was known to have got yet another new hairdo by another tony hairdresser in New York the previous Saturday. The White House had announced that the President had gone to New York to have dinner with Madeleine Albright, the UN ambassador, but in fact the dinner had been laid on quite suddenly because Mrs. Clinton wanted to get her hair cut in New York and Chelsea wanted to go to the ballet, and Mrs. Clinton wasn't authorized to use a government plane for that purpose. The President, of course, could use the government plane. The Clintons seemed to be taking too well to the perks. That was puzzling for such smart people, and was even politically dangerous self-indulgence. Clinton had, after all, run as the champion of average Americans "who work hard and play by the rules." A one-name hairdresser was alien to this world. (The photographs of Christophe, with hair down to his shoulders and shirt unbuttoned to his waist, didn't help.) And by now there had been too much Hollywood at the White House. Even some people who felt positive toward the Clintons wondered if they had taken leave of their senses.

Stephanopoulos's ordeal was made worse by the revelation that Harry

Thomason had played a hand in the travel office firings. In his briefing on Thursday, May 20, Stephanopoulos said that Thomason's aviation consulting business didn't stand to gain business from the travel office. According to Stephanopoulos, this was what Thomason had told him.

The whole sorry business began among old friends and associates of the Clintons who had been involved in travel arrangements for the campaign and were looking ahead. During the transition, Watkins had discussed future possibilities with Cornelius and World Wide—both of whom wanted to continue their work in the Clinton White House.

Starting in late December, Cornelius peppered Watkins with a series of memos, in which she proposed that the career travel office employees at the White House be fired and replaced with Clinton people who would report to her, and that World Wide be hired. After she got to Washington, where she worked in Watkins's office, she said in a February 15 memo that the travel office had been shoddily run and was "overly pro-press." Also in February, Thomason and Darnell Martens, a partner of Thomason's in the aviation consulting business—Thomason and Martens's company, TRM, had earned a commission for arranging air charters for the Clinton campaign—had inquired through Dee Dee Myers whether the White House charter business was open to competitive bidding. When, at Myers's suggestion, Martens later that month inquired of Billy Dale, the head of the travel office, about bidding for its business, he was turned away.

In April, Watkins had dispatched Cornelius, who worked for him and was bored and unhappy with her job, to the travel office, telling her to watch how it was operated and report to him by mid-May. In retrospect, this appeared to be a setup. On May 10, Thomason asked Watkins what was happening about the travel office, and then, at Thomason's suggestion, Martens faxed a memo to the White House complaining about his treatment by Dale and the way the travel office was being run.

After Martens was turned away by Dale, Thomason raised the question of the travel office with both the President and Mrs. Clinton. In April, he told Watkins he had heard rumors of corruption. According to White House staff members, after Thomason complained to Mrs. Clinton, she asked both McLarty and Vince Foster to look into the matter. On May 12, Watkins took the matter to Foster, who called in William Kennedy, his colleague in the counsel's office and his former law partner, and that afternoon Kennedy called the FBI. There were reports later that in subsequent conversations Kennedy pressed the FBI to get involved. (This would be a subject of dispute between Kennedy and the FBI, and a report later issued by the White House took Kennedy to task for some of his comments to the agency. Nussbaum issued a rule forbidding any further contact with the FBI without going through the Attorney General.) On May 13, Watkins asked the accounting firm Peat Marwick to do an audit of the travel office.

Though Mrs. Clinton's role wasn't known at the time of the controversy, she took a real interest in the matter. Thomason, who saw Mrs. Clinton fairly often, had standing as a longtime friend who had been helpful in the campaign and the inauguration. And he knew about the travel business.

At the time, Thomason had an office in the East Wing and a pass giving him entrée throughout the White House complex, and an open-ended role of trying to improve the staging of Presidential events. "Harry was more the instigator," a White House aide said afterward. "It was as if someone put a lever under the boulder and it started down the hill and hit the village at the bottom of the hill."

Thomason's urgings that something be done about the travel office were heard seriously by the First Lady. Mrs. Clinton was already suspicious of the permanent White House staff—the people who kept the place running from administration to administration. And she felt that Clinton's own White House staff hadn't been responsive enough about uncorroborated rumors of temperamental behavior on her part, printed in *Newsweek,* that were said to have originated with the Secret Service. She also thought that the Clinton group had left holdovers in too many jobs. (Later Mrs. Clinton fired a White House usher, which was usually a career job, because of her suspicions of him.)

The first public indication of Mrs. Clinton's role in the travel office affair was a May 17 memo from Watkins to McLarty, with a copy to her, that was published in a White House report on the matter issued in early July. (Copies of the memo were in about a half-dozen files, so it had to be published.) The memo itself was misleading: it suggested, incorrectly, that the inquiry into the travel office had begun "as part of the National Performance Review" (the "reinventing government," or REGO project, being undertaken by Vice President Gore). Mrs. Clinton told people looking into the matter later that she had no recollection of specific conversations in the period leading up to the firings. She was angry that a report on the travel office affair was being prepared at all and considered it too tough on various people's actions. One White House aide said, "She felt it went way too far." Members of her staff, who were presumed to be reflecting her opinion, expressed the view strongly that the travel office incident should be dismissed out of hand. Mrs. Clinton argued that there was no reason to apologize for the dismissal of the travel office people. The President felt this way at first, but in an attempt to calm things down, on May 25 he asked McLarty to look into the matter.

This was not the first, and it was far from the last, collision between the

Clintons—especially Mrs. Clinton—and the Washington culture. In Mrs. Clinton's view, the correct thing had been done, and there should be no apologies. Her husband was often bothered by Washington, but he didn't resist it as fiercely. In Washington, overreaction, loss of perspective, invasion of privacy (or what the Clintons considered privacy), were all realities and had intensified over the past couple of decades. This wasn't altogether a good development, but there it was. Worldly as the Clintons had seemed, or thought they were, they had a hard time adjusting to this.

However valid the criticisms of the travel office were, the matter couldn't have been handled worse. The picture that was drawn was of cronyism and looseness with the truth. It apparently didn't occur to anyone that hiring the Little Rock company and putting the cousin—distant or not—in charge wouldn't look particularly good. McLarty said later that he had approved the firings and had known about the hiring of the hometown travel agency but not about the cousin.

There was a systemic failure within the White House. The matter of the travel office had been dealt with haphazardly. It wasn't brought up in a senior staff meeting. On Monday, May 17, Watkins sent McLarty the memorandum (the one that also went to the First Lady) stating that he was going to "terminate" the travel office staff the next day, hire World Wide Travel on a temporary basis, and put Catherine Cornelius in charge. Later that day, McLarty went to see Watkins in his office in the White House basement; Watkins explained his plans, and McLarty concurred. That was it: no meeting, no aeration of the plan, no consideration of how it might go over in the press. McLarty and Watkins, after all, had known each other for a long time. Like the President and McLarty—and like Vince Foster as well—Watkins was from Hope, Arkansas, a tiny town of about eight thousand. There were, in fact, three Hope High School student body presidents in the Clinton White House: Watkins, McLarty, and Foster. So at the core of the Clinton White House was a group of people who had known each other for a long time and saw little reason to question each other's judgment.

No one anticipated the reaction. The travel office had done a great many favors for members of the press, facilitating their travel, making it as pleasant as possible, and helping reporters get around customs officers. After the uproar began, no one at the White House seemed to know how to step in, gather the relevant facts and get them out to the press, and put a quick end to the matter. Instead the story went on for days, each day bringing new revelations.

On Friday, May 21, at a much delayed late-afternoon briefing, Stephanopoulos, who had been closeted in meetings all day, announced that World Wide had been dropped. He also released the Peat Marwick study, which criticized the travel office for mismanagement. And he released a statement by the FBI saying that there was "sufficient information for the FBI to determine that additional criminal investigation is warranted." Stephanopoulos spent almost an hour defending the White House's actions. That night, looking white and shaken, he appeared on *Nightline* to defend the administration.

Nothing seemed to go right. On Saturday, on a Presidential trip to New Hampshire, the fuel line on the press plane broke, causing a two-hour delay. The flight, on Midwest Air, had been arranged by a New Mexico firm, Air Advantage, through Peggy Sample, a volunteer in the travel office who also happened to be the owner of Air Advantage. The travel office report said she was a "close associate" of Martens, Thomason's partner, who had recommended her for the job. According to the *Washington Post,* her firm had "arranged $9 million worth of campaign flights" through a subcontract from Thomason and Martens's firm. Air Advantage received a $1,400 commission for the New Hampshire flight. Upon the *Post*'s disclosure of the fee, Stephanopoulos termed it "a mistake," and it was returned. The maze of cozy dealing seemed to have no end. (Subsequently, American Express won the business in a competitive bid.) The series of events distracted the President and his staff and made the administration look foolish, undermining the President's serious purposes.

In New Hampshire, a member of Clinton's traveling staff asked an anchorwoman to apply Clinton's makeup. The incensed anchorwoman complained on the air.

At one of the President's New Hampshire appearances, someone held up a sign that said, "Nice haircut, Bubba."

Over the next few days, it unfolded that during the previous Friday afternoon, Stephanopoulos and others had met in his office with an FBI agent and asked him to strengthen the statement that was released to the press a little later. This and the earlier use of the FBI, calling on it to investigate the travel office, set off another round of criticism of the White House—and was to lead to serious troubles, even tragedy. It turned out that three representatives of the counsel's office—Nussbaum, Foster, and Kennedy—had been present at that meeting in Stephanopoulos's office and had raised no objection. Nussbaum said later that Stephanopoulos had simply called the meeting to get a chronology of events, and that "We didn't know that anybody from the FBI was coming to the meeting. [John] Collingwood, the FBI man, a public information person, not an investigator, walks in after the meeting started. George didn't ask him to correct the statement, he asked him to update the statement, 'Is it correct to say this?' " Nussbaum said the change "made the statement more precise."

Nussbaum continued, "Since everything is so sensitive now, would it be better not to call the FBI to the White House? Yes. That's why I put out a rule that there could be no contact with the bureau with respect to any matter, even a White House secretary losing her purse, without going through the Attorney General's office." While the travel office crisis was still going on, Reno let it be known publicly that she had called Nussbaum to protest the White House's going to the FBI without informing her.

On Tuesday, one day short of a week after the travel office people were fired, Stephanopoulos announced that five of the seven had been unfired and instead placed on leave with pay (the other two had had authority for writing checks), while McLarty reviewed the events. The story was becoming slapstick. Stephanopoulos also said that he had made "an inadvertent mistake" in releasing the FBI statement.

A very upset White House aide said at the time, "There's no brain watching these things, catching them." Later another aide said, "There was the sheer inability of anyone to just say, '*Hold it.* What are we doing?' "

Bruce Lindsey came under some criticism by a number of White House aides and Clinton friends for having sat by while the President got his expensive coif. Lindsey later said privately that it hadn't occurred to him that the haircut would blow up, because there had been earlier stories about Christophe's cutting the Clintons' hair since the Democratic Convention. "Christophe gives good haircuts," Lindsey said. "What I didn't do, which I regret, was stand back and see it in any bigger context." He added that they had been told that they wouldn't hold up any planes.

On May 25, Clinton, trying to indicate that he didn't know much about the travel office events, told reporters, "I talked to Mr. McLarty about it this morning. I said, 'You know, I keep reading this.' I know there is a feeling, at least, based on what I've read, that someone in the White House may have done something that was inappropriate or that wasn't quite handled right or something." For some time to come, Clinton took pains to say that he hadn't had much to do with what he called "that travel office thing."

The President was furious with both his staff and with the press for making so much out of what seemed to him such small matters. He was angry that the stories about the haircut and the travel office were overtaking stories about the progress of his economic program. He told a group of CEOs at a lunch on Wednesday, June 2—he lunched with a group of business executives every Wednesday—that he felt like a "punching bag." An aide described the President at this time as "frustrated, angry, disappointed." The aide continued, "He's pissed off because he asked and was told that no planes were being held."

Clinton had a seemingly unshakable tendency to walk away from responsibility for things that had gone wrong: Waco, the travel office, LAX. And, worse, to put these things in self-pitying terms: that people didn't understand him (how could they think that someone with his background would get an expensive haircut and hold up planes; how could they think he was ducking on Waco?) or that others did bad things to him (the Republicans brought up gays in the military). He threw out a blitz of excuses. Inevitably, in the back of many Americans' minds was Clinton's famous "I didn't inhale" when, during the Presidential campaign, he was cornered on his previous evasions on whether he'd ever smoked marijuana; or his dissembling about his draft record.

One of Clinton's complexities was that, on occasion, he would say, "We made a mistake." But often even then, in his view, the mistake wasn't a result of his own actions but was an outgrowth of misreading the Washington culture or of not understanding how others would misread his perfectly well intentioned actions. Other times, Clinton would say, "We made a mistake," and mean just that.

Clinton remained especially upset about the haircut episode for the rest of the year. At least, in the case of the travel office, he argued, something real had happened. In the case of the haircut, he was obsessed with trying to get across that he hadn't done anything wrong, that the whole thing was a made-up incident by people who didn't understand him—especially the press. He knew, he told people, how it looked for a President to get a haircut in a plane on a runway; then he'd go into a long explanation of how it happened to come about that way. He would emphasize that he had asked twice if other planes would be held up. (The White House managed to convince one newspaper that there had been no delays.)

Some of the President's friends concluded that this episode simply proved that one reason the President had Lindsey around when he traveled was that Lindsey wouldn't say no to him. To one friend, it didn't matter that there had been earlier stories about Christophe and the Clintons. "Now you had all this Hollywood stuff," the friend said. (Maureen Dowd, of the *New York Times,* reported in late May that Clinton had "raised eyebrows" when he ended up sitting next to Sharon Stone at a recent Democratic Party fundraiser in New York. According to Dowd, the seat next to the President had somehow turned up empty at one point, and Stone, who along with some other Hollywood figures had met Clinton at the Vancouver summit, was summoned to fill it.)

The report on the travel office, which was issued in the names of McLarty and Leon Panetta on the eve of the July 4 weekend, was critical of most of the people involved in the mess, McLarty included. In a briefing, McLarty said that Watkins, Cornelius, Kennedy, and Jeff Eller, the director of media affairs, had been reprimanded. (Eller was criticized for advocating things that were in the interest of Cornelius, with whom, the report said, he had a "personal relationship.") Thomason, the counsel's office, Myers, and Stephanopoulos were also criticized. (Watkins got in trouble in May 1994 for using government helicopters to "check out"—ostensibly for the President—a golf course in nearby Maryland and playing a round of golf there. The President accepted his "resignation" shortly after the story broke.)

The travel office report was drawn up by John Podesta, the staff secretary, and Panetta. It hadn't been issued without a fight. Nussbaum argued that the draft report was too hard on the counsel's office, and he and Foster felt that in particular it was too hard on Kennedy—and too reflective of the FBI's version of events. There was a sense among the Arkansans in the White House that they were being singled out. Podesta stood firm in the face of Mrs. Clinton's displeasure in its being issued at all, arguing—correctly—that only a tough-seeming report with reprimands would be credible, and Panetta backed him. The report was relatively tough, but it left some things, and some names, out. Some White House staff members remained bitter that no one who had brought on the mess had been fired.

In the midst of the uproar over the travel office, the indignant Thomasons, in Washington at the time, were giving interviews. This didn't help matters, but apparently no one at the White House was willing to, or could, get them to be quiet. Harry Thomason told Maureen Dowd that he and his wife, Linda Bloodworth-Thomason, were "fighting for the right to live in this country." Thomason argued that his interference in the travel office had been simply that of a whistle-blower who had seen mismanagement and tried to do something about it. On *Good Morning America,* Linda Bloodworth-Thomason said, "We make a six-figure salary weekly," and insisted that it would be "ludicrous" for her husband to say, " 'Ooh, I'm going to like take my six-figure salary a week and fly off to Washington and see if I can't get those seven little guys out of that travel office in the White House.' It's sort of the equivalent of taking over a lemonade stand."

Both Clintons were furious that the White House wasn't "on message." The President vented his anger in meetings with aides. Mrs. Clinton called some of her husband's aides, letting them know what she thought. The President recognized that in the case of the travel office episode he had paid a price for having an inexperienced staff who didn't anticipate how the press would react to the sudden firings. He was frustrated that his own people had been blindsided by the reaction. He was beginning to feel that his prior experience in Washington, as a governor working on national issues such as education and welfare, and all his Washington contacts and friendships, hadn't prepared him for governing there. He tried once to explain away why he hadn't brought to the White House more experienced people, saying that some of the people with Washington experience he had planned to bring into the White House, or even make his Chief of Staff, he had put in the Cabinet instead. But there was no evidence for this (except perhaps for brief consideration of Christopher as Chief of Staff).

In fact, the travel office and haircut episodes took a toll on the President. After sixty House members of medium seniority met with Clinton at the White House on Tuesday, May 25, one of them said, "There was a more than slightly disconcerted, almost down, feeling. It struck many of us that the President was really blown down by the last week, and at a meeting where we were expecting evangelism, the President seemed dispirited and had a very rambling and flat affect."

Late on the Sunday night of the weekend after the haircut and travel office stories blew up, Clinton called Vernon Jordan, and as he was wont to do with friends, he vented. He was upset about the press, his staff, the reception of his Presidency, and the potential impact of the recent controversies on the upcoming House vote on the reconciliation bill. He was concerned—still—about how to get the focus back on his program. Clinton asked Jordan if he and Christopher would come to the White House to see him on Tuesday evening. Jordan of course agreed.

Meanwhile, there was a great deal of swirling about on the part of the President's staff, the consultants, and his friends. White House aides were tense. Some of the meetings were with Clinton, some with Mrs. Clinton, some with both. Almost everyone agreed that some staff changes were needed. Greenberg said later, "The President was upset with both the communications and political operations."

There had been talk within the White House for some time about changing Stephanopoulos's role. For one thing, it was now more clear than ever that there was no way he could handle all the roles he'd been given. Even his close friends the consultants concluded that he wasn't doing a satisfactory job of running the communications staff. There was little long-range communications planning. Managing didn't really interest him. His true interest, and brilliance, lay in understanding the nexus between policy and politics: seeing the implications of taking various actions. By his own description, he was a tactician, not a strategist.

Stephanopoulos had mixed feelings about a change in his role. He was worried about going into some nether job, some undefined role in a structureless place. He had been considered once more as Deputy Chief of Staff, but according to someone who would have known, was blocked again by Susan Thomases. So the ongoing discussion, typically, remained ongoing. But the fractious briefings of the third week in May brought the matter to a head. The Clintons, and some others in and out of the White House, felt that the communications office was in disarray, that relations with the press were too sour, and that there was a widespread perception that the communications shop was too young and too arrogant. As early as late April, there had been rumblings within the White House that a more seasoned person was needed.

So while Stephanopoulos was still feeling torn about changing jobs, the decision was made for him. On Monday, May 24, Carville and Greenberg had breakfast with the Clintons, and then they saw Stephanopoulos and told him that they agreed that there should be a change. They put the whole thing in the most positive light possible, but Stephanopoulos was still concerned about where he would fit in.

On Tuesday evening, a warm late-spring night, Jordan and Christopher sat with Clinton on the Truman balcony, eating vanilla ice cream. They told him that he and his administration were in trouble. Clinton, at loose ends about what to do about his White House, was open to honest discussion of it and of his own mistakes. Jordan and Christopher (who had come from dinner at Citronelle) delivered a harsh analysis of the White House staff. Jordan told Clinton point-blank that he was trying to manage too much himself and should resign as his own Chief of Staff, and vest McLarty with more authority. But Clinton wasn't a delegator. He didn't delegate in his campaign until his wife forced the issue, and he hadn't given anyone in the White House real authority.

McLarty had been having conversations with David Gergen, an editor at large of *U.S. News & World Report* and a television commentator. Though Gergen had served in the Nixon, Ford, and Reagan White Houses, he wasn't particularly ideological. He was a centrist and a serious networker, part of the floating establishment that met at the Aspen Institute and Bildeberg international conferences of nabobs. He had come to know the Clintons through the Renaissance Weekends, and he and Clinton had stayed in touch. (Gergen later told a news conference that though he had worked in three

Republican White Houses, he considered himself an Independent and had voted for Clinton in 1992.)

McLarty had been discussing with the President who could replace Stephanopoulos in the communications job. He phoned Gergen on the night of Sunday, May 23, just after uproar week, and found that "he was receptive" to the idea of joining the White House staff. When McLarty reported this, Clinton told him to pursue it. "It was logical for communications to be under his definition," McLarty said later. This was to be the subject of a major misunderstanding. On Tuesday night—the same night that Jordan and Christopher met with the President—McLarty reached Gergen in Baton Rouge, where he was making a speech, and offered him a top White House job.

As McLarty and the Clintons saw it, Gergen would bring to the White House some seasoned judgment and would offer to the world a more mature visage. The addition of a prominent centrist would also help solve the "profile" problem. Mrs. Clinton was reputed, with reason, to be the true liberal of the First Couple, but she could be pragmatic when it came to her husband's interests. McLarty and Gergen discussed the job over a late, two-and-a-half-hour dinner at McLarty's house on Thursday night, after the reconciliation bill was passed by the House. Clinton called Gergen at McLarty's and said, "I'd rather you tell me directly what to do than read it in the magazine." Clinton and Gergen agreed to talk on Friday night, after Clinton returned from the rally in Philadelphia to celebrate his victory in the House on the reconciliation bill.

But Friday night, the arrangement was nearly derailed. In the early evening, before the President returned, Gergen called Gore—who enthusiastically backed bringing Gergen in—and told him that he didn't want the communications job, that it would be a "deal-buster." Gore told Gergen that they'd find another way to define his role.

Further, Gergen wanted to be satisfied on three scores: what was the philosophical direction the Clintons wanted to go in; were they enthusiastic about his coming to the White House, or was this all McLarty's idea; and would he be just another voice at the table. He insisted that he be made counselor and be allowed to sit in on meetings of the President, Mrs. Clinton, and McLarty. He won this point. Certain friends of the Clintons' felt that this concession shouldn't be made, but they recognized that Gergen was in a position to drive the bargain. As it turned out, there were few if any meetings of this sort.

McLarty—not the President—told Stephanopoulos of the pending job change on Thursday night.

On Friday, with the President still not back to the White House, Gergen met with Mrs. Clinton at about 10:30 P.M. He told her that many people on the outside thought her husband was a centrist and she was pulling him to the left, and that this was what was causing some of the zigzagging on policy. Mrs. Clinton replied that it was a complete misunderstanding; she had taken a centrist position many times in Arkansas and was very pragmatic. When the President returned, late that night, he and Gergen went over the same ground. Clinton told Gergen, "I'm way out of position, I'm way off to the left. I want to get back to the DLC."

At six-thirty on the Saturday morning of the Memorial Day weekend, Gore sat at the word processor in Mark Gearan's office and wrote out a statement for Clinton to make that morning. A leak on Friday afternoon that Gergen was coming to the White House forced an announcement. Members of the White House staff were shaken. The Clinton White House was often damaged by leaks that it should have anticipated and preempted.

Clinton's announcement was made in the Rose Garden at 7:30 A.M.—an odd time for an announcement, but things had got out of hand. His statement left ambiguous the question of whether Gergen would take charge of communications. McLarty said that the communications office would report to Gergen. The picture of Stephanopoulos standing there, his head bowed, as the President implied—despite his praise of Stephanopoulos—that he was firing him from his communications job, was painful. Clinton was graceless in the handling of one of his most loyal and talented aides. A large number of aides felt great loyalty toward Stephanopoulos and would long resent his public humiliation. It seemed that Clinton wanted the world to know that he was removing Stephanopoulos from his job. The aides' anger was compounded by background statements to the press from presumably older White House aides, who said that the change was aimed "at the idea that we need some adults here." The resentment spilled over into a grudge toward Gergen and a widespread feeling that Stephanopoulos was taking the fall for the mistakes of the elders. Nevertheless, a Clinton adviser said later, "He isn't taking the rap for things other people did; he is taking the rap for not communicating well about them."

Stephanopoulos's new role, as Clinton described it, was the right one for him. Clinton said that he "will work with me more closely, as he did in the campaign, on important matters of policy and strategy and day-to-day decision making." A Presidential adviser said later, "Someone had to be sacrificed. The pressure was building. Somebody had to be changed."

McLarty was in on the changes in order to shore up his own position as well as the President's. "Mack has never felt that he had all the help that he needed," a Clinton aide said. McLarty hadn't been able to select his own deputies, which rankled him more than he let on. Over time, McLarty built a small empire of his own within the White House, with nine assistants by the end of the year, including his own Chief of Staff and communications adviser.

McLarty's view of what was needed to steady the Clinton White House wasn't shared by the consultants, who wanted to emphasize Clinton's populism, get him more focused on the middle class. "Mack has a narrower feel," one of them said. "He's concerned with simpler left and right problems. It's an older way of looking at it: 'We've gone too far to the left.' But we've gone too far up, establishment, too elite." This person said that the Clintons wanted to be part of the elite: "He craves it. Susan Thomases reinforces it. She says, 'You need to be part of the elite.' He still doesn't get it—that it's a problem to meet with Sharon Stone in Vancouver."

The choosing of Gergen was about a lot of things. Vernon Jordan said later, "It was almost mandatory that they send a signal of substantive change. This was big substance. If you assume that personnel is policy, that it's directional to some extent, this was very important. It's also very much about process. There's nobody over there that's ever worked in the White House before." Jordan, a liberal, said, "My view was he needed help regardless of direction. With Gergen he's going straight up the middle, which from a practical point of view—it's not my position—that's how you govern."

But these changes didn't address other difficulties within the White House. Aides complained about a lack of "accountability" and an inability to get decisions made. "We have no ability to close around here," one aide said, echoing a widespread feeling. Another said, "Policy decisions aren't getting closed and don't necessarily hang together." Everyone understood that there would have to be further changes in the way the President conducted his job and the way his Chief of Staff conducted his.

By the end of May, Clinton's approval rating in some polling was at 36 percent, the lowest for any postwar President at that point. He had fallen further faster than any of his postwar predecessors. In a reflection of the zeitgeist, *Time*'s cover announced in bold letters, THE INCREDIBLE SHRINKING PRESIDENT, with a very small photograph of Clinton beneath, and *Newsweek*'s blared, "What's Wrong?" with a picture of a worried-looking Clinton.

13

HILLARY CLINTON AND HEALTH CARE

"One of the Strangest Things I've Ever Been Involved In"

The hundred days mark, by which time Clinton had promised to have a health care plan ready, came and went.

Writing such a plan was proving far more complicated than the Clintons had thought. They themselves were distracted by other things. Ira Magaziner, a businessman and FOB, who had been put in charge, had designed an immensely complex mechanism for drawing up the proposal. Some of Clinton's advisers weren't keen on the President's proposing another huge program, especially one that would require some sort of taxes, while they were still struggling to get his economic program through the Congress. Bentsen, Panetta, and Stephanopoulos felt that adding health care to an already large legislative agenda for 1993 wasn't sensible. In the face of arguments to the contrary of some of his most important advisers, Clinton was determined to propose a health care plan in 1993 for another reason: now that a Democrat had won the Presidency, other Democrats—such as Senators Edward Kennedy of Massachusetts and Harris Wofford of Pennsylvania—would push health care reform bills, and he wanted to get out ahead of them. The main reason the health care proposal was put off until after the hundred-day mark—the first of several postponements—was that it wasn't ready.

The issue had not played a large part in Clinton's campaign. Carville's famous (and oft misquoted) sign in the Little Rock War Room was "Change vs. more of the same. The economy, stupid. Don't forget about health care."

(The economy wasn't even first.) Carville and Begala were fresh from Harris Wofford's upset victory in a 1991 special election, in which Wofford stressed the need for health care.

The real impulse for Clinton's proposing a health care plan in the nominating contest was that the issue was the centerpiece of Bob Kerrey's campaign in New Hampshire. Kerrey was proposing a single-payer system, much like Canada's, to be paid for through taxes. It was a traditional Democratic approach. Clinton responded with a jerry-built plan, made up of an amalgam of ideas, that got him through New Hampshire, but he wasn't entirely happy with it, and he didn't talk much about health care through the rest of the nominating contest. But his advisers saw it as a very good issue to use against George Bush. Later Clinton began to see reform of the health care system as essential to his goal of reducing the deficit.

On September 24, 1992, Clinton made a speech at the headquarters of the pharmaceutical company Merck & Co., in New Jersey, in which he pledged to provide coverage for the thirty-eight million uninsured without raising taxes. Seeking to run as the candidate of "the third way," Clinton didn't want to offer a huge new government-controlled system, requiring big new taxes. He also objected to the "pay or play" proposal, requiring companies to cover their employees or pay into a federal system to cover them, offered up in 1991 by a commission headed by Senator Jay Rockefeller. Clinton thought this proposal too "governmental," and he had doubts about its workability. In January 1993, Clinton in fact became quite angry when the transition's health advisers—an experienced group, who were working apart from Magaziner—proposed a version of pay or play in a meeting in Little Rock. In the meeting, Magaziner reinforced Clinton's reaction.

The Clintons had had trouble figuring out what role Magaziner would play in the administration. His temperamental personality—and his history of fallings-out (with, among others, Reich)—ruled him out for a number of posts. He proposed using his business-consulting experience to work on key aspects of the "change" agenda. In January, the Clintons told Magaziner he would run the health care effort. Magaziner said that he thought he would need someone with authority to keep the project on track within the government. The Clintons replied that Mrs. Clinton would do that.

Magaziner, a Rhodes Scholar at the same time as Clinton, and also a regular at Renaissance Weekends, had a mixed record as the architect of big projects. During the campaign, he had searched for a health plan that would fit Clinton's politics. In April 1992, he had read about "managed competition." The idea, which had been drawn up by health care planners and executives from the insurance, hospital, and pharmaceutical industries who had formed the "Jackson Hole Group," named for the Wyoming resort where they met, was designed to inject more competition into the health care system. (The origins of the idea made some people suspicious.) The concept was to drive down costs by organizing insurance purchasers into large groups and have networks of doctors and hospitals compete for their business. The emphasis was on encouraging the spread of health maintenance organizations, which, through grouping practices, generally held their costs below those of the traditional fee-for-service system. But for a number of practical and political reasons (including the need to propose to Congress something that could specifically claim to control costs), Clinton's plan was never the "pure" managed competition of Jackson Hole. The Jackson Hole proposal didn't specify benefits, nor did it have the government role, or the mandatory requirements that companies insure employees, and that people join alliances, or the price controls on premiums, that the ultimate Clinton plan did.

As Clinton prepared to govern, health care took on increasing importance as his best shot at winning the support of the middle class. Polling showed that health care was a big reason people had voted for him. If he pulled it off, he might create a new Democratic coalition.

As a result of Greenberg's polling, the term "managed competition" was banished from public discourse. "Comprehensive" was a winner in the polling, so the term "comprehensive coverage" became the centerpiece. Greenberg's research also led in 1993 to a description of the program as one that provided "security": he found that while the press (and politicians) had discussed the program as one to cover the uninsured and to cut costs, what the public wanted was health care security. Greenberg's testing was to continue to bring changes in health care terminology well into 1994, when the phrase "guaranteed private insurance"—to offset the (understandable) impression that the administration was backing a big government program —became essential.

At a meeting during Clinton's first week in office with members of the health care policy-making group—Panetta, Rivlin, Tyson, Shalala, Rubin, Magaziner, Mrs. Clinton, and others—his advisers said they needed to lay out a number of options. Some of them found Magaziner's approach too limited. "Ira had drafted a policy paper that was outrageous," one official said. "It merely filled in some of the details of what the President had said in the campaign." Clinton replied, "Ira's going to do this." One of the advisers said later, "The President made a decision early on that he wanted managed competition. He didn't want to go back to single payer. He said no to broadening the discussion. He said no in that meeting, and we knew it was over." The official continued, "Everyone thought Ira's process paper was a joke because nobody's ever seen anything like it in their whole career, and everybody suddenly realized that Clinton had never seen a first-rate policy process."

Magaziner set up an extraordinary process for developing a plan. Some five hundred health experts from all over the country formed a task force, or "working group," which was broken into thirty-four subgroups, each to examine a different aspect of the question. (Magaziner told White House officials that he had identified eight hundred forty decisions that had to be made.) The task force groups were subject to "toll gates"—meetings where they were to report to Magaziner on their progress and be challenged by members of the other working groups. The meetings were so large that some attendees had to sit out in the hall of the Old Executive Office Building, and some meetings went on until the early hours of the morning. (One "toll gate" meeting lasted twenty-two hours.)

The meetings were closed to outsiders, which wasn't an untoward approach, given the size of the group and the amount of technical and other work that was to be done and the fact that the task force itself wasn't going to be actually making decisions. But on the grounds that Mrs. Clinton wasn't technically a government employee, a conservative group brought a lawsuit demanding that the meetings be open, as called for under a 1972 law saying that advisory panels not wholly composed of government employees must conduct their meetings in public. The suit arose out of the anomaly of Mrs. Clinton's position. In June, a federal appeals court ruled that Mrs. Clinton was a "de facto official or employee" of the federal government. Some advisers tried to talk Mrs. Clinton out of keeping the task force meetings secret—saying it would be a big issue with the press, that it was easy enough to at least provide briefings, that the papers could be released (this might have caused problems, given the number and types of issues that were being considered). An official said later, "They announced 'We're going to be secret' because they—the President, Hillary, Ira—were amateurs. The health working groups had a bunch of wacky ideas that they never would have gotten away with if they'd been public. You had five hundred people with every wacky idea that had ever been suggested in health care. The people now rewriting the plan never read the working group papers."

The health care task force was disbanded at the end of May, leaving behind over thirty large three-ring white binders. Even Mrs. Clinton was alarmed.

The meetings on health care of Cabinet members, economic officials, and generalists on the White House staff involved in the issue—some of the meetings with the Clintons—were the source of deep discomfort to several who attended. They found Magaziner secretive, distrustful, and dismissive.

To preserve secrecy, Magaziner ordinarily didn't distribute papers even to members of the policy-making group. (He had a point; a lot leaked from those meetings anyway.) This meant that the top officials were having some difficulty in following what was being said, or squinting at a screen showing numbers they could hardly see. Questions about the basic assumptions were ruled out of place, on the ground that, Magaziner would say, "The President has already decided that." One participant said, "Ira had two answers to everything: 'The President has already decided that,' or 'It hasn't been decided yet.' " This person added, "It's one of the strangest things I've ever been involved in."

The economic officials believed that Magaziner was coming up with far too complex a proposal, with insufficient attention to the costs of the benefits being proposed. This group—which included Bentsen, Panetta, Rubin, Rivlin, Tyson, Altman, and a couple of others—felt that the President should proceed much more slowly, dealing with the most immediate problems, try things out, and then build on the program. One economic official said in April, "My prediction is we're going to wish we hadn't done it this year."

Someone who attended these meetings said, "Originally, Ira tried to push through all sorts of decisions without numbers. That was stopped by Rubin, Panetta, Altman, Bentsen, Rivlin, and Cutter." But most of the time the economic officials were simply run over. The political advisers Greenberg, Grunwald, and Begala felt that the program had to be big, bold. Economic officials felt that the consultants didn't consider the political effects of what it would take to pay for such a program, or how the country might react to being presented with a very big program.

Donna Shalala, the Secretary of Health and Human Services, who preferred a single-payer system, was fairly open in her criticism, and this led to a falling-out with Mrs. Clinton. (The rift was mended later in the year.) Some ungallant officials attributed her discontent to the fact that the program wasn't emanating from her department. (In fact, HHS staff members did a great deal of the grunt work.) But single payer—which Clinton had rejected during the campaign—was considered politically infeasible (too much government, and taxes). A colleague of Shalala's said, "Donna learned that there were certain subjects you didn't raise." There was evidence that single payer would have been Mrs. Clinton's preference, but Mrs. Clinton was pragmatic. Also, she saw the managed-competition approach as a possible opening wedge for a single-payer plan.

Shalala also came under sharp internal criticism for floating the idea, in mid-April, that the health care program might be paid for through a value-added tax (a consumption tax on most goods)—this at a time when the administration was still struggling to save its stimulus bill. In a most unusual event, Shalala was even called on the carpet by McLarty. But what she said was accurate: a VAT *was* being considered. Clinton himself had been a bit loose-lipped on the subject.

Another source of discomfort at the health care meetings was Mrs. Clinton's presence. Some of those who attended found her intimidating—hard to argue with and uninterested in the points they made. Mrs. Clinton's style was very direct. She told people straight out what she thought. She'd say, "You're right," "You're wrong," "That's the way to proceed," "No, that's not right." One person said, "There was a little feeling on her part of 'You're not in my caste, and I'm not going to debate you'—even when she'd said, 'Great, let's debate this.' You can't debate across caste lines." Mrs. Clinton displayed a certain impatience. And her humor was biting. When the President attended, he was slower to raise questions than at the economic meetings. He knew this subject less well, and he deferred to his wife.

A showdown meeting between the economic camp and the Magaziner camp, which included Hillary Clinton, took place in late May. Before the group were two health care proposals, one (Magaziner's plan) far more generous than the other, at least at first. The less generous plan—a variation on a major-medical plan—favored by the economic advisers, would have phased in the program more slowly, eventually ending up with the more generous benefits. The issue was drawn by setting up debate teams, but the arrangement fell apart because the President asked a lot of questions. A senior economic official said later, "The process was horrible. There were fifty-some people in the room, a very high proportion of them not above kindergarten age. All of them were for the larger package. There were cheers and groans and hissing. When you have that many people in the room, senior people aren't going to conduct a real debate in front of the junior people. There are too many possibilities of press leaks, especially if you know you're talking about something the President disagrees with, and the President is volatile, and the First Lady is emphatic. You go into that room knowing that the President, the First Lady, the Vice President, and Tipper are all leaning toward the larger plan. The issue was benefits versus economic realities. In that setting, Bentsen isn't going to stand up and say, 'Mr. President, this throws into doubt your entire economic plan.' Rubin isn't going to stand up and say, 'Mr. President, if you do this, business will walk.' [Actually, Rubin did speak up that night, as did Tyson.] There was no way for the President to know the extent to which people really disagreed."

This person added, "I'm really worried that the process itself is contributing to a decision that will not be a good one. We won't blunder into the right decision."

Typically, impressions differed on where the President stood at the end of the meeting. One official was asked afterward when the decision had been made about the basic benefits package. He said, "Sometimes it's not clear when the decision has been made."

Despite Mrs. Clinton's admonition, stories about the meeting appeared in the newspapers. That was the end of large meetings. In the meantime, there were numerous private meetings of Magaziner and the Clintons—in the Oval Office, in the residence, sometimes at breakfast, sometimes late at night. Magaziner—a tall man (he was six feet three) with a prominent beaked nose, a quiet voice (he was hoarse for much of 1993), and little humor—had as the months passed a growing sense of beleagueredness. His project was being leaked, mocked, and opposed from within the administration. He felt that "the Beltway," or "the Washington establishment," was trying to kill his program. He knew that he was being accused of "mesmerizing" the First Couple, talking them into a very big and complicated program. (One member of the First Lady's staff privately referred to him as "Rasputin.") White House staff members, aware that this was Mrs. Clinton's project, lay low. A White House aide said later, "Most people in the White House felt that they were over in the OEOB secretly hatching a health care plan—that second- and third-tier aides were working with Ira as the mad scientist concocting this socialist theme. Treasury and NEC sensed the health care project was a black box. But because it was Hillary's project, everyone was nervous about criticizing it."

If the internal debate was stifled, the Clintons allowed it to be stifled. Besides, Clinton had stipulated from the outset that managed competition was the only acceptable option.

While the rest of the administration's business went on, Magaziner struggled to find a way to "close" on a health care plan. A couple of advisers suggested that the White House not try to adopt a completely written out plan but instead send Congress a detailed statement of philosophy and goals, and then work with congressional leaders to draft a plan that could be passed in 1994. (The Reagan administration had followed this formula successfully for the Tax Reform Act of 1985.) They were brushed off. (Aides to Mrs. Clinton said that members of Congress she conferred with had insisted on a specific plan.) At one point, the White House suggested it would have a plan ready in May; then it was said it would be ready in June.

For various reasons, not all of them attributable to Magaziner, it was to be months before a health care plan was ready to be presented to the Congress. It was also a very long time before Mrs. Clinton gave up on the idea that it could be passed in 1993.

In April and early May, in anticipation of the health care proposal's being ready, Mrs. Clinton's advisers, who guarded her carefully, agreed—with her approval, of course—to make her available for numerous major articles. The result was cover stories in *Time, People, Parade, Family Circle,* and the *New York Times Magazine.* The essence of these articles was a portrait of a whole woman: a working mother who struggled to keep all her roles intact, a normal, warm person. An anecdote about Mrs. Clinton making scrambled eggs for an ill Chelsea was featured in three of the articles, which served only to suggest how rare this kind of thing must have been. The softening of her image from the sometimes chilly and remote person that much of the public had perceived was obviously, and not too subtly, designed to give her more of the benefit of the doubt when the health care plan was unveiled.

The exercise raised some questions about Mrs. Clinton's judgment. She allowed herself to pose for the cover of the *Times Magazine* in a white voile suit. She couldn't necessarily know that the article would be entitled "Saint Hillary," but she did of course know what she had spoken about with the author of the article. Mrs. Clinton's (and her staff's) judgment also came into question later when, clad in a black turtleneck velour dress, she posed for *Vogue* in provocative positions. Mrs. Clinton was breaking the mold on First Ladies, and on occasion she went too far, doing something that undermined the larger point she was making. But she was experimenting. Like her ever-changing hairdos, the white-clad Hillary and the black-clad Hillary suggested that she was less centered than she professed to be.

In the *Times* article, Mrs. Clinton gave voice to a set of concerns about moral and spiritual decline, and to her searching for a political response that encompassed virtue and a greater sense of community. This was yet another Hillary Rodham Clinton, first unveiled in a speech she gave in Austin, Texas, in early April, shortly after she'd left the side of her dying father. She said that the United States suffered from "a sleeping sickness of the soul"; there was a need for "redefining what our lives are and what they should be." She used the phrase "politics of meaning" (coined by Michael Lerner, the editor of the liberal Jewish bimonthly magazine *Tikkun,* with whom she had consulted), which stuck as the definition of her search for an overarching philosophy to guide Americans toward a more noble calling and way of life.

In talking about the need for larger values and a greater sense of community, Mrs. Clinton was on to something, and she did have an authentic spiritual side, but the way she talked about it in public came off as somewhat unformed. Yet there was also a shrewd political calculus behind such talk: it was a way of no longer ceding the issues of morals and values to the right, and perhaps even preempting it. Mrs. Clinton was explicit about the necessity of not leaving these themes to the right wing. The communitarian movement that she was tapping into was very much about responsibilities as well as rights, and therefore compatible with her husband's central (if sometimes strayed from) political theme. For good reasons and otherwise, talk of "values" was becoming increasingly fashionable. In a different form, her husband was to do a similar thing later in the year.

But because her "politics of meaning" was widely mocked—by cynical and elitist journalists, her aides insisted—it played no prominent role in her subsequent speeches. However, she did continue to touch on it, as in an October speech in which she spoke of "the need for a new ethos of responsibility and caring . . . the need to restore the importance of civil society and community." Her search, and her self-definition as something beyond a crafty and ambitious believer in government programs, went on.

14

CIVIL RIGHTS

"A Ground That I Could Not Defend"

It had been a foregone conclusion at the White House for some time that Lani Guinier would be named Assistant Attorney General for Civil Rights. A noted civil rights lawyer and friend of the Clintons' (she attended Yale Law School with them, and both Clintons attended her wedding, on Martha's Vineyard, in 1986), Guinier taught at the University of Pennsylvania Law School. As a former voting rights litigator for the National Association for the Advancement of Colored People's Legal Defense and Education Fund, she had specialized in voting rights cases. She had also been a special assistant in the Justice Department's Civil Rights Division during the Carter administration. As a black woman, she fit the Clintons' criterion for diversity —but there was far more strength behind her nomination than that.

The slate for Justice Department positions was drawn up by Mrs. Clinton; Susan Thomases; Melanne Verveer, Mrs. Clinton's Deputy Chief of Staff and formerly with People for the American Way; and Eleanor Dean Acheson, a granddaughter of the late Secretary of State and a friend of Mrs. Clinton's from Wellesley, who later became Assistant Attorney General for Policy Development.

There were people in strategic positions who had misgivings about Guinier's nomination. A network of aides to members of Congress and former aides transmits a lot of the messages in Washington. In this case, more than a month before she was named, an aide to Senator Edward M. Kennedy had been tipped that her academic writings could become a political problem.

Then, having read some of the articles, the aide phoned a former colleague, Ron Klain, who had been Joseph Biden's assistant for the Judiciary Committee and was now in the White House counsel's office. These two former colleagues had been through a lot of battles together—over Clarence Thomas and other Supreme Court nominees, over Justice Department nominations during the Reagan-Bush years. They knew how seemingly safe nominations could go off the rails. But as people who had been closely allied with civil rights groups, they were in a delicate situation. To be known to be opposed to Lani Guinier could have caused them problems. But they thought that it was important to protect the President.

Klain, who was at that time busy working on finding a replacement for Supreme Court Justice Byron White, who had announced on March 19 that he would retire at the end of the term, read the articles one night and was sufficiently troubled by them that the next day he went to Bernie Nussbaum and said, "Look, I'm not involved in this, but these writings could be controversial, and they ought to be checked out before she's nominated." The Senate wouldn't beat up on a black woman, Nussbaum replied. Moreover, this was a well-known civil rights litigator and friend of the Clintons. Klain then raised the problem in a phone call to Attorney General Janet Reno, who thanked him, and that was that. (Reno, in turn, told people in the NAACP that Klain was raising questions about Guinier, which didn't help Klain with the civil rights community.) Then Klain was assured by Nussbaum that an objective, independent person—Walter Dellinger, the former constitutional law professor at Duke, then serving in the counsel's office and later named to the Justice Department—was going to read the articles. Klain felt relieved.

Nussbaum said later, "Lani was on the list very prominently. She had everything going for her: woman, African American, civil rights lawyer, respected academic, she'd served in the Civil Rights Division, she's a mother, she has a strong personality, and she was a friend of the President's and First Lady's, and they're proud of her. She had more going for her than anyone else on the list."

Despite his presumption in Guinier's favor, Nussbaum said, "I told members of my staff to read her articles." He mentioned Dellinger and an outside adviser, James Coleman, a former professor of criminal law at Duke, who was practicing law in Washington. Nussbaum said, "They described them to me. They basically said these ideas might not be good policy, and might be controversial, but they were academic ruminations and not crazy or off the wall." Nussbaum so informed the President.

What actually happened was that Coleman, a friend of Guinier's, read the articles because he heard from Dellinger, who was a friend, that questions were being raised by Klain. Coleman passed on his essentially positive comments to Dellinger, who passed them on to Nussbaum, who passed them on to the President. Subsequently, Coleman was Guinier's principal adviser as she went through her nomination process. Dellinger explained later that he was too busy to read the articles himself. He said, "I assumed that the decision was a done deal." The people in the White House sensed that the President and the First Lady wanted Guinier, and that was that.

Nussbaum said, "The President knew her very well, knew her total career. The President was just told in general terms that there were writings that may cause controversy, but taken in context over her total career, this shouldn't cause a problem. He wasn't told the details about super majorities, cumulative voting, and minority veto."

As other White House staff members—and apparently the President—understood it, two constitutional law experts had reviewed the articles. Nussbaum also assumed that everyone understood that as a fourth-level Justice Department official who would be reporting to Webster Hubbell, the Associate Attorney General, Guinier wouldn't be making policy. But the Attorney General and other top officials were busy people and didn't have the time, or the expertise, to review every action an Assistant Attorney General might take.

Nussbaum said later, "Here's where we made the misjudgment. All of us. The misjudgment was that she would be judged on her overall career, and she wasn't a policymaker. We failed. The White House failed and the Justice Department failed. When she was nominated, we wanted to cast the battle in those terms, and instead the battle was on her writings."

Another senior official said, "They gave the President the conclusion and not the facts. That's where they misserved him. Bill Clinton is a much better politician than most. He can judge from the facts what the public will tolerate and what it won't."

Bruce Lindsey had become sufficiently concerned that for three weeks before Guinier was named he held open a slot for her in the Department of Education, just in case. He knew that most of the problems would revolve around her writings about the Voting Rights Act; a job in the Education Department wouldn't raise the same sort of controversy. Upon Nussbaum's report that Guinier's writings wouldn't be much of a problem, Lindsey put her name down for Assistant Attorney General for Civil Rights, and the President nominated her on April 29, in a ceremony at the Justice Department.

On the very next day came the trumpet call from the Right that should have put everyone on notice. Conservatives had been vowing vengeance ever since liberal Democrats defeated Robert Bork's nomination to the Supreme Court, in 1987. Nominees were now no longer judged on their merits alone but also on whether they could be used as targets in the long, unforgiving, and bloody grudge match between Left and Right. During Janet Reno's confirmation, Senate Republicans repeatedly told their Democratic counterparts that they wouldn't fight her nomination—she was too popular —but they would look for someone further down in the ranks to pick off.

The trumpet blew, as it often did, on the editorial page of the *Wall Street Journal.* In an article entitled "Clinton's Quota Queens," Clint Bolick, the litigation director of the conservative Institute for Justice in America, said that Guinier "sets the standard for innovative radicalism" and laid out some of the more controversial ideas in her law review articles.

In essence, Guinier's writings advocated a results-oriented test of voting laws and procedures, and were aimed at minority empowerment. In some cases, her theories seemed to go beyond what had been contemplated in the civil rights laws, and in some cases they simply frightened people. She wrote that the term "anti-discrimination" incorporates "a result-oriented inquiry in which roughly equal outcomes, not merely an apparently fair process, are the goal." She dismissed "simple-minded notions of majority rule." She called for using the Voting Rights Act to require legislative "super majorities" for passing laws and for a minority veto. In one of her most controversial articles, in the *Michigan Law Review,* she questioned whether some elected black leaders were "authentic" representatives of the black community, and said that blacks elected by a predominantly white group might not serve black interests. She cited Virginia Governor L. Douglas Wilder in a footnote.

The administration's options at that point were to heed the warnings and drop the nomination, take some preemptive action to define the argument, or roll out the cannons and go at it. It did none of these things.

Guinier's exotic name and looks also worked against her. Webster Hubbell, whose nomination as Associate Attorney General was also in trouble, was a big, beefy man and no dreamboat, but he was a good old boy, the kind of guy senators understand. A black woman with prominent eyes and hair combed back and bursting into puffs at the sides, and with a strange name and radical-sounding ideas, was vulnerable. She was too different. She was smart and had a strong personality. She made some people uncomfortable. The white males who—all the progress notwithstanding—still dominated Capitol Hill couldn't empathize with her, joke with her. There were no grounds for the easy exchanges that stood as signs of acceptance into the club. (By contrast, Reno's bluffness and breezy self-assurance let her right in the door.)

Complicating the matter was the fact that some Jewish groups opposed Guinier (whose mother was Jewish). They had been disturbed by various remedies under the Voting Rights Act and were opposed to quotas. Some Jewish contributors weighed in with Rahm Emanuel at the White House. Therefore, Guinier's nomination threatened to divide the Democratic Party over some of the most sensitive issues it had faced—issues Clinton had managed to muffle in 1992.

Ricki Seidman, the deputy director of communications and an attorney who had worked for Edward Kennedy, was in charge of shepherding Justice Department nominations, as well as other nominations that got in trouble. Seidman had worked against the Bork and Thomas nominations. At the moment that Guinier's nomination got in trouble, Seidman was working on rescuing Webster Hubbell's. And because of the lengthy search for an Attorney General (Reno wasn't sworn in until March 12), the Justice Department was far behind in getting staffed. Normally, the Cabinet departments prepared people for confirmation; Guinier's wasn't the sort the White House usually concerned itself with. But what resources the Justice Department did have went into rescuing Hubbell. A staff aide on Capitol Hill said, "People said to contacts in the Justice Department 'There's a problem,' and they said, 'We'll deal with it as soon as we get Webb through.' "

Hubbell had come under attack for belonging to an all-white country club in Little Rock. (This was the club at which Clinton played golf during the 1992 campaign, to much criticism.) The usual explanations were offered: that the club had tried to bring in blacks, and that Hubbell had been part of the effort, and that one black actually belonged to the club. (This man was later given a job in the office of the U.S. Trade Representative.) Hubbell resisted the obvious and inevitable—that he would have to resign from the club. (McLarty resisted as well. McLarty said this would be an insult to his friends who were members of the club.) Finally, Hubbell announced in his confirmation hearing before the Senate Judiciary Committee, on May 19, that he had resigned from the club. (That same day, the White House announced that McLarty, Foster, and Kennedy had also resigned.) Committee members from both parties expressed their appreciation of Hubbell's action, calling him an "honorable and decent man."

By the time the administration was ready to help Guinier, Biden was preparing to bail out. He'd handled enough difficult nominations. He had already, several times, privately urged the White House to drop the nomination. Other Democratic senators—and not just conservatives—were becoming increasingly agitated over the number of controversial nominees the administration was sending them to vote on. At the same time that

Guinier's nomination was pending, the Senate was being asked to approve Acheson, who hadn't paid Social Security taxes on a housekeeper (the taxes were paid shortly before she was named), and belonged to a country club that had no black members, and had discriminated against women; and Roberta Achtenberg, a San Francisco city supervisor nominated to be an Assistant Secretary of the Department of Housing and Urban Development, who was an avowed lesbian and gay rights activist, had introduced her lover at her confirmation hearing, and had been critical of the Boy Scouts for barring homosexuals from becoming scoutmasters. After a bitter debate, Achtenberg's nomination was approved on May 24, but several of the President's allies voted for her reluctantly. A Senate aide said, "The word was coming back from the Senate floor: 'I'm going to vote for the lesbian but not the black radical.' "

During that same week, Biden went public with his concerns. In a much noticed Associated Press story that ran in the conservative *Washington Times* on Wednesday, May 19, Biden said that some of Guinier's writings "give me great concern." He added, "She's got to come prepared to defend her writings and give an explanation of how they comport with her view of the application of the law as the head of the Civil Rights Division." And Senator Patrick Leahy, a liberal Democrat from Vermont and a Judiciary Committee member, also expressed reservations publicly. These statements weren't made casually. In case anyone didn't understand the Republicans' intentions, Alan Simpson, of Wyoming, recalled the heated Bork hearings and said, "She's going to go through the same kind of anguish."

In late May, Guinier started making the customary "courtesy calls" on Capitol Hill, and (like Zoe Baird) she misread the reception she got. A Democratic senator said later, "When she was going around to see senators, they'd emerge from these meetings and they'd say, 'We're really impressed.' Basically, politicians—we're the weakest people in the world. When we face anyone in the office one on one, we can't help but be courteous. That's just us. We want to be loved by everybody." A Capitol Hill aide said, "She misread senatorial courtesy. People were nice to her because they thought the nomination would be pulled."

Further, Guinier had been badly advised. A White House aide said later, "She wasn't so good at the courtesy calls. She didn't understand that she was supposed to sell herself." Paster took her to see George Mitchell, and she didn't ask for his support. Afterward Paster met with her in his office and said, "Look, Lani, that was not a good visit. You have to ask for their support. You've got to explain to them why you should get the job."

Even her potential allies were lying low. Edward Kennedy quietly encouraged senators to keep an open mind, but his efforts found no takers, and he himself remained silent. On Sunday afternoon, May 23, during a meeting in the White House residence, the President and the First Lady asked Roy Neel, the Deputy Chief of Staff, to look into the Guinier nomination. The President, who had begun to realize there was a problem, said, "We have to put in motion an analysis of this and make a decision on whether to go ahead with this thing." On the same day, the *New York Times* published an editorial that had an impact on a number of politicians' thinking. If the *Times* had problems with Guinier's nomination, it was respectable for torn liberals and moderates to oppose her. The editorial said that Guinier's writings "suggest that she would interpret the Voting Rights Act in novel, even aberrant ways." If her writings were "viewed as a scholarly search," they "seem like creative theorizing," the *Times* said. "But if they represent an agenda for reorganizing democratic institutions, they seem disqualifying."

By early in the last week in May, Arkansas Senator David Pryor told Bruce Lindsey and then the President that the nomination should be withdrawn. Pryor said later, "I just said, 'Pull her.' The President was beginning to hear of trouble, but he hadn't yet been told to pull her." Pryor told Lindsey, "You don't have the capital in your bank account to do this, and you still have to get your economic program passed." Another senator told the President much the same thing. This senator said later, "I told him he could get her confirmed, but he'd be down twenty points in the polls by the time he got that done. He was in no position to fight that fight."

So Guinier was a victim not only of poor staff work but also of the President's weakened political position. Her story illustrated the perils of a President and his wife choosing a friend for a job. Moreover, the issue of her nomination came to a head at just the time that Clinton was trying to look more like a centrist. She was also a victim of the Democrats' lack of stomach for a bruising, constituency-dividing fight.

By the third week in May, it was clear to a lot of people at the White House that Guinier's nomination would have to be pulled. The consultants were for pulling the nomination, and they so informed the President. Yet it was to take at least ten full days before the matter was finally settled—days during which the issue became increasingly polarized and the consequences of whatever decision the President made became greater.

Quiet soundings of civil rights groups showed they strongly supported Guinier. By May 25, Neel recalled later, "It was apparent that we had a firestorm in the making." Neel took the deliberate decision not to anger members of the Black Caucus, whose votes were needed on the reconciliation bill—to be voted on that week—and who were becoming increasingly vocal in support of Guinier. Neel recalled, "To have opened up discussions with her advocates and her detractors at that point would have blown up the House during reconciliation and would have involved the President and the Vice President and all the senior staff, who were working on reconciliation. So we simply put it aside. There was no process that week to address the Lani Guinier situation."

By that Thursday, May 27, even Seidman, who had been a defender of Guinier within the White House, had concluded that the nomination shouldn't go forward. Stephanopoulos and Emanuel also argued that the nomination should be dropped. But still nothing happened. A few days later, Lindsey told the President that he thought Guinier's nomination should be dropped.

To make sure that Clinton understood what was going on, Biden phoned him before the Memorial Day recess. Biden recalled later, "I said, 'Mr. President, are you fully aware of Lani's views on Section Two and Section Five of the Voting Rights Act? She has written very extensively and very articulately about voting rights. I'm not setting a hearing date until you have read her law review articles. I can send them down to you.' "

The President replied, "I can get them."

Biden went on to say, "Mr. President, I'll make you a deal. If you tell me or someone else calls me and says that you have read the articles and you stand by them and you'll stick with her, then I'll support her."

As Biden recalled it, "I said, 'Mr. President, if you want to fight this I'll go to the wall with you, but I don't want to start down the road and then I get a call saying, We're withdrawing her. Mr. President, you're going to have to use up a lot of capital.' "

Other liberal Democrats also weighed in at the White House.

That Friday night, during his discussions with Gergen over the terms of his joining the White House staff, Clinton told Gergen he didn't think he could go ahead with Guinier's nomination. By this time, Mrs. Clinton was opposed to going ahead with it, and thought that the final decision had been made. She wondered aloud what was taking so long. Gore, too, was for pulling down the nomination, which he had been troubled about for some time. (A friend of the Vice President's said Gore opposed the nomination before it was made.)

A key Presidential aide said later, "Clinton was basically in the camp of dropping it several days before he did it. He knew enough about her writing to feel that there was a problem. If people had got hold of it and dealt with it, it would have saved us untold grief."

What finally drove the President and his aides to make a decision was an announcement by Dan Rather on the *CBS Evening News* on Tuesday,

June 1, that the President had decided to withdraw Guinier's nomination. Though no formal decision had been made, Rather was correct about the way things were tending. A meeting with the President was laid on for later that night, after he returned from giving a speech in Milwaukee.

The meeting was something of a rambling affair. Clinton appeared to be resigned to the certainty that Guinier had to go, but, an aide said later, "He had not yet gotten it in his gut. He was looking for affirmation of the certainty. He took comfort in Biden's and others' position—the fact that this wasn't isolated to a couple of people. He didn't seem to feel that he had to stand behind her. He clearly believed she was wrong for the job." But still no decision was made.

On Wednesday, Clinton called Biden back and said that he had trouble with some of Guinier's positions, and as Biden recalled it, he implied that her name would be withdrawn. Clinton told Biden that the situation pained him: Guinier was a good person, and he couldn't defend her. He also expressed anger that he had been told that two constitutional scholars had read the articles and said they weren't a big problem. "He was really angry about that," Biden said. "Unlike the Zoe Baird case, his tone was 'How the hell did this happen again?' "

At a photo op before his regular Wednesday lunch with business leaders, Clinton, asked about his position on the nomination, gave a very Clintonesque reply:

"I think that I have to talk to some of the senators about it because of the reservations that have been raised both publicly and privately. . . . I think any reasonable reading of her writings would lead someone to conclude that a lot of the attacks cannot be supported by a fair reading of the writings. And that's not to say that I agree with everything in the writings. I don't. But I think that a lot of what has been said is not accurate. On the other hand, I have to take into account where the Senate is, and I will be doing that and talking to them."

Thus there is evidence that Clinton was familiar enough with Guinier's writings before the day that he pulled her nomination—ostensibly because he had just read one of her articles. A White House aide said later that the President couldn't plausibly say at that point that he hadn't read the articles.

Clinton had another reason to be familiar with Guinier's written views. William Galston, a White House staff member who worked on domestic policy, had become worried enough about Guinier's nomination to compose a memo to the President. This was an unusual act; Galston had stepped out of his appointed role, and had his memo got out, it could have caused difficulty for him. Galston was one of the three former DLC members on the White House staff; Al From had warned the President in early May about the dangers of the Guinier nomination.

Galston's concern was with what Guinier posited as evidence of violation of the Voting Rights Act—for example, the refusal to fund drug treatment centers in minority areas. Galston was also troubled by what he termed the "we-versus-they" tone of her writing: that blacks and whites are competing constituencies with sharply conflicting aims. To him, this wasn't consonant with Clinton's emphasis on healing.

Two staff members recalled that Galston's memo reached the President on Tuesday. Neel said that the memo did have an impact, because "there were not many efforts to put all of this down on paper. The President read it, and it made an impression on him. It was a compelling memo."

Since Guinier had refused to get out of the way, the Clinton White House had to find a way to remove her. It was clear to Clinton that her nomination couldn't be saved. But rather than simply announce that the nomination was being withdrawn, Clinton and his advisers put on an elaborate charade. The public was later told that Gore had "confronted" Clinton on Thursday morning and told him that he must read her writings. But as Clinton had said on more than one occasion, he was already familiar with her writings.

On Wednesday afternoon, Paster, one of the few aides (Nussbaum was another) still supporting the nomination, told the President that Guinier couldn't get confirmed. At the same time, civil rights groups were speaking out in her behalf, the delays having caused them to coalesce around her nomination. Still, a White House survey of the Judiciary Committee showed that it would be very difficult to get her approved there. Even if she were, Paster reported, the situation on the Senate floor was hopeless. By now the White House was hoping that Guinier would withdraw, sparing the President any additional discomfort. But word came from the Justice Department that she had no intention of withdrawing.

The President didn't want to tell her that it was over. At a meeting in McLarty's office on Wednesday afternoon, it was decided to send a mission to the Justice Department, to give Guinier a clearer picture of her situation. After a certain amount of "You go," "No, you go," Paster and Seidman were deputized. Nussbaum said, "Look, we'll just explain that it was a failure in the confirmation process." Paster blew up. "It wasn't a confirmation failure," he said vehemently. "It was a vetting failure. Who's going to take responsibility around here?" Paster reminded the group that he had taken responsibility for the failure of the stimulus package.

Paster asked McLarty what it was that he and Seidman were supposed to do, and pointed out that they had no authority to ask her to step aside. "If she doesn't take the hint," Paster asked, "am I to ask her to withdraw?" McLarty replied, "No."

A White House official said later that though the President wasn't at that Wednesday meeting, he knew about it, and that Paster's and Seidman's excursion wasn't unauthorized. "Everyone was hoping she'd go," the official said later.

As they should have expected, Guinier declined to make it easier for them. In the Attorney General's conference room on the fifth floor of the Justice Department, at a meeting that began at about seven-thirty that evening and lasted an hour and a half, Paster laid out to Guinier and her assembled advisers the hopelessness of her situation. He told her it was the White House's best judgment that she couldn't get confirmed, and he went into some detail. He told her that she had mistaken senators' being nice to her for support. The clear message was, "Please withdraw."

Guinier replied, "I'm not going to withdraw, and what I want is a hearing." She felt that she could change people's minds. She said that the White House hadn't done enough to answer her critics. She was, of course, correct on that point, but the White House didn't want the kind of fight that she wanted and would have required. A hearing would saddle Clinton with a public debate on highly controversial and polarizing issues, and there would be charges from the civil rights community that Clinton wasn't doing enough for her.

Guinier went on *Nightline* that night, with the White House's reluctant acquiescence, and both helped and hurt herself. She strongly defended her views, and she argued that she deserved a hearing before the Judiciary Committee. But the appearance further chilled her relationship with the White House, where there was some consideration of offering her a job at the Justice Department that didn't require confirmation. Guinier's lack of cooperation ended those discussions. In the view of some of the President's advisers, Guinier was confusing a privilege—a Presidential nomination—with a right. She was looking out for her interests rather than the President's, and that was unforgivable.

Now there was yet another argument within the White House—this time over whether Guinier should be granted her hearing. Given the politics of the situation, a hearing made no sense from the President's point of view. Besides, Guinier's performance convinced White House aides that even if she got her hearing, she wouldn't agree in advance to withdraw. Moreover, neither the Judiciary Committee nor the White House was interested in having hearings that would keep the subject going.

On Thursday morning, June 3, in an Oval Office meeting, Gore led a still struggling Clinton through a list of questions to consider, designed to show that if Clinton thought about the nomination in certain ways, he would have no choice but to withdraw it. Among the questions, Gore said, were: whether her views reflect your own; whether you think she'd be injured in a confirmation process and this would affect her effectiveness; whether you think that, in the job, she would be a lightning rod for attacks on the administration.

By early afternoon, the consultants were at the White House, urging the President to withdraw the nomination. At lunch, Begala said, privately, "If at the core of everything you're doing is to fight for the middle class and revive the economy, then Lani Guinier is a no-brainer. Any fight you have, regardless of the outcome, will distract from Clinton's efforts to deal with those issues." Besides, he said, "the President doesn't have much blood left."

At around noon, after returning from touring a construction site in nearby Frederick, Maryland, Clinton said he had read some of Guinier's law review articles. Then Clinton called Vernon Jordan, who was having lunch at the Hay-Adams Hotel, just across Lafayette Park from the White House. "Where are you?" Clinton asked. He had been told that Jordan was in North Carolina. When Jordan answered, Clinton said, "Get the hell over here. Have you read these law review articles? I have just read this law review article, and this is some shit we're in, Jordan. Get yourself over here."

Jordan had been for letting Guinier have her hearing, in return for which she would agree to withdraw, but upon seeing that she considered herself an independent figure, as opposed to the President's nominee, and was therefore unlikely to withdraw, he argued in the meeting with the President that she had to be withdrawn. He also pressed Clinton to make a decision. "It's two minutes to midnight, Mr. President," Jordan said. "It's time to decide."

An aide said later, "He *had* to read her articles after she chose not to get out. He had to find a way to assassinate her." Clinton didn't want to say straight out that he was pulling the nomination because it didn't have sufficient political support. That would have made him look ineffective. And to have done that would have implicitly or explicitly aligned him with her writings. Casting a withdrawal of her nomination on the basis of her writings would align him with the sentiment of a majority of the Congress. Nonetheless, there was a strong argument within the staff over the grounds he should give for withdrawing the nomination. Clinton's chosen course caused him still further trouble with the civil rights community, which would have preferred that he withdraw her—if he did so at all—on the ground that the votes weren't there, and do so with a blast at her "lily-livered" opponents.

A Capitol Hill aide said, "Clinton did one thing 'felony stupid' in letting it go on for the last day and a half." During the delay, he said, "the civil rights groups got angry and went to the Congressional Black Caucus, so the Black Caucus held a press conference. The whole thing snowballed in the black community, and it became a storm by Thursday." A top White House aide said later, "Our delay and failure to close on a decision forced our hand." He added, "We were very screwed up."

Finally, early Thursday evening, the President met with Guinier in the Oval Office. They sat in the large yellow wing chairs used when the President spoke to heads of state. (Clinton didn't find the chairs very comfortable and couldn't understand why there couldn't be some important chairs that were comfortable, but they looked semiregal in photographs.) The meeting was coolly cordial as Clinton explained to Guinier that the question of her nomination had come down to the articles. He said that if he were comfortable with her writings, he would defend her even if there were only three votes for her. But, the President told Guinier, she had gone beyond where he would feel comfortable defending her. That was undoubtedly true: Clinton had no interest in being on the defensive about her writings for days or weeks on end. He told Guinier that he felt that proceeding with her nomination when he couldn't back her 100 percent would result in a death by a thousand cuts, and this would be bad for civil rights and bad for her. The two had a serious discussion of the substance of some of her views, such as her argument that electing blacks to legislatures wasn't necessarily sufficient to guarantee blacks' rights. Clinton said that sometimes you have to let the political process work, and the results often aren't immediate. He told her that he couldn't see how the nomination could go forward, and that a hearing wouldn't have the impact that she thought it would. Guinier argued that she could turn a lot of people's opinions around in a hearing.

Though in the conversation Clinton's thinking was clear enough, he didn't tell Guinier that he planned to withdraw the nomination. Aides explained later that this was to prevent Guinier from making an announcement of this before he had a chance to announce it himself. Perhaps, but his not telling her was in keeping with one of his strongest traits. His statement announcing the withdrawal of her nomination had already been prepared.

At a press conference shortly before nine that evening in the briefing room, Clinton read his statement emotionally. Biting his lip, a tear coming down his face, Clinton looked weary and sad as he said that Guinier's writings "do not represent the views . . . that I hold very dearly, even though there is much in them with which I agree." He expressed sorrow for the ordeal Guinier had gone through and praised her highly as a person and an attorney. He said that if he had agreed with her writings, he would stay with her nomination even if "we didn't get but one or two votes in the Senate." He said, "It is not the fear of defeat that has prompted this decision. It is the certainty that the battle would be carried on a ground that I could not defend."

In answer to reporters' questions, Clinton said something that many interpreted in ways he didn't intend. "This is about *my* center," he said, "not about the political center." He waded further into details of his views on some of her writings than his staff thought wise, because it could prejudice future court cases.

In the past, Clinton had sometimes seemed to fake a tear, but there was reason enough to think that his emotions that evening were genuine. Added to the turmoil he had gone through, he was very, very tired, and the fatigue had begun to show. But even some of his closest aides felt that he had displayed too much emotion, that he didn't look as if he were in control of himself, that, injured friend or no, a commanding President shouldn't come undone over a fourth-rank Cabinet department position.

Bruised by the Guinier episode—aware that the Clinton White House looked inept and indecisive—and determined to do better in the future, the President's aides turned to the long-postponed business of naming a Supreme Court nominee.

15

SUPREME COURT

"Of Course, If You're Not Comfortable with This . . ."

In early June, as the President's aides began to focus on the selection of a nominee to the Supreme Court, one of the most important decisions a President makes, the matter had been before Clinton for nearly three months. No other President in more than twenty-five years had taken that long. The Senate Judiciary Committee had been pressing to get the confirmation completed in time for the opening of the next Supreme Court term. But the President and his top staff had been preoccupied with other matters.

In April, there had been a strange pas de deux between Clinton and New York Governor Mario Cuomo about filling the position. Ten days after Byron White announced, in mid-March, that he would retire at the end of the term, Clinton called Cuomo to discuss the possibility of the Court seat but failed to reach him. (Cuomo said later that he was in budget meetings and his secretary didn't think she should put calls through.) Cuomo had been told by White House aides that the President was seriously considering him. During the campaign, Clinton had more than once said he would like to nominate Cuomo to the Supreme Court. He said he wanted a person with a "big heart." Clinton told his aides he would like someone like Earl Warren, someone "big," and not a judge, and Cuomo seemed to meet these standards. Cuomo would bring a brilliant mind and a politician's experience with real people—Clinton was especially interested in this point—and of course, he had a strong ethnic identity. The President also wanted an appointee who could make the rightward-leaning Court more progressive. Between them, Reagan and Bush had put five Justices on the Court; the unlucky Carter had no opportunity to appoint a Supreme Court Justice.

On April 2, a couple of weeks after White's announcement, while Clinton was flying to the West Coast for the owl/timber summit, he and Cuomo spoke. Clinton didn't ask Cuomo to go on the Court, he didn't tell him how eager he was to appoint him, he didn't say that no matter how much opposition Republicans put up, he would fight for him. He told Cuomo he was under "very serious consideration" and asked whether the White House could begin a background check. For a man of Cuomo's pride, this wouldn't do—as Clinton should have known.

According to a Cuomo associate, Cuomo's thinking was: " 'He wasn't asking me. It's not in my interest to have this thing strung out over a long period of time, and if this is the way he's doing it, how do I know whether, if the Republicans go after me, treat me like a Bork, this guy will stand with me?' " The associate said that the idea of joining the Supreme Court was tempting enough to Cuomo: he loved to think and write in solitude, some of his family was for it, it would be a distinguished way to cap a career. The associate said that if Cuomo had been asked differently, he might well have accepted. "They were ships in the night," he added. He said that Cuomo didn't fear a vetting. (For years, there had been investigations by various newspapers and magazines into rumored family ties to the Mafia, but nothing was ever found.)

On April 7, Cuomo formally removed himself from consideration, with a letter, released to the public, in which he took a subtle dig at Clinton: "I do not know whether you might indeed have nominated me...." Some Presidential aides told the press that Clinton hadn't been all that interested in him. This was ungracious and unwise. The White House didn't have a backup candidate. So the process had to start anew. Aides bragged that they had drawn up a list of fifty candidates, but clearly not many of them were real ones.

Having taken many spears for his insistence on diversity, Clinton wanted to appoint a white male. Though the "lists" circulated by the White House contained a black woman and a Hispanic, they didn't reflect Clinton's thinking. McLarty and Lindsey were arguing that it was time to take a breather from diversity. And now Clinton was trying openly to "move to the center." He asked his friend Richard Riley, the Secretary of Education, if he was interested. He wasn't; Riley wanted to keep working on education.

On June 8, there were newspaper stories, obviously leaked by the White House, suggesting that Interior Secretary Bruce Babbitt was likely to be

Clinton's choice. Babbitt had been interviewed in his office at length for the job the night before. Clinton was enthusiastic. Babbitt, another former governor (Arizona), not a polarizer, was a popular figure; he was all but told that he was the choice. And he wanted the job. But in the afternoon of the leaks, both environmentalists and some western politicians said that they preferred that he stay where he was. A Clinton adviser said later, "Babbitt met his criteria best, but the President was scared to death to lose Bruce Babbitt at Interior." The adviser pointed out that Carter had lost the West over water policy, and Babbitt had succeeded thus far in walking the line between environmentalists and other westerners. Clinton, of course, didn't want to risk losing the western states in 1996.

In addition, some conservatives, including Senator Orrin Hatch, of Utah, made it clear they would oppose Babbitt—and Clinton, having made his escape on the matter of Lani Guinier, wasn't interested in a messy fight. So Babbitt's name was set aside.

Stephen Breyer, a former Harvard Law School professor and now chief judge on the U.S. Court of Appeals in Boston, didn't meet Clinton's initial criteria—he wasn't the big political name the President wanted—but the list of candidates was narrowing and time was running out. And Breyer had powerful backing. He was relatively conservative on business regulation and a respected judge. (Clinton had said he didn't want a judge.) He was supported by Hatch and Dole, as well as by Edward Kennedy and other Democrats. In the late 1970s, Breyer had served as chief counsel to the Senate Judiciary Committee, which Kennedy then chaired. At that time, Kennedy was trying to move to the center on economics and regulation; Breyer did the navigating. Hatch served on the committee as well, and he and Kennedy had formed an unlikely but close friendship. Breyer also offered Clinton the chance of appointing to the bench the first Jew since Abe Fortas resigned, in 1969. The confirmation would be a cinch, Clinton was told.

Since Breyer was in the hospital, as the result of a bicycle accident, Vince Foster, Ron Klain, Ricki Seidman, and James Hamilton, an attorney in private practice in Washington, went to Boston on Wednesday, June 9, to interview him in his hospital room. They met with a surprise. They already knew that for a considerable period of time Breyer and his wife hadn't paid Social Security taxes on a household worker. After the Baird commotion in January sent out the alarm to all who might want to serve the government, the Breyers had checked with the Internal Revenue Service and, in late February, had paid back taxes, but for 1992 only. The advisers knew also that the remaining taxes weren't paid until after White sent his resignation letter.

What the vetters learned in Boston was that the penalties and interest due weren't paid until after it was clear that Cuomo was out of the running. (The Breyers' position was that they didn't owe the money.) Though these may all have been coincidences of timing, it was going to be hard to explain to the public.

Nonetheless, Breyer, with a punctured lung, was asked to go to Washington to meet with the President. On Friday, June 11, he arrived at Union Station, looking triumphant.

It was widely assumed among the White House press corps, and some of Clinton's advisers, that following a lunch with Breyer on Friday, Clinton would announce the nomination. Camera crews were at the ready. But an announcement was postponed. The lunch hadn't gone well. Clinton just didn't feel right about Breyer. He told aides later that he felt that Breyer was selling himself too hard, that his interests in the law were too narrow, and that he didn't have a "big heart." Even one of the President's advisers said, "Clinton tends to ask all sorts of strange questions. 'If I don't put you on the Court, who do you think I should put?' 'Who do you consider to be the best federal judges?' 'What do you consider the most significant events in your life?' " This sort of quiz was the stuff of Renaissance Weekends. Ungallantly, Clinton's aides put it about that the lunch hadn't gone well.

That evening, at six-thirty, Clinton gathered his advisers in the Oval Office for a meeting. He returned to the private quarters at eight-fifteen to entertain, with his wife, about forty people for dinner, followed by a movie *(Sleepless in Seattle)* or a basketball game. During the very busy night for Clinton, aides slipped in and out to notify him about an attack in Somalia on the neighborhood and arms depot of the clan leader Mohamed Farah Aideed and, at about eleven-fifteen, there was another meeting to discuss the Supreme Court nomination. Nussbaum, Stephanopoulos, Foster, Klain, Seidman, Gergen, Lindsey, Gore, McLarty, Rahm Emanuel, and Paster were present. Gore had taken his children to see *Jurassic Park* in the meantime. Some aides weren't entirely happy about what the President's indecision was doing to their Friday night.

If he didn't go with Breyer, Clinton asked his aides, could he appoint Babbitt? Babbitt's name had been set aside, but Clinton wanted to reopen the question.

On Wednesday, Bernie Nussbaum had put the name of Ruth Bader Ginsburg, a judge on the Federal Appeals Court in Washington, on the list of people to be seriously looked at. He thought there should be a fallback if anything went wrong with Breyer. Ginsburg had been on the long list for some time but hadn't been considered a serious candidate. Clinton wanted a white male nonjurist, someone outstanding. He'd already retreated from some of these goals. And Ginsburg could be a problem because she had been critical of the reasoning, though not the result, of *Roe* v. *Wade*. At the Friday-night meeting, Emanuel, Seidman, and Paster argued for taking a serious look at Ginsburg. There were enough complications in the Breyer case, they argued, to inspire the question: why, after three months, did Clinton send to Congress a flawed nominee? (Kennedy, Biden, and Hatch, among others, had been told about the first of the Social Security problems and had said that it shouldn't stop Breyer's nomination.) Even if Breyer was confirmed, it was said in the meeting, there would be a question of Clinton's competence if he named a candidate with a string of Social Security problems.

Something else was going on at that meeting. A Presidential aide said later, "There was an issue in this debate that was beyond Breyer. The issue is, does Bill Clinton feel he is being forced to be a centrist and *has* to pick a white male? There was an undercurrent Friday night that had to do with what is the safe course: a white male versus the Social Security problem. Everyone thought Breyer was qualified for the Supreme Court."

But Clinton seemed uncomfortable with him. He asked each person in the room how they would vote between Breyer and Babbitt. Klain said that Breyer presented too many problems and that the President should be given another option, and he argued for taking a closer look at Ginsburg. Nussbaum and Gergen were for Breyer. Stephanopoulos and Lindsey were for going back to Babbitt. The idea of Breyer bothered Stephanopoulos: he had read the twenty-five-page biographical report on him and disagreed with him substantively. He also thought that the Social Security matter was "an issue from hell" and that it would be impossible to argue away the apparent double standard applied to Baird and Breyer. Stephanopoulos thought that the fight was worth making only if the President's heart was in it—and it didn't appear to be. Foster was against Breyer. Gore was at first for Breyer but then moved away from that position. It was Gore's style to argue hard for a position and then, if he thought the President was somewhere else, to say, "Of course, if you're not comfortable with this. . . ." Gore would make his case—and remember who had been at the top of the ticket.

Clinton was listening to his instincts, but also to his divided aides. He hadn't been taken with Breyer, and he knew that the Social Security issue would cause a big ruckus. He accepted that he couldn't lose Babbitt at Interior. The meeting ended with a decision to take a closer look at Ginsburg.

Something about the Social Security story bothered Vince Foster. At 3:00 A.M. Saturday, he left his house and went back to his office and looked through the Breyers' check stubs. He noticed differing amounts of payment and deduced that some of the funds stated on the checks were to pay the woman for her work and some were outright gifts. Social Security taxes had been paid only on the wages. Therefore, the amounts paid for Social Security didn't match the amounts on the checks. This would be difficult to explain.

Later that Saturday morning, Foster went to see the Breyers, who were staying at a friend's house in Washington (Breyer had been asked to stay over the weekend to prepare an acceptance statement). Foster returned to the White House to report that the Breyers had a perfectly good explanation for the mismatched payments. The woman had been so nice to them that Mrs. Breyer would ask her how much money she would like that week. If she asked for more than the regular wages, the check would be made out for the amount requested.

Other aides were distressed that there was still more to explain. Lindsey felt obliged to put everything in the worst possible light, so that they would understand what they were getting into if they went ahead with Breyer. Though the consultants supposedly weren't involved in this decision, Greenberg, who had been meeting with the President on another matter, spoke in strong terms against going ahead with Breyer. "He was wild about not going ahead with it," a White House aide said. "He thought it would be a political disaster."

Meanwhile, arrangements had been made for the President to meet with Ruth Bader Ginsburg. She was in Vermont for a wedding, and the White House didn't want to call attention to the fact that she was being considered, so she was brought quietly to the residence on Sunday morning. Ginsburg's husband, Martin, also an attorney, had been waging a campaign for her nomination. Some aides were becoming upset over how long it was taking the President to reach a decision.

Aides said later that during an hour-and-a-half session with her on Sunday, Clinton "fell in love" with Ginsburg. He liked her "story": a woman who hadn't been able to get a job in a law firm after graduating from Cornell Law School, where she had served on the law review, had gone on to win breakthrough Supreme Court cases establishing rights for women. Breyer had had no equivalent story; Clinton liked to appoint people with good stories. Clinton's response to Ginsburg was a welcome surprise to aides who had worried that this somewhat remote and dry judge would leave the President looking for yet another candidate. (In a meeting, Gore remarked that she was "charismatically challenged.") Ginsburg filled only some of Clinton's original criteria. She wasn't the giant Clinton had been looking for —or, of course, a male. But the fact that she was a centrist did suit his political needs of the moment. (Cuomo had enough attributes to overcome his liberalism.)

Meanwhile, the President and his aides continued to test the waters. A story about Breyer's Social Security problem—only the part about the first nonpayment—was leaked over the weekend, and set off a buzz. This set a lot of people wondering whether this issue would ever go away and to what extent nonpayment should bar people from public office. On the weekend talk shows, a number of nervous senators said that they would prefer that the President not send them someone else with this problem. In part, they were concerned about appearing to be following a double standard for women and men who hadn't paid Social Security taxes on household workers.

To the administration's surprise, some women's groups said over the weekend that it was time to move past the Social Security issue. Significant liberals weighed in with the White House in Breyer's behalf. What the White House people didn't know was that the strategy behind these statements and calls was to block Ginsburg, in the hope that Clinton would pick a more liberal woman for the next Supreme Court vacancy. Besides the *Roe* v. *Wade* decision, Ginsburg had voted conservatively on a number of government-regulation issues. Her judicial record thus far was considered less than impressive.

Nevertheless, Clinton's enthusiasm for Ginsburg won out. On that Sunday night, he offered her the job, and he announced her nomination in a Rose Garden ceremony the next day, a warm and sunny afternoon. Introducing her, Clinton praised Babbitt ("among the best") and Breyer ("superbly qualified to be on the Supreme Court"), and stressed that Ginsburg was a "moderate," a word he used again and again. Ginsburg's elegant statement about her life and her family moved Clinton to tears, even though he had read it in his office beforehand. White House aides insisted that Clinton's outburst at the end of the ceremony, when Brit Hume of ABC asked him, politely, about the "zigzag quality" of the process by which Ginsburg had been chosen, was utterly spontaneous. Clinton replied angrily to Hume, "How you could ask a question like that after the statement she just made is beyond me." But the question had to do with him, not her. His response deflected a legitimate question.

Clinton's emotional approach to such a momentous decision troubled a number of people. More than any of his modern predecessors, he felt obliged to describe his emotions and publicly assigned them an important role in his governance. Partly, this was a matter of generation, but others of his generation didn't feel so compelled to tell everyone their feelings. Its most serious effect was to eat away at the dignity of office a President needs if he wants people to follow him.

• • •

Given what had gone on earlier, it could be considered surprising that thirty-seven days after Justice Harry Blackmun announced that he would resign from the bench, Clinton, on May 13, 1994, chose Stephen Breyer for the seat. Clinton did it because he was at the receiving end of a sophisticated lobbying campaign, and because he had run out of other options. History may decide that Breyer was an excellent choice, but the way Clinton got to the decision wasn't convincing that that's what he thought when he made it. George Mitchell, ostensibly Clinton's first choice—though, as with Cuomo, Clinton never formally asked him—turned down the opportunity because, he said, he wanted to be free to concentrate his energies on getting a health care bill through. But the evidence was that Mitchell, who had announced his retirement from the Senate (and was about to remarry), didn't have a strong enough desire to lead the cloistered life of a Supreme Court Justice. (One should have a love of the law, a scholarly bent, and the tolerance to work with the same eight people every day.) After Mitchell made his announcement, some White House aides, in their characteristic way, put it about that the President hadn't been keen on naming him anyway, because as a liberal Mitchell might polarize the Court rather than move it back from the dominance of Reagan-Bush appointees and toward the center. (Another said that this was pure post facto hogwash.)

As before, other names were leaked to the press, to see what the reaction would be. But the White House considered its real options to be limited. In the end, Clinton most wanted to name Richard Arnold, the chief judge of the Eighth Circuit in Little Rock, an old friend and a man of excellent reputation. Arnold was known to have had lymphoma, but Clinton aides insist that it was only in the final days before the President made a decision that he got definitive word on Arnold's condition—the prognosis, the therapy Arnold might have to undergo, and its effects—and decided that he didn't want to take a chance on what might be the last seat he would fill. One close adviser said, "If he'd known he'd have three or four more appointments, he might have made a different choice." But it was also the case that some women's groups opposed Arnold, because of rulings on women's and abortion rights. And there was the possibility that, distinguished though Arnold was, Clinton's appointing him at that time might raise charges of Arkansas cronyism.

Bruce Babbitt was dragged through this process once again, and Clinton nearly appointed him—that would have been a "big" appointment—but in the end Clinton simply decided, his denials notwithstanding, that it wasn't worth having a fight to get him approved and then have to choose another Interior Secretary, which could also set off controversy. Only a handful of senators—led by Hatch and Simpson—had said that they would oppose him, but Clinton didn't relish an open argument over his western policies, which remained contentious and unresolved. His political strength ebbing, Clinton needed all that he could muster to get an acceptable health care bill through. Midweek, Babbitt was subjected to a three-hour White House conversation, starting at midnight, with an anguished President, and at the end of the conversation he gracefully stepped aside. Afterward a White House aide said, not gracefully, that in the end it wasn't that Babbitt had such strong opposition but that he had little support, while Breyer had very strong support; another aide said that Babbitt *did* have strong support. Among others, women's groups preferred him over Arnold and Breyer. One of the more honest White House aides said afterward, "The President saw it as two qualified people, with one presenting more difficulties."

Breyer's powerful backing was even more germane this time. Once again, he was strongly supported by Edward Kennedy—who was playing a critical role in getting health care legislation passed—and Hatch. Hatch's support of Breyer and his opposition to Babbitt were undoubtedly connected.

Before choosing Breyer, the President had to get past two problems of the previous year: the belated and parceled Social Security payments, and the fact that he hadn't particularly liked Breyer and thought his interests too narrow. Encouraged by Kennedy, District Court Judge Richard Stearns, a Clinton appointee and a close friend from his Oxford days, worked to convince him that he had got Breyer all wrong; that, after all, Breyer had just left the hospital, with a punctured lung, to come to Washington. (Stearns sent a videotape of a lively Breyer giving a speech, and a handwritten note to Clinton.)

After Breyer was named, late on a Friday afternoon, White House aides told the press that the Social Security issue was politically passé and, in any event, in Breyer's case moot, because the IRS had given Breyer a refund. They explained that the IRS found that under the law, his maid was a "contract worker"—defined as one who came at irregular times or brought his or her own equipment—on whom Social Security taxes didn't have to be paid. But the story wasn't so simple. When Breyer paid the back taxes, he had challenged their validity, arguing that his maid was a contract worker because she worked for other people as well—ordinarily not a reason for exemption. But this time the IRS agreed, and refunded him for those years when she worked for someone else, though not for later years, when she worked only for the Breyers. (Breyer said they hadn't known she worked only for them.) After much discussion, White House aides decided that the Social Security issue was politically irrelevant; people no longer cared about it. Anyway, they were out of candidates.

Clinton was sufficiently unsure about choosing Breyer that a couple of hours before he announced his decision, he mused aloud in a meeting about turning to Senator Paul Sarbanes, of Maryland. Other aides were most displeased when the new White House counsel, Lloyd Cutler, candidly told a press briefing afterward that Breyer had been chosen because "problems developed with two of them, and he was the one with the fewest problems."

Typically, Clinton then made a huge fuss over his choice, inviting him and his wife to stay overnight at the White House on Sunday night, May 15, and jogging with him, before the two made their joint appearance three days after the President had announced Breyer. There hadn't been time to get to Washington between the time the President finally decided, and the time he announced his decision at the end of the day on Friday. Breyer was easily confirmed.

16

THE SENATE RECONCILES

"A Line in the Sand"

Shortly after the House passed the reconciliation bill, the President's aides decided on a new strategy: Clinton would no longer be involved in or talk publicly about the details of the legislation. He would talk "principles." This strategy was based in part on a desire to make Clinton appear more "Presidential" and in part to cover over the fact that, with Boren and Breaux opposed to a Btu tax, the votes weren't there in the Senate Finance Committee for Clinton's program. He was playing a losing hand.

The White House had been moving in this direction: the President had talked of principles in his Milwaukee speech and at the rally in Philadelphia on May 28. But the arrival of Gergen gave the strategy new emphasis. "The President gets comfort from Gergen's advice," an aide said. Reagan had stayed above the details with success—but then Reagan wasn't interested in details.

Several White House aides believed that the President's having been so involved in the details of the reconciliation bill in the House had detracted from his victory there.

Another reason to move toward principles, an aide said, was to "draw a line in the sand, show him standing for something." Another aide gave as a reason that there was no agreement within the White House on specific strategy.

But of course the White House was deeply involved in the details. McLarty was on the phone with his oil patch friends in the Senate—Breaux, Boren, and Johnston. The President, in a meeting at the White House in early June with the Business Roundtable (made up of the two hundred largest U.S. companies), talked about the reconciliation bill in some detail.

Clinton unveiled the principles in a Rose Garden ceremony for the League of Women Voters on Monday afternoon, June 7. Clinton and his wife, wearing a red suit, had entered the Rose Garden holding hands, and Mrs. Clinton spoke first. The President wore a tan suit, which emphasized his bulk. As he began, Clinton, speaking crisply, made—far more effectively than usual—the case for his economic program. The "principles" he would fight for, he said, were the $250 billion in spending cuts, tax "fairness," expansion of the Earned Income Tax Credit, and his "investments." (Of the EITC, he said, "If you want welfare reform, that's it." This was supposed to mollify conservative Democrats, who cheered whenever he mentioned welfare reform.) Given that there was no middle-class tax cut, some aides wished he would cast the Earned Income Tax Credit as help for the middle class. As he spoke, Clinton became increasingly prolix, and the principles got lost in talk about other programs he wanted.

Later that afternoon, in a photo op before the meeting with Mitchell and Moynihan, when they brought him the bad news about the chances of his program in the Senate, Clinton went through his principles again, trying for a definition: "It's an investment program, and it's a spending-cut program."

The centrifugal forces of the Democratic Party were acting centrifugally, liberals pulling one way and moderates and conservatives the other. Clinton had left the field. Rather than work to shape a coalition and fight the carnivores devouring his program, rather than lead or arouse the public, he chose to offend no one. He essentially left it to Mitchell and Moynihan to work something out. The forces of the status quo asserted themselves powerfully. The American Association of Retired Persons was fighting against more Medicare cuts. The American Trucking Association was fighting an increase in the transportation tax. The oil producers—small as well as large—were doing an effective job of killing the Btu tax, but if Clinton was to achieve his goal of $500 billion in deficit reduction, where was the $72 billion the tax was estimated to raise going to be made up? The Black Caucus was arguing against cutting the amount in the bill for empowerment zones. Other liberals were stating their opposition to further cuts in Medicare. Early concessions on the Btu tax had started the rush on taking the proposal apart. Then the jettisoning of the thing led to new political difficulties for the administration. Liberals, seeing that Boren had been propitiated, started making demands of their own.

The energy debate was fairly absurd, because so much was being made of so little. Politicians declaimed about the danger to U.S. "competitiveness" of increased energy costs, but the amount being talked about was tiny in terms of the economy as a whole and would probably have little effect on competitiveness. Bowman Cutter, of the NEC, said, "So many things intervene between the cost of energy and competitiveness in the world markets that it is nonsense to say that the Btu tax has any serious effect. We would be raising $72 billion over a five-year period when the cumulative gross domestic product will be $35 trillion. The opposition did a better job than we did. They did an effective job of putting the administration on the defense about competitiveness."

At long last, on June 28, after an abundance of meetings and negotiations and crises among the Democrats, a bill emerged from the Senate Finance Committee. It called for a gasoline tax increase of 4.3 cents per gallon—less than the difference between prices at competing gas stations. (This was to raise $24 billion over the next five years, as opposed to the $72 billion to be raised by the Btu tax.) Further cuts in Medicare were made, and spending on empowerment zones was deleted—both actions asking for trouble on the Senate floor and in the final conference with the House. The Earned Income Tax Credit, Clinton's pride, was reduced. A few tax breaks were dropped or scaled back.

The administration's plan was to beat back amendments on the Senate floor and work out the problems in the conference. But it didn't yet have the votes to pass the bill in the Senate. Fourteen Democrats were preparing to vote no or leaning in that direction, and the President had to persuade nine of them to vote yes. He met with the Democratic recalcitrants, but it was George Mitchell who set about finding fifty-one votes for Clinton's program. The senator had got something in the bill he very much desired: repeal of the luxury tax on pleasure boats, many of which were manufactured in Maine. The existing tax on small planes and other luxuries such as jewelry and furs was also repealed. All of these taxes had been part of the bipartisan deficit reduction deal of 1990; the repeal was retroactive to the beginning of 1993. Democrats believed in equity until it hit their home states.

The Republicans attacked the revised administration proposal as a tax increase plan, and questioned the numbers. The administration kept pointing out that its program had already led to lower interest rates and therefore home mortgages could be refinanced.

The administration had to make more compromises to get the bill through the Senate. A loss for the administration would have been a severe blow to Clinton's Presidency, and some Democrats didn't hesitate to hold him up for a payoff. It was widely believed that there was a real possibility the Democrats could lose control of the Senate in 1994. A half-dozen Democratic senators believed that it was in their political interest to stake out an independent, Perotian position. On the Senate floor, the Democratic leadership purchased the support of balking senators by lowering the cut in Medicare and adding tax breaks for small business. (Senators from both parties argued that the increased income tax would hurt individual owners of small enterprises, because it would tax their profits as income.) The Republicans couldn't filibuster, but they did offer a series of amendments —such as lowering the tax increase on certain Social Security beneficiaries —that were difficult for Democrats to vote against and could be used later in Senate campaigns.

Finally, at 3:00 A.M. on June 25, a weary Gore cast the vote breaking the 49–49 tie. Six Democrats—three of them up for reelection in 1994—voted against the President's plan. Actually, Mitchell had a couple of spare votes if needed (Bennett Johnston and Dennis DeConcini).

Later in the morning, Clinton held a press conference to celebrate the Senate vote, but it was marred by a mix-up in the White House over whether and how the new AIDS "czar" would be announced that same morning. (The lack of planning for the announcement, including a failure to invite interested groups, caused a blow-up at the morning's senior staff meeting.) The new AIDS policy coordinator, Kristine Gebbie, had been selected after a protracted search, some candidates having been vetoed by gay groups. Her credentials were less than spectacular. (A year later, she was forced out because of a mediocre performance and criticism from gay groups.) The announcement was tacked onto the press conference about the Senate vote, diluting the President's Senate victory.

In nine days, the Clintons were to leave for the Group of Seven meeting in Tokyo, the President's first overseas trip since taking office. In the days leading up to the trip, Mrs. Clinton sharply instructed the White House staff to shape up for the final reconciliation fight, and a flaming row broke out among the staff over a key issue in the program.

On Saturday evening, July 3, the night before the Clintons were to leave for Japan, they, Gore, most of the senior staff, and the consultants met in the solarium. (Greenberg chartered a plane to return from New Haven, where he and his wife, Representative Rosa DeLauro, lived.) The meeting lasted from 5:00 to 8:00 P.M.—in the middle of a holiday weekend. Both Clintons complained that there had been no strategy for selling the economic program. Mrs. Clinton was especially forceful. She demanded that upon the Clintons' return, the staff have a plan ready for winning the final reconciliation bill. They hadn't had a plan before, she said, and now there must be one. "We want this," she said. "When we get back, it has to be there." She commanded the staff to establish a "war room" for the final fight, modeled on the famous "war room" of the campaign, presided over by Carville.

At the solarium meeting, an internal battle that had been taking place in the White House all week was resumed. Key House Democrats had called for dropping the energy tax altogether. They didn't think it could get through the House. Stephanopoulos had taken up their cause and was accurately reporting opinion on Capitol Hill. He backed dropping the energy tax but keeping the same deficit reduction target, for fear of losing moderate Democrats if the target was lowered. The energy tax was the one tax on the middle class, and the amount it would raise wasn't worth it, he argued. Moreover, he didn't want to see much of the rest of the summer taken up with an argument over what could be portrayed as the President's trying to raise taxes on the middle class. As a fallback, Stephanopoulos suggested that the administration not try to raise the level of the energy tax beyond the Senate's number.

Gergen agreed that dropping the energy tax should be considered seriously; his concern was that raising too many taxes might hurt consumer confidence and thus the economy. Rubin, Bentsen, and Tyson opposed dropping the energy tax, as did Gore.

In the solarium meeting, Deputy Treasury Secretary Roger Altman (sitting in for Bentsen) and Panetta argued that the revenue from the energy tax was needed. Paster argued that having urged both chambers to vote for such a tax, the administration couldn't walk away; further, the money from such a tax was needed, otherwise no deal between the two chambers could be cut. "How can we ask them to cast hard votes after that?" Paster asked. "You have to look beyond the next day's event." Greenberg presented polling data that said that the energy tax was hurting the President a lot. Since it raised only $24 billion, it wasn't worth angering the middle class, he said, and he argued strongly for dropping it. But Greenberg's research also showed that people thought Clinton wasn't tough enough and didn't fight enough for his positions.

The political advisers agreed that the tax should be dropped—all but Carville, who argued that it would raise new questions about the President's commitment to principle. Clinton wouldn't look like a leader, Carville warned. Gore argued that Clinton should stand on principle and stay with the tax. A participant in the meeting said later, "Gore felt strongly against zeroing the energy tax. He was passionate about it." At one point during that week, Gore and Stephanopoulos had a shouting match in the Oval Office over the issue. This wasn't an infrequent occurrence. Gore and Stephanopoulos got along but had differing views about politics, Stephanopoulos often more willing to accommodate what he saw as political reality, Gore more concerned with "standing on principle." At times, Stephanopoulos didn't think Gore was sufficiently sensitive to the President's campaign promises—in this case, not to tax the middle class. Gore felt that Stephanopoulos was too focused on the immediate impact of decisions rather than their long-range consequences. The political consultants tended to think that Gore postured, putting "principle" over the President's real interests. On this occasion and others, Gore's response to Stephanopoulos was that he was urging the political thing to do as opposed to the right thing to do.

The issue wasn't decided before the Clintons left for their trip to Japan.

Gore didn't lose many such arguments. Clinton rarely overruled him. He was the most influential Vice President in history. He and Clinton had established and maintained a remarkably close and even amazing relationship. Here were two men of about equal age and of about equal ambitions. It was fairly impressive that Clinton had chosen someone probably as smart as he was, but Clinton wasn't intimidated by smart people. But while Clinton and Gore had the closest relationship of any President and Vice President, and while Gore had unprecedented authority, the relationship was more complicated than it seemed.

Gore and Neel had negotiated the arrangements for Gore's Vice Presidential role with Clinton and McLarty in Little Rock after the election. The issues were the things important to Gore: a lunch meeting every week; autonomy to choose his own staff; an office in the West Wing; his Chief of Staff would be an assistant to the President as well; authority to attend any Clinton meeting, unless it was a personal one; specific Presidential authority for Gore in his dealings with the Cabinet. (At the first Cabinet meeting, Clinton said, "If Al asks you for something, you should consider it as me asking.") In return, Gore would take on such things as attending fund-raising and other events, to keep them off the President's schedule. He was given environmental issues to handle, though he didn't have total authority over them. Gore had immediately got rid of Dan Quayle's Council on Competitiveness, which, as a senator, he had been highly critical of for loosening environmental and safety regulations. Gore was also put in charge of new information technologies, a subject of great interest to him. His special pet was the coming "information highway," a projected nationwide system in which business and households would have access to a vast range of interactive digital information services.

Gore was by Bill Clinton's side so much that it became something of a joke within the White House, one that even Gore shared. Staff aides to both said privately that of course the two men sometimes got tired of each other. There were occasional—rare—signs of Clinton rankling at having Gore around so much. But Clinton was very careful about this. Gore made substantial political and intellectual contributions to the White House deliberations—even if some Clinton aides thought he sometimes talked too long, pushed too insistently, and was a little heavy. But Gore was in large measure responsible for the boldness of Clinton's economic program. On one occasion, when Clinton was being briefed on a possible press question about Bosnia, staff members shuffled and then Gore stepped forward. "You say this: The position of the United States is . . ." He gave him a clear statement, his hands forming a block, chopping the air. Before a press conference, Gore would tell Clinton to "suck it up," get rid of his anger—just get it out of his system. He could help Clinton with insights about the Congress, but Gore had been a loner in the Senate and wasn't popular enough with senators to help the President much with them.

Gore cared very much what Clinton thought of him, and being by far the funnier of the two, he could make Clinton laugh. He also had the almost unique ability to force Clinton to make a decision. Gore was the more self-disciplined—they were almost opposites in this respect—and he carefully tried to instill better habits in the top man. One senior administration official remarked that Gore "is much sharper and firmer" in his decision making than Clinton. This person added, "Gore is more instinctively Presidential than Clinton."

And Gore was utterly loyal. He was extremely careful in his relations with the press. He sometimes let his staff know of his exasperation with members of Clinton's staff, but never with Clinton. Two of his close friends said that he handled the relationship so well because he had been raised as the dutiful son. When his father, a Tennessee senator, was in some reelection trouble for his opposition to the Vietnam War, the son volunteered for Vietnam (albeit as a journalist). A Gore staff person theorized that Gore's discipline, his dutifulness, was the other side of his wacky sense of humor. (Gore was quick-witted, a fine mimic and storyteller.) Gore knew that his future was tied to Clinton's success. He chose carefully the times to stand up to Clinton.

Hillary Clinton's large White House role inevitably complicated the Vice

President's. Their roles made for a complex management situation, which bedeviled McLarty and his deputies. Around the White House, Gore was known for being aggressive about his areas of interest. He got the idea early that, just as Mrs. Clinton had her own special project, he should have his. He tried for welfare reform, but Carol Rasco, who was in charge of domestic policy, and other senior staff members were wary of the Vice President's being handed such a role. The President, reluctant to decide between Gore and Rasco, let it be known that he would handle the issue himself, and Gore was eventually given "reinventing government," or REGO, as a consolation prize. Gore told his staff, "Health care has four hundred people; I want two hundred." (He ended up with two hundred sixty.)

The Clintons and the Gores had hit it off during the campaign, and the couples remained close. Some of Hillary Clinton's friends thought it unlikely that the intense Hillary and the ebullient Tipper Gore would become close, but that underestimated Tipper Gore's intelligence and her serious side. Hillary Clinton needed all the friends she could get (and trust), and Tipper Gore became one of them. But as with the two men, the relationship between the couples was complicated. A Clinton aide said, "All things being equal, they'd be equal: if they'd all graduated from college together and gone to the same law school, they'd be close friends. But one couple's the President and First Lady, and one's the Vice President and Second Lady. At night they're friends, and in the morning it's, Is mental health [a Tipper Gore interest] going to be in the health program or not? One is the boss."

In late June, the Clinton administration engaged in some international muscle-flexing that left a number of people wondering whether the real purpose was to show that it could flex muscles. On Saturday night, June 26, between 1:00 and 2:00 A.M., Baghdad time, United States Tomahawk missiles launched from ships were fired at Iraq's intelligence service complex in downtown Baghdad. The raid was in retaliation for an alleged plot by Iraq to kill George Bush with a car bomb during his visit to Kuwait in mid-April. In a televised address at 7:40 P.M., Washington time, Clinton said that the administration had "compelling evidence" that the plot had been "directed and pursued by the Iraqi Intelligence Service."

The plan had been for Clinton to go on television an hour after the raid. But since CNN wasn't on the scene, one official said, "We didn't know what the hell we'd hit." At 6:30 P.M., Clinton asked Gergen, "Are we going on the air without saying what we've hit?" Gergen called Tom Johnson, president of CNN, in Atlanta, who told him that one of their people in Amman said a relative in Iraq had called and said that the intelligence facility had indeed been hit. With that, Clinton went on the air.

Afterward Clinton officials didn't try to mask the fact that they had seen the opportunity to show their toughness. Before the raid, Stephanopoulos had asked Stan Greenberg to save room for a question in his polling for America Talks Issues; the question turned out to be whether the public approved of the raid. It did, by a large margin.

17

THE NEW WHITE HOUSE

"The Knife Edge of His Confidence"

David Gergen's arrival made a difference and also gave people in the White House an opportunity to say that things were different. Gergen, fifty-one, taller than Clinton (Gergen was six feet six), with thinning blond hair, large blue eyes, a pinkish complexion, and a soothing voice, was a calming figure for the Clintons. He was knowledgeable about Washington and about how different groups—from the press to Capitol Hill—would react to things; he understood the elite and how they could move opinion; and he was courtly. He was the southern gentleman (he grew up in North Carolina, attended Yale and Harvard Law School)—and he seemed to know everyone. Gergen had a serious interest in issues, and also a ready, deep laugh, which could be heard down hallways and through doors. Those who categorized Gergen as a "spinmeister" greatly oversimplified him and his role. (One thing the Clinton White House didn't lack was "spinners.") Gergen was a sensitive man and also a schemer, and past associates—and in time some of the Clinton people—felt that, more than the average White House aide, he leaked to the press for his own advantage.

Gergen turned his attention to large and small matters: from policy issues to how Clinton looked on television. Gergen and Mandy Grunwald studied television clips of Clinton during the campaign and Clinton as President and felt that he both looked better and talked better in the campaign—in the campaign he was talking about large matters such as the country and its goals, while as President he was talking details and process. Gergen worried that Clinton looked too young in the Oval Office and not quite comfortable there. (Before the Oval Office speech Clinton was to give on his economic plan on August 3, Gergen and Grunwald rearranged the books behind Clinton, and they framed him between the U.S. flag and the Presidential flag.)

In mid-June, Gergen told a senior official close to Clinton that the President was crushed, that his confidence was shot. Clinton had lost confidence in his staff and, for all his smiling in public, himself. He was often quite down. At one point, he was so low that Bob Rubin asked a Cabinet officer who had come to see Clinton to please try to cheer him up. A senior official said, "Sometimes when I'm going into the Oval Office someone will say, 'Do you have any good news to tell him? He needs some.' " This person continued, "It's amazing to me how many things turn on his mood. I've heard references to 'the knife edge of his confidence.' If he's thrown off his stride, he loses confidence. One of Nancy Hernreich's [Clinton's appointments director] jobs is to assess his moods and adjust the pace according to his moods. I don't know how many former Presidents were on such a sharp edge of emotion." Clinton often complained to his staff that he was working his tail off and was being beat up by the press for doing what it had criticized Bush for not doing.

One longtime friend of Clinton's was asked, in June, what had happened to Clinton that he seemed so unsteady and indecisive. He replied, "Part of it is the Oval Office. You get in there and you get so overwhelmed you begin to lose your confidence and you begin to test your ideas with your aides and they all give you their thoughts. There's no system. He has a decision-making method that is a postponement process."

Someone else who had known Clinton a long time said, "He's used to having things come fairly easily. In Arkansas, you can make mistakes and get away with them." This person wasn't the only close observer who thought that both Bill and Hillary Clinton had been somewhat spoiled and also self-indulgent. They had been huge frogs in a small pond, a couple with a large, nationwide network of supportive friends. They were smart and special.

And Bill Clinton had special needs—which helped to explain some important aspects of his style of governing. The longtime friend said, "For as long as I've known Bill Clinton, I am constantly surprised at how much he's in need of affirmation." Such a need was not an uncommon trait in politicians, but Clinton seemed to have it in greater than average measure. This was a large factor behind his wanting to please everyone. "Slick Willie" came from something deep inside him. When one of his closest advisers was asked why Clinton didn't talk about core principles more, he replied, "Because he wants to be all things to all people."

Another person who had known Clinton for a long time said that Clinton "needs reinforcement all the time." He added, "He selected people like Mack, Gore, and Gergen to provide credibility to himself rather than manage the White House. They're people who will tell him he's doing a good job. When you see this neediness in a leader again and again, you wonder why it's so necessary—and it suggests a certain malleability. Other people are in a position to give him confidence or deny it. It's always surprised me how he looks for affirmation in even the smaller things." At one meeting Clinton said, "We had a good day yesterday, didn't we?" One attendee said later, "I was surprised that a President has to have a good day." The friend added, "Sometimes you can see that Clinton needs this affirmation and Hillary doesn't give it to him. During the campaign you could see her be aloof when he needed, at that moment, just a little warmth. She can be very cold. He's alone a lot. Hillary isn't the one to provide approval. He's a very nice person, but he also works at it, so that it's a lot of effort, a lot of energy drained going into being so balanced." Notwithstanding the temper, which the public rarely saw, Clinton was very warm; the hugs seemed genuine to the recipients. He listened and focused on what guests or other casual acquaintances said—a trait that also seemed to take a lot of energy, since there was so much going on in his head. He looked at the other person intently, seeming utterly focused on what he or she was saying. The reaction this produced was, "He's really listening to me. Great. Wonderful that a President is doing this." And then one saw that he did this with everyone.

He performed more than the political average of thoughtful gestures—making a considerate phone call, doing something special for someone who had been slighted.

What part genuineness and what part need and what part political calculus lay behind all this was impossible to know. The way he dealt with long-term friends also showed his warm and thoughtful side. This helped explain why so many people who knew Clinton well liked him, even though they were sometimes exasperated by his flaws.

Sometimes these traits also detracted from his Presidentialness. They projected a certain softness. People want a President to appear tough and strong. One of his close associates said to him midyear, "You have to be seen to have a cold edge. The country needs to see you as ruthless." But Clinton never pulled this off. In his television appearances, even when he was expressing anger about something, he smiled.

At a Cabinet meeting (such meetings were rare), he would go around the table and talk about how great things were going, when everybody knew they weren't. An observer said, "This allowed for second-rate performances. He didn't demand first-rate performances." Cabinet officers got away with a lot, because they, too, did not fear him. Attorney General Janet Reno often took stands that differed from the President's, which drove his aides wild—but, apparently, not him. An administration official said, "He's amazingly tolerant and open-ended, really mild mannered, so that a Janet Reno gets away with a lot."

An old friend said the fact that Bill and Hillary Clinton were spoiled explained some of the things that had happened. "He's been waited on hand and foot ever since he became governor. I can see how they made the haircut mistake. There's a bit of the Louis XIV syndrome."

It is often said that Presidents, with their big house and large entourage and fawning aides, don't live in the "real world"—but neither do governors. The scale is smaller, of course, but the mansion, the entourage, the aides, the pampering, the currying of favor, the deference—they are addressed as "governor" by one and all—produce a similar phenomenon. Governors may be more accessible and able to meet with a higher proportion of constituents, but they come to see themselves, and are treated, as awfully important people. Business leaders fawn on them. Governors are no strangers to arrogance. The smart, serious ones—a Michael Dukakis, a Bill Clinton—can come to believe that they know more about national issues than they do. Having administered numerous federal programs at the state level, having dealt with state legislatures, having attended governors' conferences in Washington and dealt with the national press (minimally), they come to see the Presidency as simply a step up. But the Presidency, as Clinton was finding out, is of a different order.

In the course of their turbulent first year in office, Hillary Clinton came to see that the governorship, the involvement of both Clintons in national issues, the time they had spent in Washington, hadn't prepared them for the Presidency. She came to see that the difference was that in their previous roles, both of them had dealt in Washington on specific projects—welfare, education, legal services, children's issues—as opposed to having to stick around and get them passed or make them work. They had conducted hit-and-run operations rather than having to deal, day in, day out, with a large and independent-minded Congress, a critical national press corps, an intrusive foreign policy.

Though Clinton many times expressed irritation that people would think that "someone with my background" would indulge in privilege (such as the haircut), his background could work in more than one way. It could give him insights about working-class people, but it could also lead him to enjoy his perquisites.

One old friend said in May, "He's been to Yale and was a Rhodes, but he's one generation away from Hope and Hot Springs and a father with several wives and children. Just remember, he's only one generation away from all that." Clinton's mother moved to Hot Springs when he was six. He was much more the product of Hot Springs than "the Man from Hope" featured in his hagiographic Convention film. Hot Springs was a racy town. Clinton once told some reporters that he had played pool there with Minnesota Fats. His mother was a devotee of the racetrack.

One salvation during much of the Clintons' difficult first year (until their previous business dealings and personal ethics were challenged) was that they were open to listening to criticism, at least from trusted friends, and to fixing things—up to a point. Both Clintons might privately rail at Washington or at the press, but they didn't let them become the only explanations of things that had gone wrong, nor did the people around them. Had they gone into a bunker, as some preceding administrations had, they would have been in far deeper trouble—as later they did and were. Before Bill Clinton took office, they had read and thought and talked with each other about previous Presidents and noted that going into the bunker had destroyed some of them. Often it was Hillary Clinton who pushed for changing things, such as personnel. But she could have a blind eye too. Both Clintons had a greater need than was good for them to have people around them whose loyalty—and lack of independence—wasn't in question.

On matters of policy, Gergen, who was feeling his way along in a new and somewhat strange atmosphere, weighed in on everything from the President's policy on gays in the military to taxes. He wasn't enthusiastic about the reconciliation bill (he thought it didn't cut spending enough) but tried to lie low on that since it was a Presidential priority.

He urged the President to get more involved with "values" issues such as crime and welfare and national service—issues that would identify him as "a different kind of Democrat." While Gergen and his new colleagues put up a chummy front, both Gergen and the new colleagues expected that someday there would be ideological fights. (Gergen told people privately that he didn't want to wage war against the Republicans in election years 1994 and 1996.) A major reason Gergen had been brought in was that he was a centrist. Several key staff members, such as Stephanopoulos and his allies, were more liberal, more concerned with the President's campaign commitments. McLarty and Gergen formed an ideological bond. In June,

McLarty told a Senate friend, "I'm glad Gergen's here. He'll strengthen my side of the argument." In time, McLarty was Gergen's only real ally in the White House.

One of Gergen's first acts was to meet with the communications staff to try to allay its suspicions of him. But some of the communications people never forgave him for being there at all, not to mention having appeared to displace Stephanopoulos. The selection of Mark Gearan to run the communications office, something that had been considered before and that Gergen very much favored, helped to soothe feelings. Gearan, a smart, witty, low-key man, was popular among the White House staff. Though some criticized him when he was Deputy Chief of Staff as not enough of an enforcer, he was tougher than he appeared, and he made some swift changes in the communications office. Wisely, he decided not to conduct the regular briefings, leaving them to Dee Dee Myers.

Stephanopoulos now worked out of an office that was less than half the size of his former one but nearer still to the Oval Office. Only the President's private dining room separated their offices, and a peephole in the door in between Stephanopoulos's office and the dining room could tell Stephanopoulos whether it was in use. Stephanopoulos's new role was part of his former one, but expanded because he was now relieved of the briefings. He was to ride herd on policy issues, watch out for trouble, and report to the President on what he heard from his contacts on Capitol Hill. He spent a great deal of time in the Oval Office. His close relationship with the President, and his ability to read his mind better perhaps than anyone but Mrs. Clinton, made him valuable to other members of the White House staff.

Within days of Gergen's arrival, the word went out that McLarty and Stephanopoulos and Gergen had formed a "troika." This was a bit of spin that served the interests of all three: it conveyed that Stephanopoulos, despite his change of jobs, hadn't fallen; that McLarty, frequently charged with being inept, was in the company of two talented men and things were working better; and that Gergen had been accepted as part of the team. But troika talk soon faded. In fact, there had never been one. Gergen and Stephanopoulos were always courteous toward McLarty and respectful of his title as Chief of Staff, but they didn't necessarily work through him in their dealings with or for the President. Over time, the tensions between Gergen and Stephanopoulos grew.

One of Gergen's first pieces of advice to the President was to try to be on time. Gergen's friends found this news uproarious, because Gergen himself was notoriously late to most events. But Gergen's point was serious: it detracted from the dignity of the office for Clinton to be chronically late.

The tardiness had become an image problem. In a senior staff meeting, Gergen pointed out that the President's being punctual would give an impression of order, of being focused. So on Tuesday, June 8, when Clinton was on time for his meeting with the congressional leadership, some of the leaders weren't there yet, because they never expected the President to be on time. Over the next months, the drive for punctuality was a sometime thing, and it achieved only partial success. Gergen himself was frequently late for appointments. This had to do only in part with the sprawling meetings that still went on at the White House.

Gergen's strength didn't lie in organization or management, and in some ways his arrival further complicated the organizational problems. There was yet another person to check with. It wasn't clear who had what authority. A slightly more junior staff person said in June, "I try to weigh in, but I'm not sure where the place to do that is. It's more a matter of grabbing someone in the hall." Gergen added another voice to the noise. He tried to crispen the decision-making process—get people to understand when the time came to make decisions—but despite some minor progress, that problem, too, was beyond his reach.

Gergen's experience with how past White Houses had been run did enable him to offer some fairly obvious pointers. At senior staff meetings, he would try to get it made clear what was to be done that day. Even those who were skeptical about him said that he brought a sense of order to the morning meetings. He brought his sense of how to get things done within a given news cycle—though he wasn't always successful at making that happen. And he brought a sense of timing that helped determine when the President would do or propose certain things. Gergen had a wisdom that most of the less experienced didn't and couldn't have. Their resentment of him sometimes blinded them to that. After a while, the senior staff meetings in effect fell into disuse, and Gergen stopped attending them.

Early in his tenure, Gergen asked why Bruce Lindsey was on the manifest for the President's trip to Japan—especially given the numerous complaints from Capitol Hill about the slowness of the appointment process, which Lindsey was responsible for. Lindsey went to Japan. Gergen learned not to intrude in certain matters.

The Clinton White House was unlike any Gergen had known. The number of people who took the President's time, the lack of enough experienced staff people, the number of meetings, the sudden calls to the Oval Office, the inability to control his time, the fewer number of people available for certain chores (such as speechwriting), the lack of systems for moving decisions, the inability to get decisions made quickly—all came as a surprise to him, and within days he was feeling weary and frustrated.

The dinner parties for about forty people that the Clintons began to give in early June had been discussed for some time before Gergen reached the White House. Eventually, friends and staff convinced the Clintons that they were too isolated from the crosscurrents of Washington. A close friend of the Clintons' said, "You can see Hillary's hand in the new round of extensive entertaining. She understands that the country needs to see the White House and the Presidency as symbols. She felt the need to open up to Washington. They need all the surrogates and supporters they can get." The dinners, held twice a week for quite a while, were gracious affairs, with the Clintons making sure to circulate among their guests so that all were talked to. The evenings often began with drinks on the Truman balcony and included a Presidential tour of the White House. They frequently ended with a movie in the family theater.

Staff members insisted that a barbecue the Clintons threw—at the last minute—for the press on July 13 had been planned before Gergen's arrival. While this may have been true, without question Gergen urged the Clintons to relax their attitude toward the press, at least outwardly, and take certain steps to show that they had done so.

The corridor between the pressroom and what was now Gearan's office was opened—a highly symbolic move. (Gergen pointed out to the Clintons that an open passageway would enable staff members to get early warning of stories brewing in the press, and keeping it closed would cause more trouble than it was worth.) And on the day after the Ginsburg announcement came to an abrupt end, when Clinton lashed out at Brit Hume's question about the zigzag process of choosing a Supreme Court nominee, Gergen persuaded the President to hold a news conference to smooth things over. In the briefing room, Clinton, looking relaxed and friendly, called first on Hume and made a small joke about Hume's having just returned from a honeymoon, which Clinton said he hadn't had. Gergen caused some raised eyebrows among the staff and in the press by uttering, from the side of the room, in a stage whisper, like an impresario, "That was perfect." He also was noticed getting into the picture with Clinton at various events, chatting with him like an old friend.

On June 17, Clinton held his first prime-time press conference. (To the dismay of the White House, only CNN and PBS carried it in full. NBC carried it for a half hour.) Like his predecessors, Clinton used the stagy entrance: approaching the East Room on a royal-red carpet. His eyes were very puffy, and he looked unwell: allergies, his aides said.

He led with an announcement clearly designed to make news: referring to the U.S. troops in Somalia, he said, "General Powell has reported to me this afternoon that this operation is over and that it was a success." He continued, "The United Nations, acting with the United States and other nations, has crippled the forces in Mogadishu of warlord [Mohamed Farah] Aideed." In an answer to a question, he offered a technically correct but misleading statement: "The United Nations and the United States never listed getting Aideed as one of our objectives." On the previous weekend, peacekeeping forces had staged an attack, using C-130s, on Aideed's arms depots and neighborhood. The Pentagon had told reporters it was looking for Aideed (who, of course, wasn't found).

At this press conference, Clinton said, with forced joviality, "As all of you know, and as a few of you've pointed out in various ways in the past few weeks, I just got here." He was both encouraging and exploiting the public's view, as expressed in some polls, that his problems were part of the learning process. "Everyone in America knows, as I said, that I did not live and work in this city until I became President"—a good anti-Washington shot. He said, "I knew when I came here that there would be things that I would need to learn about the processes and the ways things worked."

At the end of the press conference, Clinton left the podium and shortly returned, wearing a red-and-white Mickey Mouse tie he had admired on a reporter. The President was trying too hard.

There were other changes going on in the White House. McLarty turned over the chairing of the senior staff meetings to Roy Neel, his deputy, who did try to assign people their responsibilities and hold them to them. The number of people in meetings with the President was reduced. It would go back up fairly soon. Neel also made piecemeal staff changes at the lower level, so as not to give the appearance of a massacre. A greater effort was made to not take issues to the President too soon—before they had been chewed over by the staff—and to give him options papers for policy decisions he had to make. This was of limited success, because most of the staff members were too busy going to meetings to write papers.

In early June, Bruce Lindsey said, "We're trying to structure the President's time better. I and others had sensed that meetings would be put on his schedule that weren't at a point that the President's time was needed. They weren't structured in a way that the discussion could be focused. The President does very well if you give him a memo that outlines options in a fair amount of detail." For demonstration purposes, he pulled out a memo on enterprise zones: a memo and attachments and a series of decisions, fairly detailed, to be made. But the President did like to discuss things. Lindsey said, "The big decisions around here aren't necessarily made by one person. They arise out of discussion." Stan Greenberg said that Clinton "might make some decisions from memos and options, but on major things he wants to sit down for two or three hours and talk to people about it. You need to create structure that enables him to do that. Yes, he is working from documents more, but he's not going to make policy decisions without talking to people." There were still too many meetings, and it still took too long to get decisions. And Clinton wasn't happy about it.

A lot of people blamed the lack of structure at the White House on McLarty, but that wasn't quite fair, since Clinton had chosen not to have a hierarchical structure. And McLarty was chosen late—giving him little time to prepare—"because," one Clinton adviser said, "the Clintons didn't want it to appear that some people had the inside track." The adviser said, "There was a confusion of private-sector management and knowing about government. 'Honest broker' is not the description of a Chief of Staff. Other people wanted someone who wouldn't get in their way. By the time Mack was named, there were a number of people with a direct line to Clinton, and he never empowered Mack."

In turn, though, McLarty never empowered Neel. He wasn't given real authority to do what he was supposed to do—impose order and accountability on the White House staff. Later in the summer, a senior official said, "This place isn't conducive to the charter Roy was given. The Clintons didn't want a structural, hierarchical place."

The Clinton White House was characterized by circles. One aide said, "There are circles within the White House. The first circle is folks who came from Arkansas and some people on the periphery of that circle—such as George Stephanopoulos. There are the people he respects and looks up to —Christopher and Bentsen. Tony Lake doesn't care; he's more grounded than most. Bob Rubin doesn't care, he thinks of himself as an observer on Mars. Some people it bothers—the attitude that 'We got here without you and we can do without you.' "

Political meetings in the solarium continued, held once or twice a week. Mrs. Clinton always attended, and the President did frequently. Also attending were McLarty, Stephanopoulos, Gergen, and the four consultants—Greenberg, Begala, Carville, and Grunwald. Mrs. Clinton played a prominent role at these meetings. "Hillary's the closer," someone who attended them said. "Sometimes she won't say much at a meeting at all, but when she does say something she says it with meaning. She'll say, 'This is serious,' with clarity and forcefulness. There is no beating around the bush. Her advice frequently is, Do the right thing and damn the consequences." She had been an advocate for keeping up the fight for the stimulus bill rather than cave. She argued for a stronger proposal for campaign-finance reform than the President's political advisers were urging. (She won only a partial victory.) Mrs. Clinton's combative approach sometimes helped her husband's fortunes—and sometimes it helped neither of them.

Despite all the talk of changes at the White House in the early summer, it wasn't apparent some weeks later that anything of consequence had taken place. It remained unclear who had responsibility for what. There was no coordination of policy groups—domestic, economic, national security—not to mention of policy initiatives. Legislative efforts weren't coordinated. One staff member said, "It's a floating crap game about who runs what around here. The last person who has an idea can often get it done, whether it's part of the strategy or not. The situation hasn't improved."

A source of confusion was the President. It could be difficult to know what he wanted done. Clinton gave his aides conflicting signals. He would tell one aide that he wanted more issues committed to paper and another that he did not. He would express frustration about the loose management of the White House and invite kibitzing by people inside and outside his administration. He complained about an overloaded schedule and urged that events be added. A close adviser said, "He likes a loose structure until there's a screwup. Then he gets upset."

Confusion was also caused by Clinton's virtual incapacity to say no. An outside close observer said, "One of Clinton's problems is that he raises expectations. You need someone with him all the time who can say to a Member of Congress, 'Don't get too far out with this.' " Even some of Clinton's closest advisers were thrown off by his penchant for being agreeable. One said, "Sometimes when the President says, 'That's a great idea,' or 'I really like that,' that doesn't mean 'Go do it.' It means 'Let's think about it.' He'll say, 'That's incredible' or 'I really like that, we ought to think about that,' and then launch into another subject. You had to edit out the last phrase. Even when you mention something he's adamantly opposed to, he'll say, 'I think you may be right,' and then launch into reasons we shouldn't do it. It's like a conversational tic, but people hear the part they want to hear." An aide might say to Clinton, "Mr. President, did you really promise X," and Clinton would reply, "Hell, no. I told him I thought it was a great idea, but I didn't commit to do it." Staff members often had to disabuse people of the notion that Clinton had agreed to what they had proposed.

Almost everyone fell victim to this well-intended equivocation, even Gore and McLarty. For a long time, Gore would use Clinton's positive words as an opening to advance something he felt strongly about. Only a few understood Clinton's special language: Hillary Clinton, Bruce Lindsey, Nancy Hernreich, and George Stephanopoulos. One person described this aspect of Clinton: "Failing to read the President's true meaning creates havoc from time to time."

At the end of June, Gergen pushed to get out of the way several of the President's more controversial subjects: closing military bases, resolving the owl/timber dispute, issuing the report on the travel office, and announcing the new policy on gays in the military. David Dreyer, deputy communications director, privately referred to this as "a yard sale from our little house of horrors." In announcing his owl/timber solution on July 1, Clinton said that the problem was "more difficult than I had thought." His proposal was a compromise that pleased neither side. This could be seen as perhaps a metaphor for his first year thus far.

Clinton rarely conceded that a problem was insoluble. He was in his candy store. He wanted to take on everything, from defense conversion to owls. The vitality was appealing—to a large segment of the public, much of the time—but exhausting, for him as well as the public.

On the Friday before the July 4 weekend, the White House was in a state of near bedlam. Gergen had taken charge of putting together the preparations for Clinton's first meeting with the Group of Seven industrial nations, to begin in Tokyo on July 7. Clinton and his aides had seemed quite unprepared. No one else in the White House had ever been involved in a G-7 meeting, and the planning had begun quite late. Moreover, Clinton was balking. He asked aides, "Why do I have to take this trip?" He was conducting satellite interviews with correspondents from countries that were to attend the G-7 meeting, was being crammed with briefings, and was making phone calls to other world leaders going to Tokyo. The President was to stop en route to visit the devastating floods in the Midwest. Harried aides sprinted back and forth through the West Wing lobby. Clinton summoned various advisers to the Oval Office. He wasn't in a good mood.

Yet at lunch that day with a small group of journalists, Clinton was genial and focused, and gave a clear demonstration of his potential.

At the lunch, in the yellow-walled Old Family Dining Room, on the main floor of the mansion, Clinton showed his capacity for growth, and the way his engaged mind worked. He wasn't particularly profound—his knowledge seemed to consist largely of matter that was useful to his work—but in contrast with some of his predecessors, there was nothing mentally lazy about him. The lunch performance was an impressive one, the likes of which he had yet to give publicly.

The lunch showed an evolution in Clinton: his thinking had moved beyond the pragmatic details of domestic programs, beyond the legislative battles, toward a worldview, a larger vision of what he wanted to achieve. An adviser said, "I think it finally hit him that global economics *is* domestic economics. There's damn little he doesn't understand in his gut, but during the run-up to the meeting in Japan it became much clearer to him."

Clinton also gave an insight into his unusual, and somewhat naive, way of looking at foreign policy. He said, "Part of my job is to make the Japanese people feel that I'm very hopeful, that the American people are very hopeful." For Clinton, optimism was a policy (he had read his FDR) as well as a character trait, and while he was on to something about the American people, the idea that he could cheer up the world was appealing if somewhat ingenuous. He said, "What kills people is when they think there is no tomorrow, when they cannot imagine it being better." Clinton also said something on the subject of Somalia that in retrospect raised questions about what he had said at his recent press conference, and about some of the things he said later. About Mohamed Farah Aideed, he said, "He'll continue to cause problems until and unless we arrest him." Asked about criticisms that he hadn't demonstrated world leadership, he said, "I've just been here five months."

His staff had difficulty in getting him to leave the lunch despite the fact that Chancellor Helmut Kohl was waiting on the phone.

18

WORLD LEADER

"That Way, People Will Look to You"

On July 4, a Sunday, the Clintons participated in Independence Day ceremonies in Philadelphia and flew on to inspect the floods in the Midwest, landing in San Francisco that evening. After his pre-foreign-trip speech, on trade, in San Francisco on Monday, the Clintons arrived in Tokyo that night. As happened with Clinton in other instances, the preparation could be messy, the mood bad, the fatigue deep, the prospects unappealing, and then—when the spotlight came on, when he had to perform—he summoned his raw talent, his resilience, and his competitiveness, and rose to it.

Of course, though low in the polls at home, Clinton didn't have a lot of competition in Japan. The other leaders were in a weakened condition too, at least in part because of the slumping global economy. Clinton upstaged them by his sheer energy and adroitness. By taking charge, by pushing for expanded trade and for aid to Russia, and through his impact in Japan as the young, energetic President, he managed to come off as leader of the leaders. (Mrs. Clinton was the object of great interest, given her pathbreaking First Ladyship, but to avoid offending Japanese sensibilities, she played the traditional spousal role, saying little.)

It had been solemnly decided that Clinton wouldn't jog in Japan, lest those pictures edge out pictures on the evening news of the President talking to world leaders. According to the *Washington Post* (in a story that made Clinton furious), the planners scripted "moments": the Clintons walking down a Tokyo street, the Clintons meeting the crown prince's new wife. This technique was not new, of course; Gergen was now on the scene and knew all about these things. Clinton made an "impromptu" stop at a baseball game. There had been serious debate about what he should do with regard to the parents of a Japanese exchange student who had been shot to death en route to a Halloween party in Baton Rouge, Louisiana. The American ambassador to Japan, Michael Armacost, had told the White House that Clinton had to do something. Lake drew up the options, which were dissected as exquisitely as if the subject were a major policy issue. The alternatives discussed were: bring the parents to the hotel where Clinton was staying, have Clinton go to see the parents, or a phone call. The visit to the parents was ruled out because it would have involved an hour-long helicopter ride. Gergen said later, "We didn't want it to be too dramatic or send the wrong signal to America—that the President was apologizing to Japan for American violence." The resulting phone call to the parents was generally deemed a great political success.

Clinton needed to appear successful at the summit. He had yet to demonstrate convincingly that he could play effectively on the world stage. There had been the rejection by European leaders of his Bosnia policy, and a maladroit comment to Yeltsin in Vancouver about the Japanese (that they often say yes when they mean no). His policy toward Russia was a source of pride among administration officials, but various audiences, domestic and international, needed more convincing that he was up to the entire job.

It sometimes appeared that the President was campaigning in Japan. If he wasn't the first President to do this, he seemed to do more of it. And on this trip he began the ritual of making a speech, early in the trip, to some audience in the host country, trying to persuade that country to respond to his policies. As usual, Clinton seemed to believe there was no one he couldn't persuade.

The administration successfully labeled the G-7 meeting a "jobs summit." Clinton was portrayed as pressing the other leaders to expand their economies so as to expand world trade—and thus markets for the United States. Because he was making a serious effort to reduce the deficit, he had the standing to do this. (Previous Presidents had received lectures from their counterparts about the U.S. deficit.) Gergen took over the communications function and became the briefer and the impresario. But he spun so strenuously that the effort itself stood out and detracted from the President's success. Gergen should have understood this.

The President didn't speak much in the meetings. An aide said later, "He told me, 'I've learned, in groups like this, don't speak all the time. But when you do, make it important. That way, people will look to you.' " This, of course, was a standard technique of experienced meeting-attenders. And Clinton the quick study was able to show his counterparts his grasp of the subject at hand. Still, he chafed at the formality, the structuredness of the meetings and told aides that he would argue for greater informality in the future.

The meeting produced two important developments in trade. The first got the negotiations in the Uruguay Round of the worldwide GATT (General Agreement on Tariffs and Trade) talks unstuck. (Clinton aides claimed that it was Clinton's presummit phone call to Kohl that had done it.) The other provided a "framework" for bilateral talks aimed at reducing the United States' large trade deficit with Japan. Lake disappeared in Tokyo to negotiate this, and the result came at the last minute and was much ballyhooed by administration officials.

In South Korea, the next stop, the President visited American troops at the DMZ, which produced among other things a picture of Clinton, wearing a leather jacket and a cap with a USFK emblem (United States Forces Korea), peering through binoculars at North Korea. The United States was already in a serious struggle with the North—which U.S. intelligence was saying had the capacity for making two nuclear bombs—over the limits it was placing on inspection of its facilities by the International Atomic Energy Agency. Though other Presidents had visited the demilitarized zone, Clinton was able to claim that he was the first one to go so close to the border. Clinton, still striving for approval among the military, also addressed some American troops in Panmunjom and played the saxophone for them.

Aspin flew to South Korea to join his Commander in Chief. Gergen told him not to bring any documents about the nearly completed policy on gays in the military, for fear of that subject turning up in stories about the President's trip. Gergen's request got in the news.

The exhausted President got the chance to rest in Hawaii on the way home. But neither Clinton found it possible to relax completely. Mrs. Clinton, released from her Tokyo bonds, plunged into a round of health care meetings. (Hawaii had something close to the managed-competition plan that the Clintons were fashioning.) Chelsea had joined them, and there were some attractive pictures of the family playing in the surf. (The pictures of a bare-chested Clinton weren't as bad as some of his advisers had feared; he was bulky but in quite good shape.) Clinton also played golf with Neel and others.

The pictures of the President at play misfired. And Clinton, who badly needed and utterly deserved a rest, came under criticism for splashing in the surf while midwesterners were struggling with calamitous floods. Clinton had to cut short his trip by twelve hours to get him to the Midwest before the noon news the next day. He was pained by some people's perception that he was shirking his duty. At least he could sleep in the large Presidential bedroom on Air Force One. Mrs. Clinton stayed behind to attend more meetings. The next day produced pictures of an obviously tired President, in a navy-blue polo shirt, in Des Moines, helping fill sandbags. Most of Des Moines was without safe water. When he spoke, Clinton could muster little energy. But he was able to show his empathy—and the people he had come to help were obviously grateful.

The following Saturday, Clinton's penchant for roundtable discussions was on display as he hosted a daylong meeting with midwestern governors in Arnold, Missouri, a suburb south of St. Louis. Gore and much of the Cabinet were in attendance; Clinton and Gore were dressed casually. Once again, Clinton showed off his knowledge—and Reich actually handed out checks. Gore, armed with maps, gave a weather report. In the course of the meeting, Clinton said something surprising, and encouraging to his aides. When a governor appealed for more grants instead of loans, Clinton, rather than respond right away, said, "When you get to be President, you're never supposed to say something off the top of your head."

A few weeks later, Robert Reich tried to explain a notable characteristic of Clinton's Presidency—as he put it, "Why this administration has so many summits and policy by discussion." He said, "We're almost all the products of the sixties generation, in which the process of decision making is very different from the process of decision making of the generation that went before us—people coming out of the Second World War. And the revolts of the sixties were very much in reaction to the hierarchical society we inherited. So every time I feel exasperated by how decisions are made here, why so many people are in on them and why it's so hard to get closure, I've decided a lot of it is deliberate, not just at the White House, but in my own department as well. I'm much more comfortable making decisions sitting around a table with assistants than sitting at a desk and checking a box."

19

WHITE HOUSE TRAGEDY

"You Can't Stay for the Next Half Hour"

Clinton returned from the trip to Japan to face some other important unfinished business besides the reconciliation bill—the most urgent being to decide and announce the new policy on gays in the military.

The issue had been neuralgic for the Clinton administration during the six-month period since it was turned over to the Pentagon for study. The problem wasn't only that Clinton couldn't resist answering questions. Others were keeping the subject in the news as well.

In May, Sam Nunn, the Armed Services Committee chairman, conducted sensational hearings that produced pictures of senators touring a ship, peering into closely stacked bunks and at bathrooms, and inquiring solemnly about the number of sailors per facility. (The ship's officer conducting the tour told the grave senators that "there's twenty-one men per toilet, forty-six men per urinal, and thirty-one per shower.") The biggest news out of the hearings was Marine Colonel Fred Peck announcing that his son was gay and shouldn't serve in the Marines because the colonel would fear for his safety. ("I would be very fearful that his life would be in jeopardy from his own troops.") Retired General Norman Schwarzkopf, the beefy hero of the Gulf War, also attracted attention by testifying that if the ban was lifted, the troops "will be just like many of the Iraqi troops who sat in the deserts of Kuwait, forced to execute orders they didn't believe in."

The hearings created a backlash within the Pentagon. Schwarzkopf's line suggesting that U.S. troops could be as demoralized as the Iraqi force didn't go down well with many of the senior military leaders, including Powell. They felt that the United States had the best force that had ever been fielded, and no single event would demoralize it. Marine Commandant Carl Mundy, the most opposed to a change in policy, took exception to Colonel Peck's remarks. His force was much better trained and disciplined than that, he said. Powell had already begun to shift his view, because he felt that there was too much tension within the Pentagon between the military and the civilians.

The Chiefs would have to back any new policy if it was to escape being overturned on Capitol Hill. Nunn was proposing a solution the Chiefs agreed with (no accident)—"Don't ask, don't tell": the military would no longer ask a recruit his or her sexual orientation, but a gay service member couldn't talk about it either. This left a lot of questions as to what was meant by "tell" and what would be considered banned homosexual behavior (reading gay magazines in the barracks? dancing together off base?).

With the Chiefs willing to go only so far, and Secretary Aspin having moved them as far as he could, the question was whether the President should agree to a compromise or stand up to the Chiefs and take a position that would be rejected by the Congress—the Chiefs would be required to tell Congress their views—with the probable result that the old policy would be left in place. Congress would likely write it into law.

Aspin came up with an important compromise over the existing policy's statement that "homosexuality is incompatible with military service." His compromise stated: "The Department of Defense has long held that, as a general rule, homosexuality is incompatible with military service. . . . Nevertheless, the Department . . . recognizes that individuals with a homosexual orientation have served with distinction in the armed services." The proposed new policy, termed "Don't ask, don't tell, don't pursue," said that service members would be cashiered for "homosexual conduct," which it described as a homosexual act, a statement by a service member "that demonstrates a propensity or intent to engage in homosexual acts," or a homosexual marriage. This still left a lot of questions to be worked out. Stephanopoulos, who was handling the issue at the White House, had hoped to find something that General Powell and Massachusetts Representatives Barney Frank and Gerry Studds, both openly gay, would endorse—and at one point he thought the agreement was there; but then Frank and Studds bailed out because gay groups wouldn't accept the final compromise. Frank, one of the cleverest Members of Congress, had made a good faith effort to get the gay groups to go along with the compromise. But Aspin had come up with something Powell would accept, and Powell had worked on the other Chiefs to go along.

At a meeting on Wednesday night, July 14, in the President's study in the residence, the issue was argued bitterly. Gore insisted that the President shouldn't compromise, that it was a matter of principle. The President should just lift the ban, Gore argued, even though he was sure to be overridden by the Congress. Aspin argued for accepting the compromise, saying it was as far as the Chiefs would go. The President was concerned that even private statements about one's homosexuality would largely be prohibited, and worried that the compromise was too restrictive about what constituted private conduct. (Clinton had said all along that there would be some restrictions on conduct.)

At one point, Clinton argued with Gore—this was most unusual—saying, "You can't say, 'This is the sword I'll fall on,' when I didn't for the middle-class tax cut. If you want me to die on my sword on this one, you tell me why I shouldn't have done it on the middle-class tax cut." Paster argued that picking a fight with the Congress on the gays issue would have untoward effects on the effort to win the President's economic program.

The clinching argument was made by Lake, who was generally seen as an idealist. He argued that accepting the compromise was the way to advance the cause. Lake said, "It doesn't serve a principle to stand on principle and not compromise, if that means you lose altogether."

In the following days, it was Clinton who came up with a softening of the prohibition on statements, saying that a propensity toward homosexual conduct created a rebuttable presumption that the person was gay, which the accused could challenge. Aspin got this change approved over the weekend by the Chiefs, and on Tuesday, July 20, five days past his own deadline, the President announced his new policy in a speech at the National Defense University at Fort McNair, across the Potomac. Speaking to a sea of uniforms, and with an array of flags behind him, Clinton spoke somberly, trying to touch a number of bases—pointing out that Barry Goldwater and Senator Bob Kerrey (a decorated hero of the Vietnam War), among others, favored lifting the ban. Clinton listed the military facilities he had visited and mentioned the raid on Iraq. He was virtually begging for the military's approval: "I'm here because I respect you." He didn't look like a Commander in Chief. In an echo of his January statement, Clinton said, "It is not a perfect solution. It is not identical with some of my own goals. . . . It is an honorable compromise."

The White House wasn't entirely unhappy about coming up with a solution the gay groups didn't embrace, and Presidential aides were pleased with Representative Frank's statement after the compromise was announced. "My disappointment is at the political reality, not the President," he said, adding, "Bill Clinton was quite courageous to take it on."

(The new policy was tied up in courts until the Supreme Court in late October reversed a lower court ruling and said that the administration's policy could proceed. In December, the Pentagon issued the regulations for carrying out the new policy, which continued the outlaw status of most known homosexuals in the military and left to local commanders a lot of discretion on enforcing the new code. In the meantime, Nunn had successfully led an effort in Congress to slightly tighten the new policy, a move the White House didn't feel it could resist.)

Right after the Japan trip, Clinton was also faced with the firing of William Sessions, the director of the FBI, and naming a successor. Sessions, a former U.S. district judge, and FBI director for five years (of a statutory ten-year term), had been bathed in controversy since a Justice Department report, issued in January, charged him with several ethical lapses, most of them minor. The Clinton people decided that he had to go, but Sessions wouldn't resign. Gergen and Stephanopoulos had hoped to dispose of the matter before the Japan trip, but Nussbaum hadn't come up with a successor. Normally soft-spoken (except when he was arguing with Gore), Stephanopoulos had taken to yelling at meetings about the fact that it was taking so long to get the FBI business done with. He'd say, "You've known for five months that Sessions was going, and you can't come up with a replacement?" Finally, on Monday afternoon, July 19, after Clinton made his speech about gays-in-the-military policy—this timing was deliberate, to cut into the news about the speech—he phoned Sessions to tell him he'd been fired, and, in a second call, told him that his dismissal was "effective immediately."

The timing of the firing was linked to naming a successor, and the following morning, in a Rose Garden ceremony, Clinton named U.S. District Judge Louis Freeh, himself a former FBI agent and federal prosecutor. The nomination received wide praise instantly, and Nussbaum and his colleagues, who had had a rough year, were pleased with their handiwork. Clinton, too, was happy.

That night, in the Library, on the ground floor of the White House, Clinton was to appear on *Larry King Live.* As his makeup was being applied, he was briefed by Myers, Stephanopoulos, Gearan, Dreyer, and Grunwald. The President felt good about how things were going, and his aides were encouraging him to express that. He had dispensed with the gays-in-the-military issue, Sessions had been fired and Freeh appointed, and Ruth Bader Ginsburg had begun her confirmation hearings, which were going well. Work on a House-Senate compromise of the reconciliation bill was proceeding.

While Clinton was on the air, McLarty received the news that Vince Foster's body had been found beside a Civil War cannon in Fort Marcy Park, on the Virginia side of the Potomac. An eighty-year-old Colt .38 revolver was in Foster's hand. He had been shot in the head. As the President continued the interview, McLarty and Stephanopoulos, looking ashen, were at a Secret Service station in the hallway nearby, making phone calls. McLarty got hold of Hillary Clinton, who was in Little Rock.

Clinton, in his agreeable way, had acceded to King's urging that he stay on the program for an extra half hour. At the next commercial break, McLarty said to the President, "We have an important appointment. You can't stay for the next half hour." Then McLarty led Clinton to the residence and told him. As quickly as possible—it still took thirty minutes to get the motorcade ready—Clinton and McLarty went to Foster's home, in Georgetown, to comfort his wife, Lisa. Vernon Jordan and David Gergen arrived together from a party in Georgetown. Jordan and the President hugged each other. After Clinton had just vanished from the King show, some of the press picked up what had happened and were on their way to the Foster house. So after forty-five minutes, it was decided to get Clinton out of there before the press showed up. He invited Gergen and Jordan to return with him for a drink, and back at the White House, the group gathered in the family kitchen. Clinton, rare for him, had a drink. Mickey Kantor and his wife, Heidi Shulman, arrived a little later.

Clinton reminisced about Foster, telling his consolers that in Hope, Foster's and his backyards abutted each other, and the two of them threw knives in the dirt when they were four or five. There was some discussion about what to do next. Should Clinton cancel the next day's schedule? Jordan strongly urged Clinton to stick to the business of government; it was fine for him to be seen grieving, but he mustn't appear to have been knocked off course or go into seclusion. The public and his staff had to see that he was all right, Jordan said. Both Gergen and Jordan urged him to speak to the staff the next day and make a brief appearance in the Rose Garden. Jordan also urged that Foster's office be sealed right away.

The next day, Clinton told some staff members that he had got three hours of sleep. He kept an 8:30 A.M. appointment at the White House with the Black Caucus, and gave interviews to regional reporters about the budget fight, but canceled other public appearances.

At 11:30 A.M., the White House staff gathered in room 450 of the Old Executive Office Building. The room was packed, and the audience, while it awaited the arrival of Clinton, McLarty, and Nussbaum, was silent. In his talk to the staff, Clinton spoke of Foster's life, and praised it, and said, "No one can ever know why this happened. . . . So what happened was a mystery about something inside of him." Many said later that the President's words had helped.

Shortly before noon, Clinton made a similar statement to a press pool in the Rose Garden. "It is very important that his life not be judged simply by how it ended, because Vince Foster was a wonderful man in every way," he said, and added that Foster had been "normally the Rock of Gibraltar while other people were having trouble." Clinton was obviously grieving, but his composure was reassuring.

Later that afternoon, McLarty appeared before the press in the briefing room. McLarty and Foster had grown up together in Hope, and their families were close. When Foster, a year older than McLarty, was president of the student body of Hope High School, McLarty was vice president. They were social friends in Little Rock and became very close again after they both went to the White House. Before the meeting with the staff, McLarty had broken down, and that had shaken Clinton. McLarty didn't want to make the appearance, but because it was thought important to get someone to speak on the record about Foster, and because word had got out that McLarty might hold the briefing, it was thought that if he didn't, it might look as if he were ducking. McLarty said, "Try as we might, all of our reason, all of our rationality, all of our logic, can never answer the questions raised by such a death."

Under the circumstances, these were perfectly understandable things for a grieving friend to say. But a number of officials, including McLarty, realized later that they might have appeared to be trying to discourage speculation about Foster's death—which in fact they were, but not necessarily for sinister reasons. They specifically didn't want people to conclude that the troubles over the travel office—which Foster had taken very hard—had led to his death. A White House aide said later, "We had a legitimate fear that someone who wanted to monger this would write about the travel office, and everyone wanted to make sure that the travel office didn't define his life."

The things they said publicly were very close to the things they had been saying to each other in private. These people were in shock, and feeling their way along in a situation that was without precedent. The most smoothly run White House would have had difficulty with this situation. But in its handling of the matter, what were at the least mistakes in judgment caused the Clinton White House to be haunted by the Foster suicide for a long time to come.

On Wednesday night, Clinton returned to Foster's home, and on the following night, Clinton and some friends, including Lindsey, went to Nora's, a popular restaurant where the Clintons had eaten before, and reminisced and laughed.

Gradually, shock gave way to reality and sorrow. Lindsey was probably in the worst shape of all. Inevitably, people at the White House asked themselves painful questions about whether they should have noticed more than they had that Foster seemed depressed, and whether they should have done more.

Foster, a tall, handsome, reserved man, had been very close to the Clintons, especially Mrs. Clinton. In the White House, he had handled a lot of the Clintons' personal matters (whether, as a government employee, he should have done so became a matter of debate later). White House staff members went to him with questions about how to deal with certain things regarding the Clinton family. He acted as counsel to Mrs. Clinton and her staff, who saw him nearly every day. Their offices were near each other on the second floor of the West Wing. Foster had been chosen deputy counsel before Bernard Nussbaum was chosen as counsel. Nussbaum and Foster had run the counsel's office like law partners.

On Tuesday morning, Foster had attended the President's announcement of Freeh's appointment, in the Rose Garden. Later that morning, he had gone into Nussbaum's office, where Nussbaum was watching televised accounts of Freeh's announcement, as well as Ginsburg's hearing. Nussbaum said, "Take a look, Vince, back-to-back homers. Great for the President, great for the country, and we helped make it possible." Foster said nothing, and left the White House at about one o'clock, telling his secretary he'd be back.

After Foster's death, the names of two Washington psychiatrists were found on a piece of paper in his pocket, and it was learned that a Little Rock physician had recently sent him a prescription for antidepressant medication, which he had only just begun to take.

On July 21, the day after Foster's death, the Park Police said that "the injury was not inconsistent with that of a self-inflicted wound." (On August 11, it was officially ruled that Foster's death was a suicide.) Conspiracy theorists and others out to stir trouble would later raise questions about whether it was a suicide, but everything pointed to that.

Given the evidence, it seemed entirely possible that there was nothing more involved in Foster's death than what came out at the time. Here was a former golden boy, a prince of Little Rock, a perfectionist, who had come to Washington and encountered the kind of trouble that caused him to crack. He had been a very big deal in a very small milieu. The Rose Law

Firm, where he and Mrs. Clinton and Hubbell and Kennedy had practiced law, was the third-largest firm in the nation's ninety-sixth-largest city.

But after he was in Washington for a while, Foster appeared to feel that he had let down his friends and clients—the Clintons—and that his own reputation had been sullied. Foster was very upset by editorials in the *Wall Street Journal*—which would be read by his peers in Little Rock—which attacked the Rose alumni role in the administration as some sort of cabal and in particular singled out Foster ("Who is Vincent Foster?"). Nussbaum said later, "People like Kennedy and Vince and I are from outside Washington. We don't care so much what Washington thinks. We're concerned about what people back home would say." Foster was known to have been particularly disturbed about the travel office affair and the fact that his friend and former partner, William Kennedy, whom he had brought into the case, had been reprimanded, and that a minority report by Republicans on the House Judiciary Committee (which rejected a Republican call for an investigation) had been particularly tough on Kennedy for his contacts with the FBI. The Republicans largely accepted the FBI's version of events. A colleague said later, "Vince felt responsibility for what happened to Kennedy. It was like battle responsibility, for putting Kennedy in charge." Foster told colleagues that he should have been more astute about the travel office, should have foreseen the consequences for the President and his wife. The week before he died, he had begun to make inquiries about hiring an attorney to defend him in the matter of the travel office. He told colleagues that Washington could be a vicious place and expressed his belief that the White House press corps wasn't as interested in getting the facts and reporting what happened as it was in twisting things to produce a hot story.

Foster had been the quiet, sensitive, seemingly strong one, to whom others had taken their problems. But his sense of his own worth had suffered a terrible blow. In May, Foster addressed the graduating class of the University of Arkansas Law School, where he had studied law. Giving a sense of his own high standards, and fragility, Foster told the graduates: "The reputation you develop for intellectual and ethical integrity will be your greatest asset or your worst enemy. . . . I cannot make this point to you too strongly. There is no victory, no advantage, no fee, no favor, which is worth even a blemish on your reputation. . . . Dents to the reputation in the legal profession are irreparable." He had said in an interview with Margaret Carlson, of *Time,* "Before we came here, we thought of ourselves as good people." In retrospect, that was a statement of a depressed person. Toward the end, Foster appeared to have got into a suicidal depression—a downward cycle of sleeplessness and distraughtness—that led him to his death. Close family members who were in Washington, and some members of the Arkansas crowd, were aware that there was trouble. On the day of his death, Lisa Foster and Donna McLarty had had lunch at The Four Seasons and had talked about Mrs. Foster's concerns about her husband.

But the difficulty many had in believing that nothing else—no potential scandal, no conspiracy—was involved, and the way the White House handled the matter, caused a lot of people to surmise that something was being hidden. The thought that this might be a bigger story than the White House was letting on led editors and television producers to urge their reporters to dig further. In a few cases, uncorroborated rumor made it into print or onto the air.

On July 27, a week after Foster's death, Dee Dee Myers confirmed a *Newsweek* story saying that on Monday evening, the night before Foster died, Clinton had invited him to come to the White House to watch a new Clint Eastwood movie with him and Hubbell, who was with the President when he made the call. The Hubbells and the Fosters had spent time together on the Eastern Shore of Maryland the previous weekend. Myers said that Foster had declined and that Clinton and Foster talked for twenty minutes and agreed to meet on Wednesday. Myers said that Clinton knew Foster was having a "rough time at work." But, Myers said, "There was absolutely no reason to think Vince was despondent; nobody believed that." She added, "The President did not have any inkling that Vince was about to go kill himself." Of course not, and no one was accusing Clinton (or anyone else) of not taking enough notice of Foster's despair. And Foster had been giving off mixed signals about his state. In fact, it appeared that Clinton and others were trying to help. But this episode was another sign that the White House was trying to deny that anyone was aware that Foster was in trouble. It seemed clear that Clinton must have known, given the presence of Hubbell, who had just spent time with him, and given the number of people close to both Foster and Clinton who knew that Foster was upset and depressed. Clinton and his aides seemed to be trying to avoid any suggestion that Clinton had known something was wrong and hadn't done enough about it. Gearan told the press that Foster "never said anything to indicate that anything was out of the ordinary to his colleagues." But he had.

It was entirely possible—even likely—that nothing Clinton or anyone else could have done at that point would have helped. But the Clinton White House, in its effort to deflect interest or scrutiny, went overboard in its public denials that anyone knew there was a serious problem, and this undermined its credibility on the story as a whole. In the days immediately following Foster's death, several White House aides said, word for word, that even if Foster's state had been brought about by things that had happened to him since he came to the White House, it had to have been "his own demons" that brought on his death. Or, as one aide put it, "Even if it was the White House, it wasn't the White House." While something like that was of course the case—no one else took the failures so personally and so hard—the White House people appeared too anxious to place an unbridgeable distance between what had happened in the White House and what had happened to Foster. But though Foster's "failures" were of a particular kind, affecting, as he saw it, not only his own reputation but the reputations of people close to him, for whom he felt responsible, his tragic end was obviously brought on by what had happened in the White House. There later arose speculation that he was worried about other matters, such as the Clintons' financial affairs, which he was also handling (he was working on establishing their blind trust and back taxes owed on a failed real estate investment called Whitewater), but at the time there was no sign of this. And the speculation remained just that.

Then there was the handling of Foster's office, which wasn't sealed off until ten-fifteen of the morning after his death. The previous evening, Nussbaum, Maggie Williams, and Patsy Thomasson, deputy to David Watkins, had gone to Foster's office—to look for a suicide note, they said. Originally, Nussbaum said this took ten minutes. It was subsequently learned that he and the others were in Foster's office for two hours. Nussbaum said later that the office hadn't been sealed right away "because it wasn't the scene of a crime." Two days after Foster's death, Nussbaum sorted the materials found in Foster's desk and files while representatives from the FBI and the National Park Service, which was in charge of the investigation because of where Foster's body had been found, looked on—from a distance. They weren't allowed to see the documents. Nussbaum went through the files, describing their contents to the investigators. Some of the materials, regarding the Clintons' personal affairs, were sent to their Washington attorney. But the public wasn't told about that, or about their indirect route to the attorney, until much later, and in another context.

The White House's handling—or mishandling—of a note found on Monday, July 26, nearly a week after Foster's death, also raised questions. The undated, unsigned note—in twenty-seven torn pieces from a yellow legal pad, with one piece missing—was said to have been found in the bottom of Foster's briefcase. (Once again, the story was broken by a news organization—this time CBS—rather than released by the White House.)

Numerous meetings were held to decide what to do with it. Gergen, appearing later that week on *The MacNeil/Lehrer Newshour,* explained that the delay (which had angered other aides) was caused by the desire to show it first to Mrs. Foster, who was on her way back to Washington from Little Rock, and the President, who had been traveling on Monday and was busy on Tuesday. (Breaking into the President's schedule wasn't unheard of.) The letter was given to the Park Police Tuesday evening, thirty hours after it was discovered. Key people were concerned about the questions that might arise if they made the note public—which wasn't done until August 10, nearly two and a half weeks after it was found.

Gergen described Foster's note as "an argument about why someone might resign." But it was really a list of things that obviously had disturbed Foster deeply, a list of anger and anguish, a tormented interpretation of events.

> I made mistakes from ignorance, inexperience and overwork
>
> I did not knowingly violate any law or standard of conduct
>
> No one in the White House, to my knowledge, violated any law or standard of conduct, including any action in the travel office. There was no intent to benefit any individual or specific group
>
> The FBI lied in their report to the AG
>
> The press is covering up the illegal benefits they received from the travel staff
>
> The GOP has lied and misrepresented its knowledge and role and covered up a prior investigation
>
> The Ushers Office plotted to have excessive costs incurred, taking advantage of Kaki [Hockersmith, the Clintons' decorator] and HRC [Mrs. Clinton]
>
> The public will never believe the innocence of the Clintons and their loyal staff
>
> The WSJ editors lie without consequence
>
> I was not meant for the job or the spotlight of public life in Washington. Here ruining people is considered sport.

The reference to the FBI "lying" to the Attorney General was, evidently, about his friend Kennedy's version of his contacts with the FBI not having been agreed with by the FBI. The reference to the decorating costs was subsequently addressed by a statement saying that Mrs. Clinton "has been aware of the miscommunication between the Usher and decorator and is pleased that it has been resolved. The First Lady has no reason to believe the comments in Mr. Foster's writing regarding the Usher's Office are accurate."

Foster's anguished line about Washington made a lot of people stop and think. The fact that there was some truth in what he said was a source of real discomfort. But it was also the case that few people had got caught in the fire of press and political attack—and that some had deserved to. Public life could be brutal, and did require a measure of resilience, but there was nothing new about that. Except for the *Wall Street Journal,* Foster had received little public attention. But he felt that he and people close to him had been ruined. Events that others might have endured hit him in a particular way, as defined by his own chemistry and his own way of seeing things.

The Clintons went to Little Rock to bury Foster on July 23. The grief on their faces, and on the faces of others, such as Lindsey, was stark. It would take the Clintons a while to come to terms with what had happened. The fact that they had work to get on with helped.

But the story wouldn't go away.

20

RECONCILED

"Change Is Never Easy"

When the Clintons returned from Japan, Mrs. Clinton's demands in the solarium meeting before they left had been met: a book laying out strategy for the reconciliation fight and a war room were ready. Deputy Treasury Secretary Roger Altman was put in charge of the war room, with Ricki Seidman as his deputy. Altman, forty-seven, bridged the distance between the older, more traditional economic officials and the younger, more populist campaign workers. Altman became popular with the war room workers: prime staff members from the NEC, Treasury, and communications. He made sure they had good coffee and good bagels in the morning and had them all over for a party at his Georgetown house. As a former investment banker, Altman knew about crash projects. The war room also brought back the consultants on a regular basis. Begala was there every day, and Greenberg and Grunwald came to the regular 6:45 P.M. meetings. (Carville came and went, as usual.)

In the war room, room 160 of the Old Executive Office Building, people scanned the wire services and television news programs, worked on surrogate speakers, targeted information (which members were wavering and therefore which state speakers should be sent into), supplied information to members of Congress, worked with outside groups, and proposed opinion leaders to be brought in to see the President. A major purpose was the same as the technique emphasized in the campaign's war room: make sure that no charges went unanswered within the same news cycle. (This was part of Carville's religion.) Altman, in rolled-up shirtsleeves, encouraged, advised, and made his own calls to members of Congress. The place was laden with empty pizza boxes and lots of empty soft-drink cans.

How much actual difference the war room made was impossible to tell, but it was good for morale at the White House. Stephanopoulos remarked, "If members of Congress believe it's working, that's half the battle."

On July 20, Clinton addressed the roughly two hundred House and Senate negotiators on the reconciliation bill—the final form of his economic program—and he seemed a different person. He was forceful, assured, and showed some of his real political skill. After he was elected President, those native skills—his capacity for shrewd insight, and for understanding the effect of one thing on the next thing, and for framing an issue well and delivering his views with passion—had often been lost in the confusion caused by his own and his staff's mistakes, in the babble of voices advising him, and in his loss of confidence in his staff, and in himself.

The impetus for this speech was the consultants' view that when he had fallen back to simply endorsing "principles"—also at the behest of his political advisers—he didn't seem to be for anything, to be enough of a leader. Stan Greenberg said, "Our research showed uncertainty on the President's strength of leadership. We believed it very important to take the lead. The stakes for him succeeding were very high." Starting in mid-July, Greenberg had conducted focus groups in two succeeding weeks, in New Jersey and Chicago, and then in California and Kentucky. In addition to the doubts about the President's leadership, the polling found, Greenberg said, "They hope it [the President's program] will improve their lives, and therefore they prefer the plan to inaction. They know more about the plan than we thought. They know it is deficit reduction, and they certainly know it's taxes. Above all, they want to hear from the President that it will be good for the economy. They don't know whether it's good for the economy."

Also, as usual, Clinton's advisers fell into disagreement about how specific he should be on what he wanted in the final bill. Paster and Gore were arguing against specificity, saying that that would limit the President's bargaining power and make it harder to get a deal. Closely connected was the issue of whether the "center of gravity" in the negotiations would be on Capitol Hill or in the White House. The argument was settled by Bentsen, who, with Panetta's backing, said that the President should assert leadership.

Against the advice of some, Clinton, in his talk to the conferees, was fairly (but not utterly) specific about what he wanted in the way of taxes. At the urging of some of his advisers, the President also set the deficit reduction goal at $500 billion. The problem was how to arrive at $500 billion while using the lower Senate energy tax (about $50 billion less than the House) and restoring funds for investments and fund empowerment zones as the Black Caucus was demanding. Conservative Democrats didn't want to see the Black Caucus get its way and wanted more budget cuts. House Democrats didn't want to see Senate Democrats get their way.

Wearing a navy-blue suit and standing at a podium, Clinton, who was by turns eloquent, chatty, and colloquial, told the conferees, "For a very long time there has been a kind of political paralysis in this country, where we always knew what we had to do, but we could never quite bring ourselves to do it." He said, "Our children and our grandchildren will remember whether we were bashful or bold. They will remember whether we showed courage, or whether we turned away from the challenge. They will remember whether we gave in to gridlock and the kind of easy rhetoric that has come to dominate our politics of the last few years, or whether we govern." One wondered where this man had been.

Despite the case that the President had made, and despite the fact that public opinion was beginning to swing behind his program—and was critical of Republicans for their negativism—some Democrats didn't hesitate to exploit their bargaining power. Because of the earlier close vote in the Senate, a single Democratic senator could kill the President's economic program. And so the negotiations over the final form of the bill were protracted, and agony for the administration.

Mitchell and Moynihan, along with House leaders, struggled to put together a final bill that could get through both chambers, the Senate being the larger problem. The hardest part was the energy tax. Max Baucus, of Montana, insisted that he would oppose any increase over 4.3 cents per gallon. Herbert Kohl, Democrat of Wisconsin, who was up for reelection in 1994, threatened to oppose the bill if the gas tax rose above that amount. So the gas tax was settled at 4.3 cents. Bob Kerrey suggested that his vote for final passage of the reconciliation bill wasn't a sure thing. (He had voted for it the first time around.)

Meanwhile, the White House had been trying to stave off a defection by David Boren, with whom it had had rocky relations on the economic program virtually from the start. Boren had been trying to enlist Clinton in seeking a bipartisan solution—to pull Clinton toward the center. And because of Clinton's proclivity for appearing to agree with people, Boren thought he had won the President over. The White House needed his vote to pass the final bill, but on Saturday, July 24, Boren met at the White House with Clinton, Gore, McLarty, and Gergen, and told them that the bill that would likely emerge from the conference probably wouldn't cut spending enough. He also complained that while he generally supported the President, when he offered the bipartisan compromise in May he had been attacked by the President as supporting "big oil" at the expense of the poor.

The Clinton White House had no sure instincts about how to handle opponents, especially Democratic opponents whom it might need another day. And it didn't know how to put real pressure on an opponent, or a potential opponent. Everybody knew that there was no real price for opposing Clinton.

On Sunday, August 1, on *Face the Nation,* Boren made it official that he would oppose the final version of the reconciliation bill. Boren's defection put the administration in a hole by one vote. It meant that the administration had to win the support of at least one of the six Democratic senators who had opposed the plan the first time around. Moreover, Dianne Feinstein, of California, and Joseph Lieberman, of Connecticut—both of them up for reelection in 1994—were indicating they might oppose the bill. Of the six previously negative Democrats, Shelby was a "nonstarter"; Lautenberg was out (he had made strong statements against the President); despite efforts by the President and McLarty to win him over, Johnston didn't appear to be moving; Nunn didn't seem very likely to change. That left DeConcini, of Arizona, and Richard Bryan, of Nevada.

Mitchell and Moynihan kept almost getting a deal with the House negotiators, and then it would come unstuck. On Friday afternoon, July 30, the White House was all set up for an announcement of an agreement by the conferees on the reconciliation bill—but the agreement didn't happen. To make it appear that one had, for the weekend news, Mitchell announced a partial agreement on Friday afternoon. On Saturday morning, at eight-thirty, some tourists at the White House were rounded up to provide an audience for a statement by Clinton—also planned with the expectation there would be a deal by then. Wearing bright blue pants and a navy-blue jacket (the getup was a little hard on the eyes), Clinton argued that the gasoline tax would cost the average family less than thirty-three dollars a year.

Over the weekend, the administration sought to satisfy the demands of Democratic Senator Russell Feingold, who, on behalf of Wisconsin dairy farmers, was pushing for a moratorium on the sale and use of a bovine growth hormone that would increase the amount of milk produced by cows. The problem was that Gephardt's district contained Monsanto, which manufactured the product, not yet approved by the FDA. A compromise was reached whereby the product couldn't be sold for a period of time after FDA approval, and Congress could stop the marketing of it. That and a Presidential pledge to play golf with him on the Saturday before the Senate vote contented Feingold.

Also over the weekend, the conferees agreed to raise the proposed income threshold for the increase in Social Security taxes. The aim was to win the support of DeConcini, who as a Senator from Arizona represented a large number of retirees. If DeConcini changed his position, that would neutralize Boren's defection. (DeConcini had made something of a career of being a swing vote and wrenching concessions.) Representatives of small business groups were in there to the end, trying to get a better deal—which they did. In an attempt to win over Bryan, of Nevada, restaurateurs were given a tax credit for the Social Security taxes they paid on tips. The administration also offered Bryan a compromise on the deductibility of meals, but Bryan wasn't interested, and remained opposed to the bill.

Finally, on Monday, August 2, Mitchell, Foley, and Gephardt announced a deal. The hope was to win passage by the end of the week, in time for the planned August recess to begin on Saturday (a major incentive was the fact that many members of Congress had purchased nonrefundable airline tickets). The contours of the final bill were a large income tax increase on the better off (starting at individuals earning $140,000 and couples earning $180,000), up to an effective rate of 40 percent on incomes of over $250,000, and because the tax on Medicare was to now have no cutoff point, and because exemptions and personal deductions were phased out, the result was an effective top rate of 42.2 percent; a 4.3 cent increase in the gasoline tax; a 1 percent increase in corporate taxes, to 35 percent; nearly $56 billion in cuts in Medicare; $3.5 billion for empowerment zones; and a major increase in the Earned Income Tax Credit. The agreement also included $1 billion for a new program to fund family preservation services. (The program would provide funds to states to help keep children out of foster care, through various support services.) In order to make up for some funds lost from the Btu tax, the compromise made the tax increases retroactive to January 1, 1993. Though Republicans made a huge fuss about this provision, it wasn't new. The original administration proposal, and the House-passed bill, made the taxes retroactive to that date; the Senate had set the effective date at July 1, 1993.

The compromise bill would reduce the deficit by an estimated $496 billion over five years—a quite substantial amount.

Clinton threw himself into winning the final vote in the House and the Senate. He had made some mistakes, but he was also up against total Republican opposition, congressional arithmetic, the Reagan legacy and the ethos that legacy had produced: that taxes and government spending were bad things. Ross Perot was shamelessly opposing Clinton's program without a serious alternative of his own.

Clinton jogged with undecided members, held press conferences with reporters from the states of uncertain senators, met with caucus after caucus from the House of Representatives, rallied the support of business executives, met with senators, made phone calls. The slot for running with Clinton in the morning was a precious commodity. The White House once mistakenly booked someone to run who had already committed to vote for the bill.

As the voting neared, the administration still didn't have enough votes in the Senate, and the outcome in the House was uncertain. After considerable internal debate, it was decided that the President would make an Oval Office address, on Tuesday night, August 3.

For this speech, Clinton was dressed in a very dark suit, a white shirt, and a black-and-gold tie. In his attempt to look Presidential, he looked grim. His delivery was stiff. He hadn't got the hang of this setting yet. And he offered a fairly complicated formulation of the issue, talking about "entitlement" and "abandonment." In an implicit defense of his deal making, he said, "There are always places to give and take, but from the first day to this day, I have stood firm on certain ideas and ideals that are at the heart of this plan."

Using charts, the President showed that he had inherited a deficit that was going up (red line), and that under his plan it would go down (gold line), and that his plan was fair. He said, and repeated for emphasis, "there will be no income tax increase" for working families making less than $180,000 a year. He emphasized the business incentives in the program, as well as the increases for "investments"—Head Start, the Women's, Infants' and Children's program (WIC), and immunization. He also pointed out that the EITC would help working families and said it was the "critical first step to one of the most important priorities, ending welfare as we know it." Clinton mentioned his welfare reform goal often, because Greenberg's polling found that the idea received very high approval, but he had proposed no actual welfare plan.

In a somewhat embarrassing moment, Clinton said he would issue an executive order embracing an idea of DeConcini's to put the funds that were cut into a trust fund, to make sure they were used for deficit reduction rather than new spending. It was a phony move and a bald attempt to win DeConcini's vote.

Clinton relaxed as he went along. He had to fight hoarseness. Turning to some of his basic themes, he said, "Our opponents want to bring the plan down. The guardians of gridlock will do anything to preserve the status quo to serve special interests, and to drag this thing out." He said, "Tell them to change the direction of the economy and do it now." (Some of his advisers had thought all year that he badly needed a phrase to describe what he was trying to do—his own version of "New Deal," "Fair Deal," or "New Frontier"—but they had failed to come up with one. The "New Direction" of his February 17 speech was gone.) As Clinton looked squarely into the camera, he came off as sincere and friendly, and gave a defense of his administration's achievements thus far: family leave, a Supreme Court appointment, help for high technology, international summits in Vancouver and Tokyo.

The rhetoric didn't rise above the prosaic, but Clinton's rhetoric rarely did. His address was aimed at national perceptions as much as at the Congress; polls showed that large majorities believed that the burden of the new taxes would fall on the middle class.

On Wednesday, August 4, as "wavering" members of the House and Senate (including, of course, DeConcini), stood behind Clinton's desk and looked on self-consciously, getting their picture taken for the home folks, the President made a big show of signing the executive order. Later that day, DeConcini announced that he would vote for the bill.

DeConcini's support would have provided another tie vote for Gore to break, but Bob Kerrey was still uncommitted and was telling people contradictory things as to how he would vote. On the morning of the fourth, Kerrey went running with Clinton.

Though the negotiations on the final form of the reconciliation bill were supposedly over, they continued as Democratic congressional leaders and the administration kept fiddling with it in order to attract more votes. For members of Congress, there was still some point in holding out. One official said privately that it was a mistake that the President got so involved in the details and gave things away so early. "It should be very hard to get the President to wheedle," he said. "They made it too easy." A leading House Democrat said, "He's having more trouble with the Congress than he should because he's too accessible."

Publicly, the administration was defensive about the amount of trading that was going on. Privately, Bentsen told a colleague it was the worst he'd ever seen.

The truth was that the modern Presidency didn't have a lot of leverage. And Clinton couldn't deliver strong grassroots support, since he had won only 43 percent of the vote and he had no passionate following. His efforts to put together a governing coalition were stymied by Ross Perot's open opposition. There was precious little money for distributing bridges and dams and the like. The old sense of party discipline was gone. A President has no sanctions. It didn't matter a great deal to members of Congress whether or not a President campaigned for them. (Sometimes they preferred that he not do so.) Members of Congress, especially senators, could get on local TV anytime. Though members still benefited from party fund-raising, they had their own fund-raising mechanisms, through which they raised the bulk of their campaign funds. Anyway, a President wanted his party members to be reelected. Over the past decade or so, Congress had been accumulating ever-increasing power—building large staffs and engaging in micromanaging of executive branch policies.

On Thursday, August 5, the day of the House vote, the administration didn't have the votes. Phone calls to Capitol Hill were running heavily against the bill. In some offices, the ratio was six to one and nine to one. The Christian Right, Ross Perot, and the Republican National Committee were whipping up the calls. Clinton was making calls night and day. A House member said that there was "still an odd reluctance on the President's part to forcefully advocate his own plan. He puts some distance between him and it. He discusses it with zeal, but I haven't seen any laying on of hands. There's no 'It's terribly important to me and this administration and I really need your vote.' We all have to be true to ourselves, but he could do with a little more oomph."

White House aides spread the word that if the bill went down to defeat, it would be the ruination of the Clinton Presidency. They had a valid point. Such a loss would render Clinton so weak as to be almost irrelevant in future debates. It could take months to construct another bill acceptable to a majority, and meanwhile the rest of his program would go by the board.

Democratic House leaders met with freshmen on the morning of the vote, trying to allay their concerns. The freshmen wanted reassurance that they would be able at some future point to cast a vote on a constitutional amendment requiring a balanced budget, and on a line-item veto. The Black Caucus had to be reassured. By midday, it was clear that the administration would lose at least one vote in the Oklahoma delegation because of Senator Boren's influence. Conservative Democrats, some of whom may well have been ready to support the bill, acted balky and extracted some concessions from the Democratic leadership (which was working with the White House). The administration's, and the leadership's, problem was that there were at least three Democratic parties in the House—liberals, centrists, and conservatives—and a deal made with one group had to be matched by a deal with the others. The Democratic whip organization was meeting virtually every hour to compare notes on the prospects for the bill. Some members got triple or quadruple teamed. At 5:50 P.M. on the day of the vote, David Skaggs, of Colorado, a deputy whip, said, "We don't have the votes yet. It's amazing how hard it can be to find the guys on the list of 'leaning' or 'undecided.' " Everyone knew that some of the balkers weren't motivated as much by concerns about what was in the bill as by the desire to get attention—but that didn't matter. Their votes still had to be nailed down.

At shortly after 6:00 P.M., Foley and Gephardt announced a deal with the conservatives. Foley, picking up on something that Clinton had said earlier in the day, remarked, "As the President said, this is the beginning, not the end of this process." In other words, more deficit reduction was to come, even though the administration felt that this bill went far enough. Among the concessions that Gephardt and Foley had negotiated were that in the fall the administration would submit more budget cuts for the Congress to vote on, and that there would be votes on some procedures that would supposedly rein in spending.

The leadership used various arguments on reluctant liberals. The liberals were told that Congress would probably never pass a separate bill with $21 billion for the working poor (the amount in the reconciliation bill for the EITC). Or someone particularly close to Clinton would say to a reluctant liberal, "You're going to let him fail?" To some members who said that the vote was politically difficult for them, the leadership said, in effect, "Look, if this goes down, all the Democrats will be hurt and will come under very strong press attack saying, 'You can't govern.' " A House leader said afterward, "That argument was used a lot. We said every Democrat in the House would be condemned as belonging to the party of ineffectiveness and impotence. We'll be seen as a failed party, and we should be."

For the first time in a long time, the House leaders began the roll call without being certain that they had enough votes. Two hundred eighteen votes were needed for a victory. There were a few members whose intentions were uncertain, and some who had said they would vote for the bill if their votes were absolutely essential. But it wasn't clear that there would be enough in the end. There was nothing left to do but roll the dice. Foley, who rarely spoke on the House floor, took to the well of the House and made an impassioned speech for the bill. He said, "This is not the end of the fight. It is not even the middle. It is the beginning, but it is a crucial beginning that we must make."

The roll call vote was a heart-stopper. Members stood and watched the scoreboard on the front wall of the House, with red and green lights indicating how a member had voted, or no light, indicating that the vote was being withheld. They also watched the running tally on the boards on the side of the chamber. The first, committed, votes went up first. Then, with a minute and a half remaining of the fifteen minutes allocated for roll calls, the vote slowed considerably and was 209–206. Stephanopoulos said later, "In the end, close House votes are as much about physics as about the merits of the bill. If you get to a certain number and no further, your vote will collapse." He added, "As for those who say, 'I'll be there if you need me'—the question of when that is is in the eye of the beholder." At the White House, Gergen and Gearan discussed what actions the President should take if the bill failed.

The leadership was still working on recalcitrant members. Within the final hour, three freshmen who had been holding out agreed to vote for—after the President agreed to yet another process for achieving spending cuts. In a small room right off the House floor, House leaders kept an open phone line to the President's study off of the Oval Office, sometimes putting a member on the phone to talk to the President. The President was joined in the study by Paster, McLarty, Gergen, and Stephanopoulos to watch the vote.

When the time ran out, the vote was 211–212. The leadership delayed announcing the vote. Then it was 213–213. Then, after another pause, it was 215–214. A stricken-looking Gore was doing a play-by-play on *Larry King Live.* In the back of the House, the leadership was working frantically. Soon it was at 216–214—and there was a long pause. Four Democratic votes were still at large. But Ray Thornton, who represented Little Rock, had already told the White House that he would oppose the bill. Neither the President nor Mrs. Clinton, who had been making some calls, was able to dissuade him. Thornton had won his last reelection with 74 percent of the vote, but, he told the White House and the House leadership, he had told his constituents that he had voted for the Btu tax because it was preferable to a gasoline tax, so now he couldn't vote for a gas tax. The trap he was in had been inadvertently set by Clinton. At last, Pat Williams, of Montana (where there was a tax revolt), and Marjorie Margolies-Mezvinsky, a freshman who represented Philadelphia's Main Line, a district said to be the most Republican in the country to be represented by a Democrat, voted for the bill. Knowing that her vote was a dangerous one for her career, when she phoned the President she asked in return a White House conference on entitlements to be held in her district. Clinton agreed. The fourth hang-back, David Minge, of Minnesota, voted against. That made the final vote 218–216, a one-vote margin for the administration. (A tie vote would defeat the bill.)

Later, in the Rose Garden, Clinton said, "The margin was thin, but the mandate is clear." (Upon winning the 1960 election, John F. Kennedy said, "The margin is thin, but the responsibility is clear.")

Now the problem was what to do about Senator Bob Kerrey. Kerrey, a former Navy Seal in Vietnam and a war hero, wasn't your run-of-the-mill senator. There was always something elusive about Kerrey. At times, his thought processes were hard to follow. In a linear world Kerrey wasn't always linear.

In his brief run for the Presidential nomination in 1992, Kerrey had argued for cutting the budget and the size of the government. Now he was up for reelection in Nebraska, and the deficit reduction theme was prominent. Another residue of the 1992 campaign was some bad blood between Kerrey and Clinton. Though Clinton wasn't much of a resenter, his relationship with Kerrey had remained cool. In the campaign, Kerrey had been bothered by Clinton's explanations of how he had avoided the draft, and on the eve of the Georgia primary he had said that if Clinton was the nominee, the Republicans would open him up "like a soft peanut" over his draft record. Mrs. Clinton was furious.

As the final voting neared, Kerrey called for rejecting the reconciliation bill as inadequate and proposed instead a special session of Congress in the fall to reduce the deficit by cutting entitlement programs. House leaders in particular thought this was a daft idea: a special session within a session of Congress, and one that allowed anyone to offer amendments, would be ripe for demagoguery.

During the week before the final votes, Kerrey dropped in on Gergen—he wanted to see the former barbershop that was serving as Gergen's office—and, sitting in one of the blue wing chairs in the cramped office and sipping coffee, told Gergen that if the vote were then, he would vote no. In a phone conversation that week, he told Paster, "You guys haven't changed enough. This city isn't different enough."

In a rather angry phone conversation on Thursday morning, the day of the House vote, Kerrey told Clinton that he had decided to vote against the bill. Clinton told Kerrey, "I'm sunk without this bill." Kerrey replied, "It isn't good enough."

That Thursday noon, at Gergen's suggestion, Paster, Gergen, and McLarty met Kerrey for lunch. Kerrey had proposed they meet at the American Café at Union Station, the train terminal that in recent years had been decked out with shops and restaurants and cinemas. When Gergen's assistant, Dianna Pierce, called Kerrey's office to confirm, she was told that Kerrey must have meant the American Café on Capitol Hill and gave her the address. The White House car carrying the three top officials on a most urgent mission took them to the restaurant—and Kerrey wasn't there. Gergen, upset, called his office. Finally, Kerrey was tracked down at a restaurant called America, in Union Station. When the President's emissaries found their quarry, they asked him why he particularly wanted to eat there. He replied, "Because there's a movie showing here at two o'clock."

At the lunch, there was a lot of talk about philosophy, about the moral high ground, about Kerrey's complaint that there was no ethic to the President's bill by now, that it was a bunch of deals. Gergen suggested to Kerrey that if he were his political manager, he would have to question how Kerrey's bringing down the President's bill would affect him as a national politician. Liz Moynihan, the senator's very smart and politically shrewd wife (she managed Moynihan's campaigns), who, like her husband, had helped Kerrey in 1992, had been making the same point to him. By this time, Kerrey had given up on his idea of a special session and proposed instead a bipartisan commission, to be chaired by himself, to find more ways to bring down the deficit. The President, Kerrey offered, should announce the commission after the Senate voted. The White House officials urged Kerrey to meet with Clinton the next morning. (After lunch, Kerrey asked Gergen if he wanted to go to the movie.)

So on Friday morning, the day of the Senate vote, Kerrey met with the President in the White House residence, out of the view of reporters. After the conversation, there was still uncertainty about what Kerrey would do. And his proposal for a commission was a thorny subject. After Kerrey left the White House, a sizable group—Gore, McLarty, Bentsen, Panetta, Rubin, Stephanopoulos, Gergen, and Paster—met in the Oval Office to discuss the proposal. It threatened White House prerogatives, and Kerrey's report could cause later difficulties. Gergen strongly argued that the proposal "looks like we're dividing up the Oval Office." Bentsen agreed. Then the problem was raised that the commission might take away some of the business of Gore's reinventing government project. Gore, Bentsen, and Panetta weren't happy with handing over this authority to Kerrey. "We had to make sure we didn't have a Vice President Kerrey, a Treasury Secretary Kerrey, or an OMB Director Kerrey," Gergen said later.

Clinton called Kerrey to tell him that he couldn't allow him to take over part of Gore's project, and suggested they work something out. Kerrey agreed, but the White House still didn't know whether it had his vote. That afternoon, Paster and Stephanopoulos worked on the wording of the proposed announcement. It said, "The President has named Senator Bob Kerrey as chairman of the Bipartisan Commission on Budget Discipline," and added that the President would also appoint representatives from Congress as well as from the private sector and academia. But the White House also believed that this shouldn't be announced just after the vote—that there should be, as one aide said, "a discrete interval." Otherwise, it would look like yet another Clinton concession. Privately, the President's advisers remained more than a little annoyed that Kerrey was getting away with his public statements that he didn't want and hadn't asked for anything in exchange for his vote.

On Friday afternoon, Paster made another foray to the Hill, to see whether, if Kerrey came out against the bill, any Democratic senator opposed it would change position. He had no luck.

Finally, at 8:25 P.M., Kerrey called Clinton and told him he would vote for the bill. "This one's for free," he said.

Then, on the Senate floor, he made a scorching speech, aimed mainly at the President. His unusual rationale for voting for the bill was that if it failed, "I don't trust what my colleagues will do on the other side of the aisle." The Republicans, he said, had been united against the bill and couldn't be trusted to help write a better one. He continued, "I could not and should not cast a vote that brings down your Presidency." From a lectern, reading from notes on yellow paper, Kerrey fairly shouted his speech. It was a both strong one and strange one; but Kerrey was never uninteresting. He said, "America also cannot afford, Mr. President, to have you take the low road of the too easy compromise, of the too early collapse. You have gotten where you are today because you are strong, not because you are weak."

The Clintons watched the speech in the family quarters. They were waiting for Chelsea to return from a space camp, in Alabama. The President didn't like Kerrey's speech, but he was tired and it was over. He was much more disturbed that Kerrey was getting a "free ride"—that he was getting away with saying he didn't want anything, when he did.

The vote was anticlimactic, with the Senate once again ending up with a tie vote—this one 50–50. Once again, Gore broke the tie.

To avoid the appearance of a quid pro quo, the White House delayed announcing the commission, to be headed by Kerrey, until November.

At the White House, there was jubilation. The mood was that of a campaign victory. At shortly after 11:00 P.M., Clinton went to the portico of the North Entrance, facing Pennsylvania Avenue. He said, "What we heard tonight at the other end of Pennsylvania Avenue was the sound of gridlock breaking. . . . This was not easy, but change is never easy." He added, "We're determined to stop avoiding our problems and start facing them."

21

THE SIEGE OF SARAJEVO

"The United States Is Doing All That It Can"

While President Clinton was in Tokyo for the G-7 meeting, in July, he was upset about the pictures on CNN of an intensified Serb siege of Sarajevo. (Presidents and other high officials have more time to watch television while they're on trips.) On the early leg of his trip there, Clinton had told his friend Strobe Talbott that he was troubled by the reports from Bosnia. "You know, some people are saying, 'Don't just stand there, do something,' and some are saying, 'Don't just do something, stand there.' " There were risks either way, he said, but the major peril was in doing nothing. He believed that in that case, the fighting wouldn't stop until the Serbs had obliterated Muslim Bosnia.

Clinton told Christopher in Tokyo that he was disturbed by what he had seen on CNN and that his advisers should consider options on what could be done about Sarajevo, including military options. Christopher relayed this to Lake and added that he agreed. This got Lake's attention, not only because the President was interested again in doing something but also because it signaled a change in Christopher's thinking. After his failure in May to sell the European allies on a policy of "lift and strike," Christopher had worked methodically to shut down the Bosnia policy, which he thought could threaten Clinton's domestic program.

Once burned, Christopher was loath to try to have the United States take the lead again on Bosnia. He felt that if the U.S. got out too far ahead of the Europeans and then couldn't persuade them to come along, it would hurt

American leadership on this and other issues. And that, in turn, would hurt Clinton's Presidency. This reasoning closed the circle on American leadership. A senior official who would know said, "After his European trip, Christopher put Bosnia in the 'too hard' box, and it stayed there for a long time."

In Tokyo, Lake couldn't tell from Christopher's comments how committed the President felt to taking new action in Bosnia. And then Lake more or less disappeared in Japan to negotiate the framework agreement on trade. When he saw the President at the end of the week, it was to talk about trade.

On Sunday, as the President was preparing to fly to the DMZ, Lake managed to get in a room alone with Clinton to tell him about a sensitive operation that was about to go forward in Somalia. Lake wanted Clinton's approval, and to alert him to possible questions later from reporters. The operation was a helicopter raid on Aideed's command center, where the warlord was believed to be meeting with his top aides. (It turned out that Aideed wasn't there, but several of his aides were killed.) In that conversation, Clinton told Lake, in strong terms, that he wanted various options for doing something about Sarajevo studied, including the one he had not long before said he had "never ruled in"—the use of ground troops. It was a dramatic turnabout.

Lake relayed the President's request to Aspin, who was in the next room, and the two of them arranged for a secure line from the DMZ to call the Vice Chairman of the Joint Chiefs of Staff, Admiral David Jeremiah. (Powell was in Kuwait.) From the gray and rainy DMZ, Aspin and Lake told Jeremiah of the President's request and asked him to work up some options for when they returned. Later that day, in Hawaii, as Aspin and Lake prepared to depart for Washington, Clinton told them, in the presence of others, "I hope you will be vigorously pursuing that other thing."

At a Principals meeting on Tuesday, July 13, Jeremiah said that an operation to relieve Sarajevo would require about seventy thousand troops. He explained that since the Sarajevo airport couldn't handle the number of troops needed for a ground operation, land routes would have to be opened and secured, which would necessitate a very large number of troops, working in a hostile environment. Jeremiah also suggested options involving smaller numbers of troops, but it was clear that he disagreed with them. He was asked to refine the options further.

In that same meeting, Christopher, in a major reverse, strongly pressed for the use of ground troops. One official explained Christopher's new position: "When Christopher smells the President going a certain way, that's where he goes. But the President changes his mind, and catches Christopher going the other way. The President left Christopher hanging out there in Europe." Aspin believed the idea of using troops to save Sarajevo was a "nonstarter" because of the numbers that would be required and because of the potential of a quagmire. Madeleine Albright backed the use of troops. (Albright, who generally took the more hawkish—or in this group's terminology "pro-active"—position, always accompanied her position with the argument that such an action should, and could, be explained to the American people.) Lake said it should be explored seriously. Christopher, with his European trip burning in his memory, was wary of pushing the new option openly with the allies. But one of the proposals under discussion was for unilateral action, if it came to that. Christopher now argued that if the United States acted vigorously on Sarajevo, alone if necessary, the Serbs might feel pressured to negotiate more flexibly. But this raised again a dilemma the administration had faced all along: if pressure was brought to bear on the Serbs, the Muslims might decide to wait for a better deal. Lake argued that the administration had to credibly threaten the use of airpower in order to push for a settlement, because if things went on as they were, there was no way the Sarajevans could get through the winter.

A week later, Powell offered some other ways of looking at the Sarajevo proposition. He suggested options that required fewer troops than Jeremiah's proposals but said that it would still require about twenty-five thousand soldiers. Aspin, Lake, and Christopher agreed that the number was still too high to be acceptable to Congress, and so the idea of using ground troops—which had stemmed from a Presidential impulse—was set aside.

Now another idea was revived. Before the G-7 meeting, Lake had developed a proposal for a form of cease-fire, with the United States along with the allies, through negotiations, pushing the Serbs to pull back from Sarajevo and other Muslim enclaves and to give up some captured territory. While Aspin and Albright had supported the idea, Christopher had strong reservations, because it implied bringing the subject of Bosnia back up before the President's trip to Japan and would again put the United States out in front on negotiations with the allies.

Now Lake and Christopher agreed that they wouldn't advance another American plan as such but would become more engaged in trying to get a settlement. Since they couldn't use ground troops, they should use a threat, and if necessary the actuality, of airpower to push the Serbs back from around Sarajevo. That would be phase one. The second phase would be the threat of air strikes to push the parties toward an agreement. Lake said later, "The idea was, if we're going to use power for the sake of diplomacy, let's relate it directly to the diplomacy."

After another series of meetings, another new policy evolved: threatening air strikes if the Serbs continued the "strangulation" of Sarajevo or the other "safe areas," or if they refused to negotiate a settlement. The discussions of what would constitute "strangulation" arrived at no clear conclusion. Lake suggested that it would be as the Supreme Court had said about pornography—they'd know it when they saw it.

It was also decided to make a stab at getting allied agreement, but to imply clearly that the United States was prepared to go it alone if the allies didn't agree, and to make threatening statements about the consequences for the alliance if the U.S. was rebuffed. Lake kept Stephanopoulos informed as he went along.

Then the usually very careful Christopher made a misstep. On Wednesday, July 21, the day before he was to leave for the Far East and the Middle East, he held a press conference about his trip. In answer to one of several questions about Bosnia, Christopher, despite the discussions of possible new action, said, "The United States is doing all that it can consistent with our national interest." His comment set off a storm the next day. The general interpretation was that the administration had written Bosnia off. (Christopher's aides said he was simply being literal about the policy at the moment.) And so Lake, with Christopher's concurrence, arranged for the President to correct this impression on Friday, when he met with Jean-Bertrand Aristide, whom the administration was trying to return to power in Haiti. In answer to the inevitable question whether he was giving up on Bosnia, Clinton said, "No, that's not true," and blamed the episode on the press.

Lake had suggested to his colleagues that since any talks Christopher had with the allies would be very public, perhaps he could quietly sneak over to Europe for some talks himself. So on the same day as Christopher's unfortunate remark, Lake laid out for the President—with Gore, Christopher, and Stephanopoulos present—the evolution of his plan, explaining the options for pushing for a settlement, with the threat of the use of force. Within this was a plan for rescuing Sarajevo, and also for telling the Bosnian Muslims that their leverage would never be higher. The United States would help them get the best deal they could—but it was time to deal. Clinton said he still thought that lifting the arms embargo was the better idea, but he agreed that they should try this latest proposal. "Why don't we all sleep on it," the President said, "and we can talk about it again tomorrow." On Thursday, the President confirmed his decision in a meeting with Lake and Stephanopoulos.

That same day, as he left for Singapore, Australia, and the Middle East, Christopher dropped off at the White House a memo calling for strong action on Bosnia. This was to become part of a pattern of behavior on

Christopher's—and his close aide Tom Donilon's—part. Moreover, the decision to move ahead with the new plan had already been made.

On Saturday morning, July 24, with almost no one knowing about it, Lake and Reginald Bartholomew, the Clinton administration's representative to the peace talks, boarded a small plane for Europe. From the plane, Lake called Stephanopoulos, whom he'd asked to check with the President in the morning, to make sure he still wanted him to go ahead with the mission and still agreed with a formula that Lake and Christopher had worked out: he wouldn't say that the U.S. would act unilaterally if the Europeans didn't go along, but he also wouldn't say that it would not. Stephanopoulos told Lake that the President agreed with his proceeding, and using that formulation.

Lake and Bartholomew met with the British in London on Sunday morning, and with the French in Paris on Sunday afternoon and over a good dinner. Lake argued that there was no real alternative to the path he was proposing: the alternatives were to put more troops in, which was unlikely, or walk away. He carried with him a CIA study showing the danger the Sarajevans would be in during the coming winter: body weights in Sarajevo were significantly down, as were supplies. He told the Europeans that this was no trial balloon. He said that if Sarajevo was collapsing and people were starving, it would make a mockery of the NATO summit meeting scheduled that winter to figure out NATO's role in the post–Cold War era. He also said that relationships between the United States and Europe would be very frayed if Sarajevo collapsed; there would be transatlantic recriminations no matter how hard people on both sides tried to prevent them. Further, he said, they all had interests in the Muslim world that would be badly damaged if the Bosnian Muslims were abandoned.

The British were positive, but the French were reserved. Transatlantic conversations took place over the next few days. Then the British and the French said they were sending delegations to Washington for further consultations at the end of July. It appeared that Lake's plan was starting to move. Christopher, then in Singapore, canceled the Australian part of his trip and returned to Washington before proceeding to the Middle East. The cover story was that he was returning for consultations on the Middle East, where violence had broken out in southern Lebanon and northern Israel. In the discussions in Washington, Christopher and Lake worked on their opposite numbers in the allied governments, pressing the policy of threats or use of air strikes to save Sarajevo. Neither man wanted arms embargo failure redux, and both told their counterparts that the alliance couldn't take another episode like that. The French were pushing for a very limited use of air strikes. On Saturday morning, July 31, Christopher, Lake, Powell, and Aspin met with the President in the residence—out of sight of everyone—to brief him on the operational plans for carrying out air strikes.

Clinton decided that there was enough agreement among the allies to take the matter to NATO. A meeting of the North Atlantic Council, or NAC, the political directorate of NATO, was called for Monday, August 2, in Brussels. Administration officials told reporters that air strikes could begin within a few days.

In late July, the feeling in parts of the White House, in the State Department, and in much of Washington was that, at last, something was going to be done. The newspapers ran stories suggesting a new turn. A State Department spokesman said, "As you look at the situation in Sarajevo and see that things are deteriorating there, I think it does suggest that additional steps need to be taken." Clinton himself said in a photo op on July 28, "I'm very upset by the shelling of Sarajevo."

After a twelve-hour, nip-and-tuck session, with interim reports that the talks had collapsed, the NATO members agreed, on August 2, to make "immediate preparations" for "stronger measures" in Bosnia if "the strangulation of Sarajevo and other areas continues." The resolution covered the six "safe areas" designated earlier by the UN. The stronger measures, according to the resolution, would be "air strikes against the Bosnian Serbs and others responsible" for such actions. The resolution didn't state that "strangulation" was taking place and should be acted against, or that force could be used to get the warring parties to the negotiating table. Further, the British and the French, as a price for their agreement, insisted that the NATO commanders have the UN's agreement before they could act—the United States wanted NATO to be in charge—and various details about how that was to work were put off. The administration played this as a victory, which it was of sorts, but the U.S. had failed to persuade other NATO members to approve a more specific plan to proceed with air strikes. The final communiqué said that an actual decision to use force to rescue safe areas would have to be approved by a future NATO meeting. This added still another step to the process. A week later, NATO itself adopted the gradualist plan for bombing.

The new arrangement was then made even more complicated. While U.S. officials talked of the possibility of bombing around Sarajevo within a week, UN Secretary General Boutros Boutros-Ghali insisted that only he had the authority to call for NATO intervention in Bosnia. The plan ended up with far more UN control than the administration wanted.

Despite all this confusion and uncertainty, the administration issued warnings about air strikes in Bosnia. A White House official said, "The clock is ticking."

Christopher, on his way home from the Middle East, where he had worked out an agreement between Israel and Hezbollah fighters in southern Lebanon to cease their attacks on each other, stopped at a NATO base in Italy and said, "The international community simply cannot accept the laying of siege to cities and the continuous bombardment of civilians."

Despite all these chesty statements and despite the new NATO policy, differences within the Clinton administration, even within the military, over the use of airpower still hadn't been worked out. In early August, Powell and some other military officials were arguing in interagency meetings that civilians probably would be killed by U.S. warplanes and that Serb artillery could be easily moved to places more difficult to hit. Air Force Chief of Staff Merrill McPeak was more optimistic about what could be done from the air. This was an old, unresolved argument. Also, to the fury of some people at the State Department and the White House, Aspin was giving background interviews suggesting that the Serbs would have to do something more egregious than usual before there would be any bombing. Different members of the administration had different trigger points.

As a result of a combination of Serb guile and lack of will on the part of the United States and its allies, the air strikes never occurred. The President, though he had approved the latest policy, became concerned again about getting into a "quagmire," and the political ramifications of that. On August 13, Serb forces moved down from Mount Igman, their most threatening outpost over Sarajevo. The Serbs let just enough supplies through for U.S. officials to say that "strangulation" wasn't taking place and, starting on August 16, engaged in peace talks, which though they went nowhere provided a pretext for not bombing. U.S. officials also said that the allies were reluctant to bomb and it wasn't wise for the United States to go it alone (as the administration had implied it would), since the allies had forces on the ground. In mid-August, one official said, "I'm worried about the British and the French—that a time may come when we say this is the time to bomb and they say the supplies are getting through." Thus the policymakers were back to where they had been before all the meetings, the diplomatic to-and-froing, the bold pronouncements accompanying the setting of the latest policy.

In the course of the summer, Christopher and Donilon became concerned about the criticism directed at Christopher from commentators and influential people in foreign policy circles, as well as from people in the junior ranks of the State Department, because of U.S. inaction on Bosnia. The critics weren't aware that following his May trip to Europe, where he failed to sell the allies on the policy of "lift and strike," Christopher had taken various steps to shut down the Bosnian policy. But there was ample criticism nonetheless, and it bothered Christopher a great deal. He felt that he was taking a drubbing for trying to protect the President. So he and Donilon decided to do something about it.

In August, they put forward the story to selected journalists that Christopher had favored stronger action all along and that following his trip to Europe he had urged the President to persevere. In fact, he had told the President that to try to push the Europeans could cause strains in the alliance. Moreover, he had urged the President, and some of his key political advisers, to get rid of the subject, that it would only bring the President more trouble and jeopardize the rest of his Presidency. The story now put out by Christopher and Donilon, which appeared in at least a couple of prominent places, was that Christopher was taking hits for the President's indecisiveness and for European and Pentagon stalling. It was true that Christopher was taking his lumps for the President—as well as for himself—but it was he who had worked to persuade the President to back off after the Europeans rejected "lift and strike."

The articles portrayed Christopher as the moving force behind the latest policy of threatening to bomb Serbian positions to drive the Serbs back from Sarajevo and to the conference table—whereas this was an outgrowth of Lake's plan that had been shaped into a consensus proposal. It was true that Christopher had favored an aggressive policy in the latest round of policymaking. But the stories carried some large inaccuracies. They had Christopher and Lake appealing to the President in Japan to take new action, when it was the President who brought this up—and only with Christopher. They said that Aspin and the Pentagon had been dealt out of the latest round, which wasn't the case. Christopher's July 22 memo to the President calling for new action that summer—but given to Clinton after the action had already been decided on—received prominent mention in these articles, which characterized it as "strong" and as saying that inaction was "intolerable." It was clear to others in the administration that Donilon had leaked it in order to rehabilitate his boss—and they suspected that this had been the purpose of the memo in the first place. By now, however, Christopher's colleagues couldn't be sure whether his latest change of position, toward a more aggressive policy, was based on real conviction or on where he and Donilon thought he should be in terms of public opinion and the opinion of his peers. The stories sought to restore Christopher at other people's expense, including the President's. It was then that Donilon was reminded by a senior official that he worked for the President as well as for Christopher.

The fact that peace talks were proceeding raised a new problem for the administration: how to win public and congressional support for sending American ground troops to help enforce an agreement, as the administration had promised in Christopher's statement on February 10. By September, Bosnia, and the politics of Bosnia in the United States, looked different than they had then. Now there was a greater sense of the difficulty of getting real peace among the warring groups in Bosnia even if there was an agreement, and at the same time Congress was becoming impatient about the fact that American troops were still in Somalia and occasionally coming under fire. So as the administration was trying to keep Congress from ordering the withdrawal of troops from Somalia, it was also preparing to ask Congress for authority to send troops to Bosnia. Clinton knew that this was a combustible situation.

Aspin returned worried to Washington from a mid-September trip to Europe, where he was briefed by Admiral Jeremy Boorda, the commander in chief for the area that included Bosnia. Aspin felt that people in Washington—in Congress as well as in the administration—knew that the question of implementation was coming but hadn't really focused on it. During the same trip, Aspin had said at a meeting of an international group in Brussels that the United States would commit twenty-five thousand troops. Administration officials said later that this would represent less than half the troops, but it was clear that it wasn't by much. The number had been discussed within the administration, but Aspin just came out with it. (Not everyone was pleased.) The total number represented NATO planning. When Aspin conferred with NATO planners in Italy and asked whether a thinner line could be put in—say, six thousand or ten thousand troops—which could be pulled if fighting broke out, the military officials said that that wouldn't work, that the small number of troops in Bosnia was what was bedeviling UNPROFOR.

At a September 12 Principals meeting in the Situation Room on the subject of peacekeeping (an increasingly thorny subject), Aspin suggested that the group disband and regather that afternoon at the Pentagon, where, because staff wouldn't be present and the meeting wouldn't be on anyone's schedule, there was less likelihood of leaks. Aspin wanted to be sure that the President's other advisers understood the implications of the pledge to provide peacekeeping troops in Bosnia.

Aspin also suggested to Lake that some of the President's other advisers —McLarty, Stephanopoulos, and Gergen—be briefed. "They should get the whole thing," Aspin said, "focusing on the fact that this is a major effort, it's going to overload an already crowded agenda, that it's going to take the

President's time, that it's going to be a big damned deal." Multilateralism was now coming into disfavor because of the loss of about a half-dozen lives in Somalia, and there were likely to be casualties of any peacekeeping effort in Bosnia. Moreover, congressional "hawks" on Bosnia objected to the idea of enforcing a settlement that rewarded Serb aggression. So there was the possibility of a pincer movement in Congress—on the part of those who didn't want to get involved in Bosnia and those who didn't want to enforce an agreement that ratified ethnic cleansing—against sending American troops to enforce an agreement. "If we don't do it, it doesn't happen," Aspin said at the time.

By the third week of September, a peace agreement seemed imminent, so the question of implementation was no longer theoretical. The Pentagon and the NSC worked out a set of conditions for implementing an agreement —to try to reassure the Pentagon, Capitol Hill, and the public. Among the conditions were that others had to provide more than half the total force, that NATO (not the UN) would exercise command and control, and that there had to be a clear time limit. Clinton felt that the latter was particularly important. On September 23, Christopher, Aspin, Powell, Albright, and Lake went to Capitol Hill to brief members on the plan to send twenty-five thousand troops to enforce a Bosnian peace. Sam Nunn raised a lot of questions and emphasized that the goals should be clearer and there had to be an exit strategy; several members said that the mission in Somalia had been too ill-defined. Some told the administration officials that the votes weren't there for a force to implement a Bosnian peace agreement. But the administration officials already knew that the President would have to make a major effort to get Congress's agreement. Leon Panetta was scouring the budget to find a way to pay for such troops.

At a Saturday, September 25, briefing of the President's political advisers, in McLarty's office, Aspin said, "Even if this thing works perfectly, it's still trouble. 'Works perfectly' means we go in and do what we have to do, peace is maintained, and nothing goes wrong. What have you accomplished? We've ratified ethnic cleansing. Nobody likes this deal, it's really one of those thankless tasks—but I don't know what else to do."

He also spelled out the downsides of not getting involved in enforcing a peace agreement: there would be more people killed, more refugees, more ethnic hatred in the Balkans; the war would likely spread; the United States' credibility would be seriously in question. Aspin added, "If NATO doesn't do this, you really have to ask what's NATO for."

Gergen seemed to have the most misgivings and said that the whole thing needed discussing. For Lake, there was no question that the United States would be involved in enforcing an agreement—and he was somewhat short with Gergen. (There'd been tensions between the two men anyway. Gergen wanted to be more involved in foreign policy than Lake wanted him to be.) The others felt that while enforcement wasn't an attractive proposition, the President had made a commitment. The group discussed how to start informing the American people about the enforcement plan, how to present it on Capitol Hill, and whether it was politically viable to have troops in Somalia and Bosnia at the same time.

On September 29, the pending peace agreement fell through. The Serbs had pulled back some, and the Muslims were taking advantage of the situation by trying to regain some of the territory they had lost. Officials privately offered the Muslim aggression as reason for the United States and the allies not taking strong action to try to force a cessation of the war. (The Muslims were getting arms from what administration officials said were "other Muslim states"—one of them was Iran—but they didn't have artillery and other heavy weapons.) Even if the United States wanted to act, an official explained, the Europeans might not agree that Sarajevo was being "strangulated," and it would have to go through the series of hoops established in August to govern air strikes (NAC, the UN). This was a long way from the momentary determination in the summer to act unilaterally.

For the second time in the year, the President had reacted emotionally to television pictures of what was happening in Bosnia, and had an enthusiasm for doing something—and then backed off (not before making strong statements about his intentions). He provided no steady leadership on the subject within the government, to the American people, or internationally. He was passive, and changeable—like a cork bobbing about on the waves. He was torn between his emotional responses and his domestic imperative, which always prevailed. His emotional reactions were more than once checkmated by his political instincts. He didn't think the American public would support military action in Bosnia, so he didn't ask it to. His cautious instincts may have been the right ones, but he didn't stick with them either. In the absence of steady leadership, his policy was all over the place, and his policymakers were in a state of confusion over what he wanted—and vied for his mind. His Secretary of Defense had a consistent policy, of preferring a cease-fire in place, but he wasn't very influential within the foreign policy group; his Secretary of State had inconsistent policies that seemed to change with the prevailing winds; his National Security Adviser consistently wanted tougher action but wasn't in a strong enough position to impose this on the President. His Vice President was very much in favor of a stronger policy but didn't feel that it was his place to try to rally support and try to force this on the person who had been elected President. Without leadership from the United States, the allies remained in a muddle. Whatever was the "right" thing to do about Bosnia—reasonable people could differ—the "wrong" thing was to have such an inconstant policy, or no policy at all. The President talked too much about what he was going to do —and then didn't do it. The cost in his, and the country's, credibility was potentially high. A time might come when, in an international crisis, the President would have to make a quick decision and would need to have the American people behind him, and other countries to rally, and that would require faith in his judgment and his steadiness.

The Bosnian winter was harsher than the year before. Conditions in the isolated outposts of Zepa, Srebrenica, Tuzla, and Gorazde were grim. The airport at Tuzla had been closed for two years.

In December, at an international conference in Rome, Christopher announced a doubling of U.S. humanitarian aid to Bosnia. Skeptics in the government took this as a substitute for action, which it was.

During the two-week Christmas period, ABC reported, some one hundred sixty Sarajevans were killed by Serb shelling. But in the course of the fall, other foreign policy events distracted the officials.

22

THE CALENDAR

"She Had Her Knives Out"

No sooner had the victory on the economic program been won than Clinton's advisers fell into sharp disagreement over the agenda for when Congress returned after Labor Day. Ostensibly what was at issue was the use of the President's time—the coin of the realm—but it was also over the definition of this Presidency. Involving as it did the special projects of powerful people—Vice President Gore's reinventing government, Mrs. Clinton's health care program—as well as the North American Free Trade Agreement, over which the advisers were split, the arguments were intense and sensitive. The President's advisers didn't take on Mrs. Clinton lightly.

One question was whether the White House could or should take on all three subjects at once. George Stephanopoulos was opposed to going ahead with NAFTA. Mrs. Clinton insisted that health care had waited long enough and should get high priority in the fall. Gore was insistent that REGO be given its debut in September, as the President had publicly pledged.

On Saturday, August 7, the day after the reconciliation bill was approved by Congress, the Clintons and their advisers gathered in the solarium. The focal point of the meeting was the presentation by the consultants—mainly Greenberg and Carville—of a report on the first six months of the Clinton Presidency, as seen in their focus group polling. The report was stark.

The essence of the report was that while past Presidents had been tested primarily on their ability to manage the relationship with the Soviet Union —the "threshold" test the public applied—foreign policy no longer had a substantial impact on how the public viewed a Presidency. The threshold test of a President now was his ability to deal with the Congress, the ability to govern. The consultants' assessment was that the public's view of Clinton in this respect was low, expressed by interviewees in harsh and graphic terms. The consultants said the administration had to show that it could get the Congress to move and, in a reversal of earlier advice, argued against battling the Congress. Greenberg said, "The moment things came apart was the defeat of the stimulus bill. We lost most of the public's support after that." The defeat, he said, conveyed to the public that the Clinton administration couldn't exercise control over the Congress. Also, although this loss was followed by a string of victories on the economic plan, the difficult fights and close votes (and the press's emphasis of them) gave the impression that Clinton had continued to lose.

The group then fell into an argument over what constituted "mastery" of the Congress. The consultants argued that sometimes the President should stand up for principle and sometimes he should compromise. They drew an analogy to the public's reactions to the conduct of foreign policy during the Cold War: at some moments people wanted the President to compromise with the Soviet Union and at others to stand firm. Greenberg said, "We had very explicit data on this—that at some points people were most interested in getting something done, not just posturing." But the burden of the consultants' argument was that while it sometimes made sense to fight on points of principle, even if it meant losing, the question of the President's success in advancing his program was of increasing importance. Therefore, issues shouldn't be deliberately set up in a way that would make the administration likely to lose. "The main point," Greenberg said, "was to establish effectiveness. But on some points stand on principle, even if that means you'll lose." This advice left some questions.

Out of this analysis grew a strategy for REGO: link the popular and most likely successful proposals to other things the administration wanted to accomplish. For example, since Congress was likely to go for the idea of reducing the government work force, link that to funding for 100,000 new police—taking the funds from the one and giving them to the other. At the same time, link something that powerful committee chairmen were likely to resist to further deficit reduction. The reason for this was the little-known point (the Clinton people didn't want it known) that the administration had little stomach for more deficit reduction. This was both an economic point and a political one. The President's economic advisers—especially Laura Tyson—had been worried for some time that the reconciliation bill would take so much out of the economy, especially in the early years, that it could have a contractionary effect at a time the administration was hoping that the economy would grow. Stephanopoulos most prominently wanted to get out of the "deficit reduction game." He was worried both about the number of commitments the administration was making for which there were no funds (flood relief, paying for NAFTA, and others) and about the increased pressure on the President's investments that could result from more deficit reduction. In this he had the strong support of Bob Rubin.

The consultants' analysis also led to a fundamental decision about the health care strategy. Universal coverage would be established as the one principle for which the President would risk losing the whole program. The details of the rest of it would be negotiable. This was a relief to Stephanopoulos, Greenberg, and numerous other advisers who thought that the program was too complex but didn't want to confront the First Lady.

The group also discussed the fact that the President had used up a great deal of his "political capital" on the reconciliation bill. An aide said later, "The hope was that the issues in the fall are so complex that he can't manage the legislative process the same way, and we can tell members of Congress who want to cut a deal with him, 'Sorry, the President's engaged.' "

Gergen pressed the point that Clinton had been "overexposed": the public had seen and heard him too often, and he should eschew the role of "commentator in chief." Gergen argued that Clinton didn't have to be on television every day, and he should begin to sketch the larger picture, rather than talk about details and process. Mandy Grunwald agreed emphatically. Greenberg said later, "I remember thinking that the degree of commitment to this matter may have had a direct correlation with our wanting to take a vacation. We were desperate."

Following the Saturday-night solarium meeting, there commenced an extended argument over the fall agenda. Meetings were held the following Monday afternoon and evening (over the sequencing of the issues for the fall and over the health care proposal); Tuesday (four hours on REGO); and Wednesday (more health care); and then there was another solarium meeting Wednesday night that went past midnight. The next day, the President was to depart early for a speech in St. Louis paying homage to flood victims, and then proceed to Denver to meet the Pope. The meetings were long and grueling, and Clinton and his aides were almost beyond exhaustion.

One hollow-eyed aide who had been heavily involved in the reconciliation fight the previous week said, "This week is as bad as last week." Aides were pushing themselves hard to just keep going, and several were snappish. They were strongly focused on getting out of Washington for some vacation, and lived in a state of terror that Clinton wouldn't take one. Some of the aides made pacts that they wouldn't come back for any mid-August meetings, even if the President and Mrs. Clinton called one. In the minds of several aides, the biggest questions were whether the President should proceed with NAFTA at all, and, if he did, how there could be time for health care.

Stephanopoulos argued over several days that NAFTA should be dropped. He said that winning the reconciliation fight had consumed virtually the entire White House staff, the President's full time, and every resource of the administration, and that health care would be more difficult by several magnitudes. NAFTA was a loser, Stephanopoulos said: much of organized labor was opposed, it would split the party, and it had little chance of being passed by the House, where the second- and third-ranking Democrats, Dick Gephardt, the majority leader, and David Bonior, the party whip, were opposed. The Democratic House leadership was opposed to putting its members through a rough internecine battle. Even if the administration won, Stephanopoulos argued, splitting the party wasn't worth the fight.

Stephanopoulos suggested that Mickey Kantor, the U.S. Trade Representative, "blow up" the negotiations over "side agreements" on the environment and labor, which were still going on. Clinton had stipulated during the campaign that the side agreements were his price for support of the treaty.

Clinton's campaign position had come after a considerable struggle among his advisers and apparent hesitation on his part. Negotiations for such a treaty began in the Reagan administration and were concluded by Bush in August 1992. Clinton had to take a position. A large segment of organized labor, including the AFL-CIO, opposed the treaty, arguing that it would cause U.S. companies to relocate in Mexico, to take advantage of low-cost labor. Labor felt reinforced in this view by the fact that much of business was strongly in favor of the treaty. Business was also strongly attracted by the large market in Mexico, as well as in the rest of Latin America—which presumably would be brought into the agreement over the years.

Among the most emphatic opponents of candidate Clinton's backing NAFTA were Mickey Kantor, the campaign chairman, and Hillary Clinton. The main arguments for Clinton's supporting it were that he needed to show that he was thinking beyond the borders of the United States, and to neutralize an issue Bush could use against him. Also, this was a "New Democrat" issue.

In the end, Clinton came out for the treaty, provided there were side agreements on environment and labor. It was the sort of split decision that critics saw as a sign of his trying to please everyone and others saw as evidence of his high political acumen.

Now, in the August meetings to decide the fall program, Mrs. Clinton was concerned about there being enough time to give her health care program a proper launching. Rubin and Bentsen argued strenuously for going ahead with NAFTA and even suggested that health care be put off until 1994. Mrs. Clinton was very angry with her husband's two top economic officials (who had also tried to pare back her health care proposal). "She had her knives out for them for a while," a White House aide said. The health care proposal had been postponed and postponed. Now it was vulnerable to more delay, or, as Mrs. Clinton and Ira Magaziner saw it, too little high-level attention in the fall. Magaziner had argued that he needed a month for the kickoff of the health care plan; the NAFTA people argued that that would start NAFTA much too late and, since it had to be approved by the end of the year, jeopardize it. Greenberg and Grunwald argued for postponing NAFTA so that health care would have the administration's, and the country's, undivided attention.

During this period, Mickey Kantor met with Mrs. Clinton and made a proposal that she accepted. Kantor had said publicly that health care was the administration's highest priority. In the meetings about the fall agenda, Kantor told the President that if it was best for the administration to drop NAFTA, he was willing to go along, and explained how he could negotiate in such a way that the treaty would be dead. If the President wished it, he would "blow up" the negotiations. All these things put his loyalty to the Clintons beyond question. (Kantor's willingness to give up NAFTA also won over Stephanopoulos, who had been instrumental in Kantor's not heading the transition.) Though he was willing to kill the treaty, Kantor argued that if Clinton fought for congressional approval of the treaty and won despite the opposition of labor and some of the House leadership, it would be a big win, and a big plus for him. He would have stood up to the unions and fought a bipartisan fight; he would be seen as dealing in terms of the big picture.

Knowing the White House minefield he was facing if NAFTA was to remain alive, Kantor proposed to Mrs. Clinton a way through the scheduling issue: after Labor Day, REGO could be introduced to the public, and after a few days of events surrounding that, the President could present NAFTA and give it a day or two of attention, and then NAFTA would get out of the way until close to the time the treaty would be voted on in the Congress (in late November or December), leaving the stage to health care, to which the White House could devote at least a couple of weeks. He also told Mrs. Clinton why he believed a NAFTA win would benefit the President. Ultimately, Kantor's proposal was what was agreed upon.

The consultants were divided on the subject of NAFTA. Begala remained strongly opposed to it as an "elitist" issue. He presented polling that showed that most people thought NAFTA would cost jobs and didn't see any affirmative reasons for enacting it. Carville argued that if the President abandoned NAFTA, it would look as if he were running away from a fight. It would be a "character" issue.

Given the way the Clinton White House worked, the issue came up again and again. The President said in a meeting on Monday that he wanted to go ahead with NAFTA, and he said it again in a Wednesday meeting. But the discussions kept on. (Stephanopoulos was known to reraise issues.)

In the Wednesday, August 11, solarium meeting, which lasted three and a half hours, the question of whether Clinton should proceed with all three issues was hashed over once again. The President said, presumably (but not quite) once and for all, that he wanted to proceed with all three subjects, that he *had* to proceed with all three subjects. Often, he would hear people out in a meeting and not give his response until later, when he had resolved the question in his own mind. At this meeting, however, he said, "We're going ahead with NAFTA."

Hoping that this meeting would be more conclusive than the preceding ones, Roy Neel placed a large calendar on the floor as the participants fought over the President's time. The idea was to get people to focus on concrete questions. "There was a lot of venting," one participant said later. "Everyone was exhausted. We'd had seven months of unrelenting pressure. Everybody got their gripes on the table—that we were taking on too much, that the scheduling was crazy. Everybody was very candid about the mistakes we'd made." There was a heated argument over whether the White House was showing enough solidarity on the subject of health care. Mrs. Clinton had heard that the economic advisers were belittling it on Capitol Hill, and she was displeased. A big part of the problem was the fact that these groups hadn't worked together; they were separate fiefdoms. The Clinton White House had no overall policy office, no one who kept track of the work of the various policy councils and coordinated them. There was no domestic policy coordinator, such as Joseph Califano in the Johnson White House, or John Ehrlichman in the Nixon White House. At the solarium meeting, the NAFTA faction and the REGO faction kept trying to chip away at health care's space on the calendar. The health care faction fought back. Gore had hoped for two weeks' attention to REGO and ended up with five days. Toward the end, Grunwald and Gore were crawling around the floor, poring over the schedule.

In a meeting the next week, Clinton threw everyone in the room into a fright. "We're not going," he said, referring to his vacation plans. The staff went into revolt. The issue of Clinton's vacation had not only become a traumatic subject for his staff—most had made plans—but it was close to raising questions in the public's mind about Clinton. The workaholic President, with no home of his own and no place he seemed to belong to, couldn't make up his mind. He was going to go to Roger Altman's ranch near Jackson Hole, Wyoming, but then decided it was too isolated. The Thomasons' house was now out. His advance staff had explored Telluride, Colorado, but then Clinton decided he couldn't be so far away from the White House. (This despite advanced communications equipment and a plane at the ready.)

Hillary Clinton buttonholed Presidential advisers to tell them to urge the President to go on vacation. Aides buttonholed Hillary Clinton to tell her to urge the President to go on vacation. Gergen kept up the argument that Clinton had been overexposed on the budget battle, and that he should withdraw and come back fresh on Labor Day.

For a while, Clinton considered spending his vacation at the Patuxent River Naval Base, in nearby Maryland, about sixty-five miles from Washington. This seemed to be a grim prospect. ("I don't care where he goes," one aide said. "I just want him out of here.") Then Clinton decided that he wanted surf, and the Patuxent River didn't have surf. Grand ladies offered him their homes, but there were problems with those too. Eventually, Vernon Jordan persuaded former Defense Secretary Robert McNamara to lend the Clintons his house on Martha's Vineyard. Jordan also vacationed on Martha's Vineyard, so Clinton's favorite golfing companion would be on hand. (At an early birthday party thrown for Clinton by the staff, Gore gave him a life-size cardboard replica of himself—of the sort that one can have one's picture taken with on a Washington sidewalk—telling Clinton that he could take it with him on vacation so he wouldn't miss having his Vice President at his side.)

But before he left for the Vineyard, the President visited the flooded Midwest again; went to Denver to greet the Pope; to California to talk to aerospace workers; to Vail, Colorado, with his wife and daughter, where he played golf (with Gerald Ford and Jack Nicklaus), rode horseback, and attended an outdoor performance of the Bolshoi Ballet followed by an elaborate dinner honoring the Bolshoi, at which he played the saxophone; went to Tulsa, Oklahoma, to attend a Governors' Conference; chewed out a couple of aides in front of television cameras; visited friends in Springdale, Arkansas, in the Ozarks (it was so hot that Clinton didn't come out of the house until sunset); returned to the White House for a day of work—and then, at last, departed with his family for the Vineyard at the end of the day on Thursday, August 19, his forty-seventh birthday. Vernon and Ann Jordan threw him a birthday party.

Clinton loved his vacation. The Clintons were the toast of the Vineyard; they went out every night but one during their ten days there. The place was stocked with celebrities. There was a Saturday-night dinner at Carly Simon's. Jacqueline Onassis and her family, including Edward Kennedy and his new wife, took the Clintons for a luncheon cruise. Hillary Clinton and Chelsea water-skied with Caroline Kennedy Schlossberg. Later, Mrs. Onassis took the Clintons to dinner. For Kennedy worshiper Bill Clinton, this was sheer heaven. Massachusetts's other senator, John Kerry, took the Clintons for a cruise on his motorboat. The Clintons hit the bookshop and the ice cream parlor and went clamming outside their house, and Clinton played golf nearly every day. He was having such a good time that he extended his vacation by two days.

He left behind many exhausted Vineyarders and not a few cases of bad nerves.

For the first time in years, Bill Clinton had had time to read a lot of books, rest, and reflect. He and his wife talked about where his Presidency stood.

Mrs. Clinton prodded her husband to ponder what was his message for the country, what it was that he wanted to convey, how he wanted Americans to feel and think, and what place in history he wanted. With the economic program behind him, they agreed that he was freer to talk about what he thought was important and to place what he was trying to do in context. The country hadn't elected him to fix everything under the hood, his wife told him; it had elected him to steer the car.

23

ROLLOUTS

"All Great Wars Are Lost in the Middle"

Clinton returned from his vacation in an upbeat mood. He seemed more relaxed and—for a while—was easier to work with. Two nights before he was to give a major speech, Clinton simply took a draft home with him. An aide said, "Before, we would have a three-hour meeting, with him screaming at us."

At an interfaith breakfast at the White House on August 30, Clinton told his audience that during his vacation he had read *The Culture of Disbelief,* by Stephen Carter, a Yale Law School professor. (The subtitle was "How American Law and Politics Trivialize Religious Devotion.") Clinton told the group that "the book lays a lot of these issues out that I am grappling with." He said, "I am convinced that we are in a period of historic significance, profound change here in this country and throughout the world, and that no one is wise enough to see to the end of all of it, that we have to be guided by a few basic principles and an absolute conviction that we can re-create a common good in America."

Clinton's remarks reflected in part the effect of his opportunity on vacation to think about his larger concerns—and in part his proclivity for talking his audience's language. He continued, "It's hard for me to take a totally secular approach to the fact that there are cities in this country where the average murderer is now under the age of sixteen." He added, "Now, there may not be a religious answer to the policy question of whether it's a good thing that all these kids can get their hands on semiautomatic weapons. But there certainly is something that is far more than secular about what is happening to a country where we are losing millions of our young people and where they shoot each other with abandon and now often shoot total strangers for kicks, shoot at them when they are swimming in the swimming pool in the summertime."

A clear sign that the Clinton people still couldn't make up their minds about how much to put him before the public (Clinton's poll ratings went up while he was on vacation) and couldn't resist a campaign-like moment was Clinton's suddenly appearing on Monday night, September 6, in the broadcast of the first game of the ABC fall football season. Suddenly, there on the television screen was the President of the United States, in a blue windbreaker, holding a football as if he were about to throw it and saying, "Are you ready for some football?"—the NFL slogan. There had been, of course, debate over whether Clinton should make this appearance. Robert Boorstin, of the communications office, thought it wasn't Presidential, that it would contribute to Clinton's "stature gap." Neel and Begala were for it. In the end, Gearan said, it was seen as an effective way to reach a certain segment of the population. "They thought it was a big thing for Bubba."

The Clinton White House, so lacking in competence in some respects, was at its best at staging what aides called the "rollouts" of the programs that had been so fought over in the prevacation meetings. These were campaign-like events, a genre the Clinton people knew well—perhaps too well, leading them to rely on it too often.

REGO got its rollout in a picturesque event on the South Lawn on September 7, the day after Labor Day, the traditional time for fresh starts. For props, there were two large forklifts loaded with government regulations, plus three high stacks of reports and regulations. Cabinet officers had front-row seats, with agency heads behind them. Unsurprisingly, the event started late. Finally, after ten, Clinton and Gore showed up, the two men taking long strides toward the podium. Gore "showed" Clinton the stacks of regulations, saying, "Mr. President, if you want to know why government doesn't work, look behind you." The goal, he said, was rules that work: that achieve results, put the customer first, empower employees to get results, and eliminate duplication. The idea was based less than earlier studies on reducing the size of government and more on simplifying procedures, reducing middle management, and making government more responsive to its customers. Gore was earnest and serious, as was his wont in public; he had put a lot of himself into the project. Gore, no naïf, and aggressive about his own issues, had taken the President's grant of authority and made a big thing of this.

Gore said that the project would cut spending by $108 billion, cut the bureaucracy by 252,000 people, and overhaul federal procurement practices and the personnel system. Gore and Stephanopoulos had argued almost up to the time of the ceremony over affixing a savings number to the program. In a long and heated battle over how the issue should be presented, Gore had argued for assigning a deficit reduction number to the plan's proposed changes. He felt that people would pay more attention to that than to systemic changes in the way the government worked. Deficit reduction, he argued, would give his report more punch and more urgency. He wanted to say that REGO would save over a hundred billion dollars. Stephanopoulos was vehemently opposed to getting into more deficit reduction rounds. If the administration fell short of reaching that goal, it would be attacked for that, and Congress would cut the budget by that amount anyway. He argued that if Gore's figure wasn't realistic (and he suspected that it wasn't), Congress would just assume savings of that size and take the money from Clinton's investments. He said that the Clinton administration had been careful with its budget figures, to retain credibility, and that shouldn't be jeopardized now. In the end, the President sided with Gore, as he almost always did. But the Office of Management and Budget found the figure $108 billion in projected savings so questionable that Leon Panetta refused to sign off on it.

Clinton and Gore were both truly interested in the subject of reinventing government and during the campaign had said that Democrats, believing in government, had a special burden to try to make it work better. Only if he was convincing on that score, Clinton believed, could he push for expanded government activity in various areas. Clinton had tried to apply some of the principles in Arkansas. Now, in the ceremony on the South Lawn, Clinton gave the report his approval and said, "Where it says, 'The President should,' the President will." This got big applause. Clinton also put REGO in its larger context: "To accomplish any of these goals, we have to revolutionize the government itself so that the American people trust the decisions that are made and trust us to do the work government has to do."

Clinton participated with Gore in a number of REGO events. In Washington, they went to a General Services Administration warehouse, from which the government distributed everything from yellow pads to toilet paper, to highlight waste in the government procurement process; together they traveled to Ohio, California, and Texas. Gore appeared on C-SPAN, the *Today* show, *Larry King Live, MacNeil/Lehrer,* and the David Letterman show. With Letterman, he demonstrated the funny side that those who knew him privately had seen. With mock solemnity, he made jokes about his reputation for being wooden. And he did his ashtray trick: donning goggles and smashing an ashtray with a hammer, to demonstrate ridiculous government specifications for such items. The ashtray nonsense wasn't the most important aspect of REGO, but it was something that could be got across. Over the next months, the President issued several executive orders carrying out the report's proposals; and in 1994 Congress passed legislation to change government procurement procedures. Congress also agreed to cutting 272,900 federal jobs.

In the midst of the final planning for the rollouts, a gift seemingly sent from the heavens had come: a Middle East settlement that, though the Clinton administration had had very little to do with it (Norway had secretly brokered the deal), the Israelis and the PLO, the parties to it, wanted signed at the White House. White House aides didn't learn about the possible agreement until Wednesday, September 8—five days before the signing ceremony. (The Middle East development cut short the days allocated to the REGO rollout.) The agreement wasn't a sure thing until Friday. The peripheral nature of the administration's involvement didn't stop the President from granting interviews about it over the weekend. He had a foreign policy "achievement" for his aides to trumpet. Donilon took a (partially successful) run at claiming the credit for Christopher. A White House aide said, "One of the reasons the Middle East event went so well was we didn't have time to readdress everything." How to bring about a handshake between Israeli Prime Minister Yitzhak Rabin and PLO Chairman Yasir Arafat was just one of the multitude of things to consider. But Clinton was more concerned about something else: how could he prevent Arafat from kissing him after they shook hands. In a meeting in the Oval Office shortly before the ceremony, with several aides present, Lake offered to demonstrate how to do that. With Lake playing the President, and Clinton playing Arafat—the aides dissolved in laughter—Clinton shook Lake's right hand and Lake reached with his left hand for Clinton's right arm, holding it firmly just above the elbow and locking it in place—keeping it far enough away that there was no way "Arafat" could reach "Clinton's" face. "Keep your thumb firmly on the artery," Lake advised.

On Monday morning, September 13, the day of signing, the White House was in happy bedlam. Members of the foreign press corps had streamed into Washington over the weekend. At one point on Monday morning, a young Clinton press aide, trying to establish order, said, "Israeli press over here, PLO folks over there." In the crowded Palm Room, leading to the South Lawn, an aide called out, "Make a little hole here, make room for the President"—and suddenly George Bush appeared, looking tan and fit. With only a half-smile, as he made his way through the crowd, Bush said, "Ex, Ex, Ex."

On the South Lawn, Lubavitcher Jews, Arabs (some in kaffiyehs), Jewish leaders, and Arab-American leaders milled around in the warm sunshine with the diplomatic corps, senators, and congressmen. Henry Kissinger and Jesse Jackson were there, as was former President Carter. Jackson gave numerous interviews. The state dinner planned for that night had been canceled; the Israelis thought that imbibing with the PLO was going too far. Both Rabin and Arafat had taken risks and had a job to do to sell the agreement to their constituencies. The table used for the signing of the Camp David accord between Menachem Begin and Anwar Sadat, in 1979, had been brought out. Standing on the platform with Clinton, Rabin, and Arafat were Russian Foreign Minister Andrei Kozyrev, PLO foreign policy spokesman Mahmoud Abbas, Israeli Foreign Minister Shimon Peres, and Christopher.

When Clinton spoke, Arafat, standing behind him, a full head shorter, couldn't be seen. Only the top of his kaffiyeh showed. The speech by the old warrior Rabin, who had led Israeli troops in the 1967 Six-Day War that ended with the Israeli occupation of Arab territory, some of which was now to be given back, was particularly moving. He said, "We who have fought against you, the Palestinians, we say to you today in a loud and clear voice: 'Enough of the blood and tears! Enough!' "

Clinton presided with dignity and grace. His speech, filled with biblical allusions, as well as references to the Koran, had touches of eloquence. In part, the preacher in him came out; in part, he simply rose to the occasion. He threw himself into this as he almost always did when it really counted. He understood the stakes for him, the opportunity to show himself as a world leader. When, with Clinton's obvious encouragement, a reluctant-seeming Rabin shook hands with Arafat, the audience whooped with joy and stood up.

After the Middle East signing ceremony, it didn't seem possible that Clinton could, on the very next day, pull off an event to launch NAFTA that wasn't a downer by comparison. Clinton the competitor knew that the word was around that he was halfhearted about NAFTA, that the White House, by doing nothing to encourage support for the treaty, had left the field to its opponents for months. Organized labor had mounted a serious and effective grass-roots campaign against it. Business was slow to rally behind it because business leaders didn't see Clinton as being fully behind it, and did see mixed signals coming out of the White House.

It was clear that labor was going to play rough. In mid-September, Lane Kirkland, the leathery President of the AFL-CIO, issued a not very veiled threat: "A vote for NAFTA will be regarded as a very unfriendly act . . . by

American workers." In other words, your campaign contributions just might not be there.

Ross Perot was vociferously attacking the treaty, coining the catchy phrase that it would produce "a giant sucking sound" of jobs going to Mexico. Environmentalists were divided. By mid-September, only 65 of the 258 House Democrats had said they would support the treaty. The members of the House leadership who were for the treaty said that it didn't have the votes and would fail. Clinton had his work cut out.

And his standing with the public was still tenuous. His poll ratings had risen, but he still hadn't truly won over the American people. He had leaped from ice floe to ice floe and was still standing, but he hadn't become a commanding leader. The Oval Office seemed to have become a vise for him rather than a liberator of his talents. It seemed that he couldn't move without a dozen meetings and more than a dozen advisers. His instincts had seemed stifled by the doubts and overwhelmingness of his situation. Now, in the fall, he was getting another chance.

With much of the Democratic Party's labor base essentially gone, the administration needed to form a coalition to get Congress to approve the treaty. The White House had adopted the strategy of showing that the elites were behind NAFTA. In early September, Gergen commented privately, "This is really an interesting argument over whether the establishment can still govern or, against populists, fails. Everyone in the Council on Foreign Relations is for NAFTA." The White House hope was that the elites who favored NAFTA—business leaders, former Secretaries of State, editorial page editors—would have a significant influence on members of Congress. Moreover, polling indicated that the elitist strategy could also help with the rest of the public. Michael Waldman, a White House aide in the communications office assigned to NAFTA, said later, "We found that telling people who's for and who's against NAFTA was very significant." An effective ad run later and paid for by U.S.A.*NAFTA, a coalition of business groups, listed who was for and who was against the treaty. (In favor of it were every living former President and Secretary of State, fourteen Nobel Prize economists, and Lee Iacocca and Colin Powell; against it were failed Presidential candidates Ross Perot, Patrick Buchanan, Jerry Brown, and Jesse Jackson.)

Now, on September 14, the day after the Middle East signing, with former Presidents Carter, Ford, and Bush joining him in the East Room for the launching of NAFTA (Nixon and Reagan couldn't make it), Clinton gave his most effective performance since his February 17 speech to Congress. Speaking to an audience of cobelievers—congressional leaders of both parties, other members of Congress, Cabinet officers, ambassadors—the

President compellingly laid out the case for expanding trade, in the way he had done at the lunch before his trip to Japan. Now he was expressing it to the nation. It seemed that he had grown—inwardly and outwardly—that this was a step in his development as President. He showed that he understood what was bothering the treaty's middle-class opponents, whom he of course wanted to be in his long-term constituency. He said, "In a fundamental sense, this debate about NAFTA is a debate about whether we will embrace these changes and create the jobs of tomorrow, or try to resist these changes, hoping we can preserve the economic structures of yesterday." Speaking animatedly, punching the air with his hand, showing more confidence than usual, he argued that jobs gained by American workers would outnumber those lost, that the side agreements protected American workers from a sudden surge of imports; suggested that wage increases in Mexico would keep numerous Mexicans from emigrating to the United States (anti-immigration was a subtheme used, usually *sotto voce,* by the treaty's supporters); said that the treaty would establish the largest free-trade zone in the world; asserted that there was no choice but to seek economic growth by enhancing foreign markets.

He argued that if NAFTA was rejected, the United States would have difficulty negotiating treaties to open up other markets. He said, "We are going to have a re-employment program for training in America." He did a fair amount of winging it—which he tended to do when he really knew a subject and believed in what he was saying. (The wrong text had been put before him; it was the fourth but not final version.) "Are we willing to compete and win," he asked rhetorically, "or are we going to withdraw?" Afterward Robert Dole, who had been in the audience, said, "President Clinton hit it out of the ballpark."

After Clinton spoke, ex-Presidents Ford, Carter, and Bush—all of whom had been rejected by the voters—managed to create still more excitement. Each of the three—none of whom, in office, had been a particularly effective speaker—seemed to do better than he had done during his Presidency. Even Ford, speaking without notes, was eloquent. They all conveyed an urgency to approval of the treaty. It was as if all three had been liberated, had acquired more confidence than when they were in office. Carter and Bush and Clinton (who had defeated Bush) seemed more relaxed around each other than they had the day before. Carter and Bush, already there for the Middle East signing, had stayed overnight at the White House. Bush, who had had great trouble accepting his defeat, said gracefully of Clinton's speech, "I thought that was a very eloquent statement by President Clinton, and now I understand why he's inside looking out and I'm outside looking in."

Carter took on Perot, saying, "We have a demagogue who has unlimited financial resources and who is extremely careless with the truth, who is preying on the fears and uncertainties of the American public."

As a result of internal arguments, and because of press reports that the White House was planning to give only one day to the rollout of NAFTA, thus demonstrating its lukewarm interest, a second day of Presidential activity had been laid on. And because the first day was given over to the elites, the second was to showcase labor, with Clinton making an appearance at the Port of New Orleans. But the event was rained out, and no alternative venue had been planned. Clinton returned from the long journey in a foul mood and blew up at his staff. An aide said, "When the President has a bad day, you have a bad day. You can see advisers physically pull back away from the table when he's complaining about something going wrong, as if to say, 'I didn't have anything to do with it.' "

In the midst of the rollouts, the White House unveiled the redecorated Oval Office, done by Little Rock decorator Kaki Hockersmith. The soft colors had been replaced by strong ones, making the room look garish. The rug was now a plush and loud royal blue, with a center medallion of a Presidential seal surrounded by fifty white stars. The sofas were covered in strong burgundy and cream stripes, and other chairs were covered in deep blue with a gold and burgundy motif—a design called "Little Rock Diamond." Blue-trimmed cornices had been added to the gold curtains. Aides were reduced to giggles about the Oval Office's new look. One said, "No one likes it but the President, and he loves it." Mrs. Clinton's office had told the press that she had had "no major input" in the redecoration of the Oval Office, which Clinton's aides didn't believe for a second. Other rooms in the mansion—the President's residence study, the Lincoln sitting room, as well as the personal quarters—had also been redone, with much the same effect, bold colors and noisy.

The health care rollout was the most elaborate of all. Lead-up events featuring the President, the First Lady, and the Vice President started five days before the planned Presidential speech. A health care war room had been set up. A two-day "health care university" for Members of Congress to learn about the plan was laid on on Capitol Hill, and the Clinton people were excited by the large turnout. But the problem with the staged events —the Clintons sitting with people who told of their health insurance problems, the President and Gore at a children's hospital decrying paperwork, Clinton at a hardware store—was that they looked staged. The stunts were beginning to wear thin. Radio talk-show hosts were invited to come to the

White House for briefings on the day before the President's speech, scheduled for Wednesday, and to broadcast on the day after the speech from the North Lawn—which would trample the White House's grass and its dignity. (The place was a sea of tables, microphones, headsets, and administration officials being interviewed.) On the same day, on the South Lawn, a thousand people were to be gathered in a canvas tent for a health care rally.

As Clinton's health care speech was being prepared, the customary crisis atmosphere prevailed at the White House, with Mrs. Clinton playing an even larger role than usual this time. The day before the speech, the President's wife called Gergen and Stephanopoulos and said that the President had gone to bed very discouraged, that the speech wasn't in his voice, and once again he'd have to write his own speech. She had got up at four in the morning and sketched out what she thought should be in the speech. The speech was rewritten, and as usual, as Clinton went through the rehearsal in the family theater, he made a lot of changes, and asked for new information and facts, as well as some redrafting, and the rehearsal wasn't over until 7:30 P.M. David Dreyer, who had worked on the rewrite, had to incorporate all the changes, get the facts checked, type out the latest version on Gearan's word processor, and rush the new draft to the President as his limousine was preparing to depart for Capitol Hill for the 9:00 P.M. speech. And a disaster was in train.

Dreyer handed a copy of the diskette containing the speech to Andrew Friendly, the President's personal aide, put a spare diskette in his own pocket, for later transfer to his computer, and while in the motorcade to the Capitol, for his amusement transferred the speech onto his laptop computer. When Dreyer and Begala reached the Capitol, they were met by an agitated Paster, who said that the members didn't have copies of the speech yet and asked if they could print some up. So Begala and Dreyer went to Gephardt's office in the Capitol (where they had both worked) and, using the diskette that had been in Dreyer's pocket, made copies. Begala then went off with the diskette, to have a copy of his own, and Dreyer went off to find Stephanopoulos, who was supervising the TelePrompTer operator from the White House Communications Agency (run and staffed by the military) as the operator typed handwritten changes made by the President in the limousine. Once that was finished, Dreyer and Stephanopoulos went into the House Chamber to watch the President deliver the speech. Dreyer handed a friend the shoulder bag holding his laptop, to store along the side of the chamber.

That afternoon, the TelePrompTer operator, lacking a copy of the President's health care speech with which to test the machine, had called up the

President's February 17 economic speech from the machine's hard drive, then failed to clear the old speech from the computer's memory. Thus, when the health care speech was inserted hours later, it ended up at the tail end of the earlier one. And, after he made the last changes in the health care speech, he pressed "save," thus preserving both speeches. Neither Stephanopoulos nor Dreyer had noticed this before they left for the House Chamber to watch the speech. The WHCA man then scrolled to the top, where it said, "William Jefferson Clinton: A New Direction."

Clinton entered the chamber to strong applause, said his modest thanks from the podium, glanced at the TelePrompTer, and, while the ovation continued, turned to Gore behind him and said, "They've got the wrong speech." "You're kidding," Gore replied. "No," Clinton said. "See for yourself, it's the wrong speech." Gore, momentarily leaving his chair, summoned Stephanopoulos. Stephanopoulos and Dreyer flew out of the chamber and tried scrolling down to the health care speech—"but all we could see was the economic speech," Dreyer said. They didn't know whether the health care speech was there or not. By this time, the President had begun speaking. Dreyer sent someone from the advance team into the chamber to retrieve his shoulder bag, asked the operator to wipe the disk clean, and then downloaded onto it the health care speech from his laptop—without the President's final changes. Clinton was now well into his speech, reading from the printed copy before him and also winging it. Stephanopoulos was worried that if they scrolled through the health care speech to make the changes, the President would be distracted, but the operator assured the two tense aides that the prompter feed was turned off. It wasn't. So Clinton, with tens of millions watching, was reading and winging, and seeing out of the corner of his eye his speech text whizzing down the TelePrompTer, until the changes were made and the text on the screen caught up with him.

Clinton stayed collected and delivered one of the best and most impassioned speeches of his Presidency. He covered a wide swath of political ground, praising doctors and nurses—"My mother is a nurse"—and criticizing the number and complexity of insurance forms and the fact that insurance companies "cast people aside when they get sick."

Speaking animatedly and urgently, Clinton skillfully wove together the connections between health care and the budget (the only remaining way to get the deficit under control was by containing health care costs) and the capacity for creating new jobs. Clinton was getting better and better at talking about the links between his programs. He said, "Our competitiveness, our whole economy, the integrity of the way the government works, and, ultimately, our living standards depend upon our ability to achieve savings without harming the quality of health care." When he told stories of people who had suffered from a lack of good insurance, he choked slightly, Reaganlike. Clinton, like Reagan, was a great salesman. The problem was that when it was all over, one could feel one had been subjected to a sales job.

In his speech, Clinton brought up the subject of crime, and teenagers killing each other with semiautomatic weapons—and got the biggest applause of all. It had finally happened: the easy obtainability of guns had become a mainstream issue. Some of the most terrible incidents had happened in Washington, so Clinton was faced with such news when he read the papers; and also Greenberg's polls showed a steady rise from midsummer on in concern with crime, and with moral decline.

As his advisers had suggested, Clinton stressed the point of security. He held up a blue-and-red card, like a credit card, and said assuringly that "every American would receive a health care security card that will guarantee a comprehensive package of benefits over the course of an entire lifetime, roughly comparable to the benefit package offered by most Fortune 500 companies."

Now there would be a new struggle for definition—between anxiety and disruption, between security and bureaucracy.

But, despite all the razzmatazz surrounding the President's speech, the health care bill still wasn't ready.

So, despite the success of the President's speech, there were signs of trouble. A draft of the still uncompleted bill had been leaked a few days earlier. The White House had sent a copy to Capitol Hill, supposedly to be kept under wraps, but despite the expressions of indignation from the White House, Mrs. Clinton was quite aware that it would be leaked—and had planned it that way. The idea was to float some of the proposals and get the debate started before the bill was made final. A White House aide said, "It's in the word processor; it can be changed. The idea was to draw some of the fire now." The aide said of Mrs. Clinton, "She's capable of being a very shrewd politico, and she's capable of making terrible political misjudgments."

The plan was for a complete overhaul of the nation's health care system, reshaping one-seventh of the nation's economy. It would be the most comprehensive social legislation in the nation's history. The Clinton proposal was not only to alter the way many people received their health insurance and bring in the thirty-seven million who lacked coverage, but to direct, manage, reshape, or influence the entire health care delivery system. It pledged universal coverage by January 1, 1998, and security from the inability to obtain coverage because of "preexisting conditions," or being charged more for having an illness, or having a policy revoked because one became ill or changed jobs.

In order to shape a system in which everyone had health care, and to lower costs, the administration proposed to deal with the number and distribution of doctors, as well as the kinds of doctors (pressing for more general practitioners and fewer specialists); with the education of doctors, gradually requiring a representative racial and gender mix of medical school graduates, to get more doctors into currently underserved areas; with the number and distribution of hospitals and the government's own extensive health care system (the Public Health Service and the Veterans Administration). It proposed standby federal pricing of breakthrough drugs. It proposed a system of "alliances," to be run by the states, through which individuals and companies could purchase health insurance; these would collect and pool premiums and were to produce economies of scale because of the large number of purchasers and the competition for their business. A federal board was to oversee the alliances and apply standards. Employers would be required to cover 80 percent of the cost of their employees' premiums—the "employer mandate"—with the government picking up the cost to the poor and the unemployed and subsidizing the costs to the working poor and small businesses (including each McDonald's franchise). The Clintons argued that the employer mandate was the only way of guaranteeing universal coverage, and that universal coverage was the only way to hold costs down. It would end cost-shifting from those without insurance to those who have it. They also said that this was the least disruptive approach, because so many Americans already received their health insurance through their jobs. Having decided in April, after a long debate, that holding down costs through a "global budget" covering the entire health system smacked too much of controls, the administration decided instead to provide standby authority to put caps on increases in the cost of premiums—a form of price control.

In the end, the giant program proposed five new entitlements: subsidies for individuals, subsidies for early retirees, payment for long-term home care, assistance to small businesses, and prescription drugs for the elderly. The plan offered a fairly generous and expensive standard benefits package but also proposed to tax higher benefit plans.

The complexity and disputable numbers of the leaked draft had raised a lot of questions. Earlier in the year, Representative Dan Rostenkowski had likened the program to "Star Wars." Speaker Tom Foley referred to it as the "Godzilla" of public policy issues.

Mrs. Clinton was of a firm opinion about the scale and timing of the program. "She was always of the 'big bang' school," an official said. She scathingly dismissed behind their backs those who wanted to go slower—mainly, the economic advisers—as "the incrementalists." While dissenters tended to fix the blame for such an ambitious program on Ira Magaziner, there is no evidence that either the President or his wife wanted anything less. There had been epistemological arguments within the administration over whether it was a good idea to be bold with questionable numbers, and do you want to be bold when the public is down on government and suspicious of big plans. Clinton had urged his advisers to come up with a big, bold program and was as convinced as anyone that large amounts of "waste" could be wrung from the system. Also, he understood that Congress was likely to whittle down whatever he proposed. Both Clintons indulged Magaziner in his tendency toward complexity, his insistence that the only way to deliver broader health care insurance was through an overhaul of the entire health care system (if you want to do A, you must also do B, C, and D), his taste for huge projects, and his mind that understood systems better than it did human nature. The result was that they came up with a plan that few, even in their own administration, comprehended or could explain.

A Cabinet-level official said, "Ira's modus operandi for a long time is to convene a gigantic group of people and produce a result that by its size and thoroughness overwhelms people. The problem on this one is that you had five hundred people dealing with one of the most complicated subjects in America and coming out with thirteen hundred pages of legislation which you can't explain. What Ira lacks is a sensibility about the American people and how it will react."

The question was why the Clintons didn't see the danger of coming up with such a complex program. The answer probably lay, beyond their indulgence of an FOB, in their sense that they were smarter than anyone else. For people who considered themselves masterly politicians with a fine feel for the public, and people who were of considerable political talents, they misjudged probable public reaction in this case and failed to see the material they were handing opponents. And Magaziner's view that it was the Washington establishment and entrenched interests—"the same ones who caused gridlock all those years"—who were opposing their bold endeavor undoubtedly was met with agreement on the part of the Clintons, especially Mrs. Clinton. They were reinforcing each other.

One high official had argued that the administration shouldn't be in a rush to get a program out in 1993: they should take more time to hone the program and the arguments, and prepare officials for defending it. Another high official said later, "What the public doesn't realize is that this was a rogue policy process. There's no central policy development mechanism in the White House. Everyone is suspicious of the numbers." Numerous administration officials, including Health and Human Services Secretary Donna Shalala and the economists, were troubled by important aspects of the proposal. Robert Reich was concerned too. The economists were dubious about the figures and felt that the administration was trying to do far too much far too quickly and the program should be phased in. In one August meeting, Magaziner laid out his financing scheme and, according to one participant, "Everyone looked at it and went bonkers. They were in disbelief that the whole system could be paid for the way Ira said it could." Roger Altman raised a lot of questions. Bentsen tended not to say much, but it was clear he favored a more gradual approach, and a smaller and simpler program. (Bentsen and Altman were sufficiently concerned that they interrupted their vacations—Bentsen had been supposed to visit Altman at his ranch—in order to attend some meetings in late August.) Huge amounts of money were involved—a $400 billion program over six years and a program of $130 billion a year when it was fully phased in. Altman urged moderation, so that the effects on the economy and the behavioral effects of the program would be better understood as it was put in place. Rubin, too, wanted to phase in the plan more slowly, to measure the consequences as it went along.

Rubin suggested that Magaziner was counting on cutting costs too quickly, without enough regard for the consequences in terms of quality. Rubin said, "When you try to squeeze down companies that fast, you destroy the company." Magaziner "ran right over him," according to someone who was at the meeting, dismissing Rubin's comment as irrelevant because he was talking about the private sector. Magaziner tended to dismiss others' questions. Donna Shalala argued, "Ira, I have run a public institution, and you can't do that to public institutions."

Shalala and Panetta challenged Magaziner to explain who would be for his program. Shalala said, "Ira, you're developing a negative coalition. This program will turn off liberals and conservatives; no one will be enthusiastic. All the interest groups will be mad—the doctors, the hospitals, the labs. You're building in all the negatives." Magaziner assured the group that as a result of his negotiations, a large number of interest groups would back the program. Panetta, unconvinced, said, "Ira, it won't work."

Laura Tyson was unafraid of taking on Magaziner—or Mrs. Clinton. In fact, some of the men, less courageous, urged Tyson to do so. And Shalala, looking for allies, had urged Tyson to attend certain meetings. So in a meeting in the Cabinet Room in early August, Tyson raised a series of questions. The first was how they could assume that the new insurance plans would provide the same-quality care that the country already had, and what if the providers, limited by "premium caps," or restrictions on the growth of cost in insurance premiums, couldn't do that? "What do we do then?" Tyson asked. Mrs. Clinton and Magaziner argued that savings from reducing inefficiencies and excess costs in the system would free up more resources for quality care. Tyson was also concerned that not much analysis had been made of the effects on employment, that the program might well cost some jobs. (A later study said it was very hard to tell the net effect on jobs.) Tyson also said, "I find it difficult to believe that we can slow the growth of health care spending so much and still provide the same quality of care." (Reich and Gergen in particular had urged her to raise that point.) She asked, "You proposed these dramatic slowdowns in Medicare spending. Can you be sure you can provide the same-quality care as they get now?" The President replied, "Laura has raised a good question. Let's revisit this." After that, the plan's designers came up with specific cuts.

Still, it was clear by early August that the President had decided on the large, ambitious program his wife and Magaziner had been urging. Tyson's attitude was, "OK, I've done my job."

Some of the President's advisers, including McLarty, Stephanopoulos, and Greenberg, were worried about the Rube Goldberg quality of the plan—but they were reluctant to take on Mrs. Clinton. This was one of the distortions in policymaking caused by her role. In August, one Cabinet officer said to a couple of colleagues as they were leaving a meeting on health care, "There's a deal between Ira and the President and Hillary. Don't waste your time." A Presidential adviser said privately, "We all think this thing is wired."

Magaziner had brought Greenberg and Grunwald in early and asked their advice. Greenberg began polling on health care in March 1993. One result was changes in terminology. Greenberg's polling showed that "people are radical about wanting reform of the health care system but conservative about their own health care." This should have been taken as more of a warning to the Clinton administration than it was. But perhaps Greenberg and Grunwald's most fundamental contribution was that the focus of the sales pitch for the plan be on providing security (people wouldn't lose their coverage if they changed jobs, and coverage couldn't be denied for preexisting conditions) rather than on providing coverage for the uninsured. Thus the pitch for the health care plan was aimed at the middle class, and there was little talk about insuring the poor.

Among the questionable numbers in the leaked draft was that the program would reduce the deficit by $91 billion by the year 2000 (not $90 billion, not $92 billion), when obviously this was unknowable. The administration assumed that "savings" in national health care expenditures could hold the cost of premiums to certain levels. But the savings were based on a good amount of guesswork. Mrs. Clinton estimated that the cost of "waste" in the health system was between $200 billion and $250 billion, but there was really no way to know. In order to attract support, the administration plan contained a generous package of benefits, and the proposal was going to cost a large number of people more than they paid for their existing plan. One thing that had held up the bill was that Panetta was dubious about the numbers, and insisted that they be reviewed by OMB—which led to several changes.

Moreover, in its encouragement of the use of HMOs, and its higher costs for people who wanted to continue to choose their doctors, the Clinton plan did reduce people's choices. The Clintons and Ira Magaziner didn't seem to understand how anxiety-provoking this and other changes could be. The Clintons emphasized that people could still choose their doctors; they didn't mention that people would probably have to pay more for that. There were numerous time bombs in their proposal.

The negative reaction built slowly and was encouraged by a stream of effective ads by the Health Insurance Association of America, representing small and medium-size insurance companies, which harped on the bill's complexity and the large role of government. "Harry" and "Louise," a couple who discussed the matter over breakfast or in their living room (Louise worriedly reading a copy of the bill as Harry comes home), did more damage than any of the President's real-life opponents.

In order to win the support of important constituencies, the administration had offered some very expensive items: for business, picking up the costs of premiums for early retirees, a windfall; and for the elderly, paying for the costs of prescription medicine and some long-term care. Magaziner thought that these offerings would nail down the support of business and the elderly, but that turned out to be wishful thinking. An official said that it was "often" asserted in the meetings, " 'We have to keep the AARP [American Association of Retired Persons] with us.' Everyone who had worked on health care before had in mind the catastrophic-care fiasco." (In 1989, the elderly ran a successful drive for repeal of a catastrophic-care program, enacted the year before, when the better-off elderly realized that they would have to pay for it.) Yet in the end, the administration had to struggle for these groups' support. (In February 1994, despite lobbying by the Clintons, the Business Roundtable and even the AARP declined to support the health care program.) Another official said later, "Ira was naive. He didn't know how, when someone said they'd be with us, to be sure they were with us."

Once again, the Clintons—and in this case Magaziner as well—didn't know how to drive a real bargain or how to make "agreements" stick. This was another form of their unfamiliarity with Washington, and their overreliance on their Arkansas experience. Both Clintons often pointed to Mrs. Clinton's management of the education reform proposal for Arkansas as the model for this latest exercise, but that measure was insignificant in scale beside the health care proposal. They had turned to a pal when they needed a shrewd, experienced pol, but they didn't grasp that until very late in the game.

And Clinton's handling of earlier legislation now caused him problems on health care. Numerous members of Congress recalled the Btu tax episode, and said among themselves that they didn't want to vote for something as controversial as employer mandates and then find that the administration dropped it or the Senate rejected it.

Hillary Clinton eventually understood that the complexity of the program had become a liability.

By the time the administration launched its health care program, other health care proposals had been introduced in Congress. Senator John Chafee, the moderate Republican from Rhode Island, offered universal access, with the premiums to be purchased by individuals rather than employers. It didn't go as far as the Clintons' proposal toward universal coverage. Representative Jim Cooper, a moderate Democrat from Tennessee, had introduced legislation that was closer than the administration plan to the original concept of managed competition; it had no employer mandate and didn't guarantee universal coverage. Representative Jim McDermott, of Washington, had introduced a single-payer plan, which had the most House cosponsors of all—about ninety. While no one expected the single-payer plan to be passed by the Congress, McDermott's group was large enough to have leverage, and so the administration hoped to get the single-payer advocates by allowing each state to offer a single-payer plan. Thus, the administration had numerous possibilities of forming a coalition. But while McLarty and Gergen kept in touch with the moderates in the Cooper group, Mrs. Clinton was of no mind to start talking compromise yet—with Cooper or Chafee—and later in the fall she openly attacked Cooper's plan.

She had come some distance from her view that Congress should simply endorse what the administration wanted—but she still had a way to go.

Because of all the attention to the numerous events leading up to the introduction of the health care program, an elaborate and moving signing ceremony on September 21, for the national service bill, perhaps the program closest to Clinton's heart, got lost. He had campaigned on national service, and it was popular with his audiences. Moreover, it had a DLC derivation and was important to his politics. Clinton expressed upset about the lack of attention to the signing. The program had been turned over to senior adviser Eli Segal, who had got it through by building a bipartisan base for it. But other White House officials had their own priorities. Moreover, the program had been cut back so far from what Clinton had promised in the campaign that some Presidential advisers were reluctant to make a big thing of it. But it was a start. Further, Clinton had succeeded in winning a modified version of his proposal to provide college education loans directly from the government rather than through private lending institutions, to be repaid according to income—thus making them less expensive and therefore less of a long-term burden to the borrower. Clinton was quite proud of this change. History would not measure Clinton's achievements in terms of the column inches or television seconds that were devoted to them at the time.

The three weeks that were to be devoted to the rollout of the health care program never materialized. It just fizzled out. There was no real plan for the third week, and then the President was overtaken by other matters. An aide to Mrs. Clinton said later, "Hillary was going gangbusters, but she's not the President. It needed his imprint. We'd plan events, and then there'd be no event. We were all very frustrated."

Mrs. Clinton was angry that, once again, a long-range communications strategy hadn't been worked out, and several administration figures worried about sustaining support for the program for nine months, or even a year. The President was concerned as well. He told his aides, "All great wars are lost in the middle."

The first launch of health care having sputtered, and the absence of a bill at the time of the President's speech having caused some embarrassment and loss of momentum, now that a bill was ready, the Clintons tried to relaunch the program. On October 27, an odd ceremony/rally was held in the Capitol's Statuary Hall. Members of Congress had been gathered for the event, the artificiality of which was clear. Mrs. Clinton spoke before the President did, and, in her clear, strong voice, said that she hoped for "a vigorous, honest debate." Like the President, who spoke next, she somewhat defensively explained why the plan was so complicated. In a show of flexibility, both said they had "no pride of authorship." Clinton said that the only thing he would insist upon was universal coverage. Once again, Clinton sold like mad. He concluded, "Let's start with this bill and start with this plan and give the American people what they deserve: comprehensive, universal coverage. That's what we got hired to do, to solve the problems of the people and to take this country into the twenty-first century." The bill was 1,342 pages long.

The multiple demands on Hillary Clinton were taking their toll. She was frustrated that the day before she was to begin testifying before Congress about the plan, she had to go to New York for the President's speech to the UN General Assembly and attend the requisite head-of-state wives' luncheon. After returning to Washington, she attended a parent-teacher meeting at Chelsea's school and didn't get home until 10:00 P.M.

Mrs. Clinton was privately amused by the "My, the little lady is really articulate!" greeting she got from the male members of Congress when she testified on behalf of the program before four committees or subcommittees in the last week in September. At the end of a Ways and Means Committee hearing, Dan Rostenkowski, the beefy old pol from Chicago, kissed her. Most of the members were so afraid of her, and afraid of seeming to be tough on the First Lady, that the hearings were something of a sham. Still, though Mrs. Clinton seemed to answer the mostly soft questions easily, it wasn't as easy as it looked. She was conscious that a misstep by her could jeopardize the program. The rougher questions came for the next witnesses —and Donna Shalala, who, to the fury of the White House, fumbled some answers (after all, the program was still being written), was the first victim.

By late September, the President was exhausted once more, and the mellow mood had vanished. Attempts had been made to organize his time better and give him more free time in the afternoons to make phone calls and meet with people he wanted to talk to: longtime friends, such as David Pryor, whom he could brainstorm with; black ministers (an aide said, "He's always felt he got good advice from black ministers"); someone who'd written a book he admired; members of the Cabinet who'd held elective office and whom he especially respected (Cisneros, Riley, and Bentsen); political contacts he wanted to stay in touch with (especially from states that he'd won or almost won and were important to him, such as North Carolina, Florida, and, of course, California).

But the improvements in how things worked within the White House were marginal. Clinton still got tired and frustrated. He hankered to go out and play golf on a weekday afternoon (he told an aide that he'd read that Eisenhower played four hundred rounds during his Presidency), but he never made it, both because he was overwhelmed by work and because some said it would be unseemly. He began to take occasional afternoon naps.

Of course Clinton contributed to his own problem by continuing to take on so much. But also, as Roy Neel said, "Almost everyone on the White House staff push to have their agenda get his stamp. The staff takes advantage of him. People here treat the President like he's inhuman, and they say, 'Isn't this great, he'll do this.' He says yes when he doesn't want to say no and there's nobody to say no." An aide, asked if the Chief of Staff should be protecting the President's time, paused and then said, "If we had the kind of White House—and President and First Lady—to support that kind of funnel . . ." And then he trailed off.

On Friday, September 24, the President had a day that made the point. He met for two hours with Shimon Peres and King Hassan of Morocco (the meeting was to have taken forty-five minutes, but no one suggested that the President's visitors leave). He finished up the day with chores he didn't like: videotaping satellite interviews for use at various politicians' or groups' big dinners or ceremonies. These were the kind of thing he would agree to do and would then complain about bitterly. Nevertheless, though he was late for a White House dinner, at seven-thirty, he called Roy Neel at home. The conversation lasted until eight-ten. Neel said, "Good evening, Mr. President," and "Good night, Mr. President." The rest of it was a stream of complaint on Clinton's part, a cry of pain about how his staff was "killing" him, working him to death. "Why did I have to have those satellite interviews?" Clinton asked. "And he was right," Neel said later. "I felt pain for him. We *were* killing him." Publicly, Clinton seemed to be on a roll. The introductions of the new programs and the Middle East signing had gone well. But he was getting no rest, and he wasn't getting enough time to do some of the things he wanted. He wasn't happy.

Starting in early September, some of the consultants were pushing for Clinton to make a speech pulling together the programs he was now espousing, showing their interconnections and giving some theme to his Presidency. Clinton was doing a lot, but he hadn't made it clear what his Presidency was about. There was a cohesive set of thoughts behind his activity, but he hadn't yet got that across. Robert Reich's thinking had been a major influence on Clinton for a long time. Reich's most recent book, published in 1992, *The Work of Nations,* stressed that there was now a global economy, that capital was mobile, and that the best policy for the U.S. to follow was to train high-quality workers. Clinton, reflecting that view, was beginning to say publicly what he had been saying privately to his advisers: if you want people to accept change, you have to make them more secure.

The synthesis in Clinton's own mind was reflected in the unusual degree of cooperation among his Cabinet officers. Reich and Richard Riley often collaborated on programs. When one of them was invited to a meeting, he often suggested that the other come as well—out of the ordinary for Cabinet officers. There was also broad cooperation among his domestic Cabinet officers: Reich, Riley, Shalala, Cisneros, and Reno. There were of course some rivalries within the Clinton Cabinet, but fewer than was traditionally the case. Despite the harum-scarum of the transition process, Clinton had ended up with, on the whole, a good Cabinet. Cisneros, Reich, Riley, and Shalala were the innovators.

To prepare an encompassing speech for the President, Gergen and others searched through speeches Clinton had given before, including in his campaign: there must be a theme in there somewhere. Clinton came up with the idea of using the occasion of the hundredth anniversary of the University of North Carolina, on October 12, to weave together what he was trying to do. The speech stressed the security theme, connecting his proposals or achievements on trade, health care, education, family leave, college scholarships, and personal security from violence. The personal security point fit with his proposals to put more police on the streets and limit access to guns used for the sole purpose of killing other people. (A White House aide said that Clinton and his advisers wanted to build on the moment in his health care speech that had received so much applause.) In his University of North Carolina speech, Clinton spoke of the importance of not withdrawing from the world and of embracing change.

The speech was workmanlike, no better. Because it took place just before 8:30 P.M. and because so many other things were going on, it received little attention. Also, it seemed forced—in fact, the "security" theme had come from Greenberg's polling. Stretching to make all the connections, Clinton fell short. The security theme was soon dropped.

On Saturday, September 25, Somalis fired a rocket at a U.S. helicopter, shooting it down and killing three American servicemen. Senator Robert Byrd repeated his earlier calls for the United States to withdraw its troops from Somalia.

In September, Gergen, Lake, and Stephanopoulos had been discussing among themselves the fact that the administration wasn't seen as doing much on foreign policy and wasn't getting enough credit for what it had done. Moreover, Gergen and Stephanopoulos worried that if the President lost NAFTA and health care stalled, it wouldn't look like the administration was doing much that fall. They decided there should be a set of foreign policy speeches by Lake, Christopher, Albright, and Aspin.

What no one in the White House knew was that foreign policy was about to become a prominent issue, beyond their dreams—and their nightmares.

24

IMBROGLIOS

"How Could This Happen?"

On Sunday morning, October 3, a bright, clear day in Washington, the President was preparing to fly to California. Tony Lake reached his White House office at about 9:00 A.M., as he did every Sunday. Warren Christopher was at his home in Georgetown, tired from a two-week session of the UN General Assembly. Les Aspin, after appearing on *Face the Nation,* had gone to his office in the Pentagon to confer with his deputy, William Perry, about the reports on Tailhook, the infamous convention of Naval aviators.

In Moscow, the struggle between Boris Yeltsin and his parliamentary opponents was coming to a bloody climax. CNN was showing large crowds of anti-Yeltsin demonstrators gathering outside the Russian White House, where the Duma met, and being cheered on by Yeltsin's Vice President, Aleksandr Rutskoy, who urged them to attack the mayor's office and Ostankino, the television station. Yeltsin's opponents, who also included the speaker of the Parliament, Ruslan Khasbulatov, wanted to slow reform, and were allied with some of the most retrograde factions in industry and the military, and with diehard Communists.

Lake first learned of the events in Moscow that morning from Stephanopoulos, who had turned on CNN and called him at home. Lake was highly annoyed that the U.S. Embassy in Moscow was slow to report what was going on. He wasn't notified by the Situation Room until nearly 10:00 A.M.

Strobe Talbott was at his home in northwest Washington, preparing congressional testimony on aid to Russia, when an aide called. Talbott turned on CNN and heard some in the crowd, waving hammer-and-sickle flags, chanting an old pogrom slogan, "Beat the Yids, save Russia." Using the secure phone in his study, Talbott called Thomas Pickering, the U.S. ambassador to Russia. He also called Christopher. Then he went to his office, and he and Lake set up a task force to monitor developments in Russia. Lake and Talbott, concerned that the President would have to respond to reporters at some point that day about the events in Moscow, worked on the line he should take. Shortly after noon, Clinton, looking sober, spoke to reporters in the Rose Garden. He said that the violence had been "perpetrated by the Rutskoi-Khasbulatov forces" and that Yeltsin had "bent over backwards to avoid . . . excessive force." He added, "I am still convinced that the United States must support President Yeltsin and the process of bringing about free and fair elections." Actually, officials in Washington were worried that Yeltsin hadn't moved to end the mini-coup. But later that afternoon, Washington time, tank units entered Moscow and fired on the parliament building, and troops loyal to Yeltsin put down the coup. When it was all over, at least a hundred people were dead, the leaders of the coup were in prison, and the parliament building was in flames.

From his plane that afternoon, Clinton called Yeltsin and told him, "You get stronger and better." In the succeeding days, as Yeltsin banned opposition newspapers and parties, the administration decided, in the words of one official, to "cut him some slack." They believed that Yeltsin's intentions were still good.

At eight that morning, Lake had got word at home from the Situation Room that U.S. forces had staged another raid in Mogadishu to try to capture clan leader Mohamed Farah Aideed and his top lieutenants, who were believed to be having lunch at the Olympic Hotel. As the morning went on, he was told that the operation had run into some trouble. The first reports said that a helicopter had been shot down, but also that at least two of Aideed's senior aides had been captured. The information, coming slowly through the Situation Room, was sketchy. Lake hadn't known about the raid ahead of time and was suspicious of the initial reports of any military event. The news that reached the public that afternoon was that two Blackhawk helicopters had been shot down and at least five Americans had been killed. By Sunday evening, it was clear that the events in Mogadishu, which were completely overshadowed by the CNN coverage from Moscow, were going to be the more difficult to deal with.

Early Sunday evening, Admiral David Jeremiah, now the acting Chairman of the Chiefs of Staff (Powell had retired two days earlier), briefed Aspin on the events in Somalia. At that point, the battle in Mogadishu was in full swing. An effort to rescue downed American troops was nearly completed as Aspin left the Pentagon at 11:00 P.M. By that time, Aspin had decided to send to Somalia tanks that had been requested earlier by military commanders there—a request he had earlier denied.

On Monday, most of Washington's and the media's attention was still on Moscow.

"The news out of Somalia is getting worse," a tense Gearan said, at lunch in his office. "At least eleven American soldiers are dead and fifty-eight wounded. Six are missing. There may be hostages. It's Teheran."

Later that afternoon, David Dreyer was visited in his office in the Old Executive Office Building by two reporters from a newsweekly. They were planning to write a story that Clinton had been doing so well recently, and they demanded to know how come that was. As he talked to them, Dreyer could see over their shoulders, on CNN, with the sound off, pictures of a dead American soldier being dragged through the streets of Mogadishu.

Clinton saw those pictures in his room on Monday at the Fairmont Hotel, in San Francisco. By that afternoon, there had been numerous conference calls between Clinton and his aides back in Washington—Lake, Stephanopoulos, Gergen, and sometimes McLarty, gathered in Stephanopoulos's tiny office—on the situation in Somalia. Clinton was very upset. "How could this happen?" he demanded of his advisers. To Lake and Aspin he complained that the administration hadn't been given "a realistic assessment" by the people on the ground in Somalia of "what we were up against." He said, "No one told me about the downside." He went on, "We've been jerked around for months" by the UN. He asked who was calling the shots about what American troops were being asked to do in Somalia, and who was deciding whether a mission was desirable or not. These were good, if belated, questions.

The President said to his advisers, "It strikes me as dumb at a minimum to put U.S. troops in helicopters in urban areas where they were subject to ground fire." He was angry that he hadn't been told about this mission. He compared the situation to Waco, where, he said, "At least I knew what was happening, and that it had the potential of going bad."

As the news from Mogadishu grew worse, a debate arose among Clinton's advisers over whether he should cut his trip short to return to Washington. In the running argument over this, Stephanopoulos was for Clinton's cutting his trip by a day and returning on Monday, as was Stan Greenberg. Despite the later insistence of a senior official that the consultants hadn't been involved in these foreign policy developments, throughout the ensuing turbulent week Greenberg was in regular contact with Stephanopoulos, Gergen, and McLarty. (Grunwald spoke mainly with Gergen and McLarty, and Carville phoned Greenberg from California.) Stephanopoulos thought that Clinton had to be seen to be working on the Somalia issue—and that he had to actually be working on it. Lake and Gergen were opposed to Clinton's returning earlier, arguing that it would look panicky and would "elevate" the Somalia issue. Also, Lake argued, time was needed to work out some policy options to present to the President. Clinton said he would do whatever his advisers thought best, but faced with divided advice, Clinton decided to keep to most of his California schedule; he would cut short an event on Tuesday and return about a half hour earlier than planned. And he went on to his events in California.

The battle in downtown Mogadishu was the largest firefight Americans had been involved in since Vietnam, with eighteen Americans killed, seventy-four wounded, and one captured. Official U.S. estimates were that three hundred Somalis were killed, but some officials said later that the number was quite a bit higher—perhaps a thousand. Clinton may not have been a military expert, but his instinct about a basic flaw in the planning was dead-on. Through observation of previous operations, Somalis had become familiar with the way Americans lowered themselves by ropes from helicopters, causing the helicopters to hover in place for a while—and become easy targets. The first downed helicopter had a roll-on effect, as other forces went to rescue four injured soldiers, and then a second helicopter was shot down—and a firefight broke out at three different locations. (Some mythology later developed, and was adopted by the President, that the debacle occurred because the Rangers went back to stay by the body of a dead comrade until it was recovered.) Another flaw in the operation was that to preserve the element of surprise, U.S. commanders didn't tell other UN forces of their plan; it took rescuers (other U.S. troops, plus Pakistanis driving tanks and Malaysians driving armored personnel carriers) nine hours to reach the pinned-down Americans.

Monday night's news broadcasts caught up with the Somalia story and showed the soldier's body being dragged through the streets, plus the bloodied and frightened face of Chief Warrant Officer Michael Durant, a member of the super-secret Delta force (this was not made known at the time), who was being held captive. The nation's emotional reaction was immediate, and it registered strongly on Capitol Hill, where there had already been calls for the withdrawal of U.S. troops from Somalia. (The presence of the Delta force, even the existence of which is supposed to be secret—they are trained for special missions, such as rescuing a hostage or capturing someone—was masked by their being mixed in with a force of Rangers. For cover, Deltas are also Rangers.)

The Clinton administration had come to this pass via a series of casually made decisions. There was never a Principals meeting on the subject of Somalia until after Mogadishu. Most of the work had been done in the Deputies Committee—composed of deputies of the Principals—and when it came to the higher-ups, decisions were made informally and without a lot of thought as to consequences. The Clinton administration had inherited an unthought-through mission in Somalia. Among the unthought-through questions were the varying responsibilities of the United States and the UN, which was to take over from the U.S. in May 1993. Implicit in the Bush administration's mission was that it wouldn't just dump the food and depart, but would try to leave behind something that wouldn't simply return Somalia to chaos, warlordism, and more famine. Left ambiguous was whether one goal was to disarm the warring clans. The Bush administration sent Robert Oakley, a former ambassador to Somalia, to talk to the clan leaders and try to restore stability. The Bush people said that the troops could be out of Somalia by Inauguration Day.

With that goal nowhere in sight, the Clinton administration's objective after it took office was to gradually withdraw from Somalia and hand the operation over to the UN. In May, when the transfer was made, the Security Council adopted a resolution saying the UN would in effect become involved in nation building. This implied an open-ended commitment. "Maybe we should have looked harder at it," an administration official said later, "but it wasn't couched as a fundamental shift." There were some within the administration, including UN Ambassador Madeleine Albright, who wanted to make Somalia a model exercise in multinational peacekeeping. But the UN wasn't prepared to take over.

At the same time, the Clinton administration was trying to indicate to the public that the mission to Somalia was virtually over. Thus the scene of Clinton and the troops striding across the South Lawn in early May. And thus Clinton's June 17 press conference statement that the U.S. operation in Somalia "is over."

The next step into, rather than out of, Somalia came when an attack by Aideed's forces resulted in the deaths of twenty-four Pakistani peacekeepers on June 5. An immediate emotional response at UN headquarters led to the adoption of a resolution on Sunday, June 6, calling for the arrest and punishment of "those responsible" for the peacekeepers' deaths. In Washington, the resolution, which Albright was pressing for, was considered no big deal. Lake favored it because he felt that otherwise peacekeepers all over the globe would be in jeopardy. In fact, there was no dissent within the administration. The resolution was largely drafted at the State Department. There was no Principals meeting, and no one could remember later whether the President was consulted. Aides said later that he must have been told of the need for the resolution. That resolution, and the emotions unleashed by the attack, led straight to the disaster on October 3.

From that moment on, the UN's mission re-became the U.S.'s mission—and the mission was to capture Aideed. The United States was now engaged in urban guerrilla warfare in territory it little understood—the sort of warfare that former colonial nations had learned to avoid. That wasn't the intention. A senior official said, "I don't think that on June 5 anyone could imagine where we'd be in October." Lake recalled later, "I discussed this with Colin, Chris, and Les, and we agreed that [the UN resolution] should be the response but that we should try to avoid turning this into an us-versus-Aideed struggle as we tried to apprehend Aideed and his lieutenants—that we shouldn't hype it."

It turned out to be an impossible line to draw. UN forces concentrated at first on going after Aideed's munitions and other supplies, which some policymakers thought should be considered the retribution for the June 5 killings. But inexorably the exercise became an effort to capture Aideed. Jonathan Howe, the United States' representative to the UN in Mogadishu, became, by many officials' accounts, obsessed with catching Aideed. No one seemed to consider the possibility that if Aideed were out of the way, someone like him, or worse, might take his place, or that he represented a force and might be worth trying to talk to. A few days after the UN passed its resolution, Howe put up notices offering a twenty-five-thousand-dollar reward for Aideed's capture. After the firefight in Mogadishu, administration officials tried to ascribe it to a UN mission gone awry, and referred to Howe privately as "Jonathan Ahab." But they had known all along what he was doing. Berger said later, "When Howe put up the notices, I think we felt it didn't make a lot of sense, but he was calling the shots at that point, and we weren't second-guessing him." (Howe, who had been deputy to Brent Scowcroft, Bush's national security adviser, had been chosen by Lake and Berger, who thought that he had the right credentials for the job.)

Over the course of the summer, a frustrated Howe, who had a lot of contacts within the administration, pressed for additional forces to go after Aideed. He urged that the Delta force be sent to Somalia. Also pushing for sending the force were Albright; Robert Gosende, the new U.S. envoy to Somalia; David Shinn, a State Department representative who led a fact-finding mission to Somalia in late July; and the CIA.

Christopher backed sending more forces to try to capture Aideed, as did Under Secretary for Political Affairs Peter Tarnoff, who represented the State Department on the Deputies Committee. Tarnoff said, "We didn't want to put too much daylight between Howe and us." In August, when Christopher was vacationing at his Santa Barbara weekend home, Tarnoff was in touch with him by phone. A State Department official said, "Frankly, it was a policy to which the Principals didn't pay enough attention." Donilon later suggested that Aspin was responsible for the Delta force's being sent, and that Tarnoff didn't represent Christopher's views, which was highly unlikely. Actually, Aspin tried to rein in the policy on Somalia. Aspin, Powell, and Marine Corps General Joseph Hoar, the head of the U.S. Central Command, or CENTCOM, based in Tampa (Norman Schwarzkopf's old job), were all reluctant to send in additional forces, for fear of escalating the mission or having its success measured by whether Aideed was caught. Also, congressional criticism of the seemingly open-ended mission to Somalia, with its accompanying casualties, was increasing.

On August 8, four American soldiers, on patrol in Mogadishu, were killed when their Humvee was blown up by a remote-controlled mine. This sophisticated attack, using high tech, sent a chilling message to U.S. military leaders. The fact that U.S. forces could be targeted in such a way sparked a series of consultations in the Pentagon and a recommendation by the staff of the Joint Chiefs to Powell to send the Delta force.

There was no meeting of administration policymakers on the subject of sending the Delta force, or even serious discussion of it. It was August, and officials were scattered. On Saturday, August 21, Powell called Aspin, who was sailing on Lake Beulah, in Wisconsin. Since they were speaking on a nonsecure, celluiar phone, Powell, using code, said, "You know that request that we have been talking about? I think it's time to approve it." Hoar had said that he thought the Rangers had only a one-in-four chance of capturing Aideed, while Howe and Lieutenant General Thomas Montgomery, the U.S. commander in Somalia, said that they had a 90 percent chance. Aspin recalled, "Eventually, the problem was, If Aideed is killing Americans, even if there's only a one-in-four chance of catching him, shouldn't you do everything you can?" Aspin agreed with Powell but urged that at the same time the visibility of the U.S. effort should be reduced. How this was to be done was problematic.

Powell also called Lake and said, We've got to do it, and Lake agreed. Lake's staff had for a while been pushing for sending the Delta force. Lake said later, "I thought that we would be damned if we did and we certainly would be damned if we didn't." Christopher, in Santa Barbara, agreed. Lake couldn't reach Clinton that day, so he had an NSC staff member who was in

Martha's Vineyard as part of the President's entourage tell him of the decision. An official said later, "The President didn't weigh in."

The Ranger and Delta forces were sent promptly.

The surprising thing was that Lake and Powell went along at all. Lake had written critically of the American Marines' chasing the guerrilla leader Augusto César Sandino throughout Nicaragua for years, thus making him a national hero. Powell, mindful of the frustration of the U.S. military's efforts to kill Muammar Qaddafi and capture Manuel Noriega, had been strongly opposed to getting into that kind of chase again. (Therefore, the Bush administration never admitted to trying to kill Saddam Hussein.) But Powell, a friend said later, was tired of putting himself in the way of Clinton administration policies and was looking forward to his retirement in the fall. "Colin had checked out by August," the friend said.

The Delta forces were trained to operate with stealth and surprise. (This was the group that couldn't find Noriega for so long.) Military and civilian officials who had dealt with these forces described them as very gung ho and hard to control. A former military official said, "Special ops people are hard to deal with. They are arrogant, they overestimate their own capability, and they're very secretive. This all came back to bite them in Somalia. When they needed help, nobody knew what they were doing."

These troops no sooner landed in Somalia than they swung into action. On their first day, they attacked a residence that housed UN officials. Powell was very unhappy. He felt that making a mistake on such a deadly mission was unpardonable. (Powell had them sent out into the desert for further training.) Then they shot up a house and captured a former police chief, who they insisted was Aideed. When he said he wasn't, they hit him with rifle butts and arrested him.

While all this was going on, the administration was also moving down another track. In August, officials became concerned they seemed to be going down the military track only, and that (1) this didn't necessarily offer a way out of Somalia; (2) Congress was beginning to squawk; and (3) there was the possibility of having to send twenty-five thousand troops to Bosnia to enforce a peace agreement. In addition, some military leaders began to think that the mission in Mogadishu should be reined in: there had been too much "mission creep." The officials decided that it was time to show that they wanted also to move to more political activity, and intended to withdraw from Somalia. This led to a speech by Aspin on August 27 (the day the Rangers arrived in Somalia), which was aimed at both the domestic audience and UN officials. The point of the speech was to demonstrate to Americans that there was an exit strategy, but—though the speech was cleared by Aspin's counterparts—it misfired, since it appeared to establish criteria for withdrawal that could have the U.S. in Somalia ad infinitum.

In early September, the President, disturbed by the two raids that had gone awry, told his advisers that Somalia policy needed to be looked at both in its own terms and in terms of Bosnia. Unless we can get the Somalia mission under control, Clinton said, it's going to be very hard to convince Congress to provide the forces to implement an agreement on Bosnia; and we need to get the Somalia mission under control in any event. (Members of Congress, led by Senate Appropriations Committee Chairman Robert Byrd, were drafting resolutions setting a firm date for the withdrawal of U.S. forces from Somalia.)

So a major effort commenced to turn the U.S. policy in Somalia toward seeking a political solution. A number of entreaties were made by American officials, including Albright and Christopher—and ultimately the President—to UN Secretary General Boutros Boutros-Ghali to put more emphasis on a political settlement and work with other African leaders in trying to get one. But Boutros-Ghali, an Egyptian who had been his country's ambassador to Somalia when Aideed overthrew the previous (despotic) ruler, Mohammed Siad Barrah, and disliked Aideed intensely, while never quite saying no, resisted. He knew about Somalia, he said; he was working on a peaceful exit, he said. A U.S. official said, "We thought it was inertia on the part of Boutros-Ghali. It was opposition."

The President continued to raise the problem of trying to send forces to Bosnia while there were still forces in Somalia. He also asked his aides if there was a feasible way to cordon off southern Mogadishu, where Aideed was headquartered, rather than continue to raid it. (He had got this idea from Admiral William Crowe, the former Chairman of the Joint Chiefs. At the President's urging, Crowe tried out the idea on an unreceptive Lake.) The Joint Chiefs of Staff said that this was militarily infeasible, because the U.S.'s own supply lines from the port and the airfield ran through southern Mogadishu. The President raised the question again a week before the October 3 raid.

After the raid, the question arose of why, given the fact that the administration was shifting its emphasis—or thought it was—to the political track, it had taken place at all. Why weren't the commanders in the field given new instructions? The answer was shrouded in ambiguity, if not outright confusion. Following the raid, and for a long time after that, Clinton angrily said to his aides that he thought such exercises had been terminated. But others—in their post facto explanations—said that no such decision had been made. They argued that putting more emphasis on a political settlement didn't mean that the hunt for Aideed would be called off. The theory, according to Lake, was that the military and diplomatic pressure were complementary. "The policy was never to stop trying to get Aideed," Lake said. Aspin said afterward, "The Pentagon's understanding of the policy was to move to more diplomatic efforts but snatch Aideed on the side, if you can."

Carrying out a decision made in August, the foreign policy Principals in late September gave speeches designed to explain U.S. policy. As such, they fell short. And they received little attention.

The idea was to set forth the policy as one of engagement, not retreat from the world; but because of limited resources, there had to be a strategy and priorities. Lake's speech, stressing the need for enlarging democracies and markets, seemed to strain for a theme—"enlargement"—even though there was something to what he said. His rationale for this theme was that "free markets create middle classes" and "democracies generally do not fight one another or sponsor terrorism." He added, "This is not a crusade. It is a pragmatic commitment to see freedom take hold where it will benefit us most"—for example, Russia. Indicating a lesson the administration was already learning and was about to get a major reminder of, Lake said that while humanitarian relief "has an important place in our foreign policy . . . we must be mindful of the limits and the nature of humanitarian interventions. . . . CNN is not a compass for American interests." Lake called the policy "Pragmatic neo-Wilsonian." His speech was overshadowed by events at home (the Clintons' windup to the President's health care speech, which was given the day after Lake's) and abroad (the parliamentary crisis in Russia).

Christopher's speech was a lawyerlike approach that stressed his efforts in the Middle East and, as he and Tom Donilon had hoped, made news: that the United States would convene a conference to build a Middle East peace and appoint a senior coordinator for investment in the region. The narrowness of Christopher's approach was symptomatic of a larger problem.

Albright's speech was an attempt to redefine the U.S.'s interest in multilateral efforts—more cautious now, emphasizing that such efforts would be approached on a case-by-case basis. She spelled out the requirements for American participation: clear, definable objectives; the agreement of the combatants to a UN presence; sufficient finances and personnel; and a clear end point.

Multilateralism had become an increasingly sensitive subject within the administration, which had set out with great optimism about its possibilities. During the campaign, Clinton had proposed a permanent UN force for dealing with regional conflicts. But in the course of 1993 a roaring fight went on within the government over PRD 13, a Presidential Review Directive, which was to spell out the administration's policy on the use of U.S. troops for multilateral peacekeeping missions. There were leaks to the press, and criticism from some columnists that the administration had turned its foreign policy over to the UN. The PRD had to be convincing that this was not the case and had also to work out tricky issues of command and control—and what sorts of UN reforms were needed. The experiences on Bosnia and Somalia had a sobering effect. There were difficult questions as to what to do about Russian "peacekeeping" missions in its so-called near abroad—the former Soviet republics. The Russians were threatening to take this upon themselves unless the UN joined them, but there was concern about appearing to give them carte blanche. (In the end, that's close to what happened.) The final directive laid out the criteria that would be used in discussions with the Russians on this question.

Eventually, early in 1994, the administration reached agreement on a peacekeeping policy, which was considerably more restrained about such missions than it had been earlier. It stipulated that previously warring groups must have arrived at a true peace before American troops would be sent to enforce it. It said that American interests must clearly be at stake before the U.S. got involved in peacekeeping. The use of U.S. troops in combat was subject to strict criteria.

Clinton's speech, before the General Assembly, on September 27, the final in the foreign policy series, also established strict criteria for multilateral peacekeeping and for sending troops to enforce a Bosnian peace. Clinton said, "If the American people are to say 'yes' to UN peacekeeping, the United Nations must know when to say 'no.' " Clinton's delivery of the speech gave away the difference within him when he was dealing with domestic or with foreign policy issues. He was wooden and projected little self-confidence.

When the President returned to the White House from California on Tuesday, October 5, two days after the Mogadishu raid, Stephanopoulos and Lake met with him in the Oval Office just before a formal meeting with the foreign policy advisers in the Cabinet Room and gave him some rather blunt advice. Clinton was once again venting his upset over the raid. "This is stupid," he said. "How could they be going after Aideed when we're working on the political end?" He was raising a good question, but Lake and Stephanopoulos (who had talked about this before they met with Clinton) felt that his demeanor in the meeting would be of great importance.

They urged the President not to use the meeting as an exercise in finding out what had gone wrong, that it was important that he seem in command

and looking ahead. (They were also concerned that the time was short for getting some decisions made.) Clinton agreed. He ran the meeting calmly, though occasionally he showed his frustration.

In meetings with his own staff, in and around the more formal policy meetings on Somalia, and continuing afterward, Clinton expressed his frustration strongly and often. Several times he said, "Why the hell were we chasing after him?" He expressed surprise that a raid of that magnitude could have occurred without high-level consultation in Washington. (Much of the magnitude, of course, was a result of the raid itself going wrong.) He told one of his top advisers that he thought he hadn't been adequately involved in the decisions—suggesting that the blame for this lay with his advisers. He felt that matters weren't brought to him until they had reached a crisis point. But he had made it clear, in various ways, that he didn't want to be bothered with foreign policy unless it was a crisis.

At one point, Clinton asked Gergen how it was that Ronald Reagan had been able to remain unscathed after the tragedy in Beirut in October 1983, when 219 Americans were killed in a suicide bombing of the Marine barracks. Gergen replied, "Because two days later we were in Grenada, and everyone knew that Ronald Reagan would bomb the hell out of somewhere."

About the last thing Clinton needed at this point was that his administration appear incompetent in handling foreign policy. There had been so many pratfalls in other parts of the White House; even if some people found the foreign policy group wanting, it hadn't gotten the President into trouble. Now that part of the Clinton Presidency was in question too.

In the Cabinet Room were Gore, Christopher, Aspin, Albright, Admiral Jeremiah, General Hoar, Leon Fuerth, McLarty, Gergen, and CIA Director Woolsey. Lake, working with the State Department and the Pentagon, had prepared four options: one was a big increase in the military presence and an effort to clean out southern Mogadishu, which could involve heavy fighting; the second was to build up the troops in Somalia and keep the pressure on Aideed, being prepared to fight him militarily but trying to negotiate a settlement with him; the third was to drop the military approach and try to find a face-saving way to get out; the fourth was to extend the deadline for getting out and try to negotiate a political settlement, without much of a military effort. No option proposed pulling out right away. The military had said that a withdrawal couldn't occur before March 31, because it would take that long to turn over the logistics operations to others and to move supplies and personnel. The meeting began with Hoar explaining what each option would involve militarily.

The President, to whom these proposals had been faxed as he flew back to Washington, found none of them desirable. As he often did, Clinton asked a number of probing questions. Everyone soon agreed that the first option—an all-out fight in southern Mogadishu—would involve unacceptable costs. Lake and Gergen were both quite hawkish at this meeting, Lake being adamant that the U.S. just couldn't pull out of Somalia. He argued that if it did, it would lose credibility, and peacekeepers wouldn't be safe anywhere. Further, Lake thought that the executive branch, not the Congress, should decide the timing of a withdrawal. Gergen felt that Aideed should be made to pay for the dragging of the dead soldier's body through the streets, that this was desirable politically and as an example to the rest of the world. However, he also urged that the troops be out by the date of the State of the Union address. No one favored the third option, simply finding a face-saving way to get out. That left options two and four, with most people favoring the fourth option. Both Jeremiah and Hoar said that Somalia wasn't a great place to fight a war.

The President was interested in some combination of two and four; he asked that the others stay and work something out. It was after eight o'clock, and he had to get into black tie, and was already too late for a reception at a seventy-fifth-birthday party for Robert Strauss, at the F Street Club (Mrs. Clinton showed up for a while), thrown by Dwayne Andreas, the head of Archer Daniels Midland and a major political contributor. But Clinton did go to a Democratic Senate Campaign Committee's fund-raiser at the Washington Hilton hotel.

That afternoon, there had been a briefing on Capitol Hill by Aspin and Christopher, which was universally deemed a disaster, with the major blame placed on Aspin. Paster had pressed for the briefing, saying that the situation on the Hill was hemorrhaging and Members of Congress were out of control on the Somalia issue; unless they felt reassured by the administration, they might vote for an immediate pullout.

Members of Congress were in a state of panic—the sort of unproductive and often misguided state they collectively get in from time to time, when events beyond their immediate control are riling up the country. Everything about the meeting was wrong. Room SC-5, on the ground floor of the Capitol, was windowless and had a low ceiling, and wasn't large enough for the some two hundred fifty members who turned up. (It was the largest meeting room in the Capitol.) Senators resented being thrown into the same meeting as lowly representatives. There was no sound system, so people began to shout. (Eventually, Tim Keating, Paster's aide, went out and found a microphone.) Christopher's presentation about Russia went well enough, but the members weren't really interested in Russia. And Aspin didn't have anything to tell them. His "What do you guys think" approach went over very badly. There had been a cosmic misunderstanding: the members thought they were going to be briefed, the Cabinet members went to the Hill to "consult." So when Aspin told the members, "I'm up here to get your ideas about what we should do," the response was virtually catcalls.

Aspin showed his impatience with some of the questions—never a good idea where Congress was concerned. Aspin already had important enemies in the Congress (he and Nunn had never gotten along), and now the old enmities were coming home. A Democratic member who counted himself an Aspin friend said after the meeting, "Les suffers from familiarity. We know his warts, we know his strengths. He's very bright. He knows defense, but he's not General Powell and he isn't a strong presence." Aspin was a victim of his style and the members' bad nerves and the lack of a policy. Members of Congress often carry on about wanting to be consulted. After this episode, a leading Democrat said, "I always knew they didn't want to be consulted."

Even before the meeting was over, officials at the White House got calls reporting a "disaster" on Capitol Hill.

At the Democratic dinner, Clinton heard a lot about the Aspin-Christopher "briefing" that afternoon, and none of it about Aspin was good.

Clinton was also told at the dinner by Sam Nunn and David Pryor to remember Vietnam: if he wanted more troops for Somalia, he should ask for them all at once. Vietnam was a ghost Clinton couldn't shake. He was aware that his credentials as Commander in Chief were in question. He knew that his espousing the admission of gays in the military hadn't helped his relations with the military. He knew that the men in uniform in the Pentagon looked down on him. He hoped that General John Shalikashvili, the new Chairman of the Joint Chiefs, could help him win the trust of the military, but he wondered whether anyone could.

On Wednesday, there were two more long meetings at the White House to decide Somalia policy. There was a certain amount of excuse making and seminar talk, until eventually the President said, "Let's stop all the rationalization and admit we made a mistake." Lake offered to take responsibility for the failure of the policy and said that he had been responsible for sending Howe. (Later, in a conversation with the President, he offered to resign, but Clinton wouldn't have it.) Gergen argued that they should still go after Aideed. Clinton and Gore asked good questions, and that led to a crystallization of the new policy. The President directed Albright to go to New York and speak strongly with Boutros Boutros-Ghali about reaching a political settlement. At Lake's suggestion, Robert Oakley was asked to go to

Somalia to try to arrange a settlement. Oakley had high standing both in Somalia and among people in Washington, so this was a reassuring move.

The plan was for an interim buildup of troops, to protect the forces already there, and to apply political pressure while Oakley worked for a political settlement and the U.S. disengaged—to be out by March 31. The number of troops settled on that day was what the military had said it would need. Whether or not the figure was the right one, Clinton was in no position to deny the military what it said was necessary. With less responsible military leaders, this could be a dangerous situation. If the plan had cognitive dissonance—putting in more troops in order to pull troops out—so be it. It was a way to not "cut and run" and also not get into a war in Mogadishu. Many people wished that Clinton hadn't set a date for withdrawal—on the grounds that it was a bad precedent and telegraphed plans—but if he hadn't set one, Congress would have, and it probably would have been earlier. Greenberg, Carville, and Grunwald all pushed for a pullout date before the end of the year, but Clinton told Greenberg later that that wasn't acceptable to the military.

Next came a major discussion of how Clinton was to announce his plans. His advisers were torn between wanting this to be a "high profile"—Presidential—appearance and not wishing to "elevate" the Somalia issue. (It was plenty elevated already.) Some argued that a prime-time Oval Office address was too much elevation. Clinton was initially unenthusiastic about giving an Oval Office address at all, because he thought it would draw too much attention to the events in Mogadishu. But some of his advisers saw the President's giving an Oval Office address as an opportunity to show the leadership on foreign policy that had been missing. Stephanopoulos suggested as a compromise an Oval Office address late in the afternoon, not prime time.

On Wednesday evening, the President met alone with Hoar and Jeremiah, to explore what had gone wrong militarily in Mogadishu, and then he and the military men were joined by Aspin, Lake, Gergen, and Stephanopoulos. Clinton hadn't wanted to appear to be grilling the military officials in a larger meeting. And then he questioned them on the troops and equipment they were requesting to be sent to Somalia. He wanted to be sure, he told them, that they were sending absolutely whatever was required. So at the urging of the President, the military leaders said they would come back the next day with a proposal for sending still more troops and equipment to Somalia. They weren't going to turn down an offer like that.

Thursday morning, at nine, Clinton and his advisers met with congressional leaders in the White House. Before that meeting, there was a preparatory meeting with the President that symptomized several things wrong with the way the Clinton White House was managed. Eight aides were in the Oval Office, talking to him at once. The President wasn't happy with the briefing notes that the NSC staff had prepared for him, and now there was no time to revise them, so everyone started making new suggestions—while the congressional leaders waited in the Roosevelt Room. The prepping of the President for this meeting should have taken place earlier, with fewer people, and with more clarity in the policy behind the talking points. But preparations of Clinton for a meeting were almost always on the fly.

Gergen and Lake thought that Clinton was too apologetic, or not assertive enough, to the congressional leaders in laying out what he planned to do. A number of people noticed that Christopher didn't say anything, just as some had noticed that he hadn't said much in the meetings the day before. On Thursday, he hadn't come to the usual pre-meeting meeting at the White House, and he left as soon as the session with the congressional leaders ended. The conclusion drawn by some was that he was having as little as possible to do with Somalia policy. Christopher was angry that the Somalia issue had become so big, and angry with Aspin over the briefing on Capitol Hill.

Clinton's Oval Office speech was effective—firm, well constructed, and well reasoned. He reminded the viewers why U.S. troops had been sent to Somalia in the first place, and said, "If we were to leave Somalia, other nations would leave too. Chaos would resume." He added, "It is not our job to rebuild Somalia's society." (This was to assuage Senator Bob Dole, who had made some complaints at the morning meeting.) Clinton said, "We started this mission for the right reasons, and we're going to finish it in the right way." He also made the case for sending more troops—1,700 soldiers, with 104 additional armored vehicles; and an aircraft carrier with 3,600 combat Marines offshore—while preparing to withdraw the forces already there. He pointedly said, "These troops will be under American command."

He finished by thanking the soldiers and expressing his "profound sympathy to the families of the young Americans who were killed in Somalia."

After a struggle, and the acceptance by the administration of some restrictions on the President's freedom of action, the rebellion in Congress was quelled.

Following the speech, Christopher and Aspin were to give briefings to the press. Clinton was worried about Aspin's. The Defense Secretary was having a bad week. First there was the briefing on the Hill on Tuesday; then, the next morning, the *Washington Times* revealed that in September, Aspin had denied a request from Lieutenant General Thomas Montgomery, the military commander for Somalia, for additional tanks. In early September, a division was growing among those running military policy in Mogadishu and the military brass in the United States—who felt that the UN had to scale back its objectives, as the U.S. military was being subjected to "mission creep." When Montgomery's request for Bradley fighting vehicles, M-1 tanks, and six artillery pieces reached Hoar, he scaled down the request before endorsing it in a message to Powell. Powell recommended that the request be approved—though he, too, was concerned about "mission creep"—on the grounds that the request from the commander in the field should be met. When the controversy over the tanks blew up, Aspin said later that Powell had passed it on without recommendation. Powell in fact brought up the request with Aspin at least twice. Aspin also said that he had received conflicting advice from the military about building up or building down in Somalia—which was true enough.

On September 23, Aspin turned down the request, arguing that to send the tanks at a time when the United States was supposed to be lowering its involvement in Somalia would confuse the picture and set off still more controversy in the United States. He was right on both counts. Moreover, Major William Garrison, the field commander of the special forces, presumably wouldn't have begun the October 3 mission if he felt he didn't have sufficient equipment. Pentagon sources said later that the fateful raid was the seventh Delta operation in Somalia, and none of them had called for the use of tanks.

A study by the staff of the Joint Chiefs later concluded that even if the tanks had arrived in time, they would have been of little use in the Mogadishu firefight because the vast majority of the casualties occurred within the first half hour. In late October, Garrison sent a handwritten message to the President and Aspin, via a visiting congressman. In the letter, Garrison took responsibility for the execution and planning of the mission and asserted that additional tanks wouldn't have made any significant difference in the outcome. He said that he had based his planning on "previous reaction of the bad guys," but they had reacted in a new way. He said, "Armored reaction force would have helped but casualty figures may or may not have been different." Later that month, Garrison visited Aspin and told him that the threat against his helicopters was greater than he had expected (he apparently hadn't figured out what the Somalis had—that it was easy to hit a hovering helicopter) and that if he had the decision to make over again, he would not have launched the mission.

A large group gathered in Lake's office on Thursday afternoon to prepare Aspin and Christopher for the briefings that were to follow the President's Oval Office address. In the course of the discussion, Aspin was told that the President wanted to see him in his study.

There, Clinton talked to Aspin about how he was going to handle the inevitable press questions about the tanks. Clinton had made a small suggestion and added, "What you say has got to be true, and you can't say it in a way that people don't think it's true. It's like me saying I didn't inhale. It was the God's truth, but I shouldn't have put it that way."

No sooner had the President made his Oval Office speech on Somalia than he and his foreign policy team were faced with another crisis, this time in Haiti.

During the campaign, Clinton had made some passionate statements accusing Bush of playing "racial politics" with the Haitian refugees and asserting, "I wouldn't be shipping those poor people back."

After he became President, Clinton took a strong personal interest in restoring to office Jean-Bertrand Aristide, who in 1991 became Haiti's first popularly elected President but was overthrown eight months later by the military. Aristide, a Jesuit priest, was a somewhat erratic figure, a messianic populist with a sweeping view of his own power and a radical vision for redistributing Haiti's wealth. (A CIA study, relayed in briefings on Capitol Hill, depicted him as flaky at best; some administration officials discounted the study.) But Aristide had strong backing within the United States, particularly from the Congressional Black Caucus but also in the media and among some prominent liberals, including members of the Kennedy family.

During Aristide's brief time in office, he had made some incendiary speeches and spoken approvingly of necklacing (placing a tire filled with gasoline around someone's neck and setting it on fire). There were still scores to settle. The military leaders feared, not entirely irrationally, that if Aristide was returned, they would be killed by his followers. Haiti wasn't exactly a hothouse of democracy.

The Governors Island Accord, reached in July 1993, between Haiti's military rulers and Aristide and brokered by the United States, stipulated that Aristide was to be returned to power on October 30, 1993. This was to be preceded by a series of steps showing that the military and police forces then in control were going to live by the agreement. Further, the U.S. was to send in two hundred lightly armed military trainers and engineers as part of a UN contingent, to train the Haitian military in building roads, bridges, schools, and the like, and to train some of them to be police. The

U.S. trainers—Seabees—were to stay only six months—to avoid a picture of the Americans invading and occupying the island once again. (The United States had occupied Haiti for nineteen years, beginning in 1915.)

In early September, the CIA reported that the Haitian leaders didn't intend to live up to the Governors Island agreement, and as the date for sending the Seabees approached, the leaders still hadn't honored some of the terms. Aspin argued against sending the troops, saying that it was going to be easier to get them in than to get them out, and that since it looked as if the governing powers didn't intend to leave peacefully, the U.S. could get caught in a local civil war. Aristide, too, was balking at promising amnesty to the military leaders, as he had pledged to do in the accord. At the last minute, both sides met their requirements, but there was some disagreement within the administration over whether the generals had met all of theirs.

Aspin remained doubtful of the Haitian rulers' intentions, and continued to oppose sending in the trainers. Lake, Berger, and Christopher felt that the U.S. had to show muscle to back up the agreement. Further, since the U.S. had brokered the Governors Island agreement, they said that for the administration to say it had changed its mind and wouldn't live up to its end of it wasn't an option. The President wasn't asked to rule on the question.

There was a generic split within the Clinton administration over the use of force to further diplomatic ends. It came up in questions about Bosnia, about Somalia, and about Haiti. Lake and Berger were, generally speaking, the most strongly for it. Christopher was at times more inclined to it than the Pentagon. Aspin and Powell were least in favor. The feeling in the Pentagon was that Lake and Berger hadn't had much real foreign policy experience and didn't have a seasoned understanding of the difficulties involved in using force. The Pentagon was often viewed by State and the NSC as too cautious about expending military power. The Pentagon was traditionally reluctant to use force. But the differences in outlook, along with the absence of a guiding hand, had important effects on the formulation and execution of Clinton's foreign policy.

On September 30, the *Harlan County,* with the Seabees aboard, left Charleston and stopped in Puerto Rico—the argument was over whether it should proceed from there—and after Aspin lost the argument, it proceeded to Haiti, arriving there October 11. When it was met by about forty to sixty demonstrators, some of them armed with handguns, Haitian police and military personnel stood by. The Haitian leaders—the military commander, Lieutenant General Raoul Cedras, and the police chief, Lieutenant Colonel Michel François—refused to guarantee the forces' safety. The ragtag group at the harbor wasn't the most menacing force the U.S. military had ever faced, but the lightly armed Seabees (they were carrying only small sidearms and M16s) weren't in a position to shoot their way in. Further, the dock manager hadn't removed a ship in the slip intended for the *Harlan County,* so the Seabees would have had to use force to get the ship into the harbor.

As the ship waited offshore for two days, the question in Washington was whether the United States would look worse if the ship hovered at sea, unable to land, or if there were pictures of it turning around and leaving. Gergen argued that keeping the ship there was a sign of impotence and that each day there would be a press watch to see if it could land. Lake, Aspin, and Jeremiah agreed. The decision was made to have the *Harlan County* turn around and leave. So on Tuesday, October 12, the world was treated to a picture of the mighty United States sailing away from a clutch of rioters. As Clinton left the White House to speak at the University of North Carolina that evening, he said, trying to look forceful in the face of this second humiliation in little over a week, "I want the Haitians to know that I am dead serious about seeing them honor the agreement they made."

On Thursday night, officials gathered at the White House to discuss what to do about Haiti, and the very strong emotion—on the part of Lake and Christopher as well as Gore—was in the direction of taking military action. Aristide had to be returned to power, the argument went. There were expressions of anger that the *Harlan County* had to be turned around. Aspin argued, "Be careful. Look at the last time we invaded Haiti."

After the meeting, Aspin called Gergen, who was in New York, and said, "Jesus Christ, we're about to go to war with Haiti."

Gergen replied, "You're kidding."

"No," Aspin said. "Get your ass down here."

So Gergen, in a tuxedo (he had been an honoree at an Aspen Institute dinner), was driven to JFK Airport, where he hoped to catch the last plane back to Washington, at 10:30 P.M. He missed it and stayed in an airport motel, caught a 6:30 A.M. plane to Washington, and was on time for an eight o'clock meeting of the President with his advisers. But by then emotions had cooled. It was decided to seek the reimposition of UN economic sanctions that had been lifted in August, when a government had been formed under Robert Malval, a businessman who the administration hoped could represent a compromise between the military and Aristide (who objected). Also, six ships would be sent to patrol off Haiti to enforce the sanctions—and make the United States look stronger.

On *Meet the Press* on October 17, UN Ambassador Albright said that the administration was "very concerned about the outflow of refugees" to the United States. "That's what all this was about in the first place."

After several attempts to put together an alternative government in Haiti, perhaps without Aristide at the head, by the end of the year the administration was growing weary of Aristide. Aspin thought that the policy should have been to restore democracy, not necessarily Aristide, to power. The sanctions were making a poor country even poorer. There weren't a lot of good options.

Clinton was very unhappy about these foreign policy developments. He had trouble absorbing the notion that he was responsible for eighteen deaths in Somalia. He was angry with his foreign policy advisers, sometimes calling friends at 1:00 A.M. to vent his feelings. One friend said, "When he wants to talk he wants to talk. It can go on for quite a while. At one time he was very depressed about Somalia, and he really needed some handholding." Clinton told one friend he felt he had to do something. He couldn't fire them all, because that would cause too much turmoil, and he told another friend he didn't want a "bloodbath." Clinton remained angry that the raids in Somalia hadn't been called off, as he insisted he thought they had been. He continued to bring this up in meetings. Obviously, if a President thinks he has given an order and his lieutenants think he hasn't, there's a serious problem.

The instinctive reaction of some of the President's advisers to the trouble in Mogadishu didn't necessarily help the President. One senior adviser said later, "They decided to blame the UN for Somalia policy without realizing this would make the President look inattentive and wouldn't wash." The President was more attentive than some of the analyses suggested: he had known ahead of time about at least some specific missions. But he wasn't attentive enough.

Criticisms of the President's foreign policy team rained down from Capitol Hill. The advisers themselves were in bad shape. At the Pentagon, Aspin and the people closest to him were very tense. Christopher, a proud man who had always been a success, felt besieged. Lake took the criticism very hard and fell ill with bronchitis. Clinton's foreign policy team had never jelled. Its members didn't hate each other or yell at each other, but they didn't trust each other much—and did so less as time went on. Collegiality may be overrated—if the "colleagues" come up with wrongheaded policies—but without a certain amount of trust, the policy process the President must rely on can be ragged, and in the case of the Clinton team it sometimes was. But the responsibility for seeing that it works, and for providing leadership, resides at the top. One high foreign policy official said, "If you have an engaged President, the rest of it doesn't matter."

On October 19, Christopher met with Clinton in the Oval Office. Gore was also present. Christopher had suggestions for improving the foreign policy machinery. His main message was that the President should spend more time on foreign policy. He put it very decorously, saying that Clinton's leadership was essential to his foreign policy advisers, so that they could get the full benefit of his insights and understanding of these issues. He said that the President was enormously helpful when he was "ruminating" and not just checking a box. He recommended that Clinton meet with his foreign policy team once a week, preferably for breakfast or lunch. (Christopher thought that meal meetings were more likely to stay on the schedule.) This was a small thing to request, and it was noteworthy that it had to be requested. Though the President said he agreed with the idea, between October and the rest of the year there were only two such meetings, one of them frequently interrupted by phone calls for the President. Toward the end of the year, Christopher, asked how the meetings policy had worked out, said wryly, "I would say it's not been fully implemented."

In the meeting with Christopher, Clinton complained that the national security system wasn't working well enough and that he hadn't been adequately involved in the decisions. Clinton also said that he thought there should be more Principals meetings—that the Deputies Committee was stretched too thin.

Christopher replied that the administration needed more foreign policy spokesmen—which it did, though that wasn't at the heart of what had gone wrong. Christopher suggested that the Vice President speak about it more too. But later, when Gore began to play a more active role and made some foreign policy speeches, Christopher and Donilon were known not to be happy about it.

Christopher gave Clinton some advice that reflected a concern in and out of the administration. He said, "I have a feeling you should appear in more formal settings, and not informal settings" when talking about foreign policy. Christopher said he thought that Clinton shouldn't answer foreign policy questions at the photo ops before meetings with foreign leaders. "You're in charge of that," Christopher said. The President could just say that he wouldn't take shouted questions. Though Christopher didn't say so directly, several of Clinton's aides wanted him to stop talking foreign policy in his jogging clothes.

In the immediate aftermath of Somalia and Haiti, Lake let it be known that Stephanopoulos and Gergen would be more involved in foreign policy deliberations. But this was window dressing. Both men already attended the big foreign policy meetings when the President was there, and Stephanopoulos had played a substantial if largely unknown role all year. In fact, Gergen wanted to be admitted to the Principals meetings, but Lake had resisted. He didn't want it to appear that a man essentially (if unfairly) known as a spin doctor was now playing a role in foreign policy decisions; also, like a lot of people in the White House, he considered Gergen a major leaker. Besides, there was no institutional basis for Gergen's inclusion in Principals meetings. The President avoided involvement in such squabbles among his aides.

In an appearance on *Meet the Press* on November 7, Clinton complained that Bosnia, Somalia, and Haiti were so much in the news. It was a clear sign that he thought his foreign policy had been mismanaged.

About the same time, a top White House official said privately, and with a slight smile, "The tom-toms are demanding a head."

25

NAFTA

"We're Back in the Must-Win Place"

Clinton liked to tell people, "NAFTA was dead on the day I was elected." He said this a lot in October and November, when he was struggling to win congressional approval of the trade agreement. It was both a bit of self-boostering and fact. While history demonstrated that in the end Presidents were unlikely to lose treaties or trade agreements, getting to that point could be very difficult—as it was for Jimmy Carter and the Panama Canal. So Clinton embarked on another episode of "Cliffhanger." He took on something difficult not only because there was a positive political reason for doing so (there was also a political reason for not doing so) but also because the issue fit his growing understanding of the way the world economy was moving.

The NAFTA fight took on proportions greater than the substance of the issue. It became the be-all and end-all for Clinton; once again, a loss could be a severe blow to his Presidency. The NAFTA debate was intense because it was also about real pain that people felt, and real fears that they had. Despite various estimates, nobody knew how many jobs would be lost (or eventually gained) but that was of small comfort to those who worried they'd lose their jobs. And the debate was tinged with racism—against Mexicans on both sides of the border. Also, Clinton said on some occasions that if the United States didn't make this agreement with Mexico, the Japanese would flood Mexico's markets. (A poll done for a business group backing NAFTA showed that that argument resonated high with voters.)

The real problem for Clinton was the House of Representatives. It was always assumed that the Senate would support the agreement if the House did. Because by and large senators had a more national perspective than House members, and contributions by any particular interest group made up a smaller percentage of a senator's campaign fund, free trade had always fared better in the Senate. The administration tried to get some senators to announce their pro-NAFTA position in order to give cover to House members from the same state. But some senators—remembering the Btu tax—asked why they should stick their neck out if the House wasn't going to approve NAFTA.

The rift with labor had become wider and more heated than the administration, or most of it, expected. The labor opposition was centered in the industrial unions, such as the Electrical Workers, the Machinists, Auto Workers, the Textile Workers, and the Amalgamated Clothing Workers—the declining parts of the economy—as well as the Teamsters. But the large umbrella organization, the AFL-CIO, was demonstrating (and reinforcing) solidarity in also opposing NAFTA. NAFTA was a reinvigorating, organizing issue for the labor movement. The intensity of labor opposition was much less in the sectors where there had been more stability or even growth (teachers and other government employee unions). Labor feared not only a loss of jobs but that NAFTA would accelerate the existing trend of forcing down entry wages or holding down wage increases or benefits. While Clinton had hesitated to speak out for NAFTA until the side agreements were reached, and while he was tending to domestic issues, labor organized the grassroots movement against it. There was no countervailing grassroots movement. Workers for companies that depended on exports or might increase exports after NAFTA couldn't be mobilized in the same way.

To help with the fight, Clinton had brought in William Daley (who had lost out on the Department of Transportation job). Clinton wanted to appease the Daleys, and Bill Daley could at least keep lines open to labor. Since there weren't enough Democratic votes in the House to pass the NAFTA agreement, and the White House had to build a bipartisan coalition behind it, Clinton also recruited a respected former Republican congressman, William Frenzel, of Minnesota. Daley encouraged unions—service unions, the National Education Association and others who supported NAFTA—to send checks to members of Congress who said that they'd support the agreement—and then made sure the word got around on the Hill that there were rewards for voting for NAFTA. The administration used the Cabinet as a shadow whip system for this fight; each Cabinet member was given House members to guide toward voting for the trade agreement. Though legend had it that the White House had set up brilliant machinery, led by Daley, for the fight, the real picture was messier than that. The NAFTA effort had several generals and no general. Meetings went on and on and were often inconclusive. "Nobody's empowered to do anything," an outside lobbyist complained. Even Daley despaired.

There was some thought within the administration that Clinton's merely endorsing the agreement would be sufficient—that it would be acceptable, perhaps even preferable, for him to put up a fight and lose. But that thinking didn't reckon with Clinton's temperament. Moreover, there was the counter-argument that Clinton couldn't afford to lose: the more victories he had, the more victories he'd have—and the same was true of defeats. Once Clinton put himself on the line, he had to win, not just for competitive reasons but also because the base support for his Presidency was so thin, the public passion behind him so limited.

Unwittingly, Ross Perot helped fire up Clinton. When Clinton met with Lee Iacocca, the former President of Chrysler, on September 23, Iacocca said, "You don't want to let Ross Perot beat you on this, do you?" Gergen commented later, "Lee was very good at getting him pumped up. Clinton feels he's a tremendous asset, known as a trade hawk, with huge credibility with the public." Iacocca had the friend-of-the-common-man image that Clinton and Gergen thought would be helpful against Perot. Polls showed that he was the best-known business executive in the country. A pro-NAFTA ad Iacocca made was very effective.

Once again, starting in late September, Clinton threw himself into the fight—meeting members of Congress in one-on-one sessions, making many phone calls to them, giving speeches, meeting with opinion leaders, meeting with individual members. Shortly before the vote, there were White House dinners for undecideds. Colin Powell was brought to the White House to meet with the President and endorse NAFTA.

Roy Neel, the Deputy Chief of Staff, who was then handling the President's scheduling, said, "The public events are designed less to get votes in Congress than to make it absolutely clear to members of Congress that the President is all for it." But Clinton also went directly after certain votes. He sold retail and he sold wholesale.

In the three weeks leading up to the vote, Clinton did very little but NAFTA. (Among the matters set aside was foreign policy.) Such bursts of energy, periods of dedication, were impressive in their way, but something was wrong in them too. What if the President had been faced with a foreign crisis? It seemed that the Clinton White House couldn't do more than one big thing at a time. His aides said that they knew he couldn't keep having fights like this, but now there was nothing else to do.

Clinton's retail campaign was a kind of impassioned soft sell. He talked to a member of Congress knowledgeably, explained why NAFTA was good for the economy and why it was important in a larger sense. He addressed the "constituency problems" a member might have—that is, asked them what they might need. He posed the questions members got from their constituents and provided useful answers. He talked about the international stakes, and the larger trade universe, which would, after NAFTA, involve the Pacific nations (a meeting of the Asian-Pacific Cooperation Forum, or APEC, which the President was to attend, was to occur right after the NAFTA vote), and the General Agreement on Tariffs and Trade (GATT), where negotiations were to conclude in December. The NAFTA vote was deliberately scheduled to take place just before the APEC meeting, to give the administration the argument that the President shouldn't be embarrassed on the eve of an important international meeting.

The administration offered hush-hush CIA briefings for members of Congress on the dire consequences in Mexico and the rest of Latin America if the trade agreement was rejected. The briefings were said to have turned a few votes in favor of the agreement (or they gave members another rationale to explain their vote for it). Just as in the case of the Panama Canal, the argument in favor of the agreement turned increasingly toward its implications for international relations.

The administration had a targeting plan centered on the Northeast, the mid-Atlantic coast, and the Pacific coast—all exporting areas. When Massachusetts Democrat Joseph Kennedy, son of Robert Kennedy and a leader among his generation of House members, announced on October 21 that he would support NAFTA, the President and his aides thought it was a very big thing. The same held true for Nancy Pelosi, from San Francisco, who was an increasingly influential member of the California delegation. Getting the support of Steny Hoyer, from Maryland, the chairman of the House Democratic Caucus, who had major labor backing, was particularly significant. Gephardt stayed behind the scenes, but he worked hard trying to persuade uncommitted Democrats to vote against NAFTA. The out-front Democratic leader of the opposition was majority whip David Bonior, from Macomb County, Michigan, a predominantly blue-collar district, who also knew the levers of power well. Bonior's opposition was passionate and deep-seated. None of his colleagues thought it was a political pose. He was the son of middle-class parents, and he had seen many jobs disappear. The internal split among the Democrats was bitter, with some pro-NAFTA members feeling that it was wrong for Gephardt and Bonior—party leaders —to openly oppose their President.

And the President made deals. The deals were so numerous that it seemed as if a For Sale sign had been hung over the White House. Outwardly, White House people were defensive and said that the dealing wasn't any greater than with previous Presidents—but it was. Privately, even Daley and Mickey Kantor felt that the dealing got out of hand and was unseemly. Some of the deals involved changes in the trade agreement. This particularly infuriated labor leaders, who argued that they were in an unfair fight. Under the rules, the NAFTA agreement was to be voted up or down—no amendments allowed. And here was the administration in effect making amendments.

The biggest such deal was to protect against a "surge" of Mexican exports of citrus fruits and vegetables, including tomatoes, cucumbers, and peppers, to the United States. This was aimed at the Florida delegation, where eight to ten votes were thought up for grabs; but the change didn't deliver the delegation right away, which was a bit of an embarrassment. This became a pattern. A deal would be made, but it wouldn't produce the votes a member had indicated it would. The Florida members held out to see how much more they could get, and negotiations on interpreting the deal ensued—in the end, most of the uncommitted members came around for the agreement. Clay Shaw, of Florida, was upset about a suspected rapist believed to be hiding in Mexico. At the administration's urging, the Mexican government tried to find him. (The man was found, then tried and convicted in a Mexican court.)

A limit on sugar imports was made in the hopes of winning cane growers in Louisiana and sugar beet growers in Minnesota, North Dakota, and other northern states, but some of the expected votes didn't materialize. The peanut growers, not satisfied with a deal in the reconciliation bill, returned with a demand in exchange for supporting NAFTA and got a promise of a study of peanut imports. The Black Caucus had come out against the agreement, and since the administration felt it couldn't get this position changed, it tried to lure its members one by one. Floyd Flake wanted, and got, a Small Business Administration center in Queens. An SBA office that was scheduled to be closed in the district of Bernice Johnson, of Texas, was taken off the list. Mel Reynolds, of Illinois, got a commitment from McLarty to give a fund-raiser for him.

In the hope of winning over Hispanic members, a North American Development Bank was established, to fund development along the border with Mexico—but when the funding for the bank was announced, only the one member with whom the deal was cut, Esteban Torres, of California, announced for NAFTA.

For Oklahoma, the Northern Plains states, Wyoming, and Iowa the administration agreed to negotiate new limits on exports of durum wheat from Canada.

There were deals outside the trade agreement. One involved a postponement of increases in the still contested grazing and mining fees. Another involved airline routes.

Outside lobbyists enjoyed the fruits of the bazaar. Some called the White House and said, "I can get X if you do Y." This would win the gratitude of X and of the administration. The fact that the administration was so willing to deal thus played against it, in that others, on their own initiative, started to deal on its behalf.

Labor, as it predicted, was playing rough. Several members told the White House of threats that their labor contributions would be withheld if they voted for NAFTA. William Bywater, the head of the Machinists, asked on *MacNeil/Lehrer* if he was going to work against members of Congress who voted for NAFTA, said, "You're damn right. I absolutely am. Absolutely. I've already called certain congressmen already to their face. If they vote for the NAFTA, we're going to go out to defeat you." On Saturday, November 6, Clinton played golf with three undecided House Democrats, who spoke to him about these threats. The next day, on *Meet the Press,* on location in the Oval Office, Clinton said that labor unions, in threatening members by saying they wouldn't get contributions if they voted for NAFTA, were engaging in "real roughshod, muscle-bound tactics."

Clinton aides later insisted that his statement was spontaneous, but this is doubtful. The statement was obviously quite calculated—in the manner of Clinton's taking on Jesse Jackson in 1992, through his criticism of "Sister Souljah." Once again, he was showing that he'd take on a major constituency. One aide asserted that statement wasn't planned, then said it was also meant to help pro-NAFTA Democrats characterize the opposition and convince Republicans that the President was serious. But the statement was more offensive to labor than Clinton had reckoned it would be.

Tom Donahue, secretary-treasurer of the AFL-CIO, watching from his home that day, was infuriated by what Clinton said. He felt that Clinton was playing to the negative stereotype of organized labor. After conferring with Kirkland, he said on CNN that afternoon that Clinton's remarks were a "cheap shot," part of a "desperate effort to capture votes and win passage of NAFTA."

Clinton sent a note to Kirkland, saying, "I hope my remarks didn't ruin your Sunday." The labor leaders didn't appreciate the fact that the White House made the letter public.

When Clinton, on a trip to Lexington, Kentucky, on November 4, blurted out the news that Gore would debate Ross Perot on NAFTA, most of the White House staff was taken aback and worried. (Howard Paster and Bill Daley hadn't been consulted.) It was a big gamble, they thought. But Gore badly wanted to do it, and Clinton didn't like to turn Gore down. The idea had originated with Gore's chief of staff, Jack Quinn, who reasoned that Perot wouldn't bear up well under the pressure and that if the opposition to NAFTA got identified with Perot, votes would break the administration's way. Gore was so eager that he wanted three debates. "We had to hose him down," a White House aide said. One Presidential adviser speculated that Gore, though the ultimate "team player," was always looking for ways to stand out—as Hillary Clinton did.

The Clinton people were looking for something to end the seeming impasse over NAFTA, get votes moving their way. The administration was still well short of enough votes, and its effort seemed stalled. "This is our circuit breaker," Mark Gearan said.

The mystery about Gore, which even his closest advisers couldn't resolve, was how the same person could on some public occasions be so stiff and on others relaxed, and even showing his humor. Gore couldn't resolve it either. Up until minutes before the debate, to be moderated by Larry King on CNN on Tuesday night, November 9, various attempts were made to loosen Gore up. The last thing Clinton said to him was, "Relax, be loose, but don't let the other side get the emotional edge. Make it clear we're on the side of the worker." In the studio itself, his entourage engaged in jokes with a high testosterone content. Mickey Kantor slipped him a note with a joke about Lorena Bobbitt.

Another worry was that Gore would be too heavy. This side of him had come out in debates during the 1988 Presidential campaign. During the NAFTA debate, Gore could be seen almost going too far but keeping himself in check.

Perot had already shown on television that he had a short fuse. This was what the White House was counting on, so Gore's mission was to taunt him without appearing the heavy. But Perot made such a fool of himself that Gore was in no real danger. Gore functioned at several levels during the debate. He relayed the positive message of why NAFTA would benefit the United States; he got under Perot's skin on several points (including Perot's own free-trade zone in Texas); he punctured Perot's arguments. He pushed for specifics that Perot couldn't come up with—which always upset Perot, who felt his assertions shouldn't be questioned. Perot showed his cranky, egomaniacal side and his thin grasp of the facts. Clinton remarked privately afterward that Perot hadn't been disciplined in his preparation, whereas Gore had been very much so.

When Gore asked Perot what changes he would make in the NAFTA agreement, Perot became snappish ("I can't—unless you let me finish—I can't answer your question") and never did respond. The administration was fortunate in its opponent; Dick Gephardt or David Bonior would have had no trouble responding. Gore made smart use of previous Perot predictions—including one that if Clinton was elected, a hundred banks would fail after election day, 1992.

After the debate, Gore was deemed the overwhelming victor and Perot was damaged. Gore became "hot." Perot became the face of the opposition to NAFTA. The debate took the issue beyond the elites. The White House plumped the victory hard, and there was a lot of talk about "momentum"—as if it were another election campaign. Whether or not the votes would have started breaking the administration's way without the debate, no one could know, but after the debate the votes did start falling into the President's column. Greenberg and Stephanopoulos understood, however, that in smashing Perot in the debate, the Clinton people may have created a long-range problem for themselves. They need Perot to have a respectable following come 1996. It was his 19 percent that had given Clinton his election victory.

At the White House on Friday, November 12, five days before the NAFTA vote, people were moving around from meeting to meeting with a tight, determined look. Sitting in his small office that afternoon, George Stephanopoulos seemed wired. He talked faster than usual. There was a certain giddiness. Stephanopoulos knew by then that the administration was probably going to win, but the victory wasn't nailed down.

"This is it," Stephanopoulos said. "We have to win it. We're back in the must-win place. I guess we'll be there a lot." Breaking into a laugh, he said, "We're always stuck in the small crawl space between 'must win' and 'can't lose.' "

The administration had made a pact with the Republicans that if it would produce 100 Democratic votes the Republicans would provide the other 118 needed for NAFTA to win. Though the administration—which had found itself in the unaccustomed position of working closely with the firebrand House minority whip, Newt Gingrich—had been suspicious, the Republicans delivered a sizable vote for the agreement. In the end, the vote was 234–200, not even a squeaker. The Democrats produced 102 votes, and the Republicans supplied 132 votes. (Gore delivered the entire Tennessee delegation.) The margin of Clinton's victory would cause him—once again—to be seen in a new light.

The White House of course made a big thing of the victory. The repair work with labor began. Clinton called Kirkland from the plane on the way to the APEC meeting in Seattle ("I've had better days," Kirkland told the President) and suggested that they meet as soon as possible. Kirkland coolly said that he was going to Europe for a couple of weeks; they could meet when he returned.

But despite all the outward self-congratulation at the White House, and the editorial praise, many of the President's aides took a more sober view. Roy Neel said, "Nobody around here has any illusion that this will be anything other than a short-term gain. The President will be stronger at the new year, but this has no residual effect. The issues will be different, the coalitions will be different. The press will say, What did you do today? No one here thinks we can sit on this laurel one minute. You have to win every one of them. The stimulus loss still hangs there as an example of the bumbling. We get a lot more attention to our defeats than to our victories. Maybe we spin too much and we should let others be our validators."

Later in November, the resignations of Howard Paster and Roy Neel were announced. These departures of two fairly senior officials, both of them able, before a full year was up reflected some of the serious problems in the Clinton White House. Both men had been talking privately about leaving for months. Both said publicly that they were resigning because of the strain on their families, and while there was some truth to that, there were other factors as well—in the main, the difficulty each man found in trying to do his job effectively.

In fact, Paster didn't want to leave at all. On the day of his departure he was very sad. He was walking away from the job he had wanted for a long time. But he felt that he had been in an untenable situation. He had to try to get decisions about legislative strategy made—and kept—in a milieu where there were a lot of self-designated experts on Capitol Hill. He couldn't get answers out of the White House; or the answers he got were changed. The most routine decisions were a struggle.

In August, Paster told McLarty of his unhappiness—but nothing changed. Paster took this as definitive about his future at the White House. A senior White House aide said, "Yes, Mack could have worked to keep him and didn't. Howard was in a very frustrating situation. He had a President and a First Lady who were insensitive to the problems of dealing with Congress, and they expected Howard to produce miracles. He had people working at cross-purposes, and there was no discipline. And he had to answer to five hundred and thirty-five of the worst assholes in the world. They're so demanding." This aide continued, "He was frustrated with the personnel process, that people here didn't respond to a congressional request. Mack didn't drive decisions. There are the endless meetings around here that have worn everyone out, and the consultants second-guessing everything."

This aide went on, "That's a universal frustration in the White House. The consultants probably have more time in the White House than any consultants ever. It gets to everybody—even George, who is the closest to them, thick with them." Another White House official said, "There's general frustration with the consultants coming in and at the last minute blowing things up. People here say, 'Fine. Take these hours, take this salary.' " But the consultants had played a big role in getting Clinton elected, and they could have insights that people imprisoned in the White House didn't have. They supplied the data that the Clintons depended on. The Clintons wanted to get reelected.

Neel announced his departure after only five and a half months as Deputy Chief of Staff. Neel had been worried for some time about the effect on his family of his rare presence among them, but a Presidential adviser said, "I think Roy deep down inside is leaving because of McLarty. McLarty empowers and vests and then pulls it back. With Gore, Roy got vested to do something and went ahead and did it."

The Clintons' choice—and that's how everyone viewed it—of Phil Lader to replace Neel as Deputy Chief of Staff, announced on December 7, flabbergasted a number of people in the White House. Lader, too, was a nice man, and he had some management experience, and as the organizer of the Renaissance Weekends he knew the Clintons well. But Lader had a paucity of experience in Washington or national politics. Once again, the Clintons had indulged in selecting a friend for their staff. But some other friends of theirs were bothered by the choice, feeling they had selected someone much like McLarty.

Actually, McLarty had preferred John Podesta, the staff secretary, as one of two choices for deputy (the other being Maggie Williams). But Mrs. Clinton's displeasure with Podesta's zeal in looking into the travel office affair came back to keep him from getting this slot. (Williams wasn't interested.)

Within a month, Lader had pretty much given up on trying to control who did what and who attended meetings with the President.

The problem at the Clinton White House remained that Clinton didn't empower anyone, including McLarty, and there was no empowerment down the line. The lines of authority weren't blurred; there simply weren't any. The Clinton White House didn't fit any of the traditional models: no spokes in the wheel (Kennedy), no hierarchical model, as Republican administrations had. Gergen and Stephanopoulos were freelancers, getting into nearly anything they wanted. Lindsey was freelancing as well. A senior official said, "There's still no structure to the meetings. It's just everyone talking to him. The President will sit there at his desk, with his half-glasses on, signing pictures. He just takes it in, but you don't know what he's taking in. Therefore, a lot of the time there's no decision or we revisit a decision, because no one knows what happened."

No one was yet keeping track of what was going on in the policy groups. The National Economic Council, headed by Rubin, was unanimously seen as working well, but the Domestic Policy Council, under Carol Rasco, a former aide to Clinton in Arkansas, foundered, in part because the economic team ran over her, in part because the health care policy was made elsewhere, and in part because she didn't assert herself in the near chaos.

White House aides used various sports metaphors to convey the idea that everyone raced toward the ball. One White House official said, "There are so many voices, and it only takes two or three to kill an idea. It's a damn miracle that we get anything done."

A Cabinet-level official said, "When the White House gets behind an issue, it gets things done. The bigger problem is that the President by nature wants to be exposed to a lot of views and a lot of issues, and therefore you need a disciplinarian in the White House, someone able to make decisions that need to be made and don't have to go to the President, and to control the place more."

A lot of people who dealt with the Clinton White House complained about the difficulty of getting decisions from it. A top aide to Clinton said in early December, about outsiders' complaints about getting answers, "You can get answers; they're just subject to being overruled and changed.... There is still a feeling that if we talk long enough we'll see lightning, but it doesn't always work that way. We look for consensus answers too long. There'll be an issue that we should have decided a month ago; it makes people more nervous and feeling we're subjected to pressure. And we know no more than a month ago."

Clinton himself was aware of and bothered by the long meetings and often complained to aides that a meeting was unfocused, that after forty-five minutes he didn't know any more than he did before. But Clinton didn't move to change these things, and he made his own contribution to the confusion.

He didn't compartmentalize what he told people. The top aide said, "Sometimes you have to tell him you don't know what he's talking about.

His inclination is to walk out and say something to someone, and they think he wants them to get involved. He's bad about having something on his mind, seeing somebody and saying, 'We have to call X and find out about Y,' and they don't know what they're supposed to do."

McLarty often second-guessed himself, or reopened decisions, but he had his own problems, which he divulged to very few people. One of these few said, "Mack expresses frustrations about getting his arms around the job. He says it's like Jell-O, because of the many spheres of influence around the place." In Bill Clinton's White House, the Vice President and the First Lady were formidable powers, with their own staffs and their superior access to the President. That made the life and the role of a Chief of Staff far more complicated than usual. With a President who was so prone to change his mind, it made staff work hellish.

But McLarty spent a lot of time with the President.

On occasion that fall, there were rumors that McLarty was leaving his job, perhaps to take a Cabinet post, but a Cabinet post didn't carry the prestige of being at the President's side, and McLarty showed no interest in leaving. That was a great relief to David Gergen, who was finding himself increasingly isolated. McLarty was his sole philosophical ally. Gergen had had a real impact: he had influenced numerous decisions on the basis of his sense of the timing and rhythm of things, of how Washington and the media would react and of how to lift up an issue, to get it public attention. But some of the younger staff members never accepted him. They mocked his attempts to position himself in the ever shifting firmament and resented what they saw as his leaking things that were above-average self-serving. His inviting John Ehrlichman (a former colleague in the Nixon White House) to lunch in the White House Mess didn't go over at all well. They saw him as a Republican masquerading as an Independent. They mocked (unfairly) Gergen's reaches for involvement in substance; he was just as well informed as some of them were. The early talk of a "troika" of McLarty, Stephanopoulos, and Gergen had long since ceased, and relations between Gergen and Stephanopoulos reached a point of near open warfare—and Stephanopoulos had more troops.

People had difficulty understanding how Clinton wanted the White House run, because Clinton had conflicting, even confusing, ideas of how he wanted the White House run. But what it seemed to come down to was that he didn't want any one person, other than himself, to have a great deal of power. It was Clinton's White House. Even his friends weren't sure whether it represented how Clinton wanted it to work or his confusion over how he wanted it to work.

On Saturday, November 13, the Clintons entertained at a dinner. The evening, which started early, was to include a screening of *Philadelphia.* Tom Hanks, the star, and Jonathan Demme, the director, and some others connected with the film were there. Hanks and his wife, and the actress Mary Steenburgen, who was also in the movie, were overnight guests at the White House.

Clinton, excited, told some guests, "I've just had the most moving day of my Presidency." He had gone to Memphis, first for a NAFTA event and then to speak to a group of black ministers of the Church of God in Christ. "It's the fastest-growing religious group in the country," Clinton told his guests. "And I spoke from where Martin Luther King last preached." He recited bits of his speech, obviously proud of it. In his after-dinner toast, he mentioned the speech again.

The speech, which got little press attention at first, became perhaps the most noted of his first year in office—certainly the most noted of his non-set pieces, such as addresses to the Congress. Everything came together for the Memphis speech. Clinton caught the moment—the rising national worry about violence involving the use of guns by kids. He had been struck by and cited a front-page *Washington Post* story about an eleven-year-old girl planning her funeral—the hymns she wanted sung and the dress she wanted to wear. Like any good southern politician, Clinton was quite comfortable with speaking to black audiences, especially southern black audiences. He knew the rhythms and the cadences, and he had a lot of the preacher in him. His audience interacted with him, which always made him a better speaker. As he spoke in Memphis, his face was more animated than usual, and he used his arms a lot. His accent became more southern and preacherly: "How can we justify" became "How can we jus-ti-faaayyyyy."

The situation fit right into his "third way"—neither traditional liberal nor conservative—and his theme of responsibility. Now he was talking values, usually a conservative theme. Violence inexorably raised the question of values, as a troubled public wondered what had gone wrong that kids were out in the streets killing kids. Clinton was telling his black audience of the black community's responsibility to do something about the violence. There was nothing in his speech that would be objectionable to whites. He was supposedly doing a big thing by saying these things to a black audience, but this audience agreed with him. Yet it was important for an American President to say these things, and he said them well. His audience was everyone.

The most striking part of Clinton's speech, and the one that he related to his dinner guests, was his invoking of King, saying that if King returned today, his report card on America would be that "you did a good job" on voting rights, housing integration, elevating "people of color" in the armed forces and politics and government and the middle class. But, Clinton said, "He would say, 'I did not live and die to see the American family destroyed. I did not live and die to see thirteen-year-old boys get automatic weapons and gun down nine-year-olds just for the kick of it. . . . I fought for freedom,' he would say, 'but not for the freedom of people to kill each other with reckless abandon; not for the freedom of children to have children and the fathers of the children walk away from them and abandon them as if they don't amount to anything.' "

Clinton was onto something, and he knew it. And the speech wasn't a sudden thing. Clinton drew on things he had said in a speech at Yale in early October and on *Meet the Press* in early November. A few evenings before the speech, he had dined with William Julius Wilson, a black sociologist who had written a powerful book, *The Truly Disadvantaged,* which Clinton had begun to cite. The political purposes didn't detract from the impact of the Memphis speech. That the White House hadn't advertised the speech beforehand gave it more impact; a cynical press didn't have time to discount it before it caught on. But afterward Clinton's aides couldn't resist trying to pump up the speech into legend.

Clinton had found his voice on the subject of violence. His speaking in general was getting stronger and more confident (when he was interested in the subject), as he grew more confident. Before the trip, some of his aides had tried to discourage him from adding the stop at the ministers' convention to his schedule. They thought he would be too tired. Clinton replied, "I want to go back to this group, and it's good politics."

The Memphis event, and the attention to and praise of his speech, brought home to Clinton that the Presidency was about more than getting things done—something he had lost sight of once more in his efforts to win legislative victories.

Following the President's Memphis speech, and in the light of the praise rolling in, there was talk of convening a White House conference on violence. This was a Gergen idea, but others shot it down. Stephanopoulos felt that Clinton had again been overexposed, that he had worn people out with his strenuous legislative efforts, that he should be more quiet and out of sight in December. Other reasons the conference didn't go forward, a senior adviser said, were that it wasn't clear what the conference was supposed to accomplish, that it might raise unrealistic expectations, and—perhaps most important—that it might overshadow health care. Mrs. Clinton had waited her turn, but now health care was to be primus inter pares on the White House agenda. The marching orders—no one doubted where they'd originated—were that it was time to pump life back into the health care issue.

Greenberg's latest polling figures, which he showed to the President in the Oval Office one night in early December, were encouraging, given the lows Clinton had seen. Greenberg's "thermometer"—he measured from unfavorable feelings to favorable ones on a scale of one to a hundred—had Clinton at fifty-five, his highest rating since he gave the health care speech in September. The President's advisers were pleased that, according to Greenberg's polls, Clinton was back to winning an election with 43 percent of the vote. While that might not have seemed very impressive, it was encouraging to the advisers because, one explained, the question asked was: "How did you vote last year?" He said, "When Clinton's not doing well, people forget they voted for him."

As the December 13 Bryn Mawr conference on entitlements approached —the one Clinton had promised Marjorie Margolies-Mezvinsky he would attend in exchange for her vote on the reconciliation bill—there was close to a pitched battle inside the White House over what to do about entitlements. The President's advisers were split between those, such as Stephanopoulos, who felt that enough budget cutting had gone on, and those, such as Bentsen and Gore, who thought more cutting was in order and that the entitlements should be looked at again. This would have meant taking another whack at Social Security earnings. CEA Chairman Laura Tyson argued that the Social Security program worked; it was not part of the deficit problem and to subject it to a means test would undermine a successful program. (Social Security was running a surplus but would be in trouble when the baby boomers retired.) Even such a deficit hawk as Alice Rivlin thought that Social Security should be left alone. Tyson argued that the administration had already made substantial cuts in entitlement programs and was planning to make more in connection with health care, and that enough was enough. Mrs. Clinton agreed. "We didn't come here to cut the government," she said. "We came here to get things done."

After several lengthy meetings, the President and his advisers decided not to propose more cuts in entitlements. Clinton felt that if he went at the middle class any more, it would rebel. He believed that this was what had happened in the Canadian election in October and also in the Russian elections on the day before the speech, where the reformers had done badly. (Clinton, who liked to figure the internal politics of countries he dealt with, told his aides he wasn't surprised by what happened in Russia. "You guys ought to wake up to what happens in a country," he said.) David

Gergen said that the writings of Kevin Phillips, the iconoclastic conservative, saying that entitlement reforms are "loser issues," that they had politically damaged a number of governments, and had caused the Canadian government's defeat, "had sunk into the thinking around here."

The President gave a long and dull speech at Bryn Mawr, almost as if he was determined not to make news. But that evening, at a fund-raiser for Moynihan at the Waldorf-Astoria, he made some very moving remarks, incorporating the violence theme.

Another concession the administration had made in order to get the reconciliation bill passed turned out to be more difficult to deal with. As promised, there was further opportunity in the fall for Congress to vote deficit reductions. Democrat Tim Penny, of Minnesota, a fiscal conservative, and Republican John Kasich, of Ohio, came up with a proposal to cut another $90 billion from the budget. The proposal had some holes in it and was to use up $40 billion of the cuts in health spending that Clinton planned on to help pay for the health care program. Nevertheless, it threw the Clinton administration on the defensive. The administration had made its own proposal for more modest cuts, amounting to $37 billion.

At the same time that this fight was going on, the administration was struggling to meet the terms of the 1993 budget bill, which had frozen domestic spending for five years. The reality of this concession, made in order to get its budget through, was painful. With no increases allowed for inflation, if the investments were to be funded, cuts of about 10 percent in existing programs had to be made in order to meet the spending "caps." The first round of proposals from the agencies amounted to $20 billion over the spending caps. Some of the agency heads had, in the Washington tradition, become at least in part captive of their outside constituencies, favoring existing programs over new "investments." Eventually, with a little bloodletting and a lot of meetings, the goal was met. Clinton allowed every department head to make the case directly to him. (In past administrations, the President was involved only when the budget officials and department chiefs were at a standoff.) After a big effort, Clinton had won about 70 percent of his requests for his "investments" in 1993. Now he had to struggle for them again.

In meeting the Penny-Kasich challenge, the administration had tried to figure the least amount of cutting it could get away with—and it, too, played with the numbers and engaged in a bit of double counting. It was understood in the White House that "Hillary's entitlement cuts" (for her health care bill) were to be saved. Mrs. Clinton herself lobbied on the Hill to save them. With Stephanopoulos as the key strategist, and relying unembarrassedly on committee chairmen and interest groups (CDF and the

AARP), the administration managed on November 22 to defeat Penny-Kasich by a 213–219 vote.

The vote was so close because it was politically difficult for Democrats to vote against deficit reduction, and because two days before the vote, the word spread on Capitol Hill that the President would veto Penny-Kasich, so a vote for it was a "free vote." Stephanopoulos and Foley worked to stamp that idea out.

With more difficulty than he had expected, the President did manage, on the eve of the Congress's adjournment for the year—the day before Thanksgiving—to get the Senate to adopt the Brady bill, requiring a five-day waiting period before the purchase of a handgun. The bill, named after James Brady, Ronald Reagan's press secretary, who suffered permanent brain damage and some paralysis as a result of the 1981 attempt on Reagan's life, had languished for years. Clinton had championed the bill starting in the 1992 campaign, explaining that he had grown up with hunting but this was about something else. The Republicans filibustered the Brady bill, all but killing it, and then, realizing that this didn't look good, compromised. Clinton had made some calls from Seattle on this too. Stephanopoulos asked Vernon Jordan to call a couple of Republicans he was on good terms with. When the Senate Republicans balked again, Mitchell threatened to call the Senate back in for a post-Thanksgiving session, and so another slight compromise was made and the bill was passed. Gore was in the chair. The politics of gun control appeared to have changed. James Brady, and his wife, Sarah, who had led the long fight for the bill, appeared in the Oval Office with the President, who made a statement.

(About a month later, Clinton went duck hunting in Maryland with Representative Bill Brewster, of Oklahoma, who was on the board of the NRA. The locale was the grounds of the head of DUCKPAC, a political action committee that contributed to politicians who opposed tightening restrictions on hunting fish and game. Pictures of Clinton in camouflage dress were released to the press. Only one duck was bagged.)

Also on the day before Thanksgiving, the President met with Salman Rushdie, who was still under a death threat issued by the Ayatollah Khomeini for his book *The Satanic Verses,* which had been branded as blasphemous against the Islamic religion. The last time Rushdie was in the United States, Bush had declined to see him. Whether Clinton should see him had been the subject of debate among his political and foreign policy advisers. After a lot of discussion and amid much secrecy until after the event, Clinton met with Rushdie in the Old Executive Office Building, where he was doing some satellite interviews. No photographers were allowed. Christopher and Lake had already spoken with Rushdie for about an hour, and then Lake took the author across West Executive Avenue to see the President for about five minutes.

Asked at a November 30 press conference about the meeting, Clinton downplayed it, saying, "I was in the Old Executive Office Building, and Mr. Lake brought him over there so I could see him and shake hands with him. We visited probably for a couple of minutes. . . . I mean no disrespect to the people who have that religious faith. But I do think it's important that here in the United States we affirm our commitment to protect the physical well-being and the right to speak of those with whom we may intensely disagree."

Clinton received positive press accounts of his participation in the APEC meeting toward the end of November. A speech he gave in Seattle reiterating his view of the connection between trade and growth was flacked hard by his staff and given favorable reviews. Acting on his strong preference, he hosted the other leaders at a session in a log house on an island in Puget Sound, casual clothes and all. In mid-December, with his active participation via phone with Mickey Kantor in Geneva, Clinton, through some last-minute bending, helped to bring a successful conclusion to the GATT talks, which had gone on for seven years (the formal deadline had been December 1990). The year ended on the positive note on trade that Clinton and his aides had hoped for. His increasing determination to open markets for American goods, and thus create American jobs, had become part of his political legacy.

26

SECRETARY OF DEFENSE

"Are We Sure We're Doing the Right Thing?"

On the morning of September 30, a cool and blustery day, the day of Colin Powell's official retirement ceremonies, the President and Powell sat on the Truman balcony, drinking coffee and talking for an hour. Clinton asked Powell for his assessment of Aspin. Powell told the President that Aspin didn't command the respect of the armed forces and that the President might want to think about making a change.

Two days later, Mogadishu happened.

Clinton had been hearing a lot of complaints about Aspin. Relations between Anthony Lake and Warren Christopher were tense, and more rivalrous than was generally understood, but it was about Aspin that Clinton was hearing the most criticism.

Aspin didn't get off to a particularly good start with his counterparts. The State Department saw him as a rival, since he had set up policy shops that State considered its domain. The policy shops led to charges, inside and out of the Pentagon, that Aspin was running a "think tank" and not managing what one military official called "the largest corporate entity in the world." A Pentagon veteran said, "They say he runs the Pentagon like a congressional committee. They sit around and discuss everything without making a decision. He's shortchanged the management side. Bill Perry [Aspin's deputy] is the exception."

So Aspin's aides would spin, and Christopher's aides would counterspin. This wasn't conducive to the collegiality Clinton wanted. In meetings, others found Aspin badly organized and imprecise. An official said later, "Things kept being dropped." But Aspin had a brilliant mind and was a shrewd analyst—often seeing things his colleagues didn't—and he had got some big things done at the Pentagon.

And the lack of harmony wasn't simply Aspin's fault. An experienced veteran of the national security field said, "Christopher should be leading on the collegiality, he should be encouraging it." But Christopher was too focused on his position within the Clinton group, and his standing with his peers outside government, to be the font of collegiality. Though Lake knew the President wanted peace among his foreign policy advisers and took several steps to encourage it, Lake's competitive nature sometimes went against his professed desire—and in any event, Christopher and Donilon saw the relationship as a contest. After Mogadishu, relations among the top national security figures were more strained than ever. But the President didn't want to face bickering and rivalries among his staff in general, and was an absentee landlord on foreign policy.

It was known around Washington that Aspin didn't have a particularly good relationship with the military. The high brass found his friendly, schmoozy, arm-around-the-shoulder style too casual. Military officials told their contacts outside the Pentagon, "For years [as chairman of the Armed Services Committee] he sniped at us, and then he came here and put his arm around generals and admirals, and we don't like it." One person they talked to about this said, "It's not necessary to be buddy-buddy with the Secretary of Defense. They'd have preferred a little more formality." The military spread the word on Capitol Hill and among the retired military and other allies, and the word reached the Clinton White House. Aspin had carried the White House's brief on gays in the military and after a great deal of effort had eventually won a consensus within the Pentagon. He paid a price with the military for this.

Aspin's bearing worked against him. He didn't project the commandingness people expected in a Secretary of Defense. His predecessor, Dick Cheney, had such an aura. Aspin's shambling style, his thin graying hair often awry, his posture—Aspin's head was often tilted, seeming nearly even with his shoulders, giving the impression that this large man was constantly looking up at people and had no neck—didn't offer the picture of a crisp Defense Secretary. He wore ill-fitting khaki suits, the jacket just barely buttoned over his stomach. Some high officials and friends of Clinton's felt that Aspin wasn't as articulate in public as need be and was part of the problem of the administration's inability to explain its national security policies. (Gergen advised Aspin to buy some dark suits and get a skilled media adviser. "You need a Donilon," he said. Aspin started showing up in dark suits; he insisted that he had already owned them.) This cart-before-horse thinking—that the problem was that the policies weren't being articulated well enough—was convenient for others in the administration. Something more was wrong than the fact that the Secretary of Defense didn't look enough like a Secretary of Defense.

Following Mogadishu—especially the fractious briefing on Capitol Hill—a Presidential adviser said, "A couple of very important Members of Congress gave the President a very strong report. It was clear that Aspin would never have the respect on the Hill necessary for a Secretary of Defense. That coalesced the feeling in the President's mind, and the people around him, that you can't have a Secretary of Defense who doesn't have the confidence of the military or of the Hill." Gergen had also attended the Hill briefing, and delivered a negative report to the White House. Gore already had misgivings about Aspin's performance as Secretary. Clinton talked to Sam Nunn, who had never gotten along well with Aspin. Though Aspin's decision not to send the tanks to Somalia was a justifiable one, it was held against him by some of the military and Members of Congress. A top adviser to the President said that Clinton and those close to him weren't angry with Aspin for not sending the tanks; they were angry about his changing story on why he didn't send them. (He had given conflicting responses on whether Powell had recommended sending the tanks.) Shortly after these events, an adviser quite close to the President said, "I don't think Aspin will ever have the requisite credibility. He was sinking going into that briefing and came out of it fatally wounded. He doesn't come across as a Cabinet member. A Cabinet member has to project a sense of command." A high official who insisted that Aspin's troubles had begun early in the administration also said, "Les got caught in the 'We have to do something about the foreign policy team' feeling after Mogadishu."

The President had been unhappy about his foreign policy team even before Mogadishu. But afterward he was upset that a number of his policies were going sour.

After Mogadishu, one Presidential adviser said later, "The President understood that he had to move quickly." He added that in Clinton's eyes, the real problem was "Aspin's ability as an advocate. It upset everyone. He wouldn't defend administration policy vigorously. The President wanted an advocate of his policy. He didn't want to get beat up on national security. Every time Aspin appeared on TV, he wasn't effective, and he wasn't effective with the Congress." Though this wasn't at the heart of the problem, it was true that Clinton lacked a sufficient number of foreign policy spokesmen. Aspin made nowhere near the number of television appearances that Christopher, whom Donilon was trying to stamp as *the* foreign policy spokesman for the administration, did. And often, after Aspin did appear, State complained. Lake, pursuant to his understanding with Christopher, and preferring anonymity, virtually made no appearances at all for quite a while. (Later, in 1994, Lake decided to make a few appearances, but State blocked some of them.) This adviser thought Clinton was considering more than one change in his national security team, but Clinton said to him, "I can't have a slaughterhouse right in one whack." Someone the President talked to said—and this may have really been at the core of the problem—"The Secretary of Defense wasn't taking care of national security issues; he wasn't keeping them off the President's desk."

On November 7, asked on *Meet the Press* about the longevity of his national security team, in particular Aspin and Christopher, Clinton hesitated a little longer than his usual half-second and then gave a lukewarm endorsement. The problem, a Presidential confidant said afterward, was that both names were in the question.

Meanwhile, the other members of the President's national security team were striving to secure their positions. Both Lake and Christopher had a lot to work with. Lake had his relationship with the President that went back to the campaign, and his propinquity to the Oval Office. He also had his close friendship with Stephanopoulos. Christopher had his strong relationships with two people very close to Clinton: Vernon Jordan and Strobe Talbott. And in recent months, Christopher had formed a bond with Gergen. (Gergen could tell him what was going on in the White House, and Gergen hoped Christopher would help get him in Principals meetings.) Also, the President respected Christopher and saw him as dedicated to the success of his Presidency. Moreover, Christopher was the establishment, and even if he wanted to, Clinton wasn't in a position at that point to fire the establishment.

Aspin, on the other hand, was isolated. The separation by the Potomac River of the Pentagon from the White House, the State Department, and the Capitol was both psychological and real. Aspin had no constituency—in the Pentagon, within the White House, nor, though he had some close friends there, did he have much of one within the Congress.

On October 19, in the post–Mogadishu crisis atmosphere, Christopher paid his call on the President, flattered him—told him how much the others benefited from his "ruminations"—and made some proposals for improving the management of foreign policy. (One of Christopher's closest aides said that Christopher considered Aspin a large part of the problem, and undoubtedly told the President so.) Gergen strongly urged Aspin to request a similar appointment, but Aspin didn't do that. After the President's appearance on *Meet the Press,* Christopher called him to congratulate him.

In his dealings with the White House, a Clinton aide said, "Les came over here by himself. Christopher brings Donilon. Henry Cisneros doesn't bring anyone, either, but he's around, he calls. You never had a sense of anyone getting Aspin ready for coming over here."

One morning in early November, Clinton called McLarty into the Oval Office and said that it was time to start a formal process for finding a replacement for Aspin. The President urged discretion, moving his hands around as if forming a ball: "It's a complicated theme." The two men discussed the various sectors a new nominee might be chosen from—the military, Congress, the Republicans. They concluded that the military was the most important, that that would help Clinton most at the Pentagon. Clinton had already discussed the matter with Strobe Talbott, who, as a close friend of the President's, was in touch with him regularly. Clinton had a lot of faith in Talbott's judgment, and felt that as a former diplomatic correspondent for *Time,* the author of several books on national security policy, and a regular at Aspen Institute seminars, Talbott knew more about people in the foreign policy field than he did. This gave Talbott tremendous influence, but it also put him in a tricky situation. He could not seem to be throwing his weight around or using his friendship with the President to further his own ideas, or himself. The President also sought the counsel of Gore and Admiral Crowe on the question of replacing Aspin. McLarty, Talbott, Gore, and Crowe were the only people directly involved in the early discussions with the President about whether to replace Aspin, and with whom. But others were involved indirectly.

The idea was that the search for a replacement would be "tightly held." Also, it was not to be seen that Aspin's counterparts had anything to do with his departure. Christopher didn't have to be directly involved: Talbott kept him informed and provided him cover. A participant in the process said, "Strobe drove it, but he could not do that without Christopher's OK. You have to protect that State-Defense relationship, and this gave Chris deniability." A high official said of the post-Mogadishu maneuvering, "Chris knew exactly what was going on. Strobe kept Chris absolutely informed."

Lake made it clear that he didn't want to be part of the decision about replacing Aspin, because he had to work with him every day—but he was aware of what was going on. Someone who was in on the process said, "Tony was consulted pretty closely all along." If Lake had wanted Aspin to remain on the job, he could have weighed in on his behalf.

Stephanopoulos knew that the President was thinking of replacing Aspin, but he wasn't formally brought into the process until the decision had been virtually made. Since the President had asked Lake to tell no one about this,

Lake was Delphic with Stephanopoulos, and Stephanopoulos was Delphic back—not letting on that he didn't know exactly what was happening. Vernon Jordan was in on what was going on, and expressed his concern that it would get out that Talbott was involved in the ousting of Aspin.

Just as Stephanopoulos seemed to sense what was going on, so did Gergen, who also wasn't officially brought into it until close to the end. Donilon knew. Stan Greenberg, who had been appalled by Aspin's performance in the Somalia briefing on Capitol Hill, weighed in with Stephanopoulos. If one hung around the White House enough, it wasn't hard to deduce that Aspin was probably on his way out. The only questions were timing and a replacement.

On Monday, November 8, at 5:30 P.M., Clinton, McLarty, Crowe, and Talbott—the group (plus Gore, who wasn't present) that had been designated to find a new Secretary of Defense—met in the President's study in the private quarters of the White House. The meeting lasted over an hour. Someone who knew what happened said, "Everyone in the meeting had friends in the Pentagon who had called them to complain about Les." In the meeting, Talbott said that his soundings at the Pentagon indicated that morale there was bad. Someone who knew what happened in the meeting said, "Strobe is a very persuasive advocate and enjoys the President's confidence."

When Clinton asked for suggestions for a replacement, Talbott brought up the name of Bobby Ray Inman, but he didn't push him very hard at first. (Talbott and Clinton had already had discussions about the Pentagon problem, and had met alone earlier in the day.) Talbott cited Inman's credentials as a former deputy director of the CIA and director of the highly secret National Security Agency. The President mentioned as other possible candidates some people he'd met in the campaign, such as John Young, CEO of Hewlett-Packard, who had turned down an offer to be Secretary of Commerce. Crowe brought up the names of some other industrialists, including Norman Augustine, the head of Martin Marietta, and James Kinnear, the retired chief executive of Texaco. Crowe told Clinton that in the corporate boards he sat on, there were complaints that no one "from their side of the street" was in the administration.

Talbott replied that there wasn't time for a search for such a person: they had to have a replacement ready when Aspin's departure was announced, or "the press will kill us." There were also expressions of concern that it would take an industrialist time to learn the ropes at the Pentagon, and something could happen any day that called for knowledge of the field. Crowe suggested that Aspin might agree to give them time to find a replacement, but the others said they thought that was out of the question: Aspin would get angry and walk out. "That showed," one of the participants said later, "that none of us knew Aspin very well."

Then Talbott pushed hard for Inman, arguing that not only was he very competent and highly credentialed, but there wasn't time to look for anyone else, and Inman would be quickly confirmable. Crowe suggested William Perry, Aspin's deputy, saying that he was well liked in the Pentagon. The others thought it wouldn't be politic to replace the number-one man with his number-two man. The President agreed, saying, "I think it would be considered a weakness on my part." Talbott said that he could get Inman to come to see the President the next night. By the end of the meeting, one participant said, "The assumption was that it wouldn't take time with Inman, and it was discussed in the belief that Aspin wouldn't help us. The feeling about Inman was that the minute you nominate him, he'll be on the job in a matter of days."

The next night, November 9, after the Gore-Perot debate, at close to midnight, Clinton met with Inman in the study in the residence for nearly two hours; the job wasn't mentioned. (Talbott and McLarty were also there.) The President was impressed. The next day, there was a follow-up meeting of the President, Talbott, and McLarty to review the situation.

Quiet soundings were taken, and it seemed that everybody who mattered thought that appointing Inman was a good idea. Sam Nunn reacted positively. Warren Christopher, whose proxy Talbott had, considered Inman a friend. Vernon Jordan knew Inman (Vernon Jordan knew everybody) and supported him. Gore was enthusiastic. Inman enjoyed a good reputation in Washington. He was able, and he had been accessible to powers in the Congress and to journalists.

But then Clinton got caught up in the fight for NAFTA, and it was a month before the group met again.

It wasn't that Aspin didn't have a clue that there was a problem. In November, Gergen told him in effect that the President had to do something. Though Aspin was worried, he didn't quite absorb that his job was in real jeopardy. He had been trying to calm down people at the White House about Mogadishu. In the postmortem Mogadishu conversations with the President and with Lake and Gergen, he urged them to put it in perspective. He said, "It looks bad now, but there'll be another incident, and if you handle that right, there will be a balancing." He told them that at the same time four years before, "George Bush's foreign policy team looked like it couldn't shoot straight." (On October 1989, there had been a failed coup against Noriega, and blame was being heaped on the Bush administration for not moving quickly enough to take advantage of the situation.) And all that had changed with the Gulf War. In small conversations with Aspin on the edges of meetings—they had no one-on-one meeting until the end—Clinton made it clear he felt that Somalia was a real political problem for him. He asked what could be done to make foreign policy work better. Aspin told Clinton bluntly that the policy of going from cooperation with Aideed to going after Aideed, without serious consideration, "was a real screwup—the most serious one."

On November 19, Hillary Clinton made a ninety-minute tour of the Pentagon, keeping a promise she had made to Alma Powell, the wife of Colin Powell (now retired), to speak at a lunch of the Joint Armed Forces Wives. The impression of Aspin she brought back to the White House wasn't good. Toward the end of her visit, Aspin had joked awkwardly, as he was wont to do at times. As the *Washington Post* reported the visit, a reporter asked Mrs. Clinton whether she had tried out the hot line to Moscow. "Mrs. Clinton did not know quite what to say about that, and Aspin just couldn't help himself. 'Incoming missile!' the Defense Secretary said. 'She started the war!'. . . Mrs. Clinton gave Aspin a funny look, and there was a brief awkward moment before she laughed."

"That was a stark reminder," a Presidential adviser said later. "Les behaved funny when she was there. He didn't do too well. He clowned a bit, was ill at ease. Think of that event as giving it sort of a push."

The second meeting of the search group with the President, over breakfast in the family quarters, took place on Thursday morning, December 9. By this time, the President had talked to Lake (he told the group that he couldn't proceed without telling Lake). Clinton also reported that Nunn thought selecting Inman was a good idea.

Gore spoke enthusiastically in favor of Inman. The decision, of course, had been made. No one else was interviewed for the job. The President wanted to know if anyone had changed his mind, but there was no suggestion about thinking it over further. But there was a lot of discussion about whether this was the right thing to do to Aspin. Was there a way to frame this so that it wouldn't be so damaging to him? Crowe was worried that the President would look as if he was hand-wringing when he let Aspin go. He argued that the President simply had to stick his chin out and say that he had decided to make a change. This was the President's prerogative as Commander in Chief. Anything else would be transparent. Talbott called Christopher, who was in the King David Hotel in Jerusalem, to tell him about the breakfast decision.

On November 11, Gergen paid a visit to Crowe in his office on K Street. (Crowe, the chairman of the President's Foreign Intelligence Advisory Board, which examined various intelligence matters, was soon to be named ambassador to Great Britain.) Acting on his own, Gergen told Crowe that national security machinery wasn't working right and asked if he could help, by sitting in on some of the meetings on national security policy. Crowe replied that that would make a lot of people angry—especially Lake—and that it would appear that he was second-guessing the President's military advisers. Gergen told Crowe that he wanted to play more of a role in foreign policy himself, but Lake was opposing him. Crowe declined to get into what he knew would be internecine warfare.

On Sunday, December 12, McLarty called Stephanopoulos and Gergen and asked them to come to the White House to work with Lake on changing Secretaries of Defense. The day before, Joel Klein, who had recently been recruited as Deputy Counsel (Vince Foster's old job), had gone to Austin, Texas, to vet Inman (three other attorneys had gone with him) and had reported to McLarty that it looked all right. Klein went over a list of things that he said might be problems, but said he didn't "see any show-stoppers." Klein said later, "It was designed to be a quick, one-day vet, in person." This was unusual; a vet that went that quickly, and was conducted only with the candidate, could come a cropper, and had done so in the past. But the theory was that Inman had been in government service, even in highly sensitive intelligence work, and it was unlikely that there were significant problems. Once Klein gave his report, it was decided to proceed.

Inman was coming to town on business that Sunday, providing the opportune time to name him. The idea was to get the new team settled in before the break for the Christmas holidays. The assumption was that Inman's confirmation would be a breeze. On that same Sunday, Aspin, unaware, went on *Meet the Press.* (A Presidential aide said later that Aspin's somewhat ragged performance reinforced the view at the White House that he had to be replaced. But the decision had been made.) In his appearance, Aspin in effect corrected the President's November 7 statement on *Meet the Press* about North Korea's capability of building a nuclear bomb. Clinton had said, "North Korea cannot be allowed to develop a nuclear bomb." Aspin accurately stated that there was a "range of uncertainty [that] included the possibility that they might, at this moment, possess a single nuclear device. 'Bomb' is a technical term. Some kind of nuclear device." Clinton had got his briefing notes wrong; they had advised him to say that North Korea would not be allowed to become a *nuclear power.* Such carelessness, stemming from inexperience and inattention, could have serious consequences, and in this case did.

Aspin also said that his biggest mistake all year was to not send the tanks to Somalia. He should have stuck with the reasons why he didn't send the tanks. Aspin understood that not sending the tanks may have been a political mistake, given what happened later, but that didn't mean he had made the wrong decision.

Stephanopoulos was upset. In the meetings on Sunday and Monday, December 12 and 13, called to discuss how to make the change, he said that Aspin should be given more time—perhaps a few months—to demonstrate that he could do the job. He questioned whether the process had been fair to Aspin. Shouldn't they have gone to him in October and put him on notice?

There was little in the Clinton people's discoveries about Aspin that could not have been known before.

That was what bothered Bruce Lindsey—who knew just about everything that was going on. He thought that the "management problems" at the Pentagon weren't as bad as reported. He felt that Aspin was getting more comfortable with the job. He knew that there were some management problems—some meetings started late, some people couldn't get in to see Aspin—but he believed that some of the complaints stemmed from the fact that the military was more orderly than most bureaucracies. Lindsey didn't think that these were firing offenses, or things that couldn't have been anticipated if they'd been given proper reflection before Aspin was selected.

Lindsey felt that most of the things people criticized Aspin for—thinking out loud, a rambling style—were things he and others had seen during the campaign. Lindsey also didn't like the fact that some of the criticism of Aspin was coming from the State Department. The whole national security team was being attacked, and Lindsey was bothered by the sense that others seemed to be saying, Let's push it over on Les Aspin—let him be the one. He was suspicious of some of the others' motives.

Moreover, it bothered Lindsey that Aspin had given up both a seat in Congress and the chairmanship of the Armed Services Committee to take the Pentagon job. He told all these things to the President.

In the Monday meeting, Stephanopoulos continued to raise objections to making the change then, asking, What's the rush? The rush was that Inman was in town and in various ways was making it clear that he was to be appointed now or never. Another White House aide said later, "The process got a little out of sync in terms of the Inman track moving a little faster than the Aspin track." Lake thought that the timing was a mistake: it was coming at the end of the year, the time for wrap-up stories on the Clinton administration, and it would revive Somalia stories. But Inman was forcing a decision, and the President had in effect long since made one.

So on Monday, Lake volunteered to tell Aspin that the change was going to be made. The explanation for what seemed to be yet another Presidential avoidance of unpleasantness was that Aspin would have time to think things over before he saw the President, and get a chance to leave voluntarily. Also, Lake considered himself an old friend of Aspin's, and thought Aspin should hear the bad news from a friend. On Monday afternoon, in his own office, Lake told Aspin that the President had decided that he needed to make a change. He said there had been a loss of confidence, which had started elsewhere and that the President had come to that, too. Aspin responded that he wanted to meet with the President. Lake asked Aspin if he wanted Gergen to join them, and Aspin did. The three men discussed how to proceed, and Lake and Gergen urged Aspin to do it his way as much as possible—that is, try not to make it look like the President was firing him. But this was of course impossible. A meeting between Aspin and the President was arranged for the next morning.

On Tuesday morning, in the President's study in the residence, Aspin made a strong case for keeping his job. He argued that he had accomplished several important things: he had completed his "bottom-up review" of what military forces were needed in the post–Cold War period; he had resolved such social issues as gays in the military, women in combat (they would now serve on planes and ships), Tailhook; he had worked out the relationship between the National Guard and the reserve and regular forces; he had established more military-to-military contacts with Russia and Ukraine. He argued that he was shaping things up at the Pentagon.

Aspin said Clinton was complaining about leadership, but what the President was doing—telling him that in a day he was gone—wasn't good leadership. A good leader, Aspin asserted, says, You're not doing a good job, and gives you time. "That hit home with the President," a Clinton adviser said later. At the end of the conversation, the President said that he wanted to think it over. Clinton was shaken by the conversation. He told his advisers that he felt bad about Aspin, that it was in part his fault for choosing him: he had asked a very smart strategist to take on a huge management job and had put a lot on his plate. Moreover, he liked Aspin. Clinton asked, "Are we sure we're doing the right thing?"

Meanwhile, Bobby Ray Inman, ensconced at the Park Hyatt Hotel, was getting impatient. He had been resistant at first to taking the job—Clinton had to persuade him in several phone calls—and he now felt he was being diddled by the White House. He had met with the President after Clinton saw Aspin, and he sensed a lack of commitment. Clinton had told Inman that he was getting advice from his staff to give Aspin more time. Inman said that following the meeting with Clinton, he decided that it wasn't going to work.

Gergen, worried, called Crowe to say there was slippage in moving on with firing Aspin and nominating Inman. Gore, Talbott, and McLarty were out of town, Gergen said, and "You're the only one of the original group around." Gergen said, "It's unsettling around here. We're about to lose our nerve." Gergen asked Crowe if he would talk to the President. Gergen was also in touch with Talbott, who was traveling in Russia with Gore, and arranged for him to call the President that night.

At a little after six o'clock, Inman called Joel Klein and said, "I want you to know that my family's celebrating tonight that I'm not going to be Secretary of Defense." An astonished Klein asked him what he meant. Inman said that he assumed from things that had happened that day—or hadn't happened, since he hadn't heard from the President since his meeting with him—that he wasn't going to get the job. He said he was leaving town. Informed of this, an alarmed Gergen reached McLarty, who was out of town, and the two of them contacted Christopher, who was in Washington. They couldn't reassure Inman, because they weren't certain what the President was going to decide. For that reason, they hadn't called Inman that day, either.

Then, early that evening, without telling the President, Christopher and Gergen went to see Inman. Christopher had called Inman on Sunday, to talk to him about taking the job. Now, Christopher, alluding to his previous law practice, said, "Typically, Admiral, I am in the position of asking judges for fifteen-day extensions on a case. Tonight I am asking you for a fifteen-hour extension." Inman reluctantly agreed. This was a very strange business, but the whole episode was touched with strangeness, not the least of which was the Secretary of State's playing the role he did, directly and indirectly, in the replacing of the Secretary of Defense.

Late that night, after a dinner, the President met with his advisers in the residence for over two hours, going past midnight, to decide what to do. Lake had gone to New York that day to speak to the Council on Foreign Relations and, during the dinner there, received a message to get back to Washington for a meeting with the President. Present were Gergen, Lake, Klein, Stephanopoulos, and Phil Lader, the Deputy Chief of Staff, who was filling in for McLarty. Stephanopoulos was troubled about the visit to the hotel. He felt that more concern was being shown for Inman's feelings than for Aspin's. He continued to raise the questions of whether Aspin had had a fair hearing and if he shouldn't be given more time. Gergen argued that things were now so far along that if Clinton reversed field, the story might get out, and it would look as if he couldn't make up his mind. If the story got out, Gergen warned, Clinton would be damaged, Aspin would be damaged, and Inman would be gone. Lake, who had already delivered the news to Aspin, said that his feeling was that they shouldn't make the change then, but his head said that the President was so far down the road that if he didn't go ahead, it would be a mess.

Now McLarty, who was in touch by phone, was having misgivings. He, too, wasn't sure they were being fair to Aspin, and he wasn't so sure about Inman. (He had had plenty of time to think of this before. A Presidential adviser said later, "You have to understand, Mack is always on the yellow line in anticipation of where the President's going. It's a way to survive.")

Clinton called Crowe late that night and asked him what he thought about the idea of giving Aspin more time. Crowe replied that he didn't think that that would help. Gergen said later, "We were too far down the track to slow down the train." In the course of the meeting, Clinton also spoke by phone to Gore and Talbott, in Moscow. Both of them strongly urged the President to go ahead. A Presidential adviser said later, "Strobe was very vested in Inman, and so was Gore." The next morning, Clinton was still undecided. McLarty, back in Washington, urged him to make a decision. Vernon Jordan, aware of the President's undecided state, dropped by the White House and told Clinton that he had to move ahead, that it was too late to turn back. Christopher sent word that he thought the President should go ahead. And so, after much agony, it was decided. The President called Aspin and Inman.

Aspin's "resignation" was announced from the Oval Office at 5:20 P.M. Wednesday, December 15, with little notice to the press and in time for the evening news programs. The Oval Office was meant to give the event what dignity could be bestowed upon the awkward situation, and it protected Aspin from questions from the press. Clinton, appropriately gracious, praised Aspin for his "solid leadership," his helping to launch "creative policy responses to the fundamental changes of this era," his having "led with character, with intelligence, with wisdom." Viewers could have rightly wondered what this scene was all about. Aspin's fumbling with his papers on a podium seemed metaphoric, and his announcement that he had decided to retire—"It's time for me to take a break and undertake a new kind of work"—painfully transparent. Gracefully, he said, "I know that while Bill Clinton is our Commander in Chief, our country will continue to grow in all of its strengths, our men and women in uniform will always be honored, and we will be true to our best values as a people."

Aspin had wanted a little time between his "retirement" announcement and the naming of Inman, but Gergen told him that it was best for him that the subject be changed the next day. The White House people weren't thinking of Aspin, however, when they set the next day for the announcement of Inman. When Aspin learned who his replacement would be, he warned Gergen and Lake that Inman would be trouble. "Do you know what you're doing?" he asked. "He's not an easy, compliant person." Aspin said, "Don't you realize this is the guy who quits all the time?" (Inman had previously resigned two government positions.) The Clinton people were eager to show off their new-found proficiency—the one-two punch of Aspin-Inman would do that—and get the positive press that would come from naming Inman. They had finally got it right, they said afterward—it was a long way from Lani Guinier. (They tried to make the President look magnanimous by telling reporters on background that Aspin had been offered the job as ambassador to China. He wasn't interested.)

A Presidential adviser said, "This showed Clinton could go ahead and get it done. A lot of people thought he was incapable of this."

The first signs of trouble had come before Inman was named, but the White House didn't take much notice. Inman had wriggled and squirmed and said that he didn't really want the job. He said that his wife opposed his taking the job and wouldn't move to Washington, and he would spend weekends in Austin (traveling at his own expense). His threat to leave town and not take the job if the matter wasn't settled by Tuesday was another sign.

The President's aides debated whether to ask Aspin to attend the announcement of his successor, finally saying it would be good if he came but they would understand if he didn't. Many were surprised that Aspin willingly showed up for the Rose Garden ceremony early Thursday afternoon and stood there, to the President's right, with Inman on the President's left, as Clinton made his announcement. (Lake, as usual, hovered in the background.)

Inman's startling acceptance speech—in which he referred to his turmoil over whether to take the job and said he had had to reach "a level of comfort that we could work together, that I would be very comfortable in your role as the Commander in Chief"—angered Clinton (and many others at the White House). One wondered whether Inman would have tried this in front of any other President. The thin, ramrod-straight, gap-toothed former admiral, with a high-pitched voice, talked as if he was bestowing something on the President, rather than the other way around. Some Clinton people thought Inman didn't have to go out of his way to say, as he did, that he'd voted for Bush. It was Gergen who had encouraged him to say that, to demonstrate that Clinton had reached across party lines. That was supposed to be one of the pluses of this nomination. A military man, a man known for his brilliance, a Republican to boot, would give the President the kind of political protection he needed. Most of Washington thought it was a great stroke on Clinton's part.

Immediately, however, there was some rumbling within the national security community—former Defense, State, and NSC officials now at think tanks and other roosting places around Washington, who kept in touch with their Pentagon contacts and each other and stood ready to offer their opinions to journalists and others. Some calls went on around town, asking whether Clinton and his people knew what they were getting into. Yes, Inman was brilliant, some of these people said, but he was also very prickly —stubborn and difficult. Some described him as a loner, a schemer, a leaker—and someone who would quit on a moment's notice. Now Clinton would be his hostage. If Inman disagreed with a Clinton policy, the world would know it soon enough, and Inman might well walk.

After the ceremony, Inman and some Clinton aides gathered in Lake's office. Mark Gearan heard Inman tell someone over the phone, "I'll be leaving here in six minutes." Gearan thought, He's going to have a lot to learn. The Clinton White House? Six minutes?

There were other problems. After Inman was named, the White House let it be known that he hadn't paid Social Security taxes for his housekeeper, whom he had employed for seven years—not even after the Zoe Baird events. The White House had leaked the story before Inman appeared at confirmation hearings, where it might seem a great disclosure. Inman was unhappy about it.

Inman was also annoyed that the Clinton people, with Vernon Jordan backing them up, were insisting that he resign from the all-male Bohemian Grove. Gergen had had to resign from the club upon joining the Clinton White House and thought he could convince Inman to do the same, but Inman resisted. Eventually, Gergen convinced the club to bend its rules so that Inman's name would be at the top of the list for reentry when he left government service, rather than at the bottom of the list, as per custom. Inman still refused. He said it was a matter of principle.

Almost immediately after Inman was named, the White House started receiving rumors that he was gay. Some years before, Inman had taken a lie detector test to beat off such rumors, and the recent vetting process hadn't picked up anything on the subject. The *Washington Post* called the White House to inquire about the rumors, which were coming from the gay communities in Austin and in Washington. Inman once again denied their veracity, and upon looking into this further, the White House vetters found no evidence to corroborate the rumors.

However, in the course of all this Joel Klein said to Inman, "It's pretty clear, Bobby, that your whole private life is going to come out. You have to tell me everything. I need to know what might come up. People are talking to people about all sorts of things in your private life." White House aides confirmed later that—for reasons not having to do with any of the speculation at the time—Inman decided he didn't want the press examining his personal life.

On January 6, Inman called Joel Klein to say that he was having a lot of problems with having accepted the nomination. "I knew I shouldn't have gone ahead with it," Inman said. "My family vacation has been ruined." Klein suggested that they talk it through. But shortly thereafter, Inman called Klein from the Denver airport—he had been skiing in Beaver Creek, Colorado, where he had a vacation place. He had written a letter withdrawing his name, he said, and was sending it to Klein by Federal Express, to reach him next day. Klein suggested that he think it over some more. Klein reported this to McLarty, whose dismayed reaction was, "What the hell do we have here?" The letter didn't come. Gergen called Inman and implored him to hold up any further action, because the President was about to leave on a trip to Europe and Moscow. Inman decided to wait until after the President's trip. The President left on January 8.

During the subsequent period, Jordan stayed in touch with Inman and tried to interpret his moods for the Clinton people. Klein was in contact with him as well. On Friday, January 14, while the President was in Moscow, Klein received the letter from Inman. By then Klein was persuaded that Inman would in fact pull out, and had conveyed this to other White House officials, and suggested that they start looking for someone else. In his letter, which the White House released later, Inman informed the President that he was withdrawing because "From Austin I sense elements in the media and the political leadership of the country who would rather disparage or destroy reputations than work to effectively govern the country. I do not wish to provide these elements fodder for their daily attacks." The whole thing was kept under wraps until after the President's return, on Sunday, January 16.

That Sunday night, Gore called Aspin, who had agreed to stay on until a successor was found, and said, "You aren't going to believe this."

"Try me," Aspin said. And Gore told him.

Aspin said, "You're right. I can't believe it."

On Tuesday, January 18, in Austin, Inman conducted a press conference that lasted over an hour and was one of the strangest performances by a public figure in a very long time. As viewers sat transfixed, watching this man destroy his reputation, Inman hurled charge after charge at the news media and at Republican senators, who he said were out to get him. He paid special attention to William Safire, the *New York Times* columnist, who indeed had written a tough column, which appeared on December 23. Safire had raised questions about Inman's business record (Tracor, a defense contractor he'd bought, had gone bankrupt) and claimed that Inman had an antipathy toward Israel—and he promised to write more. Inman also charged that Robert Dole was plotting with Safire against him. (On January 2, on *Meet the Press,* Dole said that Inman might not be an independent voice and predicted that he would be asked tough questions about Tracor.) Inman, rambling, said he had been "distressed" by the "rush-to-judgment distortions of my record, my character, and my reputation. . . . I'm simply not prepared to pay the current cost of public service in distortion of my record." He called himself a victim of "modern McCarthyism." (Both Jordan and Gergen had implored him not to use that term.)

One of the several odd things about this performance was that Inman's nomination had been almost universally acclaimed. He had received glowing editorials.

But not everyone who knew Inman took his remarks at face value. Inman was a practiced spook, skilled in the arts of deception and disinformation. So there was reason to think that his charges about the press, about plots against him, were designed to throw people off the trail. And they were. (Though he may well have thought what he did say was also true.) In his press conference, Inman himself brought up the rumors of homosexuality and denied them. (He also mentioned them that night on *Nightline,* describing them as rumors that had "circulated for years" because he had made a decision to keep a gay employee on the staff of the National Security Agency.) In fact, he didn't want his life subjected to such scrutiny. His wife didn't want him to take the job, he didn't particularly want to take the job—so the hell with it.

The people in the Clinton White House felt a mixture of dismay and relief. It was clear to them that they had dodged a bullet: Inman would have been trouble. Yet they knew that this episode called their competence into question once again. The "spin" they gave it was, This didn't have to do with us. It had to do with him. But they were unhappy, because the President had been embarrassed and they had been embarrassed. A senior aide said, "The President was a little stunned by this, but things bounce off him." With effort, aides joked about the fact that it was now almost one year since Zoe Baird. "Januarys are very tough on us," one White House aide said dryly.

So the search commenced again. The initial thought was that it would be good to get a Republican senator for the job. Richard Lugar, of Indiana, was believed to be planning to run for President, so he was out. William Cohen, of Maine, was approached, but declined. Sam Nunn, who had caused the President so much trouble a year earlier over gays in the military, was approached. He turned it down. Former Republican Senator Warren Rudman refused to get involved in the selection process. Names were floated by White House aides: Lloyd Bentsen, Norman Augustine. One aide floated the idea of keeping Aspin, which was quite unrealistic—the President would have looked even more foolish—and therefore was cruel. At the same time, even some of Aspin's critics agreed that he was doing a much better job as Secretary—his best yet. This flailing around confirmed that there was no philosophy guiding the President's search for a new Secretary of Defense; there was only the presumed political imperative.

William Perry, Aspin's deputy, whom the President had finally settled on over the weekend of January 22–23, was a better choice than the circumstances surrounding his being chosen suggested. A Defense official in the Carter administration, former businessman and academic, Perry was respected on Capitol Hill and by the military. Gore viewed him very favorably. But even Perry had to be talked into taking the job—by Gore. Perry offered a steady presence when steady was badly needed. But he was largely unknown outside of Washington. He was essentially a technical man, with no real policy-making or political experience, or practice as a public communicator. Perry was solid but as colorless as Lake and Christopher—so the President didn't solve his "spokesman" problem with his new choice as Secretary of Defense.

In the East Room, on Monday, January 24, one day short of a week since Inman's withdrawal, Clinton announced that he was nominating Perry to be Secretary of Defense. Aspin, his former boss, gracious to the end, stood off to one side—head cocked as usual—watching.

27

DECEMBER

"Bill Has Always Been Someone Who Has Lived on the Edge"

As the Christmas holidays neared, Clinton was riding high. The atmosphere at the White House was almost giddy. The NAFTA victory seemed to have settled the matter of his legislative prowess. In some quarters, he was being credited with having successfully pushed the most ambitious legislative program since Lyndon Johnson.

Though the Johnson comparison was an exaggeration, Clinton had accomplished a lot: his economic program, NAFTA, national service, aid to Russia, direct student loans, the Brady bill, had all been got through Congress. Winning bills that Bush had vetoed—family leave, "motor voter"—was no great feat, but they were heralded as triumphs by the White House. Other Clinton initiatives were part way through the legislative process, and he was well on the way to winning most of his "lifelong learning" proposals: national service and direct student loans were enacted; his Goals 2000 education program, which had to overcome resistance from the education establishment, was moving through Congress (and was signed into law on March 31, 1994); the school-to-work plan was moving (and was signed into law in May 1994). Legislation providing a large expansion of Head Start was under way (and was signed into law in May 1994). Reauthorization and reform of the Elementary and Secondary Education Act was moving. The Reemployment Act, to provide one-stop shopping for worker retraining, would be introduced in 1994.

Needing as he did congressional allies, Clinton talked a lot less about political reform legislation, and made less effort to achieve it, than had been suggested in the campaign. In fact, he hardly talked about it at all. He had concluded that if he wanted to get a lot done quickly, more quickly perhaps than the Congress wanted, he had to work with it, push it, be a partner to it. By the end of the 1993 congressional session, campaign finance reform bills were passed by the House and the Senate, but they didn't really get at the problem. Despite Clinton's campaign pledge to bring "change" to Washington, its lobbyist/money culture remained undisturbed.

Though Clinton's accomplishments weren't as sweeping as Johnson's, he achieved them under more difficult circumstances. (Johnson followed a martyred President and then won a landslide victory; his congressional margins were much more commanding than Clinton's, there was more party discipline then, and there were more Presidential levers, including federal projects to throw around.) Moreover, the nation's politics, Clinton's politics, and budget realities forbade legislation on the scale of the Johnson era. Most of Clinton's important victories were narrow scrapes (the economic plan) or grew out of an ad hoc coalition unlikely to be replicated (NAFTA). And despite the achievements, both Clintons now had a more sobering sense than before of the limitations on the modern Presidency—the absence of strong parties, the increased independence of Congress, and a more cynical press.

In December, Clinton's poll ratings were the highest since the first months of his Presidency. The *Washington Post*/ABC poll put his favorability rating at 58 percent, the *Los Angeles Times* at 59 percent. Significantly, a Times-Mirror Center poll in early December said that 63 percent of those surveyed thought of Clinton as someone who could get things done. Press coverage was largely positive—it was accepted that Clinton had accomplished a lot. And now he was giving good speeches more consistently than before. The unpleasantness over his foreign policy fumbles had faded from the public's mind (until the Aspin firing in mid-December). The year-end wrap-up stories, for which the staff worked hard to provide positive data and backgrounded reporters like mad, promised to be good ones.

The economy was doing well. The unemployment figure announced in early December was 6.4 percent, the lowest rate since early 1991. Inflation was low, and so were interest rates. Consumer confidence and the purchase of new homes were on the rise.

The Clintons, who had always made a big thing of Christmas, were going all out for their first one at the White House. They held at least one Christmas party or reception every day, starting December 6—in all, thirty-two events. (To avoid overcrowding, they held four for the press, for whom they still had little affection. They also gave one for the Secret Service.)

The Clintons stood patiently in the Diplomatic Room, on the first floor of the White House, while guests' pictures were taken with them, and they chatted briefly with each guest. (If a guest was thoughtless enough to start up a conversation with the President, the obliging Clinton colluded in holding up the line.) Tickets stipulating one's time for the picture taking were handed out to avoid long lines. Upstairs, in the entertainment rooms, the food was bountiful, and the guests mixed and admired the extensive Christmas decorations. Twenty-two trees were hung with ornaments crafted by artists from across the country. Clinton staff members mingled—some of them looking more relaxed than they had reason to be.

Clinton's closest aides knew—the President had known for a long time—that a story was coming alleging that as governor, Clinton had used Arkansas state troopers to help him conduct numerous sexual liaisons. A writer for *The American Spectator,* a conservative monthly magazine, had been digging around in Little Rock for some time, as had the *Los Angeles Times,* and some of the troopers were talking. The President had been alerted in August by Danny Ferguson, one of the four troopers who talked to the *Spectator*.

Something else was brewing as well. In the fall, press stories had begun to appear about an investment the Clintons had made in 1978 in a planned resort development in the Ozarks called Whitewater. The project was to be developed on two hundred thirty acres of land overlooking the White River, in northern Arkansas. There had been a brief flurry about the project during the campaign, following a story in the *New York Times* March 8, 1992, which questioned the losses on the project that the Clintons had claimed, and their relationship with their partners in the deal, James McDougal and his then wife, Susan.

McDougal was working for Clinton in the Arkansas government when the investment was made; he left the government in 1979 and in 1982 took over a small savings and loan, Madison Guaranty, and built it into one of the biggest S&Ls in Arkansas—until it failed in 1989. In the eighties, when the project got into trouble, McDougal put more money into Whitewater than the Clintons did. McDougal said later that he did this because he felt bad about getting them into the deal.

The *New York Times* piece alleged that the Clintons had put up little money and had taken improper tax deductions, and that Madison money had been used to subsidize the Whitewater project—which went bust. It also alleged that Mrs. Clinton had been retained by Madison, to help prevent it from being closed down by a state agency after it had been found insolvent, and that the closing of the bank was forestalled by Clinton's appointment of a new state securities commissioner. The *Times* reported that some of the Whitewater documents were missing. In late March, the Clinton camp produced a report by a Denver attorney and friend of the Clintons, James Lyons, that stated that the Clintons had lost $68,900 on the Whitewater project. (No backup documentation was released, and it was subsequently learned that the accounting firm Lyons had turned to had worked from incomplete information.)

This Clinton campaign exercise in "damage limitation" succeeded—as all such efforts did during the campaign—and press attention soon turned elsewhere. When, in a debate in Chicago on March 15, on the eve of the Illinois and Michigan primaries, Clinton was asked by Jerry Brown about the *Times* story, he responded with an angry defense of his wife. (This exchange was what precipitated Mrs. Clinton's famous "tea and cookies" remark.) No one knew then how many more such scenes there were going to be. Clinton won both Illinois and Michigan by landslides. The consensus was that Clinton would be the Democratic nominee. Whitewater was forgotten.

On October 31, 1993, the *Washington Post* reported that the Resolution Trust Corporation, which acquired and disposed of the assets of failed S&Ls, had asked the Justice Department to conduct a criminal investigation of Madison. This "criminal referral," as such requests to the Justice Department were called, included questions about whether Madison funds had been used to pay off a Clinton campaign debt from his 1984 gubernatorial campaign. McDougal had helped organize a fund-raiser in 1985 to help pay off the debt. The *Post* also reported that the questions about transactions involving Whitewater were part of the criminal referral. It was later learned that the RTC had also examined whether Madison funds had been siphoned into the foundering Whitewater project. The referral didn't name the Clintons as targets of the investigation, but they were mentioned as among the prominent Arkansas political figures McDougal had done business with or helped in some way. McDougal's dealings with Jim Guy Tucker, who had succeeded Clinton as governor, were allegedly far more extensive than they were with the Clintons, and were also part of the referral.

The *Post* story said that there had been a "protracted debate" within the RTC over whether the referral should name the Clintons, since the investigation primarily focused on Madison officials' handling of S&L funds. (The Madison failure was estimated to cost taxpayers about $50 million.) There had been a similar referral in October 1992, but the Republican-appointed United States attorney in Little Rock recommended against pursuing it, on the grounds that this would seem a blatantly partisan act on the eve of the Presidential election, and the Bush administration Justice Department concurred. The subsequent referral, in October 1993, in which the Clintons, while not subjects, were named, was rejected by the new Democratic U.S. attorney in Little Rock, a former law student of Clinton's, who afterward recused herself from the case.

So when the Clintons left for Washington, it was well known in political, legal, and financial circles in Little Rock that the Madison case, which was a very big deal there, was very much alive.

On September 29, 1993, White House counsel Bernard Nussbaum had met with Jean Hanson, the general counsel of the Treasury Department, who told him that the RTC was preparing a request for a criminal investigation of Madison and would name the Clintons as potential witnesses. (The Treasury Department supervised the general policies of the RTC.) In a follow-up call, Hanson told Nussbaum more details about the referral. So the White House was aware of the criminal referral at some point before it became public. Shortly after his conversation with Hanson, Nussbaum told Bruce Lindsey of the pending action. Lindsey said that a few days later, on a trip to California, he told Clinton about the referrals.

There was another meeting, on October 14, between White House aides (Gearan, Nussbaum, and Lindsey) and three Treasury officials. Those attending said they simply discussed how to deal with press inquiries about the investigation, which hadn't yet become public but which were now drawing reporters' interest. These meetings, and subsequent ones, were later to bring considerable grief to those who attended them—they could be construed as improper contacts between regulators and the White House—and to the Clinton White House itself. Public knowledge of these meetings was triggered by testimony to the Senate Banking Committee on February 24, 1994, by Deputy Treasury Secretary Roger Altman, who in the absence of an appointed head of the RTC was its acting supervisor. (The Clinton personnel system struck again.) Altman, under questioning, told the committee that there had been one "substantive" contact between Treasury and White House officials: a meeting on February 2, 1994, at which he had given a "heads up" about the statute of limitations on RTC civil suits. (Later that month, Congress passed and Clinton signed an extension of the statute of limitations.) But, shortly afterward, it turned out that there had been other meetings, and Altman had to amend his testimony four times. (White House aides realized at once that Altman's testimony was incomplete, and pressed for the amendments. The Treasury Department's inspector general later reported that there had been as many as forty contacts, including those of the most casual nature.) The disclosure of the meetings led almost immediately to subpoenas, in March of 1994, of ten White House and Treasury officials, and to the ouster of Nussbaum, who had attended all the meetings. (Nussbaum's other misjudgments—on Justice Department appointments, the travel office, and other matters, also played a role in his departure. And there was something beyond the recently disclosed meeting, which Nussbaum, as White House counsel, should have prevented. Nussbaum in general took an expansive view of the White House's relationship with regulatory agencies, and talked openly about this. An alarmed Joel Klein took the matter to other officials, and when Gore learned of it, he was very disturbed. At the end, Gore, for a number of reasons, was a strong advocate of Nussbaum's departure.) On the day after his testimony, Altman recused himself from the Madison case. (In the Whitewater hearings in the summer of 1994, it emerged that Altman had considered recusing himself from the Madison case in late January, but held off after the February 2 meeting, at which Nussbaum and others argued against it. Maggie Williams and Ickes opposed his recusing himself. No one ever doubted for whom Williams spoke. Treasury's legal and ethics offices had told Altman he wasn't required to recuse himself, but Treasury and RTC officials also told him that he would be wise to do so. Altman hadn't told the Banking Committee about the recusal discussion at the February 2 meeting.) The Clintons didn't want Altman to recuse himself and were reliably reported to be furious when Altman went ahead with it. As they expressed it to others, his presence might protect them from what they saw as "partisan" actions on the part of the RTC staff. The Clintons were particularly incensed by the RTC's hiring, in February, of the law firm of Jay Stephens, a former Republican U.S. attorney in the District of Columbia who strongly protested his firing by Reno (who had fired all holdover U.S. attorneys), to handle the Madison cases. According to a senior official, the Clintons wanted Altman to "keep the lid on." (Stephanopoulos and Ickes angrily phoned Altman about the recusal, and Josh Steiner, the twenty-eight-year-old Treasury Chief of Staff, about the hiring of Stephens—which landed Stephanopoulos a subpoena. Ickes already had one.) Also, there had been bad blood between Nussbaum and Hanson, going back to their both practicing law in New York, and Nussbaum wasn't comfortable with Hanson's having a large role in overseeing the RTC, without Altman's presence. The Clintons kept thinking they could control a situation that was rapidly spinning out of their control, and in the process made things worse for themselves and their aides.

A second strand having to do with Whitewater was making its way into investigatory channels. David Hale, a Little Rock businessman, who had managed a company that dispensed Small Business Administration funds, supposedly for minorities and women, was under investigation and threatening to charge that Clinton himself had leaned on him to make a $300,000 loan in 1976 to Susan McDougal. Hale alleged that part of the loan went to Whitewater. Conspiracy theorists made note of the fact that on the day Vince Foster died, the FBI had obtained a warrant to search Hale's offices. But by the time the subpoena was issued in Little Rock, Foster had already left his office.

To try to ensure that the case was pursued once the referral was made, there were leaks out of the RTC to newspapers and to James Leach, the Iowa Republican who, as the senior minority member of the House Banking Committee, had taken a great interest in the S&L bailouts.

Leach, a moderate with a reputation for judiciousness, was a good foil to send up against Clinton. House Minority Leader Bob Michel encouraged Leach to pursue the matter. In early December, at an embassy party, Leach told a journalist, "It's not sex that's going to bring Clinton down—it's ethics that's going to bring him down." This remark didn't comport with Leach's later claims that all he expected to arise out of the issue was a two-to-three-week investigation.

White House aides, aware that a number of reporters had turned up in Arkansas to look into Whitewater, were quietly trying to put out fires concerning the story. On December 6, a White House delegation—Lindsey, Gearan, and Gergen—went to the *Washington Post* to talk about some questions about Whitewater for which the *Post* wanted answers, as well as the *Post*'s request for some Whitewater documents. Later in December, the *Post* published a story questioning the Clintons' claimed loss. Pressure—from newspapers, from Leach—on the Clintons to release their documents on Whitewater was building.

"Whitewater" was a wonderfully apt, and ominous, metaphor.

On Friday, December 17, the *Spectator* began to fax copies of an article by David Brock around Washington. The article relayed in salacious detail stories recounted by four troopers—only two of whom would go on record—of Clinton's allegedly numerous liaisons with women, and how he allegedly used the troopers to transport him to assignations, procure women Clinton had spotted or get their phone numbers for him, deliver gifts to the women, guard him while he was having sex with them, and cover up his activities from his wife. The article asserted that these activities continued through the Presidential campaign and the transition. It portrayed Mrs. Clinton as a foul-mouthed harpy and alleged that she had had an affair with Vince Foster. It also alleged that directly (in calls to the troopers) and indirectly, Clinton had offered one of the troopers a job in exchange for refusing to cooperate with the reporters nosing around about his past sex life. The article did point out that none of the women confirmed the stories, that the troopers were hoping to make money through selling a book on the subject, and that Cliff Jackson, a Little Rock attorney who was a longtime enemy of Clinton's, was representing the troopers.

By Saturday, December 18, the White House knew that the *Los Angeles Times* and CNN were considering running pieces soon on the troopers' stories. Gergen was trying to discourage the stories, relaying rumors that the troopers had been paid for their story.

Early in the afternoon of the Saturday before Christmas, in the midst of the holiday parties, advisers gathered with the Clintons in the residence to brace them for what was coming and to talk strategy. At the meeting were McLarty, Gergen, Stephanopoulos, and Lindsey, together with David Kendall, the Clintons' private attorney at the firm of Williams & Connolly, and another attorney from the firm. The President had by then received a copy of the *Spectator* story, but aides said later that they didn't know whether he or his wife read it. (They had urged Mrs. Clinton not to read it, fearing that she would be emotionally devastated.) But both Clintons were at least aware of what was in the article. Clinton pressed his advisers for their judgments on how big the troopers story would be, where it would go, and what they should do. No one knew whether the story would be picked up in the mainstream press.

Gergen said that a storm was coming, but it wouldn't last very long. He thought that Whitewater would be a longer-term problem. Clinton was urged very strongly not to make specific responses about specific women mentioned in the article. (Gergen turned out to be right until one named by the *Spectator* as Paula—later to become famous as Paula Jones—brought a suit against Clinton the following May, for allegedly trying to get her to perform oral sex with him in a Little Rock hotel room, in May 1991, during, of all things, a governor's conference on total quality management. She first made her charges at a conference of conservative groups in Washington, where she was presented by Clinton's nemesis Cliff Jackson. The White House struggled, with incomplete success, to kill the story, and an aide dismissed Jones as "pathetic." But White House officials were plenty worried, with reason.)

Both Clintons were angry. Clinton demanded to know where this story had come from. He denounced it as "bull," said it was "crazy"; he said that some of the things in the article were "outrageous." And Clinton was perplexed about who was behind these stories—surely someone or some group was behind them.

Bruce Lindsey mentioned a story in that day's *Washington Post:* it said there was "renewed investigative interest" in papers concerning Whitewater that had been in Foster's office. (Foster handled the sale to McDougal of the Clintons' remaining interest in Whitewater for a thousand dollars in late 1992, and the payment of back taxes due on the project, and had been working on setting up a blind trust for the Clintons.) The next day, Sunday, the *New York Times* reported that "investigators" had been told that Foster had kept a file on Whitewater in his office and were trying to confirm whether the file had been taken from his office after his death; it hadn't been listed in the inventory of the items in his office conducted two days after he died.

Mark Gearan was giving a party late that Sunday afternoon at his home in Alexandria, Virginia, for the departing Roy Neel and Howard Paster. While he was out buying wine, a couple of reporters had phoned. At 4:45 P.M., fifteen minutes before his party was to begin, he participated in a conference call with Dee Dee Myers and Gergen. Gergen said that CNN was going to do something with the troopers story that night and needed a response to some questions. Also, the *Los Angeles Times* had asked to talk to him. It was decided that Gergen and Myers would miss the party and call the television networks to see if they were planning to run a story. Bruce Lindsey stayed at the White House to draft a statement. The Clintons were having a large extended-family Christmas party at the White House that night, which included several old friends from Arkansas.

At his party, as Gearan played the piano and guests were singing songs he had written teasing Neel and Paster, beepers started going off, including Nussbaum's and McLarty's. As their beepers sounded, guests would go to the phone and then leave the party—which was rapidly becoming depopulated. At eight-thirty, Gearan kissed his wife, told her it had been a good party, and left for the White House.

At six o'clock on CNN, Roger Perry and Larry Patterson, the two troopers who had gone on the record with the *Spectator,* talked about Clinton's sexual activities and said that Clinton had offered another trooper, Danny Ferguson, a job in exchange for his not talking. (Soliciting anything of value in consideration for the promise of federal employment was a federal crime.) The trooper was allegedly offered a job either as U.S. marshal in Little Rock or as a regional director of the Federal Emergency Management Agency. One former trooper, Buddy Young, who was in touch with the President and had tried to dissuade the others from talking, allegedly also spoke to them about the possibility of jobs. Young had already been made a FEMA regional manager in Texas. (The job paid $98,000; an Arkansas state trooper was paid a maximum of $25,600 after five years.) It later emerged that Lindsey—the President's consigliere and, as it happened, the director of personnel—had been having frequent conversations with Young in recent weeks.

The statement finally issued by the White House on Sunday night, in Bruce Lindsey's name, was the first in a series of nondenial denials of the allegations about Clinton's sex life. It said, "The allegations are ridiculous." It continued, somewhat misleadingly and with fractured syntax, "Similar allegations were made, investigated, and responded to during the campaign, and there is nothing here that would dignify a further response." (Allegations of this breadth had not come up in the campaign.) It flatly denied the allegations of a job offer but did say that the President "has had conversations about the fact that false stories were being spread about him."

A Clinton aide said later that the calls Clinton made to the troopers were sparked by Ferguson's phoning to say, "Mr. President, there's a lot of stuff around here." Another aide said Ferguson told Clinton that two troopers were talking to reporters and that they were being represented by Cliff Jackson. Since then, Clinton had been making calls to Arkansas to see what was going on. He had several phone conversations with Ferguson after that; the *Spectator* said Clinton had offered Ferguson a job and, through him, had made the same offer to another of the talking troopers. "He was really ripped," an aide said later.

For Clinton to have made the calls—whether or not he offered jobs—was foolish. The picture of the President of the United States calling state troopers and trying to kill a story about his sex life was dismaying. It was yet another sign, and a costly one, of the fact that Clinton had no one around him strong enough to dissuade him from doing such things. Lindsey privately admitted to knowing that the President had made some calls—and to making calls himself—and McLarty, characteristically, said he may have known about them but wasn't sure. He also said that Clinton tried to keep in touch with people who had worked with him in Arkansas, like the cook.

Some advisers attributed the calls to Clinton's "hands on" style of governing. One said later, "It may be good advice for a President of the United States that if someone calls you and says, 'There are people down here telling tales and being promised good money,' maybe he should say, 'This isn't a conversation a President should have,' but that's not his style." Another adviser said Clinton's phoning the troopers grew out of his belief in his persuasive powers. Clinton had come to think he could talk his way past anything and persuade almost anyone of his point of view. His phoning the troopers was also a sign of his need to control matters, his sense—in which he appeared to have indulged himself for a long time—that the rules didn't apply to him, and a lack of judgment about where not to venture the Presidency.

It was the phone calls that gave the troopers story currency, that gave those in the media who didn't feel that the sex story by itself was a valid one something to hang it on, raising the question of whether the President had behaved illegally as well as foolishly. Clinton later told a friend in the government that he realized he shouldn't have called the troopers—it wasn't Presidential—but he had thought he had nipped the story.

Monday, the day after the troopers story broke, was the most bizarre day thus far in this and perhaps any other administration. There were crisis meetings about what to do about the sex story. Paul Begala stopped by George Stephanopoulos's office and said, "I think I'm going to throw up."

That morning, the *Washington Times* ran the banner headline: CLINTON PAPERS LIFTED AFTER AIDE'S SUICIDE. The subhead read: "Foster's office was secretly searched hours after his body was found." The gist of the story was that papers pertinent to the Whitewater project were removed from Foster's office "during two searches"—the first one, on the night of Foster's death (which went on for two hours rather than the ten minutes originally claimed), by Nussbaum, Maggie Williams, and Patsy Thomasson. The second "search" was the one Nussbaum conducted two days later in the presence (if not within eyesight) of the Park Police and the FBI. Making the story even more labyrinthine, it was pointed out that Thomasson had been executive director of an Arkansas investment firm that was headed by a man who had done a lot of bond business with the state of Arkansas and who was convicted of distributing cocaine (including to the President's brother, Roger). The Park Police later complained to the Justice Department that Nussbaum had impeded their investigation of Foster's death.

The story went on to say what had actually happened—that the Whitewater file, being a personal matter, had been turned over to the Clintons' private attorney. (Much later, in early August 1994, it was learned that the file was first given to Williams, who, at Mrs. Clinton's direction, locked it in a closet in the mansion for five days, before it was given to the attorney. The attorney was going to Foster's funeral.) But the idea, with sinister overtones, that the Whitewater papers had somehow vanished—took hold. From that time on, news stories about Whitewater talked of "the file removed from Vince Foster's office."

Now the Whitewater and Foster stories were conjoined, enlarging and heating both. The *Washington Times* had already run stories pointing out that on the day of Foster's death, James Lyons, of the Lyons Whitewater report, had called him. But Foster didn't return the call before he left the office. (Lyons said later that he had called to leave a message about the fact that he was coming to Washington on Wednesday and was to have dinner with Foster because Foster was depressed over the travel office affair.) The Lyons call helped to feed the Whitewater theory of Foster's death.

For those who couldn't, or didn't want to, accept the simpler theory that Foster had become severely depressed by his sense that he had damaged himself professionally, especially in the travel office affair, and let down or damaged others, the Whitewater angle was grist. For those, particularly in the right wing, who wanted to exploit Foster's death and spread lurid stories about it (that he had been murdered, that he had been murdered in a nonexistent government safe house), and build Whitewater into a major scandal, the joining of the two issues was manna. But though it was possible Foster was worried about Whitewater—in the state he was in, he might have been worried about all manner of things—there was at that point no basis in fact for asserting that it had led to his suicide.

So on Monday, December 20, at the Clinton White House, while damage control was being exercised on the troopers story and a nervous vigil went on to see if it was picked up in the mainstream press, a statement had to be got out about Foster's Whitewater file. Gearan said privately, "The missing-file story is bullshit, ridiculous. We really had to shut it down. It was like the eighteen-and-a-half-minute gap in a tape [the famous gap in a tape of a Nixon conversation]. We had to work through the day to get out a statement." The statement, in Gearan's name, said that all the files on the Clintons' personal business had been turned over to their private attorney. "We know of no missing files," it declared.

Then there was also news that day that Inman had failed to pay Social Security tax for a housekeeper for several years.

And there was the news of Surgeon General Joycelyn Elders's son being arrested that day—this about two weeks after Elders had suggested a study of the question of whether drugs should be legalized. (The President had quickly knocked that down. Dr. Elders, who had been the Health Commissioner of Arkansas, often made controversial statements, but Clinton had known that when he picked her.)

In the course of the day, Gearan, asked by a reporter about the Inman story, said, "I can only deal with one nightmare at a time."

Dee Dee Myers held no briefing, so as not to have to answer questions and propagate more news about the troopers story. She held none the next day either. The atmosphere at the White House was eerie, as if someone had died.

That night, the Clintons held their Christmas party for the White House staff. The First Couple looked strained as they came down the stairs, stayed five minutes, saying little, and left.

The *Los Angeles Times* story, on Tuesday, added details about numerous phone calls Clinton had made to various women. It reported that fifty-nine calls had been placed to a particular woman's home and business between 1989 and 1991. Nussbaum told the press, "This President calls lots of people." The *Times* piece also had three troopers saying that Clinton carried on an affair with one woman into January 1993.

The troopers story had, by several accounts, a devastating effect on the Clintons. The revival of the painful Foster memory upset them all the more. The President was described by aides as "distracted." Both Clintons were described as angry, and tensions in the family quarters were said to be high. Clinton called a friend and said that it was really terrible to go through this with both his mother and his wife's mother in the house. At one point during that week, a Presidential aide called Vernon Jordan and suggested that he invite the President for some golf. Clinton had complained that he wanted to get out of the house. It's hard for a President to simply "get out of the house"—go for a drive, take a walk, drop in on a friend, as ordinary people do when they're troubled. A few days after the troopers story broke, and two days before Christmas, another top adviser to Clinton described him as dismayed, vexed, and frustrated—as well as angry.

Both Clintons were also upset that no one was defending them on Whitewater. A senior aide said, "He gets frustrated when he's not being defended. There are frequent times when they feel they're out there almost alone."

The White House's Whitewater defense was much like its trooper defense. Presidential aides said that it was an "old story," which had been hashed through during the campaign—even though it hadn't. And they and the Clintons kept the response narrow, with the aim of keeping the issue narrow. All kept insisting that the Clintons had lost money on the deal.

In coping with the troopers stories, the President's advisers pointedly avoided making flat denials of the sex stories. It was widely understood that Clinton had fooled around—he virtually admitted as much in his appearance with his wife on *60 Minutes* in February 1992, during the campaign, and his friends had never tried to dispel that widespread impression. It had been common knowledge for some time all had not been well in the Clinton marriage. Friends said that the Clintons had gone their separate ways. But on *60 Minutes,* Clinton had strongly suggested that that was all in the past.

Clinton took big risks. After the troopers story broke, a longtime friend said, "Bill has always been someone who has lived on the edge, politically and personally, for better or for worse." The friend said, "I don't think he thinks he's vulnerable." And Clinton did have a JFK fixation. His idol had been a sexual compulsive—and had taken great chances during his Presidency, some in the White House itself. But that was a different time. Questions about a Presidential candidate's personal life were fair game now—especially if it suggested a certain recklessness. It was probably only a matter of time before these questions carried over into Clinton's Presidency.

Clinton's advisers insisted that the public had elected him knowing that he was flawed and had accepted that he had strayed sexually. But they also said that if he was found to have had extracurricular sex while he was President, the public would be unforgiving. But the seamy new tales of Clinton's past, even if only partially true, were a reminder of unease about him. Clinton complained to friends that the troopers story raised the question of whom he could trust, which appeared to be a confirmation of sorts of at least some of their story.

Somewhere along the way, Clinton seemed to have become convinced that he was indeed "The Comeback Kid"—the title Paul Begala had coined to magnify Clinton's second-place showing in New Hampshire (after the Gennifer Flowers and draft episodes). Clinton was a truly resilient man. He had come out of more corners fighting than most people had ever been in at all. But inner resilience wasn't the same thing as the cumulative impression others got.

The Clinton White House's strategy for dealing with the renewed sex issue was to insist that it was all an "old story." The Clinton people were fairly confident that no other women would come forward to confirm any allegations of an affair, because Gennifer Flowers had been trashed for her public claims. (Clinton had said, according to the transcripts of the famous taped conversations with Flowers, "They don't have pictures. If no one says anything, then they don't have anything.")

White House aides and consultants also decided to combat the troopers story by saying, "It's no accident that this story is coming out when Clinton is high in the polls again." One heard the line quite often. An official who was about to proffer it at a Christmas party at the Vice President's house began with, "Stop me if you've heard this." Those who used it weren't fazed—or didn't appear fazed—by reminders that the *Spectator* was a monthly magazine, whose editors couldn't know what the polls would be in December. The fallback position was that the article was timed for when there would be a lull in the news, what with Congress gone and the holidays approaching.

The other part of the strategy against the troopers story was to trash the troopers. Betsey Wright, Clinton's chief of staff in Arkansas for several years, a damage controller during the campaign, and now a Washington lobbyist and still very loyal to Clinton, was dispatched to Arkansas. Soon stories were appearing in the papers about alleged transgressions on the part of the troopers. But the White House was particularly worried about the charge that Clinton had offered jobs to troopers if they didn't talk. At Wright's urging, and with Lindsey's involvement, trooper Danny Ferguson signed an affidavit saying that Clinton "never offered or indicated a willingness to offer any trooper a job in exchange for silence or help in shaping their stories." When the affidavit was made public, a White House aide said, "We've been waiting for that affidavit." Subsequently, however, Ferguson essentially took it back, telling the *Los Angeles Times* that all he meant was that Clinton "didn't say those words." Ferguson had told the *Los Angeles Times* that Clinton had discussed jobs for him and for Perry, the other trooper who went on the record, and he stuck with this even after the affidavit was issued.

That the troopers weren't without fault, and might have been elaborating at least some of their story and been in it for the money, didn't automatically make the gist of the story untrue. Nor did the fact that, as the White House kept pointing out, the troopers were being managed by Cliff Jackson.

The troopers story caught on and took more of a toll than most of Clinton's aides had expected. It had been receiving minor coverage (except in the tabloids), and the White House devoutly hoped that it would die by Tuesday, December 21. But on Tuesday, the *Los Angeles Times* story was published, and also on Tuesday, contrary to plan, Mrs. Clinton talked to wire services and attacked "outrageous, terrible stories" about her husband, charging that the stories were politically motivated. The "outburst" had been thought through. She was trying to redirect the story to the motives of the President's accusers, leaving out the matter of her husband's calls to the troopers and the alleged job offers. Mrs. Clinton also employed the standard line: "I find it not an accident that every time he is on the verge of fulfilling his commitment to the American people"—at what other points this was the case she didn't say—such stories come out. They were politically motivated, she said. She said that she was "bewildered" by the continuing interest in Whitewater and saw no reason to make any of the relevant files public. She said, "I think what we've said is adequate."

Mrs. Clinton's comments led the network news programs that night and put the story on the front page of the *New York Times,* which until then had run only a wire service report, on an inside page.

Aides were loath to confront her for not following the script—which was to say nothing in the hope the story would die. Her combative side and her anger got the best of her, not for the first or last time. Someone who knew the Clintons said, "They can be very hard to argue with. He says, 'I'm the President and you're not,' and she says, 'I'm the First Lady and you're not.' " This was a hazardous but not uncommon way of thought for Presidents (and First Ladies). George Bush used to tell his aides, "If you're so smart, why aren't you President?"

Though White House aides tried to brush off the troopers story (with telltale bravado), they knew it was damaging. The story became the stuff of late-night talk show jokes. And each reminder of the "character" question was erosive. Though people might have said that they knew Clinton had been unfaithful to his wife, the story was sleazy even if the troopers were elaborating. Each trivialization of the Presidency undermined both the Presidency and Clinton's moral authority, which could have real consequences.

The much planned year-end interviews with the Clintons were turning into a major headache. The network morning shows all canceled scheduled interviews with Mrs. Clinton when her staff stipulated that the questions be confined to celebrating Christmas at the White House. In a radio interview on Wednesday, Clinton, asked if he denied the whole troopers story, stammered and hesitated as he didn't on any other subject. When the tape was played on one of the network news broadcasts, the effect was very damaging.

Through the exercise of impressive foresight—he thought—Mark Gearan had arranged for Arkansas reporters to come to Washington (with enough warning that they could purchase low-fare tickets) to interview the Clintons on December 21. Mrs. Clinton passed Christmas cookies. After her outburst to the wire services, White House aides were tempted but didn't dare to cancel other interviews.

While the Republicans, wisely, kept silent about the sex issue, within a day of the "missing file" story, Robert Dole, on December 21, called for "some independent review" of Whitewater. If there were to be no congressional hearings, he said, an independent counsel should be appointed to investigate the matter.

Amid all the turmoil over the troopers issue, the Christmas celebrations, the year-end interviews, the Clintons and their staff had been immersed in an internal struggle over how to handle Whitewater—in particular, how much information to make public through the release of private papers.

The argument broke down largely but not entirely as one between, on the one hand, the Arkansans, including Lindsey, and most of the lawyers, including Nussbaum and Clinton's private attorney, David Kendall—all of whom saw it as a matter of damage control, and in terms of legal tactics—and, on the other, those who saw it as a political issue. An exception among the lawyers was Joel Klein, the new deputy counsel. Klein, forty-seven, had previously practiced law in Washington. His general view was that the information was going to become public at some point anyway; the defensive posture wasn't the best one for the Clintons to be in; and when you govern and refuse to turn over information, that only ratchets up interest in the information. Others who pushed for making information public were Stephanopoulos, Gergen, and, interestingly, McLarty. A colleague said, "Mack was just using common sense."

Mrs. Clinton's reaction was much like the one in the case of the travel office, writ large. She was strongly opposed to making any information public. She bristled at being told that she had to conform to the Washington culture and felt that the White House had been too forthcoming with the press. The irony about Mrs. Clinton's rebellion against the Washington culture was that, in the main, the best advice she was getting was from the aides most experienced in Washington. She argued that if the Whitewater papers were released, there would simply be more questions (she may have had special reason to think that); there would be no end to it.

She was right, but that didn't solve the Clintons' political problem. The impression began to grow, the charge began to be made, that—in a reach back to an earlier time—the Clintons were "stonewalling." The Watergate vocabulary was too easy to draw upon. On the basis of what was known, Whitewater was by no stretch of the imagination of the dimension or seriousness of Watergate—a constitutional issue of the abuse of power by a President. Nonetheless, term inflation was on the rise, as was disproportionality. The words "impeachment" and "cover-up" were tossed around. As of then, at the least, there was no sign of a cover-up. The Madison case had proceeded. No Presidential misconduct had been alleged.

A White House aide said later, "We treated it as a legal rather than a political issue." Another said, "Hillary reacts with her defense lawyer training: you hold things tight, you manage it closely, you reveal only what you have to." And whatever else was going on between them over the troopers story, each Clinton tried to protect the other on Whitewater. An aide said, "There may be ups and downs in the relationship, but a lot of what drives her is trying to protect him. And he won't do anything about Whitewater unless he feels she's comfortable with it." People who were looking for differences between the Clintons over how to handle Whitewater were looking for the wrong thing. The President may have seemed more "relaxed" about the issue of taking matters public, and about Washington, than his wife was, but he would let no one see any distance between them on what to do. And despite their different temperaments, his views weren't so different from hers as was widely believed. He told his aides that if he'd listened to the Washington establishment and the media, he wouldn't have become President: he got there alone, without their help.

The first argument over how to respond to Whitewater had been in regard to a *Washington Post* request on November 17 for documents, including financial records, offering proof that the Clintons had lost what they claimed on Whitewater, plus records from the 1984 gubernatorial campaign and the fund-raiser in 1985. (All of these were related to items in the RTC criminal referral.) Mrs. Clinton, her defense lawyers, Nussbaum, and Lindsey were strongly opposed to turning over the material. Lindsey and some others felt that the *Post* had been unfair to Clinton, that it was on a Whitewater kick, and that to give it the material wouldn't put an end to the issue but would probably lead to a request for more. Stephanopoulos, Gergen, McLarty, and Klein favored turning the papers over to the *Post* and making them public, even though that might have started a "feeding frenzy," as Mrs. Clinton predicted. Their view was that the papers would become public eventually, and the sooner the subject was got over, the better. Nussbaum and Kendall argued that this wouldn't end the matter. That struggle ended with a decision to not give the *Post* the papers. Lindsey sent the paper a letter saying that the matter had been examined fully during the campaign, an independent firm had written a report, and there was nothing to add. But the subject of the Whitewater papers was far from over. Now there were many demands for them.

Late in December, Gergen said wearily, "I can't say we've been a great success at putting out that fire."

By this time, the subject of Whitewater, which had been deemed by much of the media to be too complicated to explain, began to be covered on television. Newspapers were all over it. A new question about the Clintons was being raised. Whatever their virtues or flaws, and whatever the merits of the allegations, they had never been seen in the light of greed or shady dealings. They may have been simply trying to build a nest egg for their daughter's education—and Arkansas' (at $35,000) was the lowest-paid governor—but what came across was at odds with the nation's prior perception of them, and also their self-description. They had been seen as devoted to public service, as not caring very much about money. Ethics was one of their issues (even if Clinton pursued it sporadically).

The evidence produced thus far suggested the possibility of minor ethical transgressions in the past—nothing that rose to an issue on a Presidential level. The idea of "impeachment"—Leach used the word on one television program and then on a subsequent one said he shouldn't have used it (this sort of thing became a pattern)—was absurd on the face of it. But by late December, the troopers were essentially gone from the stage and a full-fledged "scandal" had taken over. Its true dimensions couldn't be divined yet, but that was almost irrelevant. Now the Republicans had a handle on something they could use to try to stop Clinton's progress, and the press had a scandal to chase. The Clintons' handling of the issue left even some of their strongest allies wondering whether they had something to hide.

On the morning of Thursday, December 23, the White House was half empty. The President was to take the day off, to relax and do some Christmas shopping. He was tired from all the receptions and all the strain. Contrary to the plan for that day, he spent a brief period in the Oval Office, where he was joined by his mother. He also dropped by the press briefing room, surprising reporters, to say hello. Those White House staff members who were in their offices planned to be gone by afternoon. Clinton aides took seriously their chances to clear out. McLarty was in his office, preparing to take his staff (what was left of it) to the White House Mess for lunch.

But the Clintons made a big decision that day. At long last, after a lot of argument—and a running discussion that morning among the Clintons, Nussbaum, Klein, Lindsey, Stephanopoulos, and Gergen—David Kendall, the Clinton's private attorney, was authorized to phone the Justice Department and offer to turn over all the Clintons' Whitewater papers, and to do this pursuant to a subpoena, in order to protect the papers—a not unusual procedure. White House officials claimed that when Kendall called, Justice attorneys said that they had been preparing a subpoena for the files that had been in Foster's office; Kendall proposed that they broaden the request. Gergen said later, "The trooper story was dying. If we could lance the boil on Whitewater, we'd have a pretty calm Christmas season and then come back and deal with the issues."

And so on the afternoon of December 23, the White House announced that all of the Whitewater papers in the Clintons' possession would be turned over to the Justice Department. (Skeptics questioned whether all the files that had been in Foster's office were intact.) The announcement said: "The President has voluntarily decided to release these documents for whatever relevance they may have to any Department of Justice law enforcement inquiries." It left out the matter of the subpoena.

The Clintons' action wasn't as magnanimous as the White House tried to make it appear. There had already been newspaper reports that Justice was considering a subpoena for the documents, so there was reason for the Clintons and their advisers to think that it was only a matter of time before they would be forced to turn them over. Moreover, Leach had just requested that Kendall turn over the documents to his staff. Leach had also just called for a special counsel to investigate the Madison and Whitewater cases.

The point of Kendall's requesting the broad subpoena was to try to hold the material as tightly as possible and at the same time appear to be cooperating with an investigation. But not telling the public about the subpoena turned out to be a big mistake. A White House official said later, "It left people here out to dry."

Hoping that they had bought a respite, the Clintons turned to trying to enjoy the holidays. After a family Christmas dinner, they went to the Kennedy Center to see *The Will Rogers Follies.*

On the Monday after Christmas, they left for a few days in Arkansas and planned to spend New Year's at Renaissance Weekend. Soon enough, they would be back in Washington to deal with health care and to prepare for the President's forthcoming trip to Europe and Russia.

They hoped for some peace, and time to concentrate on the President's agenda.

28

ANOTHER START

"I Guess the Media's Been Obsessed with This, but It Never Crosses My Mind"

The Clintons' return to Washington in January 1994 was far different from their triumphal entry a little less than a year before. The President's political position was uncertain, and the optimism and freshness of January 1993 had been replaced by the public's doubts about and perhaps overfamiliarity with him. The fact that he had achieved a lot was his strong suit with the public. But once more, he had reached a high point, only to be brought low by his own acts—this time, acts mostly in the past. It had seemed all along, beginning with his election, that even in the periods when the people gave him their approval, they didn't give him their hearts. They remained uneasy about him, held something back. The big question now was whether he and his wife could put the Whitewater affair to one side so that he could get on with the business of governing.

Clinton still had a large agenda. His health care program was in trouble —partly because of a barrage of negative advertising by the insurance industry, but mainly because the program was so ambitious and so difficult to explain. He was under pressure from Republicans as well as from centrists in his own party to deliver on his campaign promise to "end welfare as we know it." But his advisers were having difficulty finding the billions necessary to pay for his proposal to get people off the welfare rolls after two years, providing them with a government job if necessary.

Moreover, Clinton and Democratic Party leaders were very worried that the President might lose a working majority in the House in the fall congressional elections. His thin working majority in the Senate might be erased. Even maintaining control of the Senate wasn't a sure thing. Not only were there the usual midterm losses by the incumbent party, but polls taken by Stan Greenberg indicated that all incumbents were in trouble.

Greenberg's soundings also showed that the pre-Christmas period had taken its toll on Clinton's standing with the public. A close adviser said, "It's a little bit like New Hampshire, when Gennifer Flowers was followed by the draft. Flowers didn't have much effect. It's the combination of the issues of the troopers and Whitewater and the Christmas season—when the President should have been feeling good and the country feeling good. It reminded people of their difficulty in understanding Clinton and coming to terms with him." Despite their public downplaying, Clinton's aides knew, from Greenberg's polling on the subject of Clinton's alleged past sex life and from common sense, that a time could come when the "character" issue would become so large that it would undermine his legitimacy as President, and then the possibility that the public would see him in a positive light would no longer exist. Now, in January, they felt that that possibility was perilously close.

The results of the focus group polls that Greenberg and Carville presented to the President and his advisers later in January, in a meeting to prepare for the President's first State of the Union speech, were ominous. People were watching Clinton very closely, and still tied their hopes to him, and believed things were starting to move, and felt he had learned a lot. Further, they thought he was very effective with the Congress. They thought he was smart, hardworking and trying to get the country on the right track.

However, they still had doubts about whether he was real, whether he was truthful; and a substantial number believed he did things essentially to enhance his political future. The previous August, Greenberg's polls showed that doubts about Clinton's character, whether he could be trusted, had started to recede, because he was taking on issues that mattered to the public. Late in the year, as the troopers story broke and Whitewater started to get more attention, these doubts were revived. The January soundings indicated that for the moment, people could live with the dichotomy of having questions about the President's character and applauding the fact that he was getting things done. Besides, with the next Presidential election far off, they weren't being forced to consider an alternative. But how long that ambivalence would last was a question that worried Clinton's advisers.

Greenberg's conclusion was that the character issue would only become dominant if Clinton wasn't seen to be moving the country forward.

Clinton was in a race against himself. If the productive Clinton could stay ahead of the Clinton about whom people had questions, he would be successful. Therefore, it was of utmost importance to him—and his wife—to keep moving on their program.

On January 3 at eleven o'clock, in his first public event since his holiday vacation, Clinton gathered in the Roosevelt Room all the staff and Cabinet officers who worked on health care and pronounced that health care would be the year's priority. (There was some joking among the staff that, given the events of December, Mrs. Clinton now had even more sway over him.) Because of his own political situation, Clinton had to get a health care plan through the Congress. And Mrs. Clinton had been waiting a long time.

For months, there had been strenuous arguments within the White House over the strategy for winning a health care bill. The battle essentially came down to one between those who felt a compromise should be struck with Republican John Chafee or with the Democratic centrists—such as Representative Jim Cooper, of Tennessee, who had his own proposal, or Senator John Breaux, of Louisiana, who was always happy to be in the middle of major dealing—and those who wanted to hold tight to as much of the original bill as possible. McLarty and Gergen were of the first school, Mrs. Clinton and Magaziner of the second. The strategy shifted from day to day, and on some days both approaches were followed.

In January, a hydra-headed group was put in charge of managing health care strategy: Stephanopoulos, Magaziner, Patrick Griffin, who was Paster's successor as the legislative aide, and Harold Ickes, who had joined the White House staff on January 3. Authority was scattered. Of course, Mrs. Clinton played a large role. (Magaziner, who had riled a number of members of Congress, was kept out of sight.)

Ickes, a strong-willed New York attorney, a son of FDR's Interior Secretary, was now a Deputy Chief of Staff, along with Phil Lader. He had negotiated for real power before he took the position. Now that he was on the scene, the Clintons overloaded him. His main jobs were to be heading the health care effort and overseeing the various political outreach offices—which weren't coordinated and in some cases not forceful enough. And then he got saddled with Whitewater, and also the 1994 congressional elections. Some other aides saw Ickes's arrival as deliverance. He was tough, and he could talk straight to the Clintons. A White House aide said, "He's the one person most trusted by both Clintons."

Gergen wasn't deeply involved in the health care strategy. Mrs. Clinton had cooled on him because he had been making his own contacts on Capitol Hill to pursue his health care strategy, because she thought he leaked too much, and because she felt that he wasn't doing enough public defending of the Clintons on Whitewater.

Mrs. Clinton complained strongly that there was no long-term plan or central mechanism for dealing with the Whitewater problem. Lindsey had tried, but now the subject had gotten too big, and Lindsey didn't have authority over the rest of the staff. Therefore, Ickes was to take charge. Ickes could force decisions and enforce discipline. He could cut off rambling discussions, and stop people from talking at once. "I have only one good ear," he'd say, "so I can only hear one person." The fact that he could be direct with the President and his wife, and was trusted by them, gave him power among the diffuse staff.

After his arrival, Ickes convened regular meetings on Whitewater twice a day in the Ward Room. Carville and Begala got very involved, as did Stephanopoulos.

The immediate question after the holidays was whether the Clintons could or should avoid the naming of a special counsel to look into Whitewater. Again there was a division. On one side were most of the Arkansans and the lawyers (including Lindsey, Nussbaum, and Kendall, but not Klein)—who argued against a special counsel. On the other were the people who understood more about politics and communications—Stephanopoulos, Gergen, and Ickes, plus McLarty—who said a special counsel was inevitable and they might as well ask for one. Greenberg weighed in in favor of asking for one. Nussbaum was adamantly opposed. He and Kendall argued that going for an independent counsel wouldn't solve the problem. They were right, but the status quo was politically untenable.

Nussbaum also argued vehemently that the standard for appointing a special counsel or special prosecutor—a criminal charge brought by a credible source—had not been met, and going for a special counsel under those circumstances would break precedent. He had a point. (Nussbaum often had a point that was technically correct, even based on principle, but politically blinkered.) Nussbaum said he preferred hearings, distracting as they would be, over a special counsel. Klein argued that there was already an investigation under way by a career employee of the Justice Department; the information was going to come out anyway, so why draw the line there? Vernon Jordan argued for going the special counsel route; Susan Thomases' advice varied, depending on Mrs. Clinton's mood.

Mrs. Clinton felt, with reason, that a special counsel process would take a long time and be distracting and draining. Neither she nor her husband had done anything wrong, she argued. When, at a meeting of Mrs. Clinton and the staff shortly after the holidays, Stephanopoulos laid out the reasons for asking for a special counsel, "Hillary jumped down his throat," a staff member said later. "She yelled and fussed. What she was bothered by was the notion that they had to have a special counsel. She wanted a plan for handling it." In the meeting, Mrs. Clinton asked, "Well, what's the next thing?"

There was another factor, which at the time was kept well within the White House walls. A special counsel process could cost the Clintons a lot of money. Williams & Connolly, Kendall's firm, was expensive, and the process was likely to be a long one.

Mrs. Clinton argued that just because the press was clamoring for a special counsel, that didn't mean that the President should request one. She was infuriated by advisers' saying, Yes, this is an invasion of your privacy, and yes, no formal charges have been made, but that's the way this place is, and you have to do it. She argued that this wasn't something you did just to "get it behind you—there are consequences." A Clinton adviser said, "There is sort of a feeling in this town, having gone through some things in the past, that once this steamroller starts to roll, roll with it." Mrs. Clinton resisted that view.

She angrily told people, and seemed quite convinced herself, that the President's troubles were being stirred up by longtime opponents of Clinton's in Arkansas—both Cliff Jackson and Sheffield Nelson, an old political rival—who were working with right-wing groups to destroy his Presidency. And there was evidence that she was right about that. The Citizens United Organization, headed by Floyd Brown (famous for producing the Willie Horton ad in 1988) and David Bossie, his lieutenant, operating out of offices in northern Virginia, supplied news organizations with the latest goods—conspiracy theories and what have you about Whitewater, alleged sex scandals, and Foster's death. The right-wing talk show hosts—Rush Limbaugh and the evangelist Jerry Falwell and others—kept up an incessant patter, purveying salacious rumors, against the Clintons. One old enemy, bankrolled by a right-wing group, went like a troubadour from show to show, peddling lurid lies. There was no precedent for this kind of operation against a sitting President. But it didn't explain all of Clinton's problems.

The President himself felt that his staff had failed to mount a defense early in the fall. But he and his wife had rejected proposals that might have helped. A successful defense would have required getting out all the relevant information—to the extent that it was still available—and staying ahead of, or at least abreast of, the questions. The Clintons had hoped to keep the issue narrow by making it a legal one and assigning it to Lindsey. "They kept thinking they could contain it," a Presidential adviser said.

Both Clintons had a gut reaction against not fighting back. They had been that way in the campaign, when they insisted that a charge should never go unanswered, and they carried this thinking into the White House. Much of the "campaign mentality" that outsiders attributed to the Clinton staff actually stemmed from the Clintons themselves. One aide said that Clinton was happiest on the attack. The President was no happier than his wife at the prospect of people's pawing through their financial papers. Clinton displayed more equanimity, but he was plenty distressed about the situation, and he didn't display equanimity all the time. He said to his staff, vehemently, "I'm not going to be a punching bag. We just can't take this lying down."

The Clintons felt that it was wrong that they were working so hard to get things done and yet were confronted with such tangential issues and personal malice. They believed, with some justice, that opponents were using Whitewater to block the President's progress on substantive issues, to delegitimize his Presidency.

As Mrs. Clinton became increasingly upset about the assault on her as well as on her husband's character, she took to staying in the East Wing, working there rather than in her West Wing or OEOB offices. Her staff threw up a protective cordon around her. Maggie Williams suspected (not without reason) that other White House aides would leak things about Mrs. Clinton's business dealings.

The Clintons saw themselves as moral, religious people, dedicated to the public good. (The religious aspect of Clinton's life had been pumped hard by his staff in December.) That their ethics were being questioned offended them deeply. The contrast between their self-portrait—and Bill Clinton's campaign denunciations of the "greed" of the eighties—and the possibility that the Clintons had cut some corners in order to gain financial advantage was too tempting for their political opponents to let go of.

Much analysis attempted to explain Whitewater in terms of the incestuous nature of a small state capital. Arkansas was being caricatured. There were aspects of state capitals, especially small ones, that bore on the case, but the deals the Clintons appeared to have accepted from people in a position to help them out were little different from the kinds of deals that politicians anywhere might get into. Politicians who aren't rich have a lot of dealings and socialize with people who are, and are thus in a position to ease their way. They are frequently offered help in making money. The temptations to accept such favors are great.

In early January, some Democrats joined in the calls for a special counsel. The motives of these Democrats—who included Senators Daniel Patrick Moynihan, Bill Bradley, and Bob Kerrey—were mixed. They felt that Whitewater was becoming too great a distraction, and they also worried that the appearance that the Clintons were trying to hide something would rub off on them. Once some Democrats called for a special counsel, the White House could no longer dismiss the issue as a partisan one. Besides, the White House was becoming nearly paralyzed by Whitewater. A senior aide said in early January, "You can't govern in this environment. We're just consumed by it."

The President's advisers were considering four options. One was to stay where they were and fight back. "That's a loser," the senior aide said. "It puts us on the road to an independent prosecutor. Congress will pass the law and a three-judge panel will pick a prosecutor. [The law had lapsed, mainly because of opposition by Republicans.] That's a roll of the dice." The second option was to put out all the information. "That would help with the politics and the press," the aide said, "but within two weeks you'd have a call for an independent prosecutor. There are too many questions. And we don't know whether we have all the documents." Third, go for a special counsel appointed by the Attorney General, because the law had lapsed. "That won't satisfy the press," this aide said. "Soon the press would demand release of the documents." Fourth, go for a special counsel and release the documents. "That's where we're going," the senior aide said. But not quite: some documents were dribbled out over a period of time, as seemed exigent to the Clintons and the White House staff. Others had been given for safekeeping to the Justice Department. An aide said, "Everyone agreed an independent prosecutor was not a good thing if you could avoid it. The debate was over whether you could avoid it, and at what political cost."

With Republicans now calling for hearings—the Clintons' and their aides' biggest nightmare—a special counsel had to be considered, as a fallback position. The White House was intent on avoiding hearings, which would be at the least disruptive and at the worst circuslike and paralyzing. Legislative aide Pat Griffin made a lot of calls to Capitol Hill to try to head them off.

The already tense relations between the Clinton White House and Attorney General Janet Reno now took a new form. Reno had taken to saying, starting before Christmas, that it wouldn't do for her to appoint a special counsel, because the independence of anyone she chose would be questioned.

White House aides interpreted this statement by Reno as encouraging the Congress to reenact the old law to establish independent prosecutors, chosen by a three-judge court. A senior aide said in early January, "She's waving the flag to Congress to pass a special-prosecutor law." The effect of Reno's suggesting that Congress pass an independent-prosecutor law was to increase the pressure on the White House to ask for a special counsel, so as to avoid protracted congressional debate on the Clintons' case while the independent-prosecutor law was being considered. (The resignation of Webb Hubbell in mid-March of 1994, ostensibly because of a serious dispute with the Rose Law Firm over billing practices, but perhaps also because of his own work on Madison when he was there, left the Clintons feeling personally bereft and even less protected at the Justice Department. Now the only Rose partner left in the administration besides Mrs. Clinton was William Kennedy, who in March 1994 had his duties reduced because he, who had vetted job candidates, was himself delinquent on Social Security taxes for household employees and had botched the clearing of White House staff members for their permanent passes—leaving about a hundred staff members still using temporary passes and not having been subject to a background check.)

Mrs. Clinton and some White House aides believed that there would be a greater chance to limit an investigation by a special counsel appointed by the Attorney General than that by a prosecutor appointed by a court. "She thought she could control things," one adviser said. But another argument for going for a special counsel, and forestalling the appointment of a court-appointed independent prosecutor, did hold sway. Research and memories informed White House aides that court-appointed prosecutors tended to take longer with their investigations. Their nightmare was Lawrence Walsh's seven-year investigation of the Iran-contra affair. Finally, Kendall became convinced that if they didn't accept a special counsel, an independent prosecutor would be forced on them. That brought Mrs. Clinton around.

The President's advisers considered having the Clintons issue the relevant papers and submit to a long, long press conference, which would continue until the questions were exhausted. This was the device used by the Mondale-Ferraro campaign in 1984, when questions arose about Geraldine Ferraro's husband's business practices. The idea was that Ferraro would sit there until there were no more questions, and it worked. In Ferraro's case, however, all of the tax returns were available; while in the Clintons' case, some Whitewater documents were missing. (During the campaign, McDougal said he had sent some documents to the governor's mansion, which Mrs. Clinton said were lost.) Also, some aides thought such an appearance would draw too much attention to the subject. Stephanopoulos likened it to a "Super Bowl." On-and-off plans for the Clintons to air their Whitewater goods fluctuated according to White House assessments of how great the public's interest was at any given moment. White House aides tended to measure the problem (as they did other matters) in terms of whether they had had a good week or a bad week, rather than in terms of its cumulative damage. But they were also concerned that Mrs. Clinton might come off as brittle and snappish. And they were concerned that the Clintons wouldn't give the full story—and remain vulnerable to later disclosures.

It was a source of unease among the White House staff that no one in the White House but the Clintons knew what all the facts of the story might be. As one staff member put it in early January, "All of us who have gone out to defend their position have been clobbered." Stephanopoulos had been embarrassed after he had said on January 2, on *This Week with David Brinkley,* "The President has turned over all documents to the Justice Department," and the next day the White House announced that none of the papers had been turned over—that they wouldn't be sent to the Justice Department for a couple of weeks. Gearan had been embarrassed by the post-holiday discovery of the subpoena. These embarrassments made for tensions between the legal and communications sections of the White House. So one reason that the Clintons weren't being defended very well was that there were questions their defenders couldn't answer and were wary of getting into. Even Gore evaded a question on *Face the Nation* on January 12 about why, if the Clintons suffered losses on the Whitewater project, they didn't take tax deductions for that.

At the same time that the wrangling and worry about Whitewater and health care were going on, preparations were under way for the President's forthcoming trip to Europe and Russia, to begin on January 8. Clinton underwent many hours of briefings for the trip, and important questions were still to be settled as the day of departure approached. As part of the pretrip pageantry, Clinton met with the Joint Chiefs of Staff and went to CIA headquarters, in Langley, Virginia.

Just before two-thirty on the morning of Thursday, January 6, Clinton was awakened by a call from his stepfather telling him that his mother had died. Clinton had been aware that her condition was serious and had inquired into special treatments for the breast cancer she had been battling for years, but still the news came as a shock. Her last big outing, over the New Year's weekend, to Las Vegas, where she had gone to see Barbra Streisand sing, showed her in a wheelchair. By contrast, just after Christmas, the public had seen pictures of her walking from the White House along with her family, to board a helicopter to begin the trip to Arkansas. Her genes ran strong in her son. He inherited from her his ambition, temper, and resilience—and the shape of his face. Virginia Kelley had gone through poverty (whereupon she studied to be a nurse) and four husbands, having been widowed three times (the first time when she was pregnant with Bill); she had married one man, Roger Clinton, who had beat her, twice. With her streak of white hair amid raven black, her high, thinly tweezed eyebrows and long false eyelashes, and her passion for the racetrack, she was a true character. And Clinton seemed to love her without reservation. He left the next morning for Hot Springs.

No matter what sophisticated circles he entered, Clinton never lost touch with his roots. There was nothing of the snob in him. In fact, he seemed to find his roots a source of strength. Over the next couple of days, he spent time with friends from high school, visited old haunts, comforted his troublesome half brother, Roger (who was now trying to establish a singing career), and acted in every way the responsible elder son. The briefings could wait. Moscow could wait. Whitewater could wait. Clinton had gone home to bury his mother.

It was a tired and emotionally drained Clinton who climbed aboard Air Force One on Saturday night, headed for a meeting of the NATO heads of state in Brussels. Whitewater and the President's trip were hopelessly intertwined. The President's big new opportunity to show himself managing important foreign policy issues and dealing with foreign leaders was constantly interrupted by unpleasant matters back in Washington. Bruce Lindsey, who almost always traveled with Clinton, stayed behind to deal with Whitewater, and Stephanopoulos stayed back as well.

There were two major pieces of business for Clinton at the NATO summit. One was to help the alliance maneuver through the tricky business of trying to satisfy, without offending Russia, the demand of some Eastern Europe countries that they become members. As with most summits, the great bulk of the work had been done ahead of time, but it was still a delicate moment for the long-standing and successful alliance. NATO had been formed to ward off any threat from the old Soviet Union. Now that the Soviet Union was dead, and the former "satellites" in Eastern Europe were free, there was a question of NATO's purpose. Poland, Hungary, the Czech Republic, and Slovakia were asking for NATO membership. Their heads of state had made a strong case to Clinton when they came to Washington for the opening of the Holocaust Museum. They argued that unless they were affiliated with NATO, in time they might well have to yield to pressures brought by renewed nationalism in Russia.

But some administration officials, especially Strobe Talbott (who in late December was named Deputy Secretary of State), were concerned that drawing a new line to the East was fraught: it could fan the very nationalism in Russia the Eastern Europeans feared, and it could isolate other former Soviet republics. There was also the question, which wasn't given much serious consideration within the administration, of whether Americans would be willing to go to war to defend whatever countries came into NATO—it had always been presumed that all NATO allies would go to each other's defense. Aspin had argued that the United States shouldn't really want more members in NATO. He asked how, with the defense budget going down, the U.S. could take on new commitments. What happens when you put some new countries in and leave others out? Would it be saying to Russia that it's all right to attack Romania but not Hungary? He argued that ethnic struggles could drag NATO countries, including the United States, into war.

Christopher at first favored letting the new countries join NATO according to a timetable and criteria, meanwhile giving some of them associate membership, and the NSC was open to expanding membership. Eventually, the Pentagon came up with the idea of establishing a mechanism by which the NATO aspirants could participate in joint NATO planning and maneuvers and consultation, but not be granted full NATO membership. It was called Partnership for Peacekeeping, but after the events of October 3 in Somalia and the fall from grace of the idea of peacekeeping, the name was changed to Partnership for Peace. Under the new plan, all interested countries, including Russia and Ukraine, could apply. This was a way to avoid drawing a new line in Europe.

During his trip, Clinton was to sell the idea to the Eastern Europeans as an evolutionary step. So the issue was kicked down the road a bit, the real problems of what to do about the former Soviet bloc postponed.

At the end of 1993, Clinton had been once again disinclined to get more involved in Bosnia, and Christopher was once again urging that the policymakers should try to keep Bosnia off the front pages. Lake was arguing for action, but to no avail. However, as the new year came around, and preparations for Brussels were under way, the heavy shelling of Sarajevo couldn't be ignored. There were too many pictures of it on television, and accompanying stories saying that the United States and NATO had failed to act.

U.S. officials knew that Bosnia would have to be addressed in the final NATO communiqué but didn't want the subject to overshadow the summit. Since they had nothing new to propose, they proposed to repeat earlier pledges to use airpower, if necessary, to protect safe areas and to use close air support of UNPROFOR troops under fire, if requested. Britain and France wanted to strengthen that somewhat, and the United States agreed. There was a bit of cynicism behind the whole thing, because there was no clear sign that any of the countries was more inclined than before to act. Later, American officials denied reports that France was the moving force behind a resolution on Bosnia, but a high administration official admitted, "France got it on the NATO agenda."

Even with the changes, the NATO statement issued in Brussels was essentially a reiteration of earlier "commitments."

Clinton told a press conference at the end of the two-day meeting that he had said to his NATO counterparts, "Let us not put this language back in unless we mean it. Let us clearly understand that we must mean it if we put it in this time." He reenacted his little speech, complete with dramatic pauses. This seemed a stagy bit of business, since there was no sign that Clinton himself was any more inclined than before to take action.

A Christopher-leaning administration official said that Lake "deserves the credit—if that's how history views it—for stiffening Clinton's rhetoric in Brussels. Chris was less enthusiastic, because he was concerned about whether we could deliver on the threat."

In Prague, the next stop on Clinton's itinerary, Clinton said in an interview with CBS on the evening of January 11 that the issue of a special counsel would be reexamined. He added that of all the investigators who had looked into Whitewater (there hadn't been very many at that point), "not a single soul has alleged that I've done anything wrong." He said, "I can't recall anything like it in American history." As for the issue itself, Clinton said, "I've left that at home." But he hadn't, of course, because he couldn't.

That night, following picturesque scenes of Clinton and Václav Havel "strolling" through Prague (mobbed by reporters and camera crews) and walking across the photogenic Charles Bridge (to be greeted by American anchormen at the other end) and dinner with Havel in a pub (Stan Greenberg said, "Pictures of Clinton with popular figures like Havel are very helpful"), followed by Clinton playing the saxophone in another pub, the President phoned Washington after midnight, Prague time, to talk about Whitewater. In the call, which went on for over an hour, the President, McLarty, and Gergen were at one end and Mrs. Clinton, Stephanopoulos, Ickes, Lindsey, Kendall, and Nussbaum at the other.

Clinton listened as his wife said that she had concluded that a special counsel was necessary, that otherwise they weren't going to be able to get anything else done. She had also come to feel that a special counsel was inevitable, but said they had to consider the downside. It was up to him, she said. Clinton said that he wanted to "sleep on it." One factor in the President's mind, an aide said later, was that "assuming you did nothing wrong, if a special counsel came out and said so, you'd be better off."

On Wednesday, Clinton went to an old Jewish cemetery in Prague (more good pictures) and met with the leaders of the Visegrad countries—Poland,

Hungary, the Czech Republic, and Slovakia—who reluctantly accepted the proposal for a Partnership for Peace (rather than immediate full membership in NATO) and blew up in an interview with Jim Miklaszewski, of NBC. Clinton, asked about the calls for a special counsel, replied, "Basically the press has editorialized and pressured the politicians into saying, 'Here's a guy that, as far as we know, hasn't done anything wrong, nobody's ever accused him of doing anything wrong, but we think the presumption of guilt almost should be with him. He should somehow prove his innocence.' " When Miklaszewski began to pose another question, Clinton rose, removed his microphone, and snapped, "You've had your two questions, Jim," and, as he strode away, said, "I'm sorry you're not interested in the trip."

That night, as Clinton's plane arrived in Kiev, where he was to meet with Ukrainian President Leonid Kravchuk, to give him support in his effort to get through his parliament a tripartite agreement of the United States, Russia, and Ukraine to dismantle Ukraine's nuclear missiles—the stop had been added at the last minute—his plane was held at the airport while he read over a statement that had been prepared for Stephanopoulos to make in Washington that same day, Washington time, announcing that Clinton was calling for a special counsel. Then, while Clinton dined with Kravchuk, Gearan, who was in Kiev, and Ickes discussed more revisions on an open line between Kiev and Washington, and then Gearan took the proposed final draft to Gergen, at the dinner. By this time, it was late at night, and the entourage had to push on so as to be in Russian airspace by midnight: the Russians wanted to be able to say that Clinton had paid a three-day visit to their country. Clinton, talking to reporters at the Kiev airport, angrily responded to a question about his reaction to Jimmy Carter's saying that day it was time for a special counsel. Clinton said, "I have nothing to say about that on this trip, except that they have been—most of them have been denied the facts that are already in the public record before they made their comment, largely as a result of the way this thing has been discussed. But I have nothing else to say about that."

Even for Clinton, it was a grueling schedule. On all but one night, he gave an interview on *Nightline* with Ted Koppel, which took place at about 1:00 A.M. local time. (These interviews increased the pressure on Clinton to give interviews to the other networks.) Sometimes Clinton would walk the halls, and knock on Gergen's door at 3:00 A.M. to talk. And he had started out on the trip exhausted and emotionally drained.

In Washington that afternoon, Stephanopoulos announced from his old haunt, the podium in the briefing room, that the President was calling for a special counsel. Stephanopoulos said that though no credible allegations of wrongdoing by the Clintons had been made, "This controversy is becoming too much of a distraction. The President wants to get on with the vital issues facing the American people."

The Clintons and many others thought that this would be the end of the matter for a while.

On Thursday morning, in Moscow, there was a splendid scene in the Kremlin of Clinton and Yeltsin striding toward each other on red carpets, both of them smiling broadly. (Mort Engelberg, the movie producer, had done it again.) They clasped arms like dear friends. Each man had a big stake in the other.

The policy toward Russia was considered the jewel in the administration's crown. Some officials even spoke of it in those terms. When things were going bad in Somalia and Haiti and Bosnia, officials would demand to know why there was so much interest in those countries, as opposed to their policy toward Russia, which was working so well.

But in recent months there had been some bumps. Yeltsin had demonstrated authoritarian tendencies in his dissolving of the legislature in September and his temporary suppression of some parties and journals after the October 3 uprising. The elections of December 12 had been a real setback to both Yeltsin and the United States. No one, including U.S. intelligence agencies, had seen it coming. The reform parties, divided and having campaigned desultorily, did poorly. The forces of reaction, led by the demagogic Vladimir Zhirinovsky, won nearly 25 percent of the parliamentary seats, the largest bloc. Zhirinovsky had campaigned against the reform program and what he said was excessive U.S. interference in Russia's internal matters. He called for, among other things, retaking the Russian empire (including Alaska) and spending more for the military—who voted for him in large numbers.

U.S. officials made a big thing of the fact that the Russians had approved a new constitution (which gave the President expanded power) but were clearly taken aback by the parliamentary elections. Matters were made all the more sticky because Gore and Talbott, along with some other top officials, were on their way to Russia and were scheduled to arrive in Moscow on the day after the elections. No one in the administration had foreseen the possibility that they might be arriving to anything other than a triumph of the reform policies the United States so ardently backed.

Officials in Washington and on Gore's plane scrambled for what to say about the elections. In one statement, Gore bashed the international finance institutions (or IFIs) for their insistence on painful economic reform.

Gore's rhetoric about the elections became increasingly tough, culminating in his saying that Zhirinovsky's views—which encompassed anti-Semitism and threats to use nuclear power against Russia's neighbors—were "anathema to freedom-loving people in Russia, in the United States, and everywhere in the world." In Washington, Clinton termed the election "a protest vote" and painted it as a populist reaction. Inevitably, the administration came under increasing criticism for staking too much on Yeltsin. Officials denied that was the case and then took some steps to try to show that it wasn't.

On Sunday, December 19, after Talbott's return, Christopher went to his house to discuss the implications. They agreed that reform and privatization should go forward but the international community and Russia needed to ease the pain that was being inflicted. Christopher concluded that the process had been too theoretical. He and Talbott also believed that the reformers, including Yeltsin, should do more about building coalitions. The challenge was to adjust the administration's policy without appearing to be changing the policy—which might be an admission of a mistake.

In a press briefing at the State Department the next day, Talbott tried to make the simple point that there were limits on what the body politic could take. To show broad support for reformers, not just Yeltsin, he said, "We're supporting a process . . . and there are many people who are part of it." Talbott said that the reform concept of "shock therapy" should be adjusted: "There should be less shock and more therapy." It was a nice sound bite and made a lot of news. The press interpretation was that the Clinton administration was backing a slower pace of reform. Administration officials rushed to say that Talbott's briefing had been "overinterpreted." A top official said privately that the comment "contributed to the impression of postelection shock on the part of the administration. There was some truth to that."

In January, in Moscow, Clinton did the usual picturesque things (a walk in Red Square, wearing a fur hat) and made some "unscheduled" stops—at a Russian Orthodox church (where he lit a candle for his mother), at a food store. In a press conference, Clinton said, "The President gave me strong assurances of his intention to continue the reform process."

That evening, Clinton hosted a reception at the residence of the American ambassador (Zhirinovsky wasn't invited), and then he and some of his entourage dined at Yeltsin's large dacha. "Nice place you have here," Clinton joked as he arrived. For one course, the group was served moose lips, a Russian delicacy that looked like very large mushrooms and tasted, according to a member of the entourage, "disgusting."

Following the dinner, Clinton gave another *Nightline* interview, in which

Koppel referred to Clinton's stalking out of his interview with Miklaszewski the night before. Clinton, obviously very tired, said, "I literally had no idea that it was going to be asked." He continued, "You have to understand. I mean, I guess the media's been obsessed with this, but it never crosses my mind." He added, "I had no earthly idea what was going to be asked."

On Friday, Hillary Clinton arrived in Moscow, and it was widely noted within the President's entourage that "she looks like hell." Also on Friday, the President did a Clintonesque thing, holding a town meeting at the Ostankino television station, which the rebels had tried to seize on October 3, with a linkup to audiences in three other cities. Clinton was trying to cheer up Russia. ("If you choose hope over fear, then you will be rewarded.") He felt that if he could infect the country with his optimism, it would go about the reform process with a more positive attitude. In the "town meeting," Clinton showed some lack of foreign policy grasp, likening Russia's involvement in its neighbors' internal affairs to American intervention in Grenada and Panama, and making a confused statement about Bosnia.

On that same day, Clinton signed the agreement with Russia and Ukraine to dismantle Ukrainian nuclear weapons. The United States and Russia also made an agreement to retarget their own nuclear weapons away from each other, but this didn't mean much since they could be retargeted again within five minutes. (Belarus and Kazakhstan also agreed to give up their nuclear weapons.) On January 14, while Clinton was in Moscow, Russia and Ukraine announced that they wanted to join the Partnership for Peace. (Russia formally joined the Partnership on June 22, 1994.)

The day after Clinton left Russia, Yegor Gaidar, Deputy Prime Minister, resigned over the slowing pace of reform. Five days after Clinton left, the Finance Minister and reformer Boris Fyodorov quit. The Prime Minister, Viktor Chernomyrdin, announcing a new cabinet heavily made up of old bureaucrats and industrialists, said, "the period of market romanticism is now over." Clinton said later that Yeltsin had told him that Gaidar might resign. Even so, all this made it look as if Clinton had been ingenuous while in Russia.

After leaving Russia, the Clinton entourage stopped in Minsk, Belarus, because Belarus had agreed to surrender its nuclear weapons and because it had an enlightened leader—who was ousted eleven days later.

Later that day, it was on to Geneva, for a meeting with Hafez Assad, the President of Syria.

Then it was back to Washington.

Despite the glitches and the subsequent disappointments, even embarrassments, the President's trip went over well with the public. Clinton looked good and seemed more in command than he sometimes did. It gave him a real lift at an important time.

Clinton returned worried about Russia, concerned that its people would give up on trying to reform the place politically as well as economically. He felt he could sense this through his ability to read other leaders' political situations.

An aide said that as Clinton returned to Washington, he was also worried about the Democrats' losing working control of the House in the 1994 elections, and about New Hampshire. Asked why Clinton was worried about New Hampshire at that point, the aide replied, "You always have to worry about New Hampshire."

• • •

Despite the empty gestures in Brussels, Bosnia returned to the administration's plate soon enough. At a breakfast meeting in Paris, on January 24, with French Foreign Minister Alain Juppe, Christopher was pressed hard for a new U.S. effort to bring pressure on the Muslims to settle. Christopher said that the United States wouldn't do that—and a very public transatlantic argument ensued. Juppe immediately leaked details of the argument to the *New York Times,* which the following day ran a story on its front page, headed U.S. REJECTS PLEA TO ACT IN BOSNIA. On the same day, Clinton told reporters, "I don't think that the international community has the capacity to stop people . . . from their civil wars." On February 1, in Washington, British Foreign Minister Douglas Hurd gave Christopher a similar lecture over a private lunch in the Secretary's dining room. Donilon, unrelenting in his efforts to boost his boss's reputation, later spun (successfully) that Christopher then seized the initiative for coming up with a new Bosnia policy.

In reality, State Department officials had been already at work drawing up new proposals and saw Christopher's displeasure over his encounters with his counterparts, and the resulting bad publicity, as an opening for pushing a new initiative. At the same time, members of the NSC staff had been working on a new policy along the same lines. Moreover, there had been some shifts of view in other parts of the administration. The new Secretary of Defense, William Perry had all along been more inclined to use airpower in Bosnia than Aspin had been, and General Shalikashvili offered less opposition than Powell had (though "Shali," as everyone called him, did ask some hard questions). Clinton told aides that he was more comfortable with Shali than he had been with Powell.

On Saturday, February 5, at a little after 7:30 A.M., Lake was informed by the Situation Room that a large mortar shell had hit the main marketplace in Sarajevo and a large number of people had been killed. Later that morning, Christopher and Lake met in the White House, as already planned, to compare notes on the work of their respective staffs. (Perry was out of the country.) Christopher brought a proposal for a new round of diplomatic efforts, combined with the threat of military pressure, and as a cover letter a strong memorandum saying, "I am acutely uncomfortable with the passive position we are now in." But Christopher had been heavily responsible for that "passive position." To no one's surprise, the memorandum was later leaked to the press. Later some administration officials spun that the new policy had been decided upon before the marketplace bombing—but that wasn't quite the case.

Following the marketplace attack, the administration, adopting a variation on a French proposal, proposed to set up an "exclusion zone" around Sarajevo and demand that the Serbs remove their heavy weapons from the area or place them under UN control by 7:00 P.M., EST, Sunday, February 20, or face air attack. Further, the proposal said that, starting immediately after the NATO ultimatum was issued, any Serb shelling on Sarajevo would be met with air strikes. At the same time, the new diplomatic approach pressing for a settlement was put in motion. If the Bosnian Serbs rejected a peace plan that the Muslims agreed to and the allies found reasonable, there was to be military pressure on the Serbs. (Lake offered to go to Europe to sell the plan, but Christopher objected, pointing out that Lake had written in one of his books that the National Security Adviser shouldn't conduct diplomacy.) On February 9, at an emergency NAC meeting, the allies agreed—after fourteen hours of debate—to go along with the administration's plan. It had been six months and hundreds of lives since NATO first agreed to protect such areas.

Whether the administration and its allies would have done anything militarily about Sarajevo if the attack, and the terrible television pictures, had not happened cannot be known. The administration had been moving toward a new policy of diplomacy that could have used military force, but this hadn't involved setting up the special protection for Sarajevo. And there's a strong question as to whether NATO would have agreed to any new policy absent the mortar attack. An official said, "The marketplace bombing made it possible for us to get NATO agreement in general."

On Saturday, February 19, the President turned his regular radio address into a televised address, laying out the threat against the Serbs around Sarajevo. Included in his reasons for this action was that Bosnia was "in our interests." Donilon, Stephanopoulos, and Gearan had been leery of making Bosnia a prominent issue again.

To the administration's pleasure and relief, the Serbs yielded to the NATO threat—more or less. Some heavy weapons weren't put under UN control, as they were supposed to be, and not all were removed. The possibility remained (and turned out to be the case) that the Serbs would simply move some of the heavy weapons to another area. Still, this was the allies' first real threat to use force, and it essentially worked.

Almost immediately, the administration began discussing whether the Sarajevo plan could be applied elsewhere in Bosnia. Shalikashvili was dubious; the general view in the Pentagon was that factors that made the Sarajevo action possible weren't present in the other "safe areas."

Lake was nevertheless pleased and optimistic. On Monday, February 21, in his office, he said, "We have some momentum. I don't know how successfully we're going to be able to use it now. We're working on it. This is the Balkans."

In early April, when Serb shelling made it appear that the Muslim town of Gorazde, in southeast Bosnia at a strategic point on the Drina River, would fall, the administration within one week spoke with many voices. Perry, who prided himself on being straightforward and had things to learn about public communication, said on *Meet the Press* on April 3 that the United States had no intention of entering the war. Perry was saying what he thought should be the policy, but he seemed to be giving the green light to the Serb forces. Three days later, General Shalikashvili made similar but somewhat more ambiguous comments, but the nuances weren't picked up by the press. Secretary of State Christopher said in two interviews that week, "*I'm* the principal foreign policy spokesman." He suggested that a different direction would be taken. On Thursday, in a previously scheduled speech, National Security Adviser Lake said, "Let me be clear. Neither the President, nor any of his senior advisers, rules out the use of airpower to help stop attacks such as those against Gorazde." As the Serb pounding of Gorazde continued, the U.S., NATO, and the UN fumbled for a response. The multiple check-off points for air strikes—ending with the UN—paralyzed action for a while, caused friction between NATO and the UN, and then made what action that was taken look puny. The few bombs dropped were on tents, a tank, and three armored personnel carriers. A frustrated and embarrassed Clinton administration pressed successfully for a NATO ultimatum and, slowly, the Serbs complied, leaving Gorazde, much of it destroyed, encircled but no longer under heavy attack.

Next, the United States, Britain, France, Germany, and Russia—constituting themselves as the "contact group"—turned to trying to force a settlement on the Bosnian Serbs and Muslims in negotiations in Geneva.

29

ANNIVERSARY

"Though We Are Making a Difference, Our Work Has Just Begun"

Clinton wasn't to be at all allowed to ease back into his job after his trip to Europe and Russia. On Monday, January 17, the day after his return, though clearly exhausted and hoarse, he spoke at a couple of events—at the White House and at Howard University—honoring Martin Luther King's birthday.

Inman withdrew on Tuesday. The search for another new Secretary of Defense had begun. On Wednesday, Clinton was to make a day trip to California, which had been hit by a terrible earthquake on Monday. On Thursday, he was to give a speech commemorating the anniversary of his inauguration—at Georgetown University, where he had made his preliminary campaign speeches in 1991. He was to make his first State of the Union address the following week.

A year into his Presidency, Clinton's advisers were still wrestling with how he should talk to the public. The problem was how to point to progress without inviting more skepticism from an already skeptical public and, since the recovery was uneven, without looking as if Clinton didn't understand people's real situations, the way Bush had looked. Clinton felt he'd learned how hard it was to break through to the public with a message. He was still looking for a way to be more of an explainer, to assume the educative role of the President. "We had a narrower view," Stan Greenberg said. "We saw it as explaining NAFTA, period—as opposed to addressing the longing people in this country have for a long-term vision." Clinton had tried to do that at the University of North Carolina, but that speech's theme of "security" had subsequently been set aside. Greenberg said, "Within the administration, people think it's a means, not an end itself."

At lunch on the nineteenth, the day before Clinton's anniversary, Stephanopoulos said that CBS News was going to show that night that Clinton stood higher at the end of his first year than either Carter or Reagan, and that a *Wall Street Journal*/NBC poll would show a 60 percent approval rating. The *Washington Post*/ABC poll had Clinton's approval rating at 60 percent, the highest since the inauguration. Stephanopoulos said, "You take away all the mishaps and the critiques and the ugliness in the process, and we're still making progress, and that's what matters. All this debate about whether Clinton changed Washington or Washington changed Clinton—it doesn't matter very much. What happens outside of Washington is important. Most people are doing better—not everyone, but most. What people know about him at the end of the first year is that he's trying, and they give him credit for that."

January 20, Clinton's anniversary, was a gray, bleak day. The city was covered with ice, the streets and sidewalks treacherous. Many people were trapped in their homes. There wasn't enough fuel, the government was shut down, and there were occasional blackouts throughout the day. Those White House aides who could show up at all were late in reaching their offices. The President's anniversary speech, which was to be a recapitulation of his accomplishments, plus a little visionary talk, was canceled.

And on the anniversary of Clinton's first year in office, Janet Reno announced that she was naming as special counsel Robert Fiske, a Republican who had been appointed U.S. attorney for the southern district of New York by Jimmy Carter and was now a partner in a Wall Street firm.

Clinton spent a quiet day: he had his intelligence briefing, worked on his State of the Union speech, and got ready for an interview with Larry King that night—his other big anniversary event. His aides prepared him for some of the current tabloid issues: Tonya Harding v. Nancy Kerrigan, the Menendez brothers, the Lorena Bobbitt trial. The President was advised to respond that justice should be allowed to work its way. He rested in the afternoon.

On the Larry King show, broadcast from the White House library, Clinton said that "it was a little tougher to change things than I thought it would be" —a fact that he attributed to the Washington "culture." In an attempt to fix up his image after his December battering, Clinton mentioned his family several times, saying twice that it bothered him when his wife and daughter were hurt because he was in public service.

As usual, Clinton put on a smooth performance. He appeared sincere—a look he had mastered—his blue eyes looking right into the camera, right at the viewer. And he pretended to be more calm about his recent troubles than he really was.

Clinton attempted to paint himself as philosophical, to suggest that he had risen above all that: he was a President who had brushed away pesky gnats, was unbothered by untoward stories in the press, had an inner serenity that should reassure the public and help it to keep things in their proper proportion. But Clinton wasn't really like that. If he had a bad day, everyone in the White House knew it.

Clinton told King that his administration was facing "tough issues that have been ignored for too long, and everybody here gets up and goes to work every day and works like crazy." (The impression that Clinton was working hard on the nation's problems was one of his strong points in the polls.) He added, "If the bad days come with it, that's part of life."

Clinton's first State of the Union speech, on January 25, was a political masterwork. With agility and energy, and speaking for sixty-three minutes, he wove his way through the issues, avoiding ideological traps, and preempting Republican issues. He demonstrated the sweep and ambition of his domestic program; the contrast with the limited and dry section on foreign policy was noticeable. The speech went over better than it was. This was often the case with Clinton speeches. Its calculation and poll-drivenness were too obvious for the speech to qualify for greatness. It was a deliberate attempt to push Clinton's numbers up and put more steam behind his program. The address was aimed at the public mass, not the people in the hall or the press. But Clinton was now master of the speech to the big hall, with the political audience as his prop. He showed more confidence than he had a year earlier, when he also had done well. He had become comfortable with speaking with eloquence and passion about domestic issues. To people familiar with his rhetoric, the speech had a ring of Clinton's greatest hits, but, David Gergen had argued, most people hadn't heard all his rhetoric, and this was his biggest opportunity to reach them.

Whether this would move the members of Congress was another question. Theirs would be a complicated calculation, to be made only when necessary and to be based on, among other things, Clinton's staying power, factors at home, the pressures of contributors.

As had become the custom by now, Clinton's speech reached Capitol Hill moments before he was to speak. It had gone through ten drafts and, as usual, was essentially rewritten that day during the rehearsal in the family theater. The draft was too thematic for Clinton's taste: he wanted to list things, spell things out.

The Reaganesque touches were striking. The Clintons carried the guest-in-the-balcony routine to new lengths. Lane Kirkland was on one side of Mrs. Clinton, and on the other was Jack Smith, the CEO of General Motors. With both sides in NAFTA, and two very important forces on health care, seated by the First Lady, it went on from there. Also in the gallery were Tom O'Neill, son of Tip, who had died in early January a popular figure; T. Berry Brazelton, a childhood development expert (who had also been there for the President's health care speech); a community policeman who patrolled a tough neighborhood in New York; James Brady. Like Reagan, Clinton was anecdotal, even reading a letter to Mrs. Clinton from a couple who had lost their health insurance and been forced into bankruptcy.

Clinton resolved the question of how to claim achievements without seeming insensitive to people whose lot hadn't improved measurably, by citing the achievements—the deficit reduction program, NAFTA, the Brady bill, the investments, more affordable college loans, national service, and others—and then saying, "Though we are making a difference, our work has just begun." He added, "Many Americans still haven't felt the impact of what we've done. The recovery still hasn't touched every community or created enough jobs. Incomes are still stagnant. There's still too much violence." (The speech was regionally conscious.) And then he called for action on many other programs: his Goals 2000 education program, revamping the unemployment system, health care reform, welfare and anticrime measures.

Clinton's embrace of anticrime legislation wasn't a new thing for him: an anticrime position had long been part of his New Democrat identity. But now the issue had taken on a new urgency—and political salience. A punitive crime bill was already moving through the Congress (the death penalty was applied to about sixty new crimes, though just federal ones). According to the presentation Greenberg had made to Clinton advisers a week earlier, crime was far and away the issue uppermost on people's minds—way beyond the economy. (The fact that the economy was doing well may have had something to do with that.) Clinton endorsed a proposal called "three strikes and you're out" (jail without parole for committing three violent crimes), which gave his Attorney General and some Democratic congressional leaders great pause and was largely irrelevant to what was upsetting people (it, too, only covered federal crimes). In fact, the incidence of violent crimes was down from 1981, but the use of guns by youths was way up. The famous recent incidents—such as the kidnap and murder of a twelve-year-old girl from a slumber party in her home in Petaluma, California—intensified television coverage of violence, and the seemingly rampant gunning down of kids by kids had led to a sense of national crisis. Clinton adroitly sidestepped the prevention/punishment issue (his Attorney General was outspokenly for emphasis on prevention) by calling for a "tough and smart" bill. Though Clinton didn't emphasize it, given the politics of the moment, there were also substantial funds in the crime bill (eventually, about $9 billion) for "prevention," including job training for youths and making schools into community centers. And he renewed his request for more community policemen, pointing to the guest in the balcony.

Despite the rhetoric about the importance of changing the welfare system, there wasn't a dollar in the new budget for welfare reform, nor was a proposal ready. But welfare reform was one of Clinton's New Democrat touchstones, and a way of preempting Republicans and of assuaging Senator Moynihan, who would preside over the Finance Committee's deliberations and who had said recently that there was no health care crisis but there *was* a welfare crisis, and of pleasing the governors, who were about to come to town again.

Clinton made a strong case for the health care reform program—this was its third launching. It was now called "guaranteed private health insurance," to get away from the idea that it was a large government insurance program. The proposal had been limping, and Clinton was worried about the program's fate. His theatrical brandishing of a pen, saying that he would veto any bill that didn't contain universal coverage, repeated his sole nonnegotiable demand—one that left room for interpretation. But it was theatrical, and gave him his headline. The intent was to establish that he was resuming command of the health care debate (even though it didn't work out that way). The political burden of the health care section of the speech was to offset the insurance industry ads and make the case that the program would be a net gain for the middle class.

Clinton gave a little *tour d'horizon* of his recent trip and expressed his goal of a great united Europe through the Partnership for Peace. The only thing he had to say about Bosnia—after lecturing the allies in Brussels—was to mention the fact that the military were "carrying out the longest humanitarian airlift in history." He said, "we will continue to press for the restoration of true democracy in Haiti." (At that point, the administration had fallen out with Aristide over the terms of his return and was deliberating on what to do next.) And he made a sweeping pledge "to support the advance of democracy everywhere."

Like Reagan, the President talked values—deploring "the loss of values" —but in Clinton's case this wasn't a substitute for inaction. Yet Clinton understood the political appeal of the issue and sounded most Reagan-like, in cadence as well as in thought, when he said, "We can't renew our country until we realize that governments don't raise children, parents do." Clinton was going right at Reagan's base; it was the crossover of some of that base that had made Clinton President. Welfare and crime were good issues for Clinton's "profile"—a subject his advisers still had in mind. Behind the rhetoric lay an activist agenda.

His passage on what he meant by values had a touch of eloquence: "Let's give our children a future. Let us take away their guns and give them books. Let us overcome their despair and replace it with hope. . . ."

He ended on an optimistic note. Reagan had perfected the politics of optimism, but Clinton was quite good at it himself. As Jimmy Carter learned painfully, the American people don't want to be told that they're depressed. Referring to the natural disasters that had occurred during his Presidency—the floods in the Midwest, the California earthquake—where the American people "rose to the occasion . . . showing the better angels of our nature," he concluded, "Let us not reserve the better angels only for natural disasters, leaving our deepest and most profound problems to petty political fighting. Let us instead be true to our spirit, facing facts, coming together, bringing hope, and moving forward."

But the White House had no plans for the President to stay with the "violence" and "values" themes (other than continue to fight for the crime bill), to rally the nation to new action, to make a crusade of his rhetoric that no one should go without opportunity and responsibility. His rhetoric on violence fit the mood of the times and he was on to something big, but he left it there.

Following the speech, Clinton stopped in the Old Executive Office Building, where he took some of the calls from citizens.

The next day, and the next, Clinton's throat was so sore, and he was so hoarse, that a doctor ordered that his public events be canceled. Clinton's voice had finally given out.

At the end of Clinton's first eighteen months in office the public remained hesitant about him, and, if anything, had grown increasingly so. The cluster of defects that could be listed under the term "character"—his "Slick Willie" aspect and all that that conveyed, his inclination to avoid responsibility for some of his acts, his lack of discipline, and his reckless streak (at least in the past)—endangered his Presidency.

He and his aides were facing the possibility that the public trust essential to governing was evaporating and might soon be gone, and perhaps irretrievable. His closest friends and aides were quietly worrying that this was the case. His high poll ratings early in the year evaporated in the face of Whitewater, the Paula Jones suit, his stalled domestic program, and his patchwork foreign policy. Clinton's apparently successful press conference on March 7 didn't—as was so often the case with him—settle things for long. Mrs. Clinton's surprise press conference on April 22, where she was the epitome of calm, saying she was pleased to be asked this or that, laid little to rest—including how she made $100,000 in commodities futures in one year. Clinton himself knew his Presidency was in trouble. In the instance of the all-important health care bill, he and his wife had overreached, and had lost control of the debate. If there was to be salvation, others would have to deliver it.

Because of the public doubts about him, and because of the "character" issues, and also because he had been undisciplined in talking about his efforts, Clinton, to the great frustration of the White House, wasn't getting credit for his substantial achievements. His Presidency was a blur. Moreover, his leverage with the Congress had diminished. Members had long since learned that there was nothing to fear from opposing him, but now his lack of popularity with the public provided little reason to stand with him. He received scant praise for an improved economy and 4 million new jobs.

The things that went wrong because of Clinton's loose, lax governing style distracted him and his staff and drew public attention away from his substantive efforts. They contributed to a lessening of confidence in him.

Some of Clinton's problems in foreign policy could be attributed to the fact that he inherited a messy post–Cold War world, and problems that his predecessor had ignored (Bosnia, Haiti, North Korea) or left unresolved (Somalia). But Clinton's failure to pay sufficient attention to foreign policy was a form of self-indulgence, and costly. His pollsters had told him the public didn't want their President spending a lot of time on foreign policy, so he got into a self-perpetuating cycle of not making it an important part of his Presidency, and not leading the public on the subject because the public was presumed not to care about it, nor to want him to spend much time on it. But the public did want a President to demonstrate competence in foreign policy. There were some positive aspects of the Clinton administration's foreign policy efforts—the relationship with Russia, and the nudging of Middle Eastern countries toward a broader settlement after the breakthrough agreement between Israel and the Palestinians. But, as on domestic issues, the successes were far overshadowed by negative developments and mishandling of certain foreign challenges. By the spring of 1994 the danger Clinton had been courting materialized: the lack of public confidence in his management of foreign policy spilled over into a lack of confidence in his Presidency as a whole. By the summer it was the largest negative in his poll ratings.

Clinton's deliberate demystification of the Presidency came back to hurt him. In his frenzied efforts to "get close to the people," to be accessible, to popularize the Presidency—telling a questioner on MTV that he wore briefs—he wiped away much of the mystique of the office, took risks with the authority of the office. In due course, he was out there without its protective wrapping. Clinton became an undifferentiated President. Staff members said he had become so familiar to the public that when he was on television people at airports didn't stop to watch. (That more than one said this in precisely the same terms suggested how much it was on the minds of his aides.)

Bill Clinton was well motivated, and serious about using his time in office to serious purpose. He had a sense of where he wanted to take the country—even a "vision"—and how he wanted to improve the lives and potential of its citizens. He reached high. He was an activist President in a cynical age. He didn't, as some charged, lack a core. In trying to win office, and then to govern from a minority position and with narrow congressional margins—and, of course, to be reelected—he moved within a spectrum. The spectrum may have been too wide for some Democrats' taste and too narrow for others' (Democrat or no). His famed "flexibility" in some cases accounted for his legislative success, but it also made it increasingly difficult to convince a number of legislators—at least twice burned—to take a chance for him. His abandonment, early in his Presidency, of the stimulus bill and the Btu tax haunted his legislative efforts from then on.

But Clinton was a grower and a learner, and in late June 1994, frustrated and concerned that his Presidency was in serious trouble, he yielded to the importunings of friends, and by now, also his wife and his Vice President, and made changes in the White House staff. (Gore played a large role in the rearrangement.) Clinton replaced his lifelong friend Mack McLarty as Chief of Staff with Leon Panetta, the Director of the Office of Management and Budget, and gave Panetta a franchise to change the way the White House staff worked. (Alice Rivlin became OMB Director.) This action represented a painful and belated recognition on Clinton's part that the place had to be more disciplined; that he would be better served by someone who knew Washington well; that governing *was* different from campaigning, and that he had relied too heavily for too long on former campaign aides—that he needed more experience and maturity around him. The consultants (who didn't know about the shake-up before it happened) were to be reined in. Clinton showed that he was now willing to confront the fact that his Arkansas friends might not have been up to the jobs in which he had placed them. McLarty would stay as a counselor, so he could continue to spend time at the President's side, and play the role of ambassador to moderate and conservative Democrats and the business community, but the reduction in the number and roles of the Arkansans in the Clinton administration by the end of his first year and a half was of striking proportions. David Gergen (who was planning to leave by the end of the year anyway), increasingly isolated and now without the one ally (McLarty) in a position to help him, was sent to the State Department, but he got his long-coveted seat on the Principals Committee. Making these changes was also a way of braking the criticism of Clinton's governing style, of (as in the instances of changing Stephanopoulos's job and bringing in Gergen) "getting some space," as one adviser put it.

Still, the dangers to his Presidency were real enough. Whitewater could remain alive, or even grow. Even if it didn't, and despite the Clintons' perhaps valid claim that it was all minor stuff that had happened long ago, it had caused damage. It raised new questions about the Clintons; it was another distraction—a big one. A number of their aides who tried to lessen the damage to the Clintons were damaged themselves.

Clinton also faced potentially paralyzing party losses in the November midterm elections. In that regard, he was right to try to achieve as much as possible as early as he could. That the strength of his Presidency rested almost entirely on legislative achievements—not on a strong public affection for him, or even respect for him, or an ideological identification with him—put his Presidency at constant risk. This shaky base could cave from under him if he stopped having legislative successes—but it was the only base available to him. The "third way" was an electoral strategy, and a technique, if only a partially successful one, for governing by breaking longstanding impasses. It wasn't a clarion call, or something that would capture public imagination.

Despite all the difficulties, Clinton had accomplished a great deal, and turned the country in a new direction. And this man, who had been so resilient in the past, personally and politically, was still in a position to be seen as a successful President—albeit one with a rocky tenure in office.

But surviving crises wasn't the same thing as deepening, or even holding on to, the public trust. This trust kept eroding, largely, but not entirely, because of his own traits. Each crisis undermined his position further, and made it more difficult to achieve his large goals. To the end, Clinton's Presidency would be a war between his ambitions and his flaws.

EPILOGUE

"I've Got to Be More Like John Wayne"

Leon Panetta wasn't long in the job of Chief of Staff before differences from the former regime were apparent. Clinton and Gore had decided that the two largest problems were the management of the White House and foreign policy—on which the President continued to draw heavy negatives in the polls. When Panetta met with the Clintons and the Gores at Camp David on the weekend of June 25–26, before he was named on Monday, he asked for and was given a large writ of authority from the President to make changes. Panetta knew enough about the Clinton White House to obtain the same authority also from the Vice President and the First Lady.

Shortly after he moved into McLarty's office on July 17, there was a general tightening up. Meetings with Clinton were fewer, with fewer people in attendance, and were less likely to be held before the subject was ready for the President's attention. Walk-in privileges to the Oval Office were drastically reduced; even Lake, Lindsey, and Stephanopoulos had to go through Panetta. No decision papers, not even from the National Security Council, went to the President without Panetta's review. If he felt that the President wasn't given enough options, Panetta would send a paper back. By many accounts, Panetta ran meetings crisply, moved sessions in the Oval Office along, and had little tolerance for the reopening of previously decided subjects. White House aides said with relief that it was easier to get decisions made, and more likely that they would stick. Panetta also took over the scheduling operation, which had been chaotic.

Panetta moved to reduce the freelancing by staff members with no clear line of authority or responsibility. Stephanopoulos spent a great deal more time in Panetta's office than he had in McLarty's, talking policy and Capitol Hill strategy with Panetta, in effect serving as his Deputy Chief of Staff on these matters—the job Stephanopoulos used to covet. Stephanopoulos understood that the President was in such trouble that things had to change. And he appreciated the fact that the White House now had a center where things got decided. Lindsey was given specific legal chores (such as the baseball strike), and Panetta planned to make him part of the counsel's office. McLarty would spend most of his time making speeches to business groups. (Gergen was already at the State Department.)

Panetta also reined in the consultants, who were now to report to Harold Ickes. When Stan Greenberg met with the President to give him his poll findings, Panetta and Ickes were also present. A White House official said, "The Chief of Staff runs the White House, the pollster doesn't run the White House." (Panetta also pushed out David Wilhelm, the well liked but miscast chairman of the Democratic National Committee.) Panetta instituted a 7:30 A.M. meeting with a small number of top staff people—much smaller than the senior staff meetings, which had become largely useless. These meetings set the agenda for the day, and also for the longer run.

National Security Adviser Tony Lake was asked to attend these 7:30 meetings. Panetta wanted to make the foreign policy part of the White House less of a separate entity and get more consideration of the political implications of foreign policy decisions. Panetta put himself on the Principals Committee and sat in on the President's national security briefings. Panetta was taking on an awful lot, which had its own dangers, and because more changes were looming, there was unease among the White House staff.

Panetta himself spent a lot of time with the President, and the effects of his influence were soon seen—in a more disciplined Clinton. The President was now more likely to stick to one subject a day in his public appearances. There were far fewer photo ops, at which Clinton might be asked to pronounce on any subject and usually did. When Clinton made a statement on foreign policy, he now declined to take questions on other subjects. When he went out on the South Lawn to make a statement on the morning after the defeat of a rule for debating the crime bill, he obeyed instructions to not take questions.

Clinton, aware that his Presidency was in serious trouble, was willing to listen to advice. This was the Clinton who could be objective about himself and his situation. As Panetta saw it, one of the first and most important orders of business was to try to restore the President's stature. Panetta understood that it had been eroded by, among other things, a President who had become too familiar and had been on too many talk shows. Panetta started reducing the amount the public saw of the seriously overexposed President and increased the ratio of press conferences to other appearances, because Clinton looked more Presidential standing behind a podium. He emphasized to Clinton the importance of the stature of the office. Accepting the point, Clinton replied, "I've got to be more like John Wayne."

Panetta also felt that Clinton needed to move to the center. Panetta himself, as a popular former Member of Congress, and a powerful one, spent a great deal of time during his first weeks on the new job on congressional strategy—especially as the White House was faced with crises over health care and the crime bill. Some of the rearranging, including personnel changes, had to wait until after the legislative crises.

Panetta laughed easily and hard, but he could also be quite tough—he had been a popular choice as the new Chief of Staff. Some said that if he hadn't been on the scene, the shake-up would have been far more difficult to pull off.

According to reliable reports, Mrs. Clinton had concluded a long time before the shake-up that it was necessary, and the President had accepted it but had a hard time removing his friend McLarty from the Chief of Staff job. ("That's been the fundamental mistake all along," an adviser to the Clintons said.) Mrs. Clinton and her husband spent the weekend of June 18–19 alone at Camp David, presumably discussing it. (By mid-1994 the Clintons had come to appreciate escaping to Camp David.) Gore, too, felt a change was of critical importance, and it was he who finally confronted a wavering McLarty with this, just a few days before the changes were announced.

As he took over, Panetta somewhat clumsily let it get about that he was considering replacements for Mark Gearan, the communications director, and Dee Dee Myers, the press secretary, before talking with them. For the second time in the Clinton Presidency, the target was the communications office, on the ground that Clinton's achievements weren't getting across. Clinton was particularly upset that his signing, on May 16, of his principal education bill, Goals 2000, went virtually unnoticed by the public.

The other Clinton, the one who blamed others and outside forces and the times and enemies and a cynical press for his troubles, was also much in evidence. Both Clintons continued to feel beleaguered. Clinton complained privately that the public was in 1965 in terms of what it wanted government to do and in the 1980s in terms of what it trusted government to do. He'd tell aides, "It's only when I lose or when there's tremendous controversy that what I'm doing gets covered." An aide said, "What frustrates him most is the idea that he was doing what he was elected to do, and in large part succeeding, and he wasn't getting credit for that."

While there was some truth to what the Clintons were complaining about, some of these factors were surmountable; others came with the Presidency and weren't unique to theirs. The First Couple flirted with coming off as whiners. And their thinking in these terms could get in the way of self-corrective actions.

The Whitewater hearings by the House and Senate Banking Committees, which ran from July 25 to August 5, were more damaging to the administration than it had expected. A White House official said, "The hearings took a lot of time and focus here, and did have an impact on the public mind." On June 30, Special Counsel Robert Fiske issued reports saying that Vince Foster had definitely committed suicide, and that the contacts between White House and Treasury officials over the Resolution Trust Corporation's investigation of Madison Guaranty didn't constitute criminal behavior. Though the hearings were limited to only those matters on which Fiske had completed his investigation, they did their damage. The White House's goal was to make the case that no effort had been made to stop the RTC investigation, which had gone forward. While the hearings didn't establish that there had been such an effort, they did show that there had been a great deal of scurrying around on the matter on the part of Treasury and White House officials, and that a high-level effort had been made to keep Deputy Treasury Secretary Roger Altman from recusing himself from the Madison case.

The mere fact of the hearings—the sight of so many Clinton aides having to go before the Congress to explain their actions—was damaging enough, but this was compounded by the large quantities of conflicting testimony and memory lapses. The conflicting testimony of Treasury Secretary Lloyd Bentsen, Altman, and Treasury Counsel Jean Hanson over whether Altman had "tasked" Hanson to tell Bernard Nussbaum about the criminal referral and whether she had informed Bentsen of the White House meeting indicated the sensitive territory these people had been traversing. The main target of the Senate hearings was Altman, who had been less than forthcoming in his testimony before the committee in February—leaving out, among other things, the fact that at the February 2 meeting, the fateful one, he had been pressured by White House officials not to recuse himself. Even some Democrats were disturbed by Altman's lack of candor, because that went to the point of congressional prerogatives and the ability of the Congress to discharge its oversight function.

It was clear enough through leaks before the hearings began that Altman was for some people the designated fall guy. But one or two White House officials genuinely thought that Altman had an insuperable problem with the Senate committee; others had lingering resentments over some of Altman's behavior in the case. In the hearings, Altman denied that he had misled the committee, and after the hearings ended he tried to stick it out. But the White House let it be known through leaks that Donald Riegle and his successor as chairman, Paul Sarbanes of Maryland, one of the most respected senators, had told White House officials that they would have problems with Altman's staying in his job. Altman bowed to the building pressure and resigned on August 17. An able public servant, the kind that the government needs, had made a mistake and paid a large price. Hanson, as expected, resigned the next day.

On the Friday afternoon, August 5, that the hearings ended, the sudden news that a three-judge panel, acting under the reenacted independent prosecutor law, had decided to replace Fiske with a conservative Republican came as a body blow to the White House people. They had just begun to feel relief that the hearings they'd spent many hours preparing for, and about which they had been extremely tense, had ended and nothing terrible had happened. Now there was the grim prospect that the independent prosecutor process would take longer and that some subjects might be reopened. The anger and dismay went all the way up to the Clintons. The appointment of Kenneth Starr, a former Solicitor General in the Bush administration, raised questions because Starr had been involved in writing a legal brief for a conservative women's group opposing Clinton in the Paula Jones suit, and had engaged in other partisan activities. It was decided that no one in the White House, from the Clintons on down, could complain publicly—but others were encouraged to do so. (In late August, it was reported that Fiske had already broadened the inquiry to include the financing—by an Arkansas bank—of Clinton's 1990 gubernatorial campaign.)

It turned out that the three-judge panel—headed by Appeals Court Judge David Sentelle, a Reagan appointee and a Jesse Helms protégé—had been petitioned by Republican senators unhappy with Fiske, and by Floyd Brown, and that while the panel was considering whether to replace Fiske, Sentelle had lunched on Capitol Hill with Helms and Senator Lauch Faircloth, also of North Carolina, and a vociferous critic of Fiske.

Though it wasn't so much in the news, the Paula Jones suit continued to hurt Clinton as well. The greatest nightmare at the White House was that Clinton would have to go into court to defend himself against the lurid charges. Clinton's lawyer's argument that while a President holds office, he is immune from civil suits against actions before he took office, a new theory, was now in the courts. In July, a federal judge in Little Rock ruled that this issue would be heard before Jones's actual charges, thus giving Clinton plenty of time to appeal the issue through the courts, if need be. The Clintons had attracted a lot of criticism by setting up an unprecedented legal defense fund, in late June, to help them pay their burgeoning legal bills. Individuals, including lobbyists, could contribute one thousand dollars each to the fund.

Clinton's problems couldn't be isolated. A leading Democrat said, "Because he's had personal problems it's harder for his defenders to defend him on the substance of his work."

The President's poll ratings on foreign policy continued to sink. Pictures of fleeing Haitian refugees and stories about the administration's shifting policies dominated the news while Clinton was attending his second G-7 meeting, in Naples in early July. Clinton's two trips to Europe during the summer didn't do much to help his standing in the polls. A White House official said that the Naples trip was "snake-bit"—that while the President was attempting once again to show his world leadership, Haiti policy was spinning, the dollar was plummeting, and an inadequately prepared proposal on trade was rejected by the President's counterparts. By contrast, the President's visit to Normandy in June had gone well. Clinton had given good speeches. But he wasn't given much credit; there was an undertone of questioning his legitimacy.

In the spring, the administration had succumbed to pressure from the Congressional Black Caucus, a stronghold of support for the ousted elected Haitian President, Jean-Bertrand Aristide, and from others, such as Randall Robinson, the head of TransAfrica Forum, who was conducting a hunger strike, and changed the policy of forcibly returning refugees fleeing to America by boat. It also fired Lawrence Pezzullo, a career foreign service officer who was special envoy to Haiti and who had been trying to put together a coalition government over Aristide's objections, and replaced him with William Gray, a former Democratic House whip who was now president of the United Negro College Fund. The administration had thought that the new policy might lead to hundreds of refugees, but instead there were thousands, and havens for them outside the United States had to be found. Many ended up at Guantánamo Naval Base, in Cuba.

There was deliberately open talk out of the administration of invading Haiti if its military leaders didn't depart voluntarily. Officials kept up the talk of invasion. Clinton himself said, "I do not believe that we should rule out any option." The problem with threatening invasion was, of course, that the administration had to mean it if the threat was to be effective.

But the administration was divided. Defense Secretary William Perry and the military were strongly opposed to an invasion and felt that building a "stable environment," as some officials termed it, by means of an international force would be a long and perhaps impossible job. An invasion of Haiti had, a Pentagon official said, "too much of a Mogadishu possibility." Publicly and privately, Perry urged that all other methods of removing the military be exhausted before an invasion was undertaken. Officials said often that Clinton hadn't made up his mind about an invasion, but the real question within the administration was when to bring the matter to a head—a question that was spoken of in terms of whether to "slow walk" it or "fast walk" it. There were other considerations, of course—such as the fate of the Clintons' health care program.

An invasion would be highly controversial on Capitol Hill, dividing the President's allies. Yet (not unlike the case of Somalia) the administration was taking steps that could force it to take military action. On July 31 it asked for, and got, a resolution from the UN authorizing a multinational force "to use all necessary means" to remove the Haitian military leadership. (A Pentagon official said, "If we go in, we're going in alone.") Officials then said that once such authority was given—the first authority for military action in the Western hemisphere—it was important to use it, and to use the "momentum" that it provided. A top official said that the UN resolution "settled the matter" as to whether the U.S. would use force if the Haitian leaders didn't leave. The hope was that if all else failed and at some moment the U.S. set a deadline by which, if the Haitian rulers didn't leave, the Americans would invade, the rulers would believe the message and depart. At the end of August, an official said that the moment was coming "soon."

The Clinton administration did have one big foreign policy breakthrough in the summer of 1994: avoidance of a potentially awful collision with North Korea over its handling of nuclear reactors. The International Atomic Energy Agency said that North Korea had destroyed some evidence of past plutonium production, in violation of the nuclear Nonproliferation Treaty (NPT), and North Korea was still blocking full access of inspectors to its plutonium plants. The administration held numerous crisis meetings to examine North Korea's intentions and the implications of another Korean war.

It was agreed that North Korea's activities were a threat to the nonproliferation regime—such as it was. North Korea had warned that it would consider the imposition of sanctions an act of war. The administration found it difficult to agree on what the sanctions should be, and the Pentagon, which would have to fight the war, was less concerned than other agencies over North Korean destruction of evidence of past nuclear activity, as opposed to its current efforts to perhaps build a nuclear device. China and Japan expressed reservations about the sanctions; Russia and South Korea were hesitant. (The desired cooperation of China on the North Korean issue had been one of the reasons expressed for Clinton's decision in late May to renew most-favored-nation treatment of China, despite its lack of progress on human rights—a reversal of another campaign pledge.)

So the administration was in a jam when former President Jimmy Carter insisted on going to North Korea to try to resolve the crisis. Despite misgivings on the part of some officials and despite embarrassments to the administration—Carter praised the regime of North Korean leader Kim Il Sung and criticized the administration's drive for sanctions—Carter's trip did lead to a breakthrough. On June 22, Clinton announced that North Korea had agreed to freeze its nuclear program and allow IAEA inspectors access to its facilities, that the U.S. would drop its drive for sanctions, and that high-level talks between the two countries, broken off a year ago, would resume. It was a rare opportunity for Clinton to announce a positive foreign policy development, and his pleasure showed.

By the end of August, the Clinton administration's policy on Bosnia had just about come full circle. Having virtually run out of options, the administration was headed back toward the "lift and strike" proposal of May 1993: lifting the arms embargo against the Bosnian Muslims and conducting air strikes if the Bosnian Serbs took advantage of the situation in the interim. But the administration was divided on this, too. The Congress was pressing for a unilateral lifting of the arms embargo. This was a cheap vote, one that ran the risk of a bloodier war in Bosnia and a wider war in the region. In a letter to Sam Nunn, the President pledged to seek a lifting of the arms embargo by the UN by mid-October, and, if the UN refused, to consult with Congress on lifting the ban unilaterally, which the administration had long opposed.

The administration did consider the threat to lift the arms embargo one of its levers to try to get the Bosnian Serbs to agree to a peace proposal drawn up by the "Contact Group," composed of the United States, Britain, France, Germany, and Russia, and announced on July 4, which gave 51 percent of Bosnia to a federation of Muslims and Croats and 49 percent to the Serbs. The Contact Group's position was that if a plan met the bedrock requirements of the Bosnian government and the Serbs didn't agree to it, the allies would put military pressure on the Serbs. The Muslims accepted, and the Serbs, who controlled about 70 percent of Bosnia, in effect turned it down. The Contact Group, meeting in Geneva at the end of July, eschewed the use of air strikes, on which they'd been split all along, and instead decided on a three-step approach: impose stricter sanctions on Serbia itself;

extend the concept of "exclusion zones," already applied to Sarajevo and Gorazde, to the four other Muslim "safe areas" designated by the UN more than a year before, requiring the withdrawal of heavy weapons from those areas, and threatening air strikes if the terms were violated; lift the arms embargo. Plans for the military action were to be ready by late August. As before, some European countries threatened to withdraw their forces if the arms embargo were lifted. And in late summer Russia objected.

When the Serbs violated the Sarajevo exclusion zone in early August by removing some of the heavy weapons under the protection of UNPROFOR, the UN, the U.S., and NATO agreed to retaliation—which consisted of one strike on one gun emplacement in an abandoned area. Meanwhile, both the Serb and Muslim forces were on the move in Bosnia. Once more there was sniper fire on Sarajevo, and the Serbs closed the road to the city. In Geneva, Warren Christopher said, "We are not prepared to see this process be strung out indefinitely."

But the prospect was for continued fighting in Bosnia—unless the Serbian leader Slobodan Milosevic, his country already suffering from sanctions, exerted strong enough pressure on the Bosnian Serbs to quit. One weary and resigned official, explaining the idea of lifting the arms embargo, said, "The hope is that at some point they'll all feel they had enough. The way they're going now has no other end in sight."

About the last thing Clinton needed on top of everything else that was going on was the outpouring of refugees from Cuba, which began in early August. Worsening economic and political conditions in Cuba and a liberalized exodus policy by Fidel Castro sent boatloads of Cubans headed toward Florida. Like Bill Clinton, Florida politicians had seen this before and would brook no repeat of the Mariel boatlift of 1980, in which Castro had released some 125,000 people, many of them mentally ill and criminals. (The ones sent to Fort Chaffee, in Arkansas, had rioted.) At a Principals meeting on Thursday, August 18, it was agreed that it was essential to "demagnetize" the U.S. to avoid a continuing flow of Cuban refugees, and also that the U.S. couldn't be harsher on the Cubans—by turning them around—than it was on Haitians. "Safe havens" would be found. On Friday, Clinton announced a change in a nearly thirty-year-old policy on Cuban refugees. But the new policy had been drawn up in haste as Clinton was pressed by Florida Governor Lawton Chiles (who was up for reelection) to stop the flow. Clinton still harbored the idea (illusion, perhaps) that he might carry Florida in 1996. (He lost it in 1992.)

When Cuban-American leaders, meeting with the President on Friday night, with Chiles in attendance, let the administration know that they were less satisfied with the new policy than the administration had expected, Clinton tightened the economic sanctions on Cuba by barring remittances and charter flights. Afterward the fact that Clinton had treated the exodus as a South Florida problem, and had met with and tried to appease wealthy Florida Cuban leaders, Republicans to boot—whose outright goal was the overthrow of Castro—rather than seek a broader range of opinion was criticized from within the administration and by some members of Congress. Clinton's actions also reflected the fact that immigration had become a "hot-button" issue nationally. Despite efforts to discourage the Cubans from setting out for the United States, they kept coming by the thousands. Refugees from both Cuba and Haiti now were being crowded into Guantánamo. Clinton was criticized by members of his own party for not opening a "dialogue" with Cuba, a relic of the Cold War, but administration officials at first said that there was no point in broad talks with Castro, who had been obdurate to all comers over the years, and that even if there was some point, talks shouldn't be undertaken under the threat of a refugee crisis. But they did decide to resume lapsed talks with Cuba over migration policy.

Then, as the domestic criticism increased, Christopher and others sent signals that the U.S. was willing to discuss further matters if Castro showed some sign of moving toward a more democratic regime. The administration wanted to make it clear to the public that it wasn't bending to Castro because of the refugee crisis, and that the onus for changing the relationship was on him.

In June, as Clinton's poll ratings on foreign policy continued to sink, he seriously considered changing his foreign policy team, but after giving it some thought he decided that to do so at that point would be disruptive and look like scapegoating. But a lot of people expected him to make changes within a few months. The relationship between Christopher and Lake still wasn't good. No one who knew the situation thought that Christopher would go without trying to take Lake with him. A neutral official said, "Each is maneuvering to see that it's the other one."

August turned into an almost unbearable trial for the Clinton White House. The Whitewater hearings had hurt and the health care bill was in trouble, but the Clinton people saw a victory on the crime bill as the beginning of a reversal in his fortunes. If Clinton won the crime bill, he would have "momentum" for the health care bill; if both were passed before Congress took its August recess, the press and public would see the Clinton Presidency in a whole new light—which would be helpful in the November congressional elections.

But it soon became clear that Republicans had in mind exactly the reverse, and would try to stop Clinton's initiatives across the board. The President understood that and was angry. But the difficult fix the President was in in the last days of August wasn't just a result of Republican partisanship—it was also a sign of his diminishing political strength. Mid-August polls showed his approval ratings at the low forties. One poll also showed that by a large margin people didn't think Clinton had broken "gridlock" in Washington or had accomplished very much. Even Stan Greenberg was advising his congressional clients not to link themselves closely to Clinton. Greenberg also advised that the crime issue was of far more importance to people than health care. Doubts about Clinton's character were deepening, and people were getting tired of him. The legislative troubles were symptoms.

The defeat in the House on August 11 of a rule for debate on the crime bill came as a shock to most people at the White House, where everyone understood that it had larger implications than the loss of the crime bill itself. The National Rifle Association had been working successfully to peel off Republicans and conservative Democrats who had voted in May for a ban on nineteen types of assault weapons, which was now in the bill, and the Republican National Committee had put pressure on the thirty-eight Republicans who had supported the ban when it passed the House. But more embarrassing for the administration was that a total of fifty-eight Democrats walked away from their prior support of the crime bill—some on the right because of the ban on assault rifles, some on the left (especially within the Black Caucus) because of the more than sixty new applications of the death penalty and because they had been forced to drop an "equal justice" provision, which would allow defendants to challenge death sentences as discriminatory, using racial statistics. Republicans and some conservative Democrats also decried the amount of money in the bill for crime prevention that had been in the bill when the House passed it in April, with the votes of sixty-five Republicans.

Clinton went on the kind of offensive that his aides thought made him look like a fighter—"It energized him," they kept saying—but turning around the eight votes needed to get the rule adopted proved a lot harder than the White House expected. Gun control and the death penalty were emotional issues (almost like abortion) on which people couldn't easily change their position. With difficulty, he did get three members of the Black Caucus who strongly objected to the death penalty provisions to say that they would vote for the rule, but not the bill itself.

Since Clinton couldn't pick up enough votes from his own party, not eight votes, he had to bargain with the Republicans. House Democratic leaders urged him to drop the ban on assault weapons in order to win with the votes of enough Democrats, but no one in the White House thought Clinton should—or could, given how it would be seen—do this. In a press conference on August 19, in a bit of silk-pursing, he praised his attempt to win over Republicans as a worthy bipartisan approach, of the sort he said he had used since NAFTA—but he hadn't used it much and only did so now because he was forced to. The eleven Republicans who had supported the rule the first time had come under pressure from their party leaders, so they had to exact a price for voting for it again, and other moderate Republicans who had voted against the rule but had earlier supported the assault weapons ban were being criticized by constituents for this, so they needed cover for switching once more.

In virtual round-the-clock negotiations, Democratic leaders and administration officials, led by Panetta—who got no sleep one night over the weekend of August 20–21—shuttled among the anti-ban Democrats, the Black Caucus, and the Republicans. With indirect participation by Newt Gingrich, who had led the effort to defeat the rule, the Republicans demanded cuts in the prevention funds before they would vote for the rule again. Republicans took to charging there was "pork" in the bill, and (in a throwback to the stimulus bill) derided some specific projects. (There was far more money in the bill for building prisons.) It was all shadowboxing, maneuvering without substance, but that didn't really matter. Clinton grudgingly recognized that the Republicans were scoring effective political points—coming up with good catch phrases—and that they were generally better at that than the Democrats.

The crime bill wasn't a legislative monument in any event: its title was more important than its substance. It was a hodgepodge of programs and established several new types of federal crimes, which by definition would be limited in their effect. (Only 5 percent of violent crimes come under federal jurisdiction.) The proposal authorized an additional one hundred thousand police, a Clinton initiative, but the funding for this was in question. Politicians wanted to be able to say that they'd passed a crime bill. For that reason, the Republicans didn't want to go to the voters having blocked the bill entirely. That the President and the leadership did turn around the vote on Sunday, August 21, was, of course, touted by the White House as yet another glorious chapter in the legend of "the Comeback Kid." But everyone knew what the first loss had meant.

A myth grew up that the initial setback on the crime bill was yet another one for the storm-tossed health care program, collapsing any possibility that either the House or the Senate could produce a bill before the recess, which was supposed to begin in mid-August. But the health care bill wasn't going anywhere anyway, and, if anything, the dramatics over the rescue of the crime bill masked the trouble over health care. The Clinton plan was dead, and the Clintons were becoming less and less a factor in what, if any, health care program ultimately passed.

With the President's plan foundering, the Democratic leaders had gone to the White House on the night of July 21 and told the Clintons that their bill could not pass and that the leaders would try to wrest some new health care plan from the Congress. Administration officials, with straight faces, called this a "relaunch" of the health care bill (the third or fourth, depending on how one counted). When House Majority Leader Dick Gephardt unveiled his plan, he was at pains to say that it wasn't "the Clinton plan," and he had charts at his side enumerating the differences between his proposal (which had an employer mandate in five years, to cover eighty percent of the cost of premiums) and the Clintons'. The mandatory "alliances," or large purchasing cooperatives, in the Clinton plan, with their bureaucratic overtones, had long since become politically dead, and the "employer mandate" of the Clinton plan was in serious political trouble, as, therefore, was the goal of universal coverage. Majority Leader Mitchell worked to come up with something he thought he could get past his chamber but also met the President's minimal requirements. In the White House meeting, Mitchell, depressed by how far he seemed to have to go to compromise, said that he doubted he could get the Senate to agree to a "hard trigger," the automatic triggering of an employer mandate if a certain level of coverage wasn't reached by a specified year. The President and others persuaded him to try. Finally, Mitchell came up with a proposal that provided that an employer mandate to cover 50 percent of the costs wouldn't come into effect until the year 2002 if it was found that fewer than 95 percent of a given state's citizens were covered. His proposal was a long way from the Clinton plan's "universal coverage" by the end of 1998.

It was a low moment at the White House, especially for Mrs. Clinton, who was severely disappointed. Through a series of misjudgments—not having a bill ready in time for its big rollout, producing a bill that was highly complex, far-reaching, and nearly impossible to explain, being unwilling to compromise for too long—the Clintons had undermined their own major initiative. Rejecting the advice of McLarty, David Gergen, and others, Mrs. Clinton for too long resisted negotiating with moderate Republicans such as John Chafee of Rhode Island, or Democrats such as Representative Jim Cooper of Tennessee. She preferred to proceed with a "fifty-one-vote" strategy: get enough votes from Democrats (with one Republican ally, Senator James Jeffords of Vermont) to pass something as close to the administration's bill as possible. But several conservative Democrats didn't want to vote for a bill that didn't have some Republican support. A number of people warned that it wasn't wise to launch such a big new social program on such a narrow base, but this view was rejected at the White House until it was almost too late—or until necessity forced its hand.

Now, in August, even the Clintons' one "nonnegotiable" demand, universal coverage, was at risk. When in his State of the Union speech the President had theatrically brandished a pen, saying he would veto any bill that didn't provide universal coverage, everyone understood that the definition of that term was somewhat elastic. But now the White House was agonizing over what was acceptable as meeting that goal. Mrs. Clinton resisted for some time giving up on the goal of 100 percent coverage (never very realistic), but a Clinton adviser said, "There's been an increasing sense of realism about what you could get through the Congress."

A decision was made not to talk about what percentage would be considered "universal"—until the President, speaking to the National Governors' Association, mused aloud about 95 percent perhaps meeting that goal. The next day, after an uproar, particularly on the part of liberals, the President more or less took his words back, but he had been reflecting reality. (Aides said that Clinton couldn't resist wonk talk when he went before his old pals the governors.) Clinton, the adviser said, accepted the less-than-100-percent goal before Mrs. Clinton did because "it came out of a policy process, whereas she is more committed to an affirmation in law of a right to health insurance. As governor, he was more aware of the consequences of laws; as a lawyer, she's more concerned with establishing a right within the law."

When Clinton endorsed the Mitchell proposal at an August 3 press conference, he alluded to his own proposal as if it were an alien creature. He said that the Democratic leaders' proposals were "less bureaucratic" and "more flexible." Six days later, Mrs. Clinton let it be known that she preferred Gephardt's proposal. She also attacked Senator Phil Gramm of Texas and Senator Robert Dole. Shortly afterward, Mrs. Clinton accepted that she had become a liability—aides said this was because her image had been "distorted"—and stayed largely out of sight. This was a long way from what the Clintons had thought she would bring to his Presidency.

As a result of earlier reversals of White House positions on the Btu tax and the stimulus bill, House members were loath to vote on the Gephardt bill if the Senate was going to reject any form of employer mandate, so House leaders decided to wait for the Senate's vote. But the Senate debate, which opened on August 9, soon bogged down—a combination of delaying tactics on the part of some Republicans and a search to see if a bipartisan "mainstream coalition," led by Chafee and consisting of a floating group averaging fifteen senators, might offer proposals Mitchell could accept, providing enough votes to pass the bill. Neither Mitchell nor Gephardt had the votes to pass his own proposal. Gephardt wasn't anywhere close, nor was there a House consensus on any other bill. Gramm and Dole were both positioning themselves to run for President in 1996, with Gramm far to the right and Dole not wishing to leave too much distance between them. So, for a number of reasons—including public reaction, and lobbying by business groups (whom the Clintons thought would be with them)—the congressional sentiment on health care kept becoming more conservative. Even the moderate Chafee backed away from some parts of his earlier proposal.

Inside and outside the Capitol, sentiment for dumping the whole thing and starting over was growing. Members of Congress, panicked, were slapping together packages of proposals that they hoped would win enough votes. This was no way to legislate on something so complex. White House aides were aware that Clinton might have to reject a bill on grounds other than the fact that it didn't meet his criterion of universal coverage. If he signed a bill that was soon seen as unworkable, he could be worse off than if he'd signed no bill at all. The mainstream group's proposal, unveiled on August 19, presented a lot of political problems. It made deep cuts in Medicare without giving the elderly new benefits, such as payments for prescription drugs; it limited the tax deductibility of plans over a certain level, which would include most union plans. It was estimated to reach 92 percent of the public by 2004. (All such estimates were dubious.)

After the defeat of the rule for the crime bill, House leaders put off debate on health care proposals indefinitely, ostensibly because they didn't yet have a report from the Congressional Budget Office on Gephardt's proposal, but mainly because they didn't have the votes. Members of Congress become very cranky when their recess starts to slide away, especially in an election year, and especially when it's their summer recess. At some point it becomes counterproductive to keep them in session. As the final days of August neared, the atmosphere on Capitol Hill was chaotic—there were meetings all over the place. Debate was becoming snappish. At the White House, meetings went on from early morning until nearly midnight, the atmosphere very tense. The stakes for Clinton were enormous.

After resurrecting and passing the crime bill, the House began its recess. Foley told reporters that consideration of major health care legislation should be put off until the following year, or perhaps a minimalist bill could be passed after the recess. While Senate Republicans tried to tie up the crime bill, negotiations between Mitchell and the mainstream group continued, but weren't getting very far. There were limits to what Chafee could do without losing some members of his group. White House officials knew that the possibility of completing action on comprehensive health care reform in 1994 was slipping away. "The clock is running on us," one said as the end of August neared. When, on August 25, Senate Democrats, with the help of six moderate Republicans, mustered the sixty votes (plus one) needed to defeat a Republican procedural move designed to hopelessly tie up or even kill the crime bill, Clinton took credit for another bipartisan achievement. But all but one of the six had voted for the weapons ban before. Mitchell, who had threatened to keep the Senate in session until it passed a health care bill, decided to recess once the crime bill was dealt with. Moods were too bad to get any more done, and some senators were threatening to depart anyway. So after the Senate passed the crime bill, Mitchell sent them home.

Though Mitchell would continue to negotiate with Chafee, and some White House aides said a major bill might still emerge, it was recognized in the White House as well as on Capitol Hill that the possibility of a comprehensive health care bill in 1994 was all but gone, that all that remained possible was a "minimalist" bill, perhaps containing insurance reforms and a few other things, that was even less ambitious than "incrementalist" proposals Mrs. Clinton had once derided. The President could sign such a bill, a White House official said, as long as he didn't call it health care reform. Some aides even hoped that nothing would come from discussions with the mainstream group so that Clinton wouldn't be faced with an embarrassing question of whether to sign a bill that fell short of universal coverage.

On Friday, August 26—a week late—the Clintons left for Martha's Vineyard.

Sitting in the White House at the end of August, a top adviser said that when Clinton returned after his vacation, "he has to strike broader themes going into the general election." He added, "We've lost our compass a bit in the hurly-burly, and people have lost a sense of why he came here and where he wants to take the country." This adviser said, in what was becoming at the least an annual refrain in the Clinton White House, "The President has to redefine what his Presidency is about."

Author's Note

This book is based on regular interviews with every high official in the Clinton White House on the broad range of issues, foreign and domestic, that the President confronted—or was confronted with. My interviewing also involved frequent sessions with Cabinet officers involved in these issues, and others in the various agencies, as well as Members of Congress and Capitol Hill staff members whose angle of vision and expertise could shed light on the Clinton Presidency. Not-so-famous White House aides were also tremendously helpful in clarifying issues and helping me understand events.

Because this book was written while these people (most of them) were still in their jobs, and because various issues and relationships remain sensitive, in many instances the sources are not quoted by name. All quotations are from direct sources. Any thoughts or views attributed to anyone came from someone with direct knowledge. As a journalist should, I kept asking myself, "Why is this person telling me this?" The information was screened for, among other things, self-aggrandizement, rivalry (and even vendetta in some cases), and puffing of the boss.

This is a genre of middle-distance journalism, intended to catch events and people's involvement in them or reactions to them while they are still fresh and before they have been fuzzed over, and retouched, in recollection. It is also intended to offer the analysis and perspective of someone close to the events, seeing them unfiltered, but not under the compulsions and restrictions of daily or weekly journalism.

Index

ABOUT THE AUTHOR

ELIZABETH DREW is a much-honored writer who appears frequently on "Meet the Press" and other public affairs programs and is the author of seven books, including *Washington Journal: The Events of 1973–1974* and *Politics and Money.* She lives in Washington, D.C.